The Nature of Slavery

The Nature of Slavery

Environment and Plantation Labor in the Anglo-Atlantic World

KATHERINE JOHNSTON

OXFORD
UNIVERSITY PRESS

Oxford University Press is a department of the University of Oxford. It furthers
the University's objective of excellence in research, scholarship, and education
by publishing worldwide. Oxford is a registered trade mark of Oxford University
Press in the UK and certain other countries.

Published in the United States of America by Oxford University Press
198 Madison Avenue, New York, NY 10016, United States of America.

Portions of Chapters 3 and 5 appeared in Katherine Johnston, "Endangered Plantations:
Environmental Change and Slavery in the British Caribbean, 1631–1807," *Early American Studies:
An Interdisciplinary Journal* 18, no. 3 (Summer 2020): 259–286.

This book is derived, in part, from an article published in *Atlantic Studies* in
December 2013, available online:

http://www.tandfonline.com/10.1080/14788810.2013.835591.

CIP data is on file at the Library of Congress

ISBN 978-0-19-751460-3

DOI: 10.1093/oso/9780197514603.001.0001

1 3 5 7 9 8 6 4 2

Printed by Sheridan Books, Inc., United States of America

CONTENTS

ACKNOWLEDGMENTS

It is with great pleasure and joy that I express my gratitude for the people who have encouraged and supported me over the years. Many friends, colleagues, family members, and institutions have contributed to this book in various ways, and I owe sincere thanks for insightful comments, financial support, practical assistance, and timely reprieves.

For funding that allowed me to conduct research in international as well as domestic archives, I am grateful to the Harvard Atlantic History Seminar, the Institute of Historical Research, the Humanities Research Centre at the University of Warwick, and both the history department and the Graduate School of Arts and Sciences at Columbia University. I visited many libraries and archives on my travels and want to extend special thanks to Bernadette Worrell and Michael Thomas-Hannibal of the National Library of Jamaica, as well as to Sheila Sedgwick, archivist at the Farquharson of Invercauld Estate in Braemar. I am also grateful to Breanne Hewitt of the Georgia Historical Society for help with images. For providing me with access to family papers in Scotland, I thank Simon Blackett of Invercauld Estate, Archie Orr Ewing of Cardross House, and Jamie Stormonth-Darling of Lednathie. For excellent research help closer to home, I thank Kelly Leahy at the Beloit College Library. Finally, my sincere thanks to the artist Carlton Murrell for permission to use his painting, *Sugarcane Harvest*, on the cover.

Fellowships at the American Philosophical Society, the Massachusetts Historical Society, the Library Company of Philadelphia, and the John Carter Brown Library provided me with spaces and communities to expand my work, and I am grateful for the companionship of fellow researchers as well as the fantastic librarians and staff at each one. I am particularly grateful to the JCB for both a short- and long-term fellowship, and especially to the staff and fellows during the spring of 2019, when I held a fellowship funded by the National Endowment for the Humanities and also had a baby. The flexibility, encouragement, and excitement of the JCB staff and fellows made the whole experience unforget-table and quite wonderful. Thanks especially to fellows Fabrício Prado, Dana Leibsohn, and Hannah Tucker for helping us move rental apartments with a newborn and for signing crucial papers.

Readers and attendees at various workshops, seminars, and other venues have provided thoughtful feedback on different iterations and sections of this book. For the opportunity to present my work, I thank the organizers of the Summer Academy of Atlantic History, the Brown Bag Seminar at the McNeil Center for Early American Studies, the Boston Environmental History Seminar, the Humanities Research Centre, as well as the Early Modern and Americas Research Seminars at the University of Warwick, the Center for the Study of Slavery and Justice at Brown University, and the conveners of the Atlantic Environments and the American South conference. I am also particularly grateful to members of the Breakfast Club for their careful reading and con-versation. I have presented portions of this work at meetings of the American Historical Society; the Omohundro Institute of Early American History and Culture; the Society of Early Americanists; the Society for Literature, Science and the Arts; the History of Science Society; the American Society for Environmental History; and the Southern Historical Association. I thank the commentators, audiences, and my fellow panelists at all of these gatherings for helpful suggestions and thoughts on my work, and especially Sean Morey Smith for invitations and sustained scholarly engagement. Finally, I am grateful to the conveners and participants of the 2017 Omohundro Scholars' Workshop. Spending a sticky couple of weeks in Williamsburg with a brilliant group of people turned out to be a great stimulus for my work and a solid foundation for friendship. I am especially grateful for the encouragement, advice, and friend-ship of Kate Mulry and Nadine Zimmerli, and I feel fortunate to have kept up those conversations over the years.

Many years ago, Megan Kaste encouraged me to write, and although I had no idea the direction that writing would take, I am grateful to her for cheering me on at an early stage. Later, after a period of wandering, I had the good fortune to find a group of mentors in Washington, DC. Eileen Findlay, Alison Games, Kate Haulman, Katharine Norris, and Phil Stern guided and encouraged me, and my career as a historian began with them. My studies continued in New York, where I was fortunate to have the guidance of Karen Ordahl Kupperman, Natasha Lightfoot, Pamela Smith, and especially Chris Brown. I will be forever grateful to Chris for his sage advice and unflagging support at every step of the way. His insights improved my work enormously, and his calm assurance led me through some rough patches. Chris challenged me and, perhaps most importantly, had faith in me, and his advice throughout graduate school and beyond has meant a great deal to me.

As I traveled to libraries and archives all over the UK, as well as around the Caribbean and the United States, I sometimes had the delightful opportunity to be able to stay with friends and family. For supporting my itinerant lifestyle during years of research, I am grateful to Dick Norris, Rogers Smith and Mary Summers, Liz and Dave Newton, Chris and Laura Dennis, Becky and Charles Amis, and Alison and Bruce Garrett. All were gracious hosts and gave me warm food and sociable evenings after long days in the archives. Simon Sleight and the late Hayley Maher welcomed me to London and took me for a much-needed holiday to the Lake District, where I had the pleasure of drinking hot thermoses of tea while perched atop wet and windy rocks in the middle of a hike. I am also grateful that I was able to spend time with family while in England. Special thanks to Gillian and Adrian Dawson for adventures in Dorset and Dartmoor, as well as to Naomi and Matt Kenny for hosting me in Manchester and to Laura Dawson for entertaining evenings in London. Thanks also to the Andrews and Gluckman families for welcoming me to gatherings. Above all, I thank Julia, Julian, and Sancha Markson for making me feel so welcome and for providing me with a home for so many summers. Although this book took longer than they ever imagined, I am so grateful to have had the chance to grow closer to them during that time.

Friends and colleagues who supported me in numerous ways over the years have nourished this project both directly and indirectly. I am especially grateful for the insights, support, and friendship of Zara Anishanslin, Martha Brough, Phil Chen, Chad Diehl, Maria John, Jacob Lee, Lisa Maguire, Mary E. Mendoza, Melissa Morris, Matthew Mulcahy, Jordan Smith, Christina Snyder, and Peter Walker. Jordan and Maria both keep me sane and entertained on a regular basis in various ways, and I am grateful for their ability to keep me from my hermetic tendencies. Ann Little offered encouragement at various points, and Suman Seth's excellent comments on the manuscript improved it substantially. Pablo Hernández Sau gave me several thoughtful suggestions on the introduction, for which I am thankful. Elena Abbott generously shared her manuscript with me before it was published, and I learned a great deal from her outstanding work. Susan Ferber reached out to me at exactly the right time, and I am grateful for her careful editorial eye and for her patience. My colleagues at Beloit, particularly the members of the history department, have been supportive since my arrival a few years ago, and their warm welcome has helped to make Beloit a home. I am also grateful for my wonderful students. Their smart and insightful questions, as well as their belief in my work, have pushed me to make this a better book. I look forward to their enthusiasm each day.

Finally, I am grateful for my family. Victoria Johnston has been a hiking companion across many parts of the country and an excellent host in some of them as well. Derek Mills joined for some of these excursions and co-hosted others, and I look forward to more adventures to come. The extended Davies clan has welcomed me with open arms, and I am thankful for their warmth and generosity. My parents, to whom this book is dedicated, I cannot thank enough. Wendy and David Johnston have been more supportive than I could ever have dreamed. I have thrown challenges their way over the years and they have remained steadfast. I so appreciate how often they have rented a car and spent days on the road to visit us these last few years, particularly when we needed it the most. They both have my profound thanks. Sam has been intrepid from the beginning, weathering various iterations of final drafts of this book since his birth during a fellowship. He is a source of constant joy and delight and watching him grow is one of the greatest pleasures of my life. Ann Davies is simply extraordinary. Astute editor, wise co-parent, generous and loving partner and wife, and so much more, she fills life with love, strength, and brilliance. I feel so lucky to share my life with her.

The Nature of Slavery

Introduction

When the ship from Scotland reached the harbor in St. Vincent on a bright April day in 1791, its passengers caught sight of a small town with a handful of buildings along the coast, flanked by steep hills. The lush greenery sloping away from the sea provided a stark contrast to the bleak, windswept hills of Scotland. Unlike the gentle inclines of the Highlands, where sheep dotted a terrain of exposed rock and grass, St. Vincent's peaks rose sharply out of the ocean. Thick forests covered some of the slopes, and rows of coffee plants grew along the sides of others. In place of the numbing winter mists they had left behind, the Scottish travelers found the vibrant environment of their new home warmed by strong sunlight and the steam of spring rains.

Many of the passengers had undergone extensive journeys across Scotland even before boarding the ship. After suffering through a harsh winter with little food or heat, the travelers had faced six to eight weeks of sailing, depending on the prevailing winds. As the ship charted a course across the Atlantic, they had endured increasingly stale and meager food rations, along with a dwindling supply of stagnant drinking water. Yet for many of the voyagers the journey represented opportunity: they had heard that some of the West Indian islands needed laborers, and they were eager to work.

As they disembarked, the migrants encountered some fellow Scots on the island, many of whom eyed their countrymen with suspicion. "Have you no employment for your young men in Scotland?" one St. Vincent inhabitant, Thomas Fraser, wrote to his cousin a few days later. Fraser had worked for many years as a carpenter in Grenada and Tobago before establishing himself as a coffee planter in St. Vincent. The ship from Glasgow had deposited so many new arrivals, Fraser continued, "that it was said she was a Scotch *Guinea man* and that in spite of Mr. Wilberforce and the Parliament we would get white negroes from Scotland enough to cultivate our plantations without buying them."[1]

The Nature of Slavery. Katherine Johnston, Oxford University Press. © Oxford University Press 2022.
DOI: 10.1093/oso/9780197514603.003.0001

Fig. I.1 Kingstown, St. Vincent, from Charles Shephard's *An Historical Account of the Island of St. Vincent* (London: W. Nicol, 1831).

While Fraser likened the Scottish ship to a "Guinea man," or a slave ship from West Africa, and termed its passengers "white negroes," members of Parliament in London were engaged in a heated debate regarding the future of the trans-atlantic slave trade in the British West Indies. The enslaved population in the Caribbean was not self-sustaining; enslaved laborers died more frequently than they had children, and planters had constructed an economy that depended on a constant flow of new arrivals from Africa to work plantations. William Wilberforce, the voice of the abolitionists in Parliament, denounced the Atlantic slave trade on the grounds of its cruelty and inhumanity. Meanwhile, blithely ignoring ships such as the "Scotch Guinea man" docking in St. Vincent, planters argued that abolishing the slave trade would doom lucrative West Indian planta-tions.[2] Slaveholding planters insisted that enslaved Black laborers were essential to the cultivation of the islands because white laborers would never be able to stand the heat.[3]

These debates resounded across the Atlantic: concurrent arguments about the future of slavery in the new United States Congress repeated the same rhetoric. The climate in the Georgia and South Carolina lowcountry was inhospitable to white laborers, slaveholders argued, and as a result this region required enslaved Black laborers. In both Parliament and Congress planters announced that the ec-onomic fallout of abolishing the transatlantic slave trade would be catastrophic. Industries would be ruined and land laid to waste. Slaveholders demanded the continuance of the slave trade as the only way to avert utter disaster. Desperate to save the trade, white planters depicted racial slavery as subject to an unalterable law of nature: they insisted that Black bodies were suited to hot climates while white bodies were not.[4]

Framing the issue of racial slavery in this way allowed planters to deny their own culpability in enslaving human beings. But their use of climatic language had much larger consequences. Planters' climatic defense of racial slavery in the late eighteenth century became a retroactive explanation for its establishment in these colonies. British slaveholders pointed to the influx of Africans to the Caribbean starting in the mid-seventeenth century as evidence that white laborers were incapable of plantation labor. In the American South, slaveholders turned to the history of Georgia, a colony whose early years were marked by an explicit ban on Black slavery, to argue that the region's experiment had faltered for climatic reasons. In each case, slaveholders argued that previous planters' experiences with white laborers had failed because white people were incapable of field labor in hot places. Although slave traders and others had occasionally made climatic excuses for racial slavery before the late eighteenth century—most notably in colonial Georgia—the perceived threat to the transatlantic slave trade provoked slaveholders to forcefully articulate this climatic defense. Their climatic justifications spurred a reinvention of the history of plantation societies in the Anglo-Atlantic world. Thus, a defensive maneuver in the slave trade debate during the eighteenth century turned into an explanation for the establishment of racial slavery in the colonies in the first place.

This explanation became part of the prevailing narrative of labor in the Atlantic world. As planters' claims entered published works in the late eighteenth century, historians began repeating this account of the labor transition. Histories of the Americas, for example, contained passages explaining that in early Georgia "a very short experience" proved "that Africans, or their descendants" could work the land in hot places where Europeans could not. Scholars continued to reiterate this version into the twentieth century, applying the same explanation to accounts of the early West Indies. During the second half of the twentieth century, scholars began searching for epidemiological explanations to support this argument. They assumed that planters were articulating their own understandings about Black labor in hot climates, rather than constructing a narrative to suit a particular political moment. Over time, slaveholders' justifications became an essential element in histories of labor in plantation societies.[5]

Planters' rhetoric about climate made racial slavery appear to be rooted in nature. This use of environmental language drew divisions between Black and white bodies that seemed innate and even immutable. This portrayal stood in stark contrast to predominant theories of bodies in the eighteenth-century Anglo-Atlantic as changeable entities, altering with varying environments and surroundings. The rhetoric in defense of slavery, then, transformed incoherent, contradictory, and varying notions of bodies into a binary theory of bodily difference.[6]

By arguing that Black and white bodies naturally suited different environments, slavery's defenders contributed to emerging scientific theories of biological race. The climatic defense of slavery strengthened theories that Black and white bodies were physiologically and biologically different from one another. The timing was critical: slaveholders made their arguments just as scientific disciplines investigating bodily difference grew in strength and significance. Practitioners of anatomy, biology, physiology, and phrenology theorized conceptions of race based on a belief in people's external and internal bodily differences.[7]

The repercussions of planters' arguments were significant. Over the following decades, particularly in the United States, slaveholders presented multiple defenses of slavery, but none was more insidious and damaging than the idea that Black and white bodies were fundamentally, biologically distinct from one another. The climatic argument was foundational to this theory because it presented Black and white bodies as physiologically suited to different climates. The climatic rhetoric became so prevalent and so pervasive that even those people adamantly opposed to slavery were inclined to believe it. White abolitionists, for example, argued that the climatic argument was an inadequate defense of the institution of slavery, but many of them did not question the premise that Black laborers were best suited to hot climates. Instead, they insisted that those laborers did not have to be enslaved. While significant numbers of Black people, especially those living in colder climates in the American North, dismissed the climatic argument as patently false, others accepted it. Regardless of individual beliefs, the racialized rhetoric of climate was a powerful force that endured well beyond the era of slavery.

The Nature of Slavery argues that slavery's stakeholders developed and manipulated the climatic defense of racial slavery despite their experiences, not because of them. Through a careful examination of private correspondence—letters sent between friends, family members, and absentee planters and managers—as well as official correspondence, medical manuals, pamphlets, newspapers, minutes of government hearings, public testimonies, natural histories, and other sources, this book demonstrates the ways in which those with an interest in maintaining racial slavery in the Anglo-Atlantic constructed and perpetuated a rhetoric that had no basis in their own observations. In the same way that theories of biological race are groundless and yet have caused incalculable harm, so too was the climatic defense of slavery a manufactured rhetoric purporting to have a foundation in reality and yet utterly lacking in evidence. Nonetheless, this rhetoric served as an excuse for white people to consistently place Black bodies in environmentally hazardous situations, even after the official end of slavery in both the Caribbean and the United States. For this reason, the climatic rhetoric can be considered an early iteration of environmental racism, or a way of systematically placing people of color in dangerous environments. Ultimately, the language that slaveholders constructed to defend racial slavery had an extensive legacy.[8]

This rhetoric also generated a myth about the rise of African slavery in parts of the colonial Americas that became foundational to the history of these places. As planters' claims circulated around the Atlantic, they entered history books and a collective consciousness as a historical explanation of the transition to African slavery in American plantation societies. This explanation permeated the literature to such an extent that it became accepted as historical fact. But the argument that planters in the Anglo-Atlantic turned to African laborers at least in part for climatic reasons rests on three premises: that planters noted health differences between Africans and Europeans on plantations, that Europeans could not labor in hot places, and that Africans suited the climate in American plantation societies. This book dismantles each of these premises. It shows that prevailing conceptions of health and illness in the Anglo-Atlantic world were environmental, not racial; that there was no real evidence that Europeans were categorically unable to work in these places, but that European slaveholders were highly motivated to perpetuate this idea; and that slaveholders well knew that Africans suited labor in American plantation environments no better than Europeans did. Personal correspondence from plantation societies makes clear that this labor myth developed as a strategic move designed to protect planters' economic livelihoods, which then grew into a rhetorical tool used to justify racial slavery for many years thereafter.

Places and Peoples

The British and Anglo-Americans were not alone among imperial powers in theorizing about various climates' effects on bodies. Settler-colonists and other agents of empire speculated on the ways different climates transformed and ravaged bodies in places all over the globe, including Africa, India, and the Americas.[9] In all of these places, visitors, colonizers, theorists, and others engaged with ideas about climatic and bodily difference at various points during the seventeenth and eighteenth centuries and beyond, particularly as these ideas related to health and other bodily changes. Climate also figured into other imperial ventures to the warm regions of the Americas, such as the French expedition to Kourou, and it remained part of the larger rhetoric about colonization.[10]

Within that global context, this book focuses on the Anglo-Caribbean islands and the lowcountry region of the present-day United States, an area currently part of Georgia and South Carolina. This region, dubbed the Greater Caribbean, was distinctive in its plantation economy, vast population of enslaved laborers, and environmental conditions. Unlike the Chesapeake and areas north, the lowcountry and the West Indies had secured a reputation for being unhealthy places by the middle of the eighteenth century. And unlike West Africa, which held an even worse reputation for European bodies, plantation colonies in the Americas were not native spaces for either Africans or Europeans. European intrusions onto Indigenous land created plantation spaces where white planters held Black laborers in bondage, and both Africans and Europeans had to adjust to an unfamiliar place. In addition to being critically important to the empire's economy and culture, plantation societies in the Greater Caribbean were essential to the emergence of ideas about race and the body during the eighteenth century. On multiple occasions the British and Anglo-Americans explicitly defended transatlantic slavery on the grounds that Black laborers were essential to the cultivation of the Americas. For this reason, these slaveholders perpetuated a rhetoric about climate, labor, and bodies, and turned it into a central part of an Anglo-American narrative of slavery.[11]

Indigenous peoples were in some ways involved in every piece of this history: they labored on plantations, their bodies were integral to white theorists' developing ideas about race, and they too changed their conceptions of race and bodily difference during this period. Yet the particular rhetoric about climate and labor focused on the bodies of Black and white laborers, leaving little room for Indigenous bodies. The physical presence of Indigenous peoples draws attention to the political expediency of planters' rhetoric. According to planters' reasoning, Indigenous people should in theory have been ideally suited to labor in their own environments. But white settler-colonists were quick to portray Indigenous bodies as unsuited for labor.[12] The unabated colonial violence against Indigenous peoples, including the rapid spread of infectious diseases as part of the colonial invasion, contributed to a myth that they were quickly disappearing. Although this characterization did not stop colonists from enslaving Indigenous peoples, it did largely exempt Indigenous bodies from slaveholders' binary climatic rhetoric. Planters regularly grouped Indigenous and Black bodies together in their records, particularly where Indigenous slavery was technically illegal, but settler-colonists did not make a sustained argument for the necessity of Indigenous bodies on plantations. Instead, the correlation of climate and labor emerged in direct response to threats to the transatlantic slave trade and to African slavery in the Americas. Abolitionist efforts in the late eighteenth century sparked the solidification of this climatic rhetoric, which subsumed all bodies into a Black and white dichotomy.[13]

Although there were a handful of statements to the effect that English bodies were "not fit" for work in plantation colonies in the seventeenth century, these scattered claims did not crystallize into any kind of meaningful rhetoric until the eighteenth century.[14] In the nineteenth-century United States, climatic language about race affected emigration and colonization, and this rhetoric continued into the twentieth century. This book goes back to the formative years of the era of transatlantic slavery to illuminate the development of this particular rhetoric of climate, labor, and bodily difference.[15]

Climate, Environment, and Bodily Health

This book connects the history of health and the environment with political events and economic concerns to show that concepts of biological race did not emerge naturally from people's experiences in plantation societies. Planters in the lowcountry and the West Indies were economically savvy, making calculated decisions designed to boost their financial, social, and political capital. Given their concern with their status, they were highly sensitive to threats to the system of forced labor they had created. The proposed abolition of the slave trade imperiled the structure they had refined. If they could no longer import people stolen from Africa and force them to work on plantations until they died, planters feared that their labor system and source of wealth would collapse. They had every incentive, therefore, to counter threats to the slave trade with any argument they could muster. The racialized rhetoric of climate was one of the ways slaveholders appealed to legislators.[16]

Planters' arguments about the effect of climate on people's bodies were rooted in ancient Greek and Roman theories. Aristotle had declared in *Meteorology* that the heat in the tropics was so intense as to make the region uninhabitable, and early European travelers to the Americas found themselves having to persuade those at home that people could live, and even thrive, in tropical places. Even so, Europeans remained skeptical of a different climate's effect on their bodies. In the early modern period, Europeans considered climate to be indistinguishable from latitude; the closer a place was to the tropics, the hotter that place would be. These perceptions of latitude and climate continued to affect European expeditions across the Atlantic well into the colonial era.[17]

Moreover, the Hippocratic text *Airs, Waters, and Places* drew direct connections between bodies and their surroundings, with climatic and environmental implications for bodily health. Historians of medicine have shown that European medical practitioners relied heavily on Hippocratic theories during the seventeenth and eighteenth centuries. Environmental concepts of health and bodily change continued into the nineteenth-century United States, even as theories of biological race overtook those of changeable bodies around the turn of the century. According to Hippocratic theories, environmental conditions, including the strength and direction of winds, the presence of stagnant or flowing water, the composition of soil, and the amount of shade or the angle of sunlight a place received played a central role in determining bodily health. These ideas about bodies and environmental conditions lay at the core of Anglo-American understandings of the body.[18]

As a result, many settler-colonists in the Anglo-Atlantic developed extraordinarily nuanced understandings of localized environments or microclimates. For these colonists, becoming familiar with the winds and the waters of a particular place and organizing infrastructure according to local environmental conditions could mean the difference between health and illness. In addition, prevailing medical theories held that good health resulted from people's internal elements operating in harmony with external environmental conditions. Galenic writings, which also influenced early modern Europeans, stated that a person's fluids, or humors, had to maintain a specific proportion to one another for that person to be healthy, and this proportion varied from body to body. Humoral and environmental balance working in tandem translated into good health, and physicians theorized that illness was often the result of the external environment throwing off a person's internal balance.[19]

These climatic, environmental, and medical theories had several implications for slaveholders' arguments. English travelers harbored considerable fears about the dangers of hot climates for their bodies. Because bodies were calibrated to particular climates, a substantial change in climate could throw off this careful balance and trigger illness. Climate, then, played a significant role in a collective English and European imagination; for European inhabitants, it was not difficult to conceive that an unfamiliar climate could threaten their bodies. Slaveholders' arguments about the climate in plantation societies touched upon these fears, and longstanding suspicions of the dangers of unfamiliar climates supported planters' rhetoric.

On the other hand, settler-colonists considered environmental nuance, rather than simply changes in latitude, to be essential to bodily health. This meant that local conditions, such as the presence of flowing water and fresh breezes, could be more important than broader climatic conditions in assessing whether or not a place would be healthy. While the impact of local environments on bodily health did not negate the importance of climate, settlers often believed that living in a place away from stagnant water and its accompanying dangerous miasmas, for example, was more important to the preservation of their health than seeking a place in a familiar latitude. As medical manuals in the eighteenth century announced, all climates had healthy and unhealthy spots, and differences existed across incremental spaces. Naval physician James Lind, who wrote one of the most cited and well-known books on the health of Europeans in hot climates, observed that the heat in a particular place did "not altogether depend upon a proximity to the Equator," but was instead determined by a place's elevation and soil, which varied across "inconsiderable distances." At the same time, concerns about bodily health led settler-colonists in the Americas to try to alter both local environments and the climate on a larger scale. Colonists in North America cut down trees to encourage air flow, drained swamps to remove standing water, and convinced themselves that their surroundings were gradually warming or cooling, depending on where they lived.[20]

Colonists' perceptions of their ability to alter their surroundings, as well as their sense of environmental nuance, reveal some of the smaller cracks in planters' climatic arguments for racial slavery. The attention that Anglo-American settler-colonists gave to environmental conditions, and the extent to which they planned and built around them, demonstrates that the concept of a hot climate was for many of them an outdated and oversimplified rhetorical device. Those living in plantation societies in the Greater Caribbean recognized that they inhabited a hot climate. But just as colonists had discredited ancient fears that life was altogether impossible in the tropics, so too did they recognize that the concept of a uniform hot climate was far too imprecise to describe the places in which they lived. Yet slaveholders used this term in their arguments to defend the transatlantic slave trade because it had ideological power. Drawing upon established fears of hot climates gave slaveholders a rhetorical advantage, in part because such a concept meant more to legislators far removed from plantation societies than it did to those living on plantations themselves.

Larger cracks in planters' arguments begin to appear through a close look at contemporary concepts of health and bodily difference. Writings of physicians in the West Indian colonies show that they did not consider race to be a cause of medical difference for much the eighteenth century. Instead, they largely focused on place, theorizing that environmental conditions, rather than innate differences, caused illness. Similarly, white Americans did not note differences in diseases between Black and white bodies during this period.[21]

In addition to published medical manuals, private letters—from managers in the West Indies to absentee planters, from struggling settlers in early Georgia to their patrons, and from family members to one another across the Anglo-Atlantic world—reveal a great deal about the ways settler-colonists thought about health, bodily difference, and the environment in plantation societies. Letter after letter explains that slaveholders and others believed that environmental conditions affected all bodies in the same way. Prolonged periods of rainy weather, for example, made everyone sick, Black as well as white, and drier spells improved people's health. Personal correspondence clearly shows planters' understandings that everyone was vulnerable to the same environmental threats, regardless of skin color. The main difference in susceptibility, according to several sources, was people's amount of exposure to dangerous environments. Enslaved people, therefore, often fell ill more severely than others because they were the most exposed, and planters and physicians recognized this vulnerability.

Regardless of their recognition that exposure to environmental hazards, including the dangers of field labor, harmed enslaved laborers, slaveholders managed to turn their beliefs about the origins of illness onto enslaved people themselves. Eighteenth-century concepts of health and illness became increasingly tied to behavior, as medical practitioners began to see certain diseases as a consequence of moral failings. This behavioral link with illness applied to both Black and white populations in the colonies, and slaveholders embraced this theory as a way to avoid their own responsibility for enslaved people's illnesses. That is, planters and managers regularly blamed bondspeople for their exposure to dangerous air by claiming, for example, that they spent too much time dancing at night. Settler-colonists considered night air to be especially humid and harmful, and slaveholders repeatedly cast blame on enslaved people who gathered during the only time they had free from direct supervision. Regardless of responsibility for illness, however, planters' recognition that enslaved people regularly fell ill on plantations and that these illnesses were often the result of exposure to environmental conditions demonstrates some of the weaknesses of the climatic defense of racial slavery. In other words, the frequency of illness and death among enslaved populations on plantations casts doubt on planters' claims that Black people were especially suited to labor in the hot climates of the Americas.[22]

Finally, the concept of seasoning reveals some of the most significant fault lines in planters' rhetoric about climate and slavery. According to colonial understandings of bodily health, as people moved from one climate to another their bodies became acclimatized, or seasoned, to the new environment. This process could take years, and it entailed a permanent bodily change. Crucially for slaveholders, Africans as well as Europeans needed to adjust physically to the unfamiliar climate in the Americas. West Indian and lowcountry environments differed significantly from various parts of Africa, and planters recognized the need for Africans' bodily adjustment upon arrival in the Greater Caribbean. Settler-colonists viewed unseasoned bodies of any skin color or point of origin as significantly more vulnerable to environmental threats than seasoned bodies. Planters considered that neither Africans nor Europeans had bodies suited to environments on the western side of the Atlantic, but both could adapt. This is an essential point, as it demonstrates that white colonists did not, in fact, view Black laborers as especially suited to plantation environments. Under careful scrutiny, and with due attention to prevailing concepts of environmental nuance and seasoning, planters' arguments about the necessity of Black laborers on plantations because of their particular ability to labor in hot climates begin to unravel.[23]

Race

The notion of seasoning also signified the fundamental fluidity of bodies. This bodily ability to change applied to physical appearance as well as to health. Bodies were malleable, porous entities, and environmental forces inscribed themselves upon people's faces, limbs, and skin, affecting posture, gait, complexion, and countless other bodily characteristics. British Atlantic travelers believed, for example, that the texture and tone of their skin might alter or that the shapes and contours of their faces and eyes might shift to accommodate a change in the angle of sunlight if they moved from one environment to another. A person's bodily fibers could tighten, toughen, or relax according to the climate; pores might widen or narrow along with the heat and moisture in the air; and internal organs could adjust along with the body's external appearance. All these physical changes that accompanied environmental fluctuations underscored the widely held conviction among colonists that bodies were changeable.[24]

Settlers' writings from the eighteenth century demonstrate that they did not hold concepts of fixed bodily difference. Instead, personal correspondence reveals an array of ideas about mutable bodies contingent on environmental factors. Writing about the relocation of a group of bondspeople from one plantation environment to another, for instance, a Jamaican planter noted that they "appear to me not the same looking People." Similarly, a West Indian resident from Scotland wrote that his siblings had "both much altered in their looks" after prolonged residence in the Caribbean climate. In each of these cases, as well as in many others, planters, travelers, and merchants all noted that people's bodies physically changed as they adapted to different environmental conditions. This book argues in part that the notion of bodies in flux with their environments undermines planters' rhetoric about definitive and innate bodily difference justifying Black labor in early American plantation societies. Bodies changed as they moved from one environment to another, and slaveholders recognized that bodies were only compatible with particular environments until they became seasoned to another. Once they became seasoned, bodies suited that particular environment best, so, for example, there was no reason that a white body seasoned to a hot climate could not labor there.[25]

At the same time, racial prejudice existed long before the advent of biological racial theories. Racist practices, or differential treatment based upon skin color and ethnicity, abounded in the early modern Atlantic world, and many of these practices were codified in law. Social norms governing labor on plantations, for example, strengthened and reinforced racist practices as field labor became increasingly associated with Blackness during the colonial period and after. Preexisting racial antipathy deepened and strengthened along with racial slavery in early America. This racism was not irreconcilable with concepts of malleable bodies; white Anglo-Americans saw their own bodies and the bodies of others as changeable and adaptable even as they simultaneously constructed a hierarchy with themselves at the top.[26]

Yet even as racial prejudice flourished during the eighteenth century, the turn to biological race was neither natural nor inevitable. Even on a theoretical level, intellectual conceptions of bodily difference were inconsistent and contradictory. Eighteenth-century European philosophers who engaged in robust theoretical discussions about the origins and rankings of human bodies around the globe sometimes drew upon ancient theories of climate and environment.[27] In *Politics*, for example, Aristotle had argued that climate affected people's characters, intelligence, and political situations, and these assertions influenced early modern Europeans. In the sixteenth century, French philosopher Jean Bodin used Aristotle's theories as a basis for his own writings, and these same theories undergirded philosophical discussions about whether or not populations native to the Americas could or should be enslaved, particularly in the Spanish context.[28] By the middle of the eighteenth century, philosophers and naturalists such as Montesquieu had reiterated and refined ancient theories, proclaiming that a region's climate strongly affected its inhabitants' bodies as well as their societies. These European theories of self-superiority prompted Euro-Americans to assert that they had not deteriorated in a different climate, but rather, in the most famous example, Thomas Jefferson insisted that the North American climate had made Euro-Americans more robust than their European counterparts. Nevertheless, inhabitants of hot climates remained a favorite target of European philosophers, and Jefferson himself had complicated but decidedly racist views of Black Americans. More to the point, an "intellectual genealogy" of European thinkers does not often reflect the reality of people's lives on plantations, and even those planters who subscribed to or participated in these debates did not translate their theories into direct practice. In other words, planters' writings on bodies reflect their understandings that bodies were changeable and malleable regardless of whether or not philosophers and naturalists believed in fixed racial differences.[29]

Concepts of biological race did not develop inevitably from colonial lived experience with bodily health. Plantation managers and colonial medical practitioners remained deeply embedded in environmental theories of health and illness that considered seasoning, not skin color or other bodily difference, as the most important factor in determining health. Moreover, concepts of seasoning held that bodies could change and adapt to different climates, throwing planters' claims about Africans' suitability for American climates into serious doubt. When faced with the potential end of the slave trade, slaveholders presented arguments that demonstrated a consciously constructed public narrative of deep certainty and cohesion about physiological bodily differences between Black and white bodies, in contrast to a private set of indeterminate and fluctuating understandings of bodies. Varying opinions about climate, health, and bodies coalesced into strong convictions about racial difference.

This book makes the case that a rhetoric of bodily difference gained strength and power as slaveholders and others imbued it with a language of nature. The case of Georgia is emblematic. Settlers in the colony's early years had no reason to believe that Europeans were incapable of laboring in the lowcountry climate, and sources show how aspiring slave traders adopted a rhetoric about the necessity of Black laborers in Georgia's climate as a smokescreen for other grievances. Nevertheless, the turn to racial slavery in Georgia seemed to outsiders to be incontrovertible proof that places with hot climates required Black laborers. The arguments over climate and labor in Georgia became foundational to the larger climatic justification for Black slavery throughout the Anglo-Atlantic. By the nineteenth century, white people defending racial slavery in the American South relied upon a language of climate and race that had become a maxim. This rhetoric appeared in Parliamentary and Congressional debates, and in pamphlets and other public writings supporting slavery in plantation societies. Because this language dealt directly with the body, and because it separated Black from white bodies through a supposedly natural division, it contributed to the construction of theories of biological race.[30]

Slavery's defenders resorted to a rhetoric about race and climate as ideological support for their larger economic motives. Threats to the slave trade and the institution of slavery pushed to the fore an unambiguous picture of Black and white bodily difference in contrast to the fluid and inconsistent notions of bodies prevalent at the time. At the end of the eighteenth century and into the nineteenth, a binary racial rhetoric flattened and erased colonists' nuanced conceptions of bodily difference.

Framing a Narrative

For those living in plantation societies, death and illness were everywhere. All people in the colonial Americas "suffered extraordinary mortality rates, but certain peoples were always considered more expendable than others."[31] Both Africans and Europeans experienced alarming levels of mortality in the seventeenth-century West Indies, and even if Europeans in eighteenth-century Jamaica died in slightly higher proportions, Africans died in larger numbers. Upon visiting his Jamaican plantation in the early nineteenth century, Matthew Lewis commented that "the climate" did not seem particularly suited to Black laborers, whose lives seemed "very precarious." High death rates on his plantation gave Lewis no choice but to observe the tenuousness of Black lives on a West Indian plantation. None of these high death rates suggests that white people could have considered Black people to be particularly healthy on plantations, and personal correspondence supports this conclusion. The reality was that all bodies suffered from labor in dangerous environmental conditions, but white planters placed Black bodies in these spaces much more readily than white bodies. This was a deliberate situation, and an illustration of the way in which environmental racism was central to Atlantic slavery.[32]

This context of death, and particularly the death of Black plantation laborers, is essential to re-framing the narrative of the transition to African slavery in the Greater Caribbean. For example, historians seeking to understand the transition to enslaved African laborers on plantations have sometimes looked to differences in immunities, suggesting that some groups of Africans may have held immunities to particular diseases that Europeans did not. In particular, they have argued that certain Black populations had immunities or resistance to malaria and yellow fever and that these immunities led planters to select Black laborers because they were healthier. Regardless of the uncertainties inherent in diagnosing the past, this approach to history accepts planters' arguments that only Black people could labor in the heat as a premise and seeks to find a modern medical explanation to support that premise. Historians taking this approach appear to want to find a logical reason for racial slavery that is separate from racism. By assuming that planters' arguments, made in defense of the slave trade, had validity, this approach diminishes the outrageous death tolls of Black plantation laborers by focusing more on the death rates of white people. This approach is also problematic because of its overreliance on published material; the extent of slaveholders' claims had a long reach, and histories that rely largely on those published sources are predictably partial to those sources.[33]

The Nature of Slavery demonstrates that the story told in printed material can differ substantially from the one told in private. This is a deceptively simple but essential observation. Personal correspondence, along with other sources, reveals no sense of slaveholders' ideas about racial or inherent bodily difference when it came to health on plantations. Environmental conditions affected all bodies, and planters did not note that Black people were healthier than white people on plantations, especially during the transition to African slavery in the seventeenth century. It is anachronistic to look for evidence of racial disparities in health during this period; planters and other settler-colonists believed that seasoned people, Black or white, would be healthier than unseasoned people. Race was simply not a factor in colonial understandings of bodily health.

This book is based on a rigorous examination of personal correspondence, scattered in archives across the United Kingdom, the United States, and the Caribbean, as well as on published sources. Although only a fraction of the voluminous correspondence between friends, employers, and family members in plantation societies survives, the existing letters provide significant insight into the beliefs, desires, and frustrations of planters and managers in the Greater Caribbean. Some of these letters are well catalogued and preserved in libraries and historical societies, while others remain in the care of planters' descendants. Overall, these sources reveal significant differences between planters' public claims and their private writings and actions. These differences matter because they exemplify the way that a public story can become the dominant—and often the only—narrative, despite the ways it may differ from a wealth of other evidence.

This story involves economics, politics, the environment, and conceptions of the body, particularly those related to bodily health and bodily difference. And yet this story is also necessarily partial because it recounts the creation and use of a rhetoric from the perspective of those who created and used it and not from the perspective of those it affected most. It is difficult to determine what Black people themselves thought of the climatic rhetoric during the eighteenth century. Focused on the horrors of the experience, slave narratives do not often address ideological defenses of slavery. The best sources available are nineteenth-century newspapers, written largely by and for Black people in the United States. These newspapers give insight into the ways in which some Black people firmly rejected the climatic argument while a minority of others accepted parts of it. In a sense, the most remarkable aspect of these articles is that the climatic argument appeared at all. That it did—and that Black people engaged with it in a variety of ways during the nineteenth century—demonstrates the extent to which it had become an integral part of American culture.

Structure

The book is organized into six chapters that examine race, labor, climate, and health from the seventeenth through the nineteenth century. The first chapter considers the labor force in the early English Caribbean, analyzing both the transition to a majority of enslaved African laborers on plantations and European conceptions of hot climates. Although colonial residents overcame ancient theories of the dangers of hot places, a series of events solidified the region's reputation as dangerous and unhealthy. Ultimately, white residents of warm climates learned that they could capitalize on this reputation to achieve various ends.

One of the most spectacular examples of colonists taking advantage of the supposed dangers of hot climates to white bodies was the case of Georgia in the 1730s and 1740s, the subject of the second chapter. The colony, which was conceived as an experiment without enslaved Africans, lasted less than two decades before capitulating to the demands of aspiring slaveholders. Although residents repeatedly insisted on the need for Black laborers in the heat, archival evidence shows that white people could labor in Georgia but that those interested in profiting from the Atlantic slave trade argued that they could not. The implication of this argument—that Black labor really was necessary in the heat—served as a lasting justification for race-based slavery across hot climates of the Atlantic.

The next two chapters examine places and bodies in depth. Chapter 3 shows that colonial residents thought of their environments in highly localized and nuanced ways, and these differences played a role in determining patterns of settlement. Crucially, rather than considering Black bodies healthier than white bodies in dangerous environmental conditions, white people perceived the suffering of Black people in hazardous environments. Chapter 4 demonstrates that far from relying on a sense of racial difference in susceptibilities to disease, physicians and laypeople alike understood bodies as products of their environments, consistently subject to change. Just as Britons understood that their own bodies would adjust to the unfamiliar environment on plantations, so too did planters believe that Africans would adapt to the climate in the Americas. This need for African bodily adjustment lays bare the deep contradictions between planters' private beliefs about bodies and the public claims they made in hearings over the slave trade.

Elucidating these contradictions in greater depth, Chapter 5 focuses on Parliamentary debates in the 1780s and 1790s over the abolition of the transatlantic trade. West Indian planters insisted that plantations could never be cultivated without African labor. But others maintained that European bodies could stand the heat of the Americas as long as they were inured to labor. In their repeated petitions to Parliament, though, planters dismissed all history of European labor in the West Indian colonies, insisting instead on its impossibility.

Thanks in large part to the public arguments over plantation labor, the link between skin color and the ability to work in warm climates had become a maxim by the nineteenth century. The sixth chapter shows some of the ways in which this climatic rhetoric operated in the United States. A variety of people, both Black and white, drew upon the theory of Black people's bodily suitability for hot places to promote different causes. They made cases for and against emigration out of the country; they argued about the westward expansion of slavery; and they theorized about bodily differences between Black and white people. Black activists both used and condemned the racialized language of climate as they fought against a tide of racism that questioned their place in the country.

* * *

Ultimately, private letters from plantation societies demonstrate the ways in which people with an interest in African slavery created and disseminated a rhetoric about climate, race, and labor even though it did not accord with their experience. White planters did not choose to cultivate plantations with enslaved Black laborers for health reasons because they did not observe noticeable differences between Black and white bodily health during the seventeenth or eighteenth centuries. By focusing on a variety of sources from the West Indies and the lowcountry, this book re-centers a discussion about race away from European scientists and thinkers and toward people's experiences in plantation societies. Most historical work rests on the assumption that a fairly continuous line exists from English uncertainties about hot climates in the seventeenth century to a biological theory of racial difference during the eighteenth century. This book aims to show that no such continuum existed. Instead, unpublished sources reveal the prominence of varying perceptions about bodies, race, and the environment during the eighteenth century. These sources show the ways in which those with an interest in racial slavery manufactured arguments to defend the institution.

At first glance, it might seem that a straightforward explanation resolves the question of how planters could insist upon the need for enslaved Black laborers while in some cases exclaiming how healthy they felt in the heat. Perhaps, as some planters insisted, white people could live, but not labor, in hot climates. Yet the story is not so simple, and this solution skirts the central issue of how and why planters made categorical declarations about Black and white bodily responses to warm climates despite their own experiences. It is true that some planters did operate under the assumption that, although white people could live in a hot place, they could not labor there. But it is also true that others had vastly different understandings of the capacity of white people to labor in the heat. Several West Indian planters, for example, sought out Scottish plowmen, reasoning that Highlanders accustomed to one kind of harsh climate would easily adapt to another. Although the "white negroes" Thomas Fraser observed arriving in St. Vincent in 1791 would most likely have looked for work as artisans rather than as field workers, this labor system reflected a social hierarchy based upon skin color that was well established by the late eighteenth century. The American South looked similar—white people did not labor on southern plantations because a social system created and maintained a division of labor tied to skin color. As abolitionists and others pointed out, white people in both the southern lowcountry and in pockets of the Caribbean labored in fields for subsistence. Perhaps most importantly, planters and managers wrote consistently about how unhealthy enslaved Black laborers actually were on plantations. Only in public did planters construct an image of Black bondspeople happily laboring in fields under a hot sun; in private, planters and managers constantly noted the heavy death tolls on plantations and the poor health of many laborers. Clearly, enslaved people suffered extremely from the conditions under which they labored, and planters knew this.

This book demonstrates the origins of a rhetoric about climate, labor, bodies, and race in Anglo-American plantation societies, as well as how it developed over the course of the eighteenth century. It also shows some of the ways white people manipulated and used this rhetoric to defend racial slavery and to separate themselves from Black people, both ideologically and physically, in changing political and social contexts. It makes the case that planters' rhetoric created a myth about the labor transition in the colonial period that is not only misleading but damaging. The assumption that planters turned to enslaved African laborers for climatic or health reasons perpetuates an environmentally racist fallacy and seems to excuse some of planters' racism. The point here is not simply to call planters' bluff. Instead, revealing the hollowness of their arguments about climate and labor demonstrates the ways that slaveholders' baseless claims provided fodder for theories of biological race and helped to excuse practices of environmental racism across the Atlantic world. Despite their experiences with health, labor, and the environment in plantation societies, slaveholders perpetuated a climatic rhetoric that proved foundational to Anglo-American constructions of race.

1

Labor in Hot Climates

The Seventeenth Century

In the early decades of the seventeenth century the trip from the British Isles to the Caribbean tested people's bodies. The motion of the ship caused many passengers to fall seasick. Food became stale, moldy, and riddled with vermin, making meals unappetizing at best. The air below deck was stifling and uncomfortable. Sounds and smells of unwashed bodies in close proximity to one another, as well as to frightened livestock, assaulted the ears and noses of travelers. Deprived of fresh food and crowded together, crew and passengers alike might suffer from any number of illnesses. For a passenger from England, Scotland, or Ireland bound for St. Christopher, Antigua, or Barbados, these conditions only exacerbated the anxiety and uncertainty over a larger concern: what would happen to their bodies once they arrived?

Regardless of whether voyagers from the British Isles traveled to the West Indies as prospective planters or as laborers, they would have been familiar with popular lore about the dangers of the climate. Ancient theories about the tenuousness of life in hot climates proved difficult to overcome, despite repeated European voyages to the Caribbean throughout the sixteenth century. Beginning in the 1620s, however, a steady flow of migrants from the British Isles arrived in the West Indies, the majority of them as laborers. These laborers cleared wooded land to create fields, then planted cotton, indigo, and tobacco. They constructed buildings and tended fields, trying to coax potentially lucrative products from the soil. They harvested crops seasonally, sending them to ports to be shipped and sold. In the process, some laborers fell ill and died, while others survived.[1]

Over subsequent decades, ships from the West African coast began arriving on the islands, and by the 1650s their numbers had swelled. The passengers on these ships fared considerably worse than did those from the British Isles. They were enslaved and thus substantially more crowded together, spending much of their time chained to one another below deck. There was no room to

The Nature of Slavery. Katherine Johnston, Oxford University Press. © Oxford University Press 2022.
DOI: 10.1093/oso/9780197514603.003.0002

stand up, and they lay awash in human waste that sloshed across floorboards with the motion of the sea. These passengers' health fared poorly; they did not have enough to eat, and sickness spread quickly in the confines of their maritime prison. Sharks trailed in ships' wakes, feasting on the refuse tossed overboard. Sometimes these sharks also feasted on human bodies.[2]

None of these migrants—all of them forced—came to the West Indies as planters. All arrived as laborers. They cleared forests, planted and harvested crops, and built structures for processing and storing the crops. Some of these laborers fell ill and died within a few weeks, months, or years, while others survived longer. Although they had more pressing concerns, much like the laborers from the British Isles, these enslaved migrants also found themselves in an unfamiliar climate.

Laborers from both Africa and Europe, along with enslaved Indigenous laborers from various parts of the Atlantic region, performed difficult tasks in demanding environmental conditions. They withstood long days of preparing, planting, and harvesting crops in the searing sun, and they encountered snakes, rats, and razor-edged vegetation in forests thick with disease-carrying mosquitos. Dense patches of sugarcane harbored similar threats, and tasks such as digging holes for the cane along with hauling, spreading, and turning dung on the fields led to high mortality rates.[3]

Most histories of this period note that in the 1640s, planters began turning to sugar as a particularly profitable crop, first in Barbados and then in other islands. As they did so, they also began relying heavily upon enslaved Africans to perform the difficult labor of sugar production. Although Europeans continued to labor on plantations and even cultivated and harvested sugar in the early decades of the sugar boom, enslaved Africans replaced indentured Europeans as the majority of laborers by the second half of the seventeenth century.[4] The numbers of enslaved Indigenous people are more difficult to estimate; issues of legality meant that enslaved Indigenous peoples went largely undocumented in English archives. For the most part, planters grouped them together with enslaved Africans in their records and often failed to distinguish them. The positions of enslaved Indigenous peoples were similar to those of enslaved Africans on Barbados plantations, with both groups performing the same roles and facing the same treatment. Still, this archival absence contributed to the erasure of Indigenous peoples in later British accounts of labor in the seventeenth-century Caribbean.[5]

In many later accounts of the transition to a predominantly African workforce, beginning with late eighteenth-century debates over the slave trade, planters minimized the role of European laborers in the seventeenth century. When they acknowledged European labor, defenders of slavery claimed that planters turned to Africans because their bodies suited the hot Caribbean

climate better than European bodies did. But these arguments relayed a decep-
tive history. Seventeenth-century planters did not embrace African slavery for
climatic reasons, nor did they note health differences among African, European,
and Indigenous bodies. How and why, then, did later generations of planters
make these climatic arguments so vigorously and to such great effect? The first
piece of this puzzle can be found through an understanding of labor conditions,
assessments of bodily health, and reports of the climate circulating in the seventeenth century.

This chapter makes two central arguments. First, it demonstrates that
planters' perceptions of bodily health played no role in the seventeenth-century labor transition. This was in part because other factors, particularly the
supply of available laborers, determined who worked on plantations, and in
part because neither planters nor physicians noted categorical differences in
African and European bodily responses to the Caribbean climate. Even after
the transition from mostly indentured European to mostly enslaved African
laborers in mid-century, both planters and colonial officials continued
to recruit and petition the English government for indentured servants
throughout the second half of the seventeenth century. Planters seeking
laborers, whether from northern Europe, the Americas, or West Africa, primarily looked for workers who were available and economical. Colonial
understandings of climate and bodies had no bearing on the makeup of plantation labor forces.

Second, although fears of hot climates abounded in early modern England,
settler-colonial populations developed nuanced understandings of Greater
Caribbean environments. Colonists understood that the heat was neither an au-
tomatic death sentence nor a miraculous cure. Still, residents of the British Isles
received conflicting reports about these climates. Promotional material extolling
the virtues of the lowcountry and West Indian environments portrayed them as
ideal places for human habitation, while reports of disasters such as the English
military expedition against the Spanish in 1655 known as the Western Design
and the Port Royal earthquake of 1692 appeared to portend serious danger for
European bodies in warm latitudes. By the early eighteenth century, those in the
metropole remained unsure of the effects of heat on northern European bodies,
but in general they did not categorically dismiss the possibility of British labor
on colonial plantations.[6]

Settler-colonial understandings of climatic complexity, as well as Europeans'
bodily fitness for such places, did not traverse the Atlantic intact. While Euro-
Caribbean residents often found that their experiences in warm climates did not
conform to their expectations, they primarily transmitted this climatic knowledge through personal correspondence. Meanwhile, disastrous occurrences
like the Western Design and the Port Royal earthquake were newsworthy items.

Accounts of illness and mortality accompanying these disasters fueled English perceptions of the Caribbean climate's potential dangers.

The transatlantic disparity regarding beliefs about bodily health and hot climates allowed inhabitants of the Greater Caribbean to harness the power of climate as a rhetorical tool. Through a combination of pre-conceived European notions and publicized reports of devastating events, Euro-Caribbean residents used entrenched English suspicions about the dangers of hot climates to further their own economic prospects. Some colonial officials, for example, demanded higher wages to compensate for the health risks of residing in the heat. Although their employers in England did not always take colonial officials at their word, governors and other civil servants in the colonies deliberately used the English fear of hot climates to make their cases.

This climatic rhetoric laid the groundwork for later climatic justifications for African slavery in the Greater Caribbean. Although planters transitioned from mostly European to mostly African laborers around the middle of the century, this transition had nothing to do with the actual climatic effects on African versus European bodies. Yet by portraying this transition in part as a climatic move—by speculating that planters switched to Africans because hot climates suited their bodies better than the bodies of Europeans—later writers naturalized the transition to slavery, portraying it as an inevitable development of labor in a hot climate. In fact, nothing about the transition to slavery was natural, nor did climatic concerns motivate planters to shift the labor force during the seventeenth century. This chapter presents evidence countering this historical explanation and demonstrates the ways in which a climatic rhetoric developed and grew throughout the seventeenth century.

The political and economic savvy of Euro-Caribbean residents regarding climatic prejudice in England should not eclipse the sincere trepidation many of them felt about a hot climate's effects on their bodies. While some English settlers may have felt healthy in the warm regions of the Greater Caribbean, natural disasters, such as earthquakes and hurricanes, revealed the precariousness of environmental conditions in these places. Many inhabitants were not without qualms, and several questioned the stability both of the local environment and of their own bodily health. Yet rather than viewing hot climates as unequivocally dangerous for European bodies, sources show an ambiguous Euro-Caribbean approach towards bodily health and potential change in an unstable climate.

From Skepticism to Optimism—and Back Again

Travelers' concerns had deep roots. Although the seventeenth century witnessed significant change in the scientific and medical community, prevailing ideas about the body still relied heavily on ancient Greek and Roman concepts. According to these theories, people's bodies reflected and responded to their surrounding environments. Atmospheric elements, including temperature, moisture, and air quality of particular places, affected peoples' health, characters, appearances, and identities. A healthy body maintained a stable equilibrium between its internal humors and the external elements. Bodies were permeable, and a constant movement of fluids and vapors throughout the body, as well as between bodies and their surroundings, contributed to good health. While bodies could adjust to gradual external changes such as seasonal transitions, more significant fluctuations, such as sudden weather events or travel to a different climate, could cause a change in health.[7]

In addition, Aristotle had theorized that the earth could be divided into sections based on latitudinal bands, and only the middle parts—between the torrid center and the frozen poles—could be inhabited by humans. As increasing numbers of Iberian, French, Dutch, and English travelers ventured to West Africa and the American tropics during the sixteenth and early seventeenth centuries, many of them felt compelled to reassure inhabitants of Europe that warm climates did not induce swift and sure death.[8] Insisting upon the value of their own "eyewitness experience," some of these travelers published reports detailing lush and vibrant lands in the Americas, full of thriving greenery and capable of supporting both animal and human inhabitants.[9] These accounts challenged Aristotle's model of a zoned earth with a parched, burning central region certain to extinguish all life. Some parts of the ancient theory remained true—the Torrid Zone was indeed hot—but other parts of it, including its inhospitable nature, could be tossed out in the face of new evidence. But human existence in the American tropics did not in itself allay fears that Europeans, let alone northern Europeans from the British Isles, could thrive in such a hot place. Residents of the British Isles who considered traveling to the hot climates of the Americas in the early part of the seventeenth century continued to worry about their health, as well as about other potential bodily changes in a different climate.[10]

Scattered reports of English voyagers in hot climates began appearing in the mid-sixteenth century. Describing an expedition from England to West Africa in 1554–1555, one writer declared that Africa was so hot that even the moon radiated heat. Residents "curse[d]" the sun when it rose, he wrote, and the intense heat curled people's hair and made their skin "very blacke." In contrast, the West Indian islands had a more moderate climate. The air was "very temperate," and the inhabitants' bodies displayed this difference. Their straight hair complemented skin "the colour of an Olive," a marked change from people in both Africa and Europe. These descriptions reflected prevailing ideas that climatic conditions shaped bodily appearance. Prior to the seventeenth century, though, English ideas about the effects of hot climates on their own bodies were still largely speculative rather than experiential. Traveling to a hot place was one thing, but living there might have significant bodily consequences.[11]

English settler-colonists who began establishing permanent settlements in the Caribbean in the 1620s and 1630s had only a smattering of reports to guide them. Henry Colt, who arrived in St. Christopher in the summer of 1631, found that the island's constant breezes made the air "fresh & coole." Although he noted that the summer sun could cause fevers, Colt wrote that his health had not suffered, in part because he had carefully calibrated his diet and wardrobe to the climate. Richard Ligon, who traveled to Barbados in the late 1640s, found the air "torridly hot" and wondered how "bodyes comming out of cold Climates, could indure such scorching without being suffocated." After a short time, though, Ligon observed that his body began to adapt. Like Colt, Ligon appreciated the cooling sea breezes that blew throughout the day and thought colonists could take precautions to preserve their health. Notably, neither Colt nor Ligon seemed bothered by fundamental bodily changes. Explaining that the West Indian climate made little impression on English bodies, Colt declared that the sun "neuer freckles nor tannes ye skinn, except of such as works in ye heatt therof all day." Responding to northern European theories that proximity to the equator determined skin tone, Colt clarified that light-skinned people would neither automatically nor necessarily darken in the Caribbean.[12]

Colt's comment reveals the prevalence of light-skinned manual laborers in the Caribbean. Some English, Scottish, Welsh, and Irish people noticed changes in their skin precisely because they did work in the heat all day. In fact, Colt provided an extensive account of several such laborers who cleared a plot of land in St. Christopher and began work on an estate for him. Servants from the British Isles cut through dense tropical forest and carried building materials uphill from the coast. The labor was so demanding that Colt wrote to his son requesting more servants. "I want at least 40 men moor," he wrote. "I haue a great plantation, & I will . . . pay all men y^t wch is due vnto them next yeer." Colt's writings are silent on the precise labor he expected these servants to perform and on whether or not he intended to use any other laborers, such as enslaved Indigenous peoples. Even so, Colt's desire for servants reflected his understanding of the Caribbean labor force in the early seventeenth century: if he promised payment, he would be able to procure European laborers for his nascent plantation.[13]

By the time Colt traveled to St. Christopher, the English had established settlements on several Caribbean islands. Most of the wealthier inhabitants owned plantations worked by European indentured servants who cleared brush, prepared fields, and cultivated and harvested crops including tobacco, indigo, and cotton. These servants learned to cultivate crops from Indigenous peoples, many of whom had themselves been enslaved and transported to the islands from elsewhere. Although planters relied on the knowledge and labor of Indigenous peoples, the market for European indentured servants thrived, especially as English officials began sentencing convicts to be shipped to the islands. As Colt's narrative makes clear, his reliance on indentured servants as well as his request for more attests to their prevalence and importance in early Caribbean settlements. His desire to invest in servant laborers, moreover, leaves no doubt that he expected them to survive in the Caribbean. Colt surely would have hoped that any investment of his would pay off, which would require that Europeans be able to work in the West Indian climate.[14]

Several years later, Richard Ligon was both shocked and impressed with the hard labor servants were expected to perform on plantations. After spending the night in crudely constructed cabins, servants worked in the fields "with a severe Overseer to command them" from six in the morning until six in the evening. They were allowed a meager midday meal of gruel, beans, or potatoes before returning to the fields, and they ate the same thing again at night. Servants in the Caribbean, Ligon reflected, were "put to very hard labour." This labor, though, was not impossible for Europeans to perform. Nowhere in his history did Ligon indicate that European servants were unable to work, nor did he write that such physical exertion in the heat would sicken workers because they were European or constitutionally incapable of work. In fact, Ligon noted that even during the hottest part of the year "servants, both Christians, and slaves, labour and travell tenne hours in a day." "Christians," then, or Europeans, could indeed adjust to the tropical climate. As Ligon observed, many had adapted to the extent that they could labor all day in the Caribbean heat.[15]

At the time Ligon wrote, the population of Caribbean laborers was rapidly changing from primarily indentured Europeans to enslaved Africans. Some scholars have argued that racial prejudice and racist attitudes in Europe facilitated, or at least enabled, slavery based on skin color. Others maintain that Caribbean planters switched from indentured European to enslaved African laborers because of economic factors. While there is little doubt that racial prejudice contributed to planters' promulgation of African slavery in the Americas, a variety of economic reasons likely ranked highly in planters' decisions to turn to an enslaved labor force. As sugar became a lucrative crop, planters wanted to increase its production and therefore sought large numbers of laborers. Although in previous decades planters had been able to obtain servant laborers from the British Isles, the population of readily available European servants shrank markedly in the mid-seventeenth century due to increasing economic opportunities in England following the Civil War and the mid-century English Navigation and Trade Laws that limited planters' access to Scottish servants. The economic opportunities in England encouraged many potential servants to stay rather than leave for the colonies, or to choose mainland colonies with greater post-indenture opportunities. While the earliest generations of indentured laborers could acquire land upon the expiration of their terms, small Caribbean islands such as Barbados, Antigua, and St. Christopher had rapidly diminishing available land. At the same time, larger planters consolidated smaller estates into plantations that primarily grew sugar. The English continued to import enslaved Indigenous laborers, but never in the enormous numbers required to cultivate swiftly growing sugar estates. Given the relative scarcity of available servants, planters began turning to slave traders to fulfill their labor needs. Perpetuating this pattern, as increasing numbers of enslaved African laborers appeared on plantations, white servants who had previously worked the land proved increasingly unwilling to labor alongside enslaved Africans, particularly when opportunities arose elsewhere.[16]

Economically minded planters desired the most readily available laborers for the least amount of money and began relying upon enslaved Africans. Although in several cases European servants did work with enslaved Africans, their reluctance to do so contributed to the changing labor force. Moreover, as servants from the British Isles contemplated traveling to the Caribbean, the fear of the islands' unhealthiness and poor labor conditions could have affected their decisions. Some early accounts like Ligon's and Colt's emphasized the surprisingly benign nature of the climate, remarking upon the cooling breezes that blew from the sea all day long. Potential servants encountering reports like these might conclude that the West Indies would not be so unhealthy for Europeans. At the same time, these accounts also noted the difficult manual labor expected of servants. Even if potential servants could imagine that the Caribbean climate itself would not slay them, reports seemed to indicate that the labor might. But most people from the British Isles would have had limited access to reliable reports. Ligon's published work was expensive and not widely distributed, and personal accounts like Colt's reached a small audience. Unfortunately for planters who still sought to attract indentured servants, in the 1650s the reputation of the West Indian climate suffered a well-publicized and serious setback through the campaign known as the Western Design.[17]

In 1654, General Robert Venables, naval Commissioner William Penn, and a fleet of English ships arrived in the Caribbean in an attempt to oust the Spanish from Hispaniola. Landing far from the capital of Santo Domingo, in 1655 Venables conducted a mortifying campaign on land, in which his troops were "tormented with Heat, hunger, and thirst." They brought only enough food with them to last a day or two, and they found wells blocked by the Spanish. The soldiers suffered through constant rain, were "extreamly troubled with the Flux," and had to carry "fainting and almost famished Men" to try to find shelter.[18] Eventually they gave up on Hispaniola and left for Jamaica, which they managed to capture from the Spanish despite the deplorable condition of the English army. Upon their return to England, Venables and Penn found themselves imprisoned for their incompetence and the failed attempt to capture Santo Domingo. Venables tried to excuse the botched expedition, insisting that he had been ill supplied with provisions from the first. He had insufficient food, water, tents, and stores, and feared his troops, "raw and unseason'd to the Climate," quickly became ill through exposure to the seasonal rains. In an extreme reversal of Aristotle's vision of a parched tropical land, English officials, believing that the Caribbean's abundant forests and vegetation would provide plenty of provisions for the armed forces, had neglected to supply the troops with enough food.[19]

Ultimately, Venables's grievances with his commanders made little difference. Although his troops had fallen ill from poor diet, unclean drinking water, and inadequate protection from persistent rain, English officials, unwilling to admit their own lack of foresight, blamed the Jamaican climate (along with Penn and Venables's ineptitude) for the deaths. Despite Venables's explanation of many of the preventable conditions causing illness, the situation reinforced lingering English suspicion of the Caribbean's general unhealthiness. As one contemporary account explained, "the excessive heat of the Sun, the want of water in many places, with other defects and impediments naturally incident to the place, and disagreeing to English constitutions, enweakene[d] and disable[d]" the troops. Through such interpretations, the bungled Caribbean adventure heightened English fears about the dangers a tropical climate posed to English bodies. The Navy, already hard pressed to find recruits, found it next to impossible to do so. Sailors in 1656 reputedly preferred to be hanged than to work on a ship bound for the West Indies. In the wake of the fiasco on Hispaniola, accounts like Colt's and Ligon's could do little to persuade skeptical readers that the Caribbean climate was not inimical to English bodies. In contrast to Ligon's writing, accounts of the Western Design spread widely, and the expedition received publicity for its significant human toll as much as for its colonial gains. The outcome appeared to be clear: the West Indian climate itself was dangerous to Europeans, and venturing to the islands was likely nothing short of a death sentence. A disastrous campaign with high rates of illness and mortality led observers from afar to distill a variety of causes into one primary culprit: climate.[20]

The notoriety of the Western Design, and of the ill health it caused so many of its participants, sparked a flurry of promotional literature commending the virtues of the Caribbean climate. To counteract negative perceptions and to induce migration to the islands, the colonial office in London encouraged reports promoting the salubriousness of warm climates for English bodies. Accounts from mid-century, for example, noted the "very healthfull aire" of Antigua, and the "Coole, and temperate ... delightfull arye" in Barbados which "agree[d] with the temper of the English." Early descriptions of Jamaica were likewise positive. "We finde not yt there is such an antypathy between ye Constitution of the English and this clyme," one report stated. Although "foavors and auges" sometimes debilitated people, they were only "troublesome" and "never mortall." Moreover, according to the report, these fevers resulted in large part from people's behavior: from their refusal to labor or exercise, and from poor diet as well as the excessive consumption of alcohol. Another report from 1664 claimed that the Jamaican mountains were "most healthfull & fruitfull land" and that although newcomers might experience fevers if they arrived in the summer months, and agues could result from rainy weather in the fall, "ye up lands and hills are as healthfull" as parts of England. According to the report, the good health of these elevated spots could be proven by the people, both "Blacks & Whites," who lived "in those parts all ye worst months, & never any one sick." Others who had been "sent sick from the low lands" had recovered, further evidence of the healthy climate in Jamaica's mountainous regions.[21]

Through reports such as these, colonial promoters hoped to attract English settlers to the Caribbean. The English had asserted dominance in Jamaica, but the Spanish did not leave for over a decade. The best way to maintain control of the island was to send colonists, particularly those who could serve as a defense force. Attracting settlers was therefore a priority, and counteracting fears of the West Indian climate was crucial to this process. These writings cannot, then, be taken entirely at face value. They are promotional by their very nature and thus prone to exaggeration. At the same time, they likely contained a modicum of truth: some English inhabitants of the Caribbean did actually find that the climate agreed with their bodies.[22]

Persistent Labor Problems

Despite these promotional writings, as the reputation of servitude in the West Indies reached England and Scotland, some potential laborers chose to forego the brutal passage and hard labor that awaited them across the ocean. Moreover, strict laws against free trade with Scotland limited the numbers of potential workers for frustrated planters. In 1667, Barbados representatives petitioned the King for free trade with Scotland so that the island might have a steady supply of Scottish servants. While they waited, the representatives pleaded for a "transport of one or two thousand of English servants" to work plantations. Promotional literature may have worked to attract planters, most of whom were admittedly drawn by reports of fabulous wealth to be gained on sugar plantations. But without enough laborers to work on plantations, planters found their prospects stymied.[23]

Petitions requesting a free trade for laborers continued for decades. In 1680, Barbados governor Jonathan Atkins complained to the Council of Foreign

Plantations about the shortage of Europeans on the island. Some servants refused to come to Barbados, and a "great number of people" had left over the past six years for Jamaica, Carolina, and Antigua, where they hoped to acquire more land, he wrote. Atkins believed that part of the problem lay with Parliament. The "strict Acts in England for Trade," he explained, hindered "any white servants" considering the Caribbean as a destination. Three years later his successor Richard Dutton agreed. Barbados was in need of "a yearly supply of white servants," he wrote, both to work plantations and to compose a militia. Dutton requested that the Council ask the King to allow "such a proportion yearly of servants from Scotland as may supply the necessities of the Island, [planters] finding by long experience that [Scots] are much better servants, than any that are sent thither from any other place." As these letters and petitions attest, West Indian representatives and governors believed English laws were hurting the colonies. Repeatedly complaining about a shortage of servants, these writers insisted that Scots made good workers and that English lawmakers were to blame for the scarcity of indentured laborers in the islands.[24]

Letters from West Indian planters confirmed the desperate shortage of servants. Planter Christopher Jeaffreson, for example, repeatedly wrote from St. Christopher to his cousin in England requesting more servants. When he first arrived on the island in 1676 he immediately implored his cousin to send carpenters and masons, and over the course of the following six years his demands increased. He wanted "any laborious and industrious men," whom he promised to house, feed, and clothe, rewarding them with significant amounts of sugar when their indentures expired. By 1681 he found himself in need of "some white servants, especially a mason, carpenter, taylor, smith, or any handy craftsman," as well as a clerk. He would take "any sorte of men, and one or two women," including "labourers and menial servants." Jeaffreson informed his cousin that he believed numbers of both Scottish and English people "would willingly change their clymate" to venture to St. Christopher upon the terms he offered. Jeaffreson, then, saw no immediate danger to English or Scottish bodies in the Caribbean climate. In fact, his comment implies that a hot climate, far from deterring migrants, was actually an inducement to laborers used to raw wind and rain. West Indian colonists did not all think that the climate was a drawback, and several saw it as an asset.[25]

Jeaffreson's growing frustration with the lack of servants echoed the complaints of many contemporary planters. An earlier report, issued by the Council of Foreign Plantations in 1660, noted the difficulty of procuring laborers for the colonies. According to the report, although servants were "the wealth of planters, and the seed of plantations" they were not easy to obtain. The report explained the difficulty: "either they must bee Whites, or Blacks; if

Whites, they must bee drawn out of gaoles, and prisons: and such servants are but ill-fitted to the beginnings of a plantation . . . or [they] must bee invited out of Scotland, by faire proposicions." As for "Blacks," the report continued, the Council did not want to risk the dangers of a large African population working for a "paucitie of planters." The report reflected the growing unwillingness of Britons to travel to the West Indian colonies. Even Scottish laborers facing a bleak economic situation at home refused to travel without an acceptable contract. By Jeaffreson's time, the population of enslaved Africans on the islands had significantly increased, even as planters continued to complain about the lack of white servants.[26]

Plantation owners, though, compounded the supply problem themselves as their personal economic calculations added to the servant shortage. "[S]ince [planters] have found the conveniency by the labor & cheap keeping of slaves," Governor Atkins of Barbados complained, "they have neglected the keeping of white men with whome alone they formerly carried on their Plantations." Several years later, Edwyn Stede of Barbados registered a similar grievance. Because planters found white servants to be "less profitable" to them than "the Negroes," he explained, "they keep but few Christian servants." To maximize profits, planters funneled their resources into acquiring enslaved Africans over indentured Europeans.[27]

Colonial governors and councils battled a dual opposition in their desire for European inhabitants. Expanding the population of white servants on an island appealed to colonial governors because such men would serve as a colonial defense force. After decades of writing to Parliament, though, governors found themselves repeating the same requests. In the early 1690s, the Jamaica Council instructed agents in England working on their behalf to "encourage a trade with Scotland, that we may have white people from there . . . and also a trade with Wales may be obtained for white people." The Council wanted both "servants & tradesmen" and reminded the agents to press for measures "encouraging the importation of white servants or free people from all countrys that you shall think fitt." But English laws prohibiting free trade on the one hand, and planters' preferences for cheaper laborers on the other, together stymied colonial governors.[28]

Letters from the colonies communicated perennial frustration with English laws that prevented easy access to potential servants. Although laws also restricted access to enslaved Africans, a growing international market in enslaved people meant that colonists in the Caribbean could more easily acquire African laborers. Planters also calculated that enslaved laborers, who could be purchased for life, were a better economic investment than temporary servants. As a result, planters began to purchase enslaved Africans rather than indentured Europeans. Moreover, servants had increasing economic opportunities both at home and in other colonies as the empire expanded. They could demand higher wages than West Indian planters were willing to pay.

Promoting Good Health

In the meantime, colonial promoters began enticing settlers to the Carolina lowcountry. From the 1660s through the early eighteenth century, dozens of promotional pamphlets appeared in England encouraging potential colonists to settle in Carolina. These pamphlets stressed the "*Healthfulness* of the *Air*; the *Fertility* of the *Earth*, and *Waters*; and the great *Pleasure* and *Profit*" that colonists would experience. One from 1666 emphasized that Carolina's "wholsom Air" made it "so desireable" for English migrants. Expanding upon the climate's suitability for potential English settlers, the pamphleteer assured them that "The Summer is not too hot, and the Winter is very short and moderate, best agreeing with *English* Constitutions." Although the English did not establish a permanent settlement in Carolina until 1670, a few short-lived efforts in the mid-1660s inspired promotional material encouraging migration. The incentives for planters to settle were considerable: according to one pamphlet, English men venturing to Carolina by late March 1667 would receive a 100-acre land grant for every free man, woman, child, and male servant accompanying them, and 50 acres for each female servant or slave. Urging those without means not to "be troubled at the thoughts of being a Servant for 4 or 5 year," the writer encouraged artisans as well as "diligent Husbandmen and Labourers," who wanted to "live in a most pleasant healthful and fruitful Country" to indenture themselves. According to these pamphlets, Carolina's climate was its best asset.[29]

In an attempt to assure potential travelers that they would remain healthy, the pamphlet writer advertised that no one from a group of settler-colonists living by the Charles River in the early 1660s had fallen ill. These settlers apparently experienced good health despite their situation, "when they had no house nor harbor, but wrought hard all day, in preparing Wood to build, and lay in the open Air all night." The pamphlet did not elaborate on why this settlement did not succeed, but it assured readers that the local environment was not at fault. If these early colonists had performed hard labor day after day in the Carolina heat with no proper shelter at night and still remained healthy, subsequent colonists and servants should rest assured that the Carolina climate would not damage their English bodies.[30]

Other promotional pamphlets made similar claims. One advertised that colonists would immediately notice the beneficial effects of the Carolina air: men would find their bodies "more lightsome, more prone, and more able to all youthful Exercises than in England;" women would be "very fruitful," and children would quickly gain "fresh sanguine Complexions." Another colonial promoter explained that the Carolina air was "of so serene and excellent a temper, that the Indian Natives prolong their days to the Extremity of Old Age." Meanwhile, "English Children there born, are commonly strong and lusty, of Sound Constitutions, and fresh ruddy Complexions." The pamphlets, both published at least a decade after English settler-colonists had established a settlement in the region, assured potential colonists of the wonderful health they would experience in Carolina. Significantly, there was no sense of racial distinction here; the second pamphlet implied that English colonists would enjoy the same good health as Indigenous peoples did. Indeed, the Carolina air would improve English bodies, making them strong and healthy, and perhaps even as robust as Indigenous people who had benefited from the climate their entire lives.[31]

While pamphleteers devoted considerable space to assuring English readers of Carolina's healthy climate, private letters divulged more nuanced views of local environments. Thomas Newe, who arrived in Charleston in 1682, found to his surprise that the Carolina climate was not, in fact, quite the picture of health the promotional pamphlets had advertised. "One thing I understand (to my sorrow) that I knew not before," he wrote to his father, was that "most have a seasoning." This seasoning entailed a period of ill health while the body's internal workings struggled to adapt to the change in climate. Still, he continued, few people actually died from this seasoning, and Newe expressed his desire to stay in the country. He asked his father to send over a male servant as soon as possible, "for such will turn to good account here." Newe's private letter displays a measured perspective on the lowcountry climate. It was neither the universally dangerous place that it might be, given the stark climatic difference from England, nor was it the earthly paradise promoters advertised.[32]

When travelers or settlers in the lowcountry or the Caribbean fell ill, colonial promoters, officials, and even colonists often blamed the people rather than the climate. South Carolina's governor John Archdale explained that any illness in the colony resulted from "carelessness," including "the Intemperance of too many." Archdale proudly proclaimed that in his own five-year residence he had only ever suffered from a cold. One colonial enthusiast claimed that sickness in Carolina was due to people's "bad Conduct, and not knowing how to regulate themselves suitably to the Country where they live."[33] West Indian writers expressed the same belief. The Caribbean region was not unhealthy by nature, these writers claimed; settlers experiencing illness had only themselves to blame. In 1665 Jamaica colonist John Style assured the Council of Foreign Plantations that "the clymat" was "most healthy" and that he had never enjoyed better health since arriving on the island. Coastal breezes mitigated the heat, "so it is not the country but the deboystness [debauchery] and intemperance of the people in the country that brings the evill vapours," Style announced. Similarly, planter-turned-governor Thomas Modyford reported that he "enjoyed as great a measure of health" in Jamaica as he had in England since his "natural inclination" was to be temperate.[34]

Colonial physicians agreed with this reasoning. Physician Thomas Trapham, who lived in Jamaica in the late seventeenth century, published a treatise in 1679 specifically for English travelers hoping to preserve their health in warm climates. According to Trapham, a hot climate in and of itself was not dangerous for English bodies. The daytime sea breezes were "healthful," and even the night air was less damaging to Europeans, whose pores were closed thanks to their ac-customed cold air, than it was to longtime island inhabitants, whose pores had opened and would allow dangerous vapors into the body. Instead, when settlers fell ill, Trapham implicated the "over-copious drinking of Rum and other spir-ituous liquors," which caused "Distempers" among residents, and a tendency to spend too much time in damp places. To "fundamentally secur[e] life and health" in "the Tropicks," colonists needed to shift their behavior. Like many of his contemporaries, Trapham explained that alcohol and moisture caused the vast majority of illnesses he observed in the otherwise benign Jamaican climate.[35]

Physician and naturalist Hans Sloane agreed with Trapham's assessment. Although he found "Fevers and Agues" to be "very Epidemic" in Jamaica, Sloane concluded that these were due to the frequent rains, much as similar fevers appeared in the "fenny and marshy" parts of England. In fact, Sloane believed that nearly all the diseases he observed in Jamaica were merely variations of those he had seen in England. The Caribbean air itself, Sloane wrote, "not-withstanding the heat, is very healthy," in part because of the constant breezes. Although he observed high rates of dropsy among his patients in Jamaica, Sloane attributed them to "intermitting Fevers, and drinking extravagantly." Sloane's original Jamaica patient, the Duke of Albemarle, whom he accompanied to the island, died shortly after arrival following a long illness. Sloane thought the Duke's sickness resulted from late nights spent "drinking great draughts" and "being merry with his friends." Years later, the physician remained convinced that excessive drinking, more than the heat of the climate, caused much of the illness he observed in Jamaica.[36]

Colonial promoters circulated similar narratives blaming people's behavior, rather than the climate, to explain soldiers' deaths during the ill-fated Western Design. According to cartographer Richard Blome, irresponsible behavior caused the high mortality rates following the campaign. "The only reason that can be given for the great Mortality in the Army upon their first Arrival" in Jamaica, Blome wrote, was "their want of Provisions, and their discontent, together with their unwillingness to labour and exercise themselves." Fevers, agues, and other illnesses settlers or travelers might experience in the Caribbean resulted from their own laziness or "excessive drinking." The climate itself was not at fault, Blome assured readers. "It is confirmed by a long experience, that there is no such antipathy betwixt our *Britanick* Temper and the Climate of *Jamaica*," he insisted. Another report also explained that the Jamaican climate did not "inevitably" cause disease despite its heat. Instead, sickness resulted from overeating, under-exercising, or inadequate clothing and lodging. All these reports blamed people's behavior for their illnesses. By avoiding damp places and limiting or eliminating the consumption of alcohol, people could decrease the likelihood of falling ill.[37]

In no cases did these physicians, colonial promoters, or officials express concern about the inherent unhealthiness of hot climates for Europeans. Rather they stressed the contingencies of ill health, pointing to avoidable causes: proximity to damp situations and overindulgence in alcohol. Those who subscribed to this view, and who reported their own good health in the warm climates of the Americas, could claim a moral high ground. Their superior health obviously reflected good behavior and temperance, a deduction that sometimes led to self-satisfied reports of personal health in the Greater Caribbean. By blaming peoples' behaviors, though, colonial promoters could encourage settlers, including servants, to venture to hot places. In this interpretation, servants could expect to remain healthy provided they regulated their own behavior.

Yet the shortage of European servants in the Caribbean continued, and planters' treatment of servants only exacerbated the problem. Writers who observed European laborers often focused on their harsh labor conditions. In the 1660s, for example, a visitor to Barbados wrote that on plantations he had "seene 30, sometimes 40, Christians, English, Scotch and Irish at worke in the parching sun, without shirt, shoe or stockin." Similarly, Richard Ligon wrote that some Caribbean planters treated their indentured servants extremely poorly, and John Taylor, an English visitor to Jamaica in 1687, wrote that planters were "verey severe to [their] English servants." These servants were "keept verey hard to their labour att felling of timber, hewing staves for casks, sugar boyling and other labours, soe that they are little better than slaves." They had poor food, lodging, and clothing, and faced "hard labour in the open feild (*sic*), allmost burnt up with the sun." Even as they commented on the plight of servants, none of these writers noted any actual obstacle to the ability of white people to labor in the Greater Caribbean.[38]

Most importantly, these reports did not claim that Africans would be healthier than Europeans in these places. None of these writers insisted that white people were less suited than Black people to manual labor in the Caribbean, nor did they maintain that white people were more subject to illness and disease. Writers who

did note differing rates of illness among Europeans and Africans often observed
that Africans were actually more subject to diseases such as dropsy and yaws than
were Europeans, even if some noted a greater European propensity for yellow
fever.[39] John Taylor, for instance, believed that Africans were "naturally afflicted
with the French pox in a more higher degree than evere any Europian bodys
were, and this they here call the yaws, and they are also subject to the dropsie in
a verey high manner." According to Taylor's observation, then, Africans were actually less healthy in the West Indies than were Europeans. Although physicians
Thomas Trapham and Hans Sloane disagreed about some aspects of the West
Indian disease environment, neither believed that white people were more subject to illness in the West Indies than Black people were. Trapham wrote that
the same behaviors caused illnesses in both Africans and Europeans, and Sloane
recorded roughly equal cases of Black and white patients. Both physicians held
firm beliefs that wet weather and alcohol consumption, not skin color or origin,
were the primary culprits in causing illness for everyone on the islands. Toward
the end of the seventeenth century, then, neither planters nor physicians nor
colonial officials expressed the opinion that Black people would make better
laborers than white people in the West Indian climate, nor did they claim that
white people were incapable of labor in hot places. But if by the last decade of
the seventeenth century colonial promoters had any hopes that the Caribbean
was finally beginning to recover from the legacy of the Western Design, in 1692
the region's reputation suffered another violent blow, this one even more severe
than the first.[40]

The Earthquake

On a Tuesday morning in early June a tremendous earthquake hit Port Royal,
the most populous town in Jamaica. Taking the merchant town by surprise, the
earth opened up and much of the flourishing port sank into the sea. "We felt the
House shake, and saw the Bricks begin to rise in the Floor," wrote one witness.
He watched as neighboring houses were destroyed; "some swallowed up, others
thrown on Heaps" and saw "the Sand in the Street rise like the Waves of the Sea;
lifting up all Persons that stood upon it, and immediately dropping [them] down
into Pits." Another writer suggested that "for its Violence and strange Effects" the
earthquake "may perhaps be compared with the greatest, that ever yet happened
in the World." The tremors that shook Port Royal and the nearby Liguanea plain
caused mass destruction. Scores of houses tumbled to the ground, a mountain
collapsed in on itself, and two-thirds of Port Royal fell into the harbor. Churning
waves drowned hundreds of people, and many survivors found their homes and
businesses destroyed.[41]

Fig. 1.1 Port Royal tumbling into the sea during the earthquake, depicted alongside an account of the quake. The caption under the image describes various events, each represented by a letter in the image. Letter P, for example, in the lower left corner, reads, "Dr. Trapham, a Doctor of Physick, hanging by the Hands on a Rack of the Chimney, and one of his Children hanging about his Neck seeing his Wife and the rest of his Children a Sinking." [Captain Crocket], *A True and Perfect Relation of that most Sad and Terrible Earthquake, at Port-Royal in Jamaica* (London, 1692).

Jamaica resident Joseph Norris was among the thousands affected by the earthquake. His father perished in the violent upheaval, and he himself experienced a "strange sort of agony." A few days later, though, Norris began to recover, and found his body "strong and healthy." But during the long, hot summer following the quake and into the autumn, some observers noted changes in the atmosphere. "The Weather was much hotter after the Earthquake than before;" one person wrote, "and such an innumerable quantity of *Musketoes*, that the like was never seen since the Inhabiting of the Island." Another noticed alterations in the usual wind patterns: "since the Earthquake, the Land-breezes often fail us," he wrote. These atmospheric changes, along with physical aftershocks in the earth, appeared to cause bodily effects in survivors. In the wake of the disaster, the general health of the inhabitants declined. "We have had a very great Mortality since the great Earthquake," wrote one person the following September. "[A]lmost half the People that escap'd upon *Port-Royal* are since dead of a Malignant Fever, from Change of Air, want of dry Houses, warm Lodging, proper Medicines, and other Conveniencies." This time Joseph Norris was among the dead, having succumbed to ill health three months after the initial quake.[42]

Some of Port Royal's residents rebuilt on the remaining narrow strip of land jutting into the sea while others left for a more secure foothold on the mainland. "After the great shake," one witness recounted, some people "went to the place called *Kingstown*," a small settlement across the harbor from Port Royal. But the results were deadly: "from the first clearing of the Ground, and from bad Accommodations . . . not sufficient to keep out Rain, which in great and an unusual manner followed the Earthquake, lying wet, and wanting Medicines, and all Conveniencies, &c. they dyed miserably in heaps." In fact, "a general Sickness" prevailed "all over the Island" and "few escaped being sick." The earthquake, the writer speculated, by releasing foul air from the depths of the earth, bore responsibility for the illness and deaths. Kingston, as "yet an unhealthy Place," suffered the brunt of this mortality, "supposed to proceed from the hurtful Vapours belch'd from the many openings of the Earth." Making matters worse, dead bodies regularly floated around the harbor "as the Sea and Land-breezes blew them, sometimes 100 or 200 in a heap." Some were newly dead, and others had washed out of cemeteries in various stages of rot, which "may be thought to add something to the Unhealthfulness of this Place."[43]

Those in Jamaica tended to offer explanations for the illnesses ravaging the island that stressed the particular environmental circumstances of the earthquake. These reports noted that intense heat seemed to follow the earthquake, and breezes appeared to be less frequent. Mosquitos swarmed, and rainy weather combined with "hurtful Vapours" caused a "Change of Air" in the island. Notably, for witnesses living in Jamaica, these environmental changes left the island less healthy than it was before. Although several of the reports emphasized that damaged infrastructure, a contaminated water supply, and inadequate shelter actually caused much of the sickness, the high incidence of death seemed to signify that the climate of Jamaica had changed for the worse. This change was, in fact, the opposite of what many colonial promoters hoped would occur.[44]

When news of the earthquake and its aftermath reached England, religious leaders claimed that Port Royal's inhabitants brought the destruction upon themselves through their immoral behavior. The town held an unsavory reputation as "a Sink of all Filthiness" and "one of the Ludest [places] in the Christian World." A pirate's haven, the port witnessed constant "Drinking, Swearing and Whoreing," and many of the earthquake's first victims included a large number of men in taverns at eleven in the morning. The quake was clear evidence of divine vengeance for evil behavior, a sign of holy wrath. The misery inflicted upon the area, these writers insisted, demonstrated the consequences of vice. The earth had opened and swallowed the sinners, leaving those behind the chance to repent and redeem their souls. In these interpretations, unsanctioned behavior had led to otherworldly intervention in the form of an earthquake, which then caused widespread illness and death.[45]

Regardless of the explanations, the earthquake further damaged the Caribbean's already suspect reputation. As one eighteenth-century historian of Jamaica wrote, after the quake and the sickness that followed, "many persons were so terrified that they removed to other countries . . . and strangers were so discouraged, that very few would venture over and become setlers [sic] for many years after." And in the early nineteenth century, historian Robert Renny reiterated the dangerous ramifications of the quake: a "malignant fever" followed the initial shock, he wrote, which "snatched thousands of unresisting victims to the grave." By the autumn, "the rich and flourishing island of Jamaica was considerably depopulated." Even a century later, Renny continued, people continued to believe "that the climate of this island is less genial, the air less salubrious, and the soil more unfruitful than formerly." If the colony had struggled to attract settlers—particularly servants—before the earthquake, its prospects certainly seemed doomed afterwards. In the decades that followed, especially as Jamaica suffered a series of further disasters including fires and hurricanes, European migration dwindled to a scant trickle.[46]

Jamaican residents emphasized that contingent factors, such as the proximity of rotting bodies and miasmas rising from newly cleared land in Kingston, caused illness and death following the quake. These conclusions were consistent with contemporary concepts of illness. Those not exposed to unhealthy situations would not fall ill nearly so frequently as those whose locations rendered them vulnerable. But to residents of the British Isles, news of the quake and of the illness and death that followed signified a more generalized threat. If the Caribbean was prone to unexpected calamities, surely it was a dangerous place. In this way, news of and reactions to traumatic events, such as the Western Design and the Port Royal earthquake, overtook more nuanced evaluations of the Caribbean environment. Although some English and Scottish residents were aware that not every person from the British Isles fell ill and died in the West Indies, catastrophes with high death rates appeared to confirm theories about the climate. To these observers, alarming rates of illness and death were merely the inevitable consequences of the hot, damp climate, and they verified inherited fears about the Torrid Zone. Entrenched opinions were slow to change, and despite the work of promotional writers, English people with no experience of their own were inclined to stick to long-standing ideas.[47]

Some colonial officials took advantage of those ideas. Several governors, for example, found themselves disenchanted with the realities of island life once they arrived in the West Indies. Many expected ample living quarters and a full staff as part of their position, but upon arrival found that they were actually worse off than many of the planters they were meant to govern. Disappointed with small salaries and with the expenses they incurred on the islands, these governors wrote to the Council of Foreign Plantations in London requesting permission either to return to England or to relocate elsewhere. Almost all of these requests were framed as complaints about the climate. Richard Dutton, governor of Barbados in the early 1680s, wrote to the Council of Foreign Plantations in 1682 that he was "impaired in my health by ye violent heate . . . having not had one day of perfect health since my entrance upon my Government." Finding himself unable to recover in Barbados, Dutton requested a leave of absence. "I am perswaded to believe," he wrote, that "nothing but my native ayr can restore mee to a perfect state of health again." A few years later, John Witham also wrote from Barbados that he would "never recover my health perfectly in this continual hott, & moist air, but must returne to my native Country, by ye advice of my Physitians, to recover my full health, & strength." Whether or not these colonial officials actually experienced ill health and attributed that sickness to the climate is almost immaterial; both realized that complaining about the climate was likely their best shot at convincing their superiors in England to let them return. As both men would have known, the reputation of the West Indian climate as dangerous and debilitating for English bodies remained strong in England.[48]

Some officials learned to use the reputation of the region's climate as a bargaining chip. Lieutenant Governor of Jamaica William Beeston, for example, wrote to the Council in 1699 requesting a health leave, but the Council had good reason to believe that Beeston was angling for more money rather than truly suffering from poor health. Beeston had spent much of the past forty years in Jamaica by then, his body fully adapted to the climate. He sent regular reports to England about the healthy condition of the island, stating over the course of several years that it was improving. He had also repeatedly complained about his meager salary. In a report of the Council of Trade and Plantations in October 1699, Jamaica agent Gilbert Heathcote suggested that Beeston's uneasiness in Jamaica likely resulted from his financial situation, rather than from any medical condition. As it happened, Beeston himself had dealt with a similar situation: six years prior to his own request, Beeston had fielded a complaint from Jamaica's Attorney General who wanted a leave of absence "for his health." Explaining the request to his superiors, Beeston suggested that, rather than suffering from any effects of the climate, the Attorney General was really going to England to complain about his position in Jamaica. When Heathcote surmised that Beeston was using a similar ruse, the Council of Trade and Plantations informed Beeston that they would increase his salary and make him full governor rather than grant him such leave.[49]

A decade after the earthquake, colonial appointees continued to manipulate climatic fears to improve their own positions. In 1703 Barbados's new governor Beville Granville arrived to find the island "very sickly & ye sickness very mortall." A "dangerous distemper" raged, and Granville believed that Barbados was "more unhealthy than it was ever yet known to be." The illness, "very catching and very mortall," soon afflicted Granville, although not seriously. Even so, he found the heat "painfull & insufferable" and was unable "to digest ye heat, air, meat or drink." Granville sent several letters to various members of the Council of Trade and Plantations complaining about the disappointing island that had failed to live up to his expectations. He pleaded to be moved to a "more moderate" climate, especially Virginia (his first choice) or New York. After these pleas proved ineffective, he added that, if a transfer was not an option, he would settle for a higher salary. When that, too, seemed to elicit no positive response, he suggested that he return to England but keep his position, appointing instead a Lieutenant Governor to serve in his place. London officials' apparent refusal to improve Granville's situation suggests that they may have become all too familiar with health complaints, whether genuine or exaggerated.[50]

It is likely that it did not suit the interests of London officials to change Granville's position, so they declined to do so despite prevailing views of the West Indian climate in Britain. This indicates that multiple views of hot climates circulated in the eighteenth century, and Britons without experience of their own encountered an array of contradictory reports. Perhaps the climate was not as unhealthy as some accounts claimed, but it was difficult to judge without consistent information. At the same time, Granville probably recognized that writing about a dangerous illness afflicting the inhabitants of a hot climate might be his best opportunity for leaving Barbados while retaining the position of a colonial governor. By the end of the seventeenth and into the eighteenth century, the idea of hot climates as dangerous for British bodies had become a rhetorical tool available for use and exploitation. People in a variety of situations, from potential servants to colonial officials, could cite fears or bad experiences with hot climates as a way to further their interests.

Complaints by colonial officials acknowledging that health was not the real issue exemplify the ways in which people took advantage of the climatic rhetoric. A few years after Granville, Naval Officer Charles Cox was infuriated with his situation in Barbados and wrote to the Council of Trade and Plantations. "I desire you to procure H.M. leave for my coming to England, alledging it's for the recovery of my health, for here is no living under such management," Cox wrote. Although he admitted his frustration to the Council, he recognized that framing his request as a health complaint would increase the chances of it being granted. Colonial officials dissatisfied with their positions for any number of reasons—climatic, financial, or otherwise—could stress the prevalence of disease or the unhealthful nature of the colonial environment. As Cox's letter shows, people sometimes deliberately used an excuse they knew would be the most convincing.[51]

Private letters, though, sometimes told a different story. Many Britons who spent time in the Greater Caribbean gradually shifted their opinions about the climate after a period of time. James Barclay, who traveled from Scotland to Jamaica in the 1720s, illustrates the divergence between British and colonial conceptions of the climate. Upon arriving in Jamaica, Barclay described his situation to his uncle. "I believe you are not unacquainted with the sickliness of this climate," he wrote, "which I do assure you is no better than it is said to be." Despite Barclay's initial confirmation of the climate's unhealthiness, his own experience differed from his expectations. As he informed his uncle, "I have kept my health perfectly well, & except a small intermitting fever with which I was seized on my first coming here, I have not had the least reason to complain of sickness since I have been in the Island." A year and a half later, his health suffered slightly; he wrote to another uncle that he had "kept my health pretty well hitherto, tho not altogether free from sickness." Still, he found "the place agrees with me better than I expected." Barclay arrived in the Caribbean with preconceptions about its dangerous environment, but nonetheless found that he maintained relatively good health. Even if he had been ill, he had recovered well, and his writings reveal his changing views about the Caribbean climate.[52]

But Barclay's letters were private documents; only his uncles, and perhaps a circle of friends and family, read his measured reports of Jamaica's environment. These letters and others like them did little to improve the poor reputation of the West Indian climate circulating in Britain by the turn of the eighteenth century. Some people would have had access to Ligon's, Trapham's, and Sloane's texts, in which they explained the beneficial qualities of the refreshing breezes on the surprisingly moderate West Indian climate. More might have heard about Venables's and Penn's expedition and the numbers of soldiers who contracted mortal illnesses while in the islands. Even more people would have heard about the Port Royal earthquake and the devastation it caused, both to the natural environment and through its considerable death toll.

* * *

By the end of the seventeenth century and into the eighteenth, there was no consensus about the effects of a hot climate on British bodies or on the ability of white people to labor in a hot place. While some European travelers to the Greater Caribbean found that the change of climate did not agree with their bodies, most did not believe that no white people could ever thrive or physically labor there.

Planters' personal letters consistently contained requests for servants. Nowhere did these letters confirm, or even imply, that white laborers would fall ill or be unable to labor in the tropical heat; rather they contained repeated pleas for servants, sometimes with promises of advance payment. West Indian residents who wrote to friends and relatives requesting more servants would have had to pay for their passages, and thus would have regarded these servants as an investment. They would have expected that most servants would at least live long enough to fulfill the terms of their contracts. Servants from the British Isles performed many types of difficult labor on plantations, from clearing forested land to planting and harvesting crops, sugar cane included.[53]

Although some seventeenth-century writers remarked on the surprising ability of people, both Europeans and Africans, to labor in the heat, they did not express the opinion that white people were unable to labor in such a climate. Yet the growth of the English sugar industry and the large-scale replacement of European servants with enslaved Africans occurred as portrayals of the West Indian climate became increasingly negative. Thus, the transition from primarily European to primarily African laborers may well have been related to the Caribbean climate, but not in the way that planters (or historians) later portrayed. Planters did not believe that white people were constitutionally unable to labor in a hot climate, and many of them repeatedly attempted to acquire European laborers. But along with other factors, the reputation of the West Indian climate—regardless of people's actual experiences—may have deterred enough potential servants to push planters to look elsewhere, in this case to enslaved Africans, for laborers.[54]

Because of competing agendas—to attract European settlers, but also to support those planters who were increasingly turning to enslaved African laborers—promoters and other writers contorted their arguments in multiple ways. Blaming settlers' behavior for illness was one of these ways: the climate itself could not be entirely at fault for people's ill health. Other reports simply gave positive assessments. Surveying Carolina in 1701, John Lawson wrote of the "very healthful" climate that was becoming daily more so as it was cleared. He found the weather "very agreeable to *European* Bodies, and makes them healthy." As a result of all this conflicting and competing information, Britons in the early decades of the eighteenth century still harbored a degree of uncertainty about the climate in the Caribbean and the lowcountry.[55]

A growing number of Britons and colonists, though, had also learned that the rhetoric about climate and labor could serve various interests. Crucially, negative perceptions of hot colonial climates helped support a growing system of African slavery whose defenders were beginning to occasionally adopt climatic justifications. One of the promotional pamphlets from South Carolina, for example, explained that Africans would naturally suit the Carolina climate.

"Negroes by reason of the Mildness of the Winter thrive and stand much better, than in any of the more Northern Colonys," one pamphlet claimed. Samuel Wilson, who wrote the pamphlet, cited no evidence that Black people in the North fell ill from the climate. Moreover, he insisted that white people would thrive in Carolina because the summers were "not near so hot as in Virginia or the other North American English Colonys." Apparently, Carolina's "nearness to the Tropics" exposed it to constantly refreshing breezes, making the climate ideal for all bodies. Even so, Wilson's claims about Black bodies attest to the persistence of deep-rooted climatic theories, as well as to the utility of these theories in promoting a system of racial slavery in plantation societies.[56]

Other pamphlets began appearing in the last years of the seventeenth century and into the first decades of the eighteenth, some arguing that only Black people could labor in the "sultry" West Indian climate. It is essential to note that many of these pamphlets were promotional material generated by both the Royal African Company and its competitors in an attempt to advance the slave trade. The writers of these pamphlets had a direct economic interest in stimulating and increasing the market for enslaved African laborers and used various methods to persuade readers that Africans were necessary to cultivate plantations. These pamphlets, therefore, cannot be taken as evidence that planters themselves believed that only Black people could labor in the heat. Instead, they point to the persistence of climatic tropes among British pamphlet writers, despite a multitude of evidence to the contrary. They also reduced the language around labor and bodies to an African/European, Black/white binary, contributing to the erasure of Indigenous laborers in histories of the Caribbean.[57]

Although they did not suffer the same erasure from the record as Indigenous laborers did, European laborers' presence became minimized over time as the prevailing rhetoric equated labor in the West Indies with Africans and their descendants. But even as Black laborers became more prevalent in the late seventeenth century and into the eighteenth, laborers from the British Isles did not disappear from the Caribbean. In the early 1750s, when Alexander Baillie arrived in Nevis from Scotland, he found the heat "very uneasy & disagreeable." But he soon learned to adjust his habits, he wrote to a relative, and the climate no longer bothered him. Indeed, he considered himself lucky, "when I see so many of my poor countrymen . . . toiling & fatiguing in the field exposed to the excessive heatt of the sun from morning till evening after a parcell of Negroes." These men, he wrote, "may be truly said to earn their bread with the sweat of their brows." Even in the 1750s, then, Baillie observed Scottish manual laborers doing the work usually reserved for Black people. But Baillie's letter was not part of the public narrative that was developing around Black and white people's abilities to labor in hot places.[58]

This narrative had not solidified, however, and in the early decades of the eighteenth century uncertainty about the climate in the Caribbean and the lowcountry prevailed in Britain. Perhaps Europeans could work in hot places, but a multitude of competing reports were inconclusive. Across the Atlantic, some colonial officials and settler-colonists recognized that they could use the power of the climatic rhetoric to their advantage. Particularly when corresponding with people with no experience of their own in the colonies, some people began relying upon British fears of hot places to further their own agendas. Sometimes taking advantage of this climatic uncertainty and trepidation had serious and longstanding consequences.

2

A Colony "on Fire"

The Georgia Experiment, 1732–1750

One of the most dramatic and influential cases of colonists using an emerging climatic rhetoric to their advantage occurred in Georgia. The succinct version of the colony's history is relatively straightforward: the group of London Trustees who founded Georgia in 1732 conceived it as a place that would be populated and cultivated by free and indentured European laborers. The Trustees believed that these settler-colonists, to be drawn largely from the ranks of the unemployed in Britain, would demonstrate the value of free labor. This system directly contrasted that of other Anglo-American colonies, which were becoming increasingly dependent on enslaved labor. To promote industrious work habits among these settlers, the Trustees prohibited African slavery in Georgia not long after the colony's founding.

Rather than showcasing a model of European productivity, the colony's initial two decades without African slavery brought it to the brink of collapse. British settlers and servants who moved to Georgia to create small farms soon refused to cut timber, clear land, and cultivate crops. Worse, a group of disgruntled settlers known as the Malcontents argued that white people could not possibly work the land in the lowcountry environment and that the colony would only succeed with enslaved Black laborers. Many of these settlers, frustrated with the prohibition on slave labor, deserted Georgia in protest. Eventually, the Trustees capitulated, and planters began legally using enslaved Africans in 1750.

Letters from Georgia in the 1730s and 1740s point to factors other than climate in the demand for slavery. Facing chronic shortages of European servants and unable to cultivate their lands as quickly or efficiently as the Trustees envisioned, some Georgia settlers saw African slavery as an opportune answer to the struggling colony's problems. After unsuccessfully petitioning the Trustees with economic arguments, the Malcontents turned to the climate instead, well knowing that in Britain warm climates had a reputation for being inhospitable to Europeans. Lacking any real evidence that white bodies were unfit for Georgia's

The Nature of Slavery. Katherine Johnston, Oxford University Press. © Oxford University Press 2022.
DOI: 10.1093/oso/9780197514603.003.0003

environment, the Malcontents relied on older ideas about climatic determinism and counted on the Trustees' willingness to accept climatic rhetoric as truth. These arguments directly benefited slave traders, who used white people's fears of ill health for their own economic ends. Social and economic forces drove the Malcontents' calls for African slavery and lay behind their excuses for working Black laborers to death in place of themselves.

Although historians since the eighteenth century have portrayed Georgia as an outlier, characterizing its experiment with white labor as an isolated incident, the climatic argument for slavery had implications far beyond Georgia's Trustee period. Historians of the 1760s and 1770s explained that the colony had struggled during the 1730s and 1740s because white people simply could not perform labor in the heat. In these interpretations, the experiment in Georgia proved "the necessity" of using enslaved African laborers in the lowcountry climate. In one account, minister Alexander Hewatt wrote of "the utter inaptitude (*sic*) of Europeans for the labour requisite in such a climate." If the clearing and cultivation of the lowcountry had been left to Europeans, Hewatt wrote, they "would have exhausted their strength in clearing a spot of land for digging their own graves." According to these histories, the Trusteeship in Georgia clearly indicated that enslaved Black laborers were necessary in hot, humid environments. This same climatic reasoning reappeared in later defenses of African slavery, during debates over abolition of the transatlantic slave trade and of slavery itself. While these debates occurred long after the colony's founding, the specific ways that the climatic argument emerged in Georgia and the way in which a group of people employed it to serve their own ends are crucial to understanding—and undermining—later defenses of African slavery.[1]

Archival evidence shows that the climatic argument served as a justification for introducing African slavery into the colony and creating a plantation economy. Yet the reverberations of the decision to allow African slavery had profound consequences for the development of a climatic rhetoric used to perpetuate ideas of racial difference across the Atlantic world. Georgia's legacy influenced white perceptions of different people's abilities to labor in warm climates and gave slaveholders a convenient crutch in their defenses of slavery for many decades thereafter. Moreover, the colony's story reveals the power of ideology over experience in constructing a language of race.

Envisioning a Colony

Georgia's inception was directly linked to the recent history of neighboring South Carolina. By the late 1720s, several decades after the first promotional pamphlets appeared, South Carolina had developed into a flourishing colony.

Enticed by the promise of vast tracts of land, aspiring planters from Britain joined a contingent of Barbadians who left the heavily cultivated Caribbean island for a colony with significantly more space. Many of these Barbadians brought enslaved Black laborers with them from the West Indies; the planters possessed human capital but not enough land to cultivate lucrative crops. Within a generation of Carolina's founding, rice had emerged as the colony's staple crop, and by the early decades of the eighteenth century the parts of Carolina best suited for growing rice—those prone to tidewater flooding—were rapidly becoming enveloped in large plantations worked primarily by enslaved Black and Indigenous peoples.[2]

Despite the alluring promises of promotional material, the colony faced significant problems. Like settler-colonists elsewhere, South Carolinians traded weapons with various Indigenous groups for deerskins and captives. Planters relied on the labor of some of these captives, and traders sent others to the Caribbean. As Indigenous people competed with one another for weapons to ensure their status as enslavers rather than slaves, their debts to colonists who demanded increasing numbers of captive people grew. After colonists began seizing their trading partners' family members, the Yamasee, Catawba, and Lower Creek fought back. The ensuing Yamasee War (1715–1718) left both sides shaken, with some Indigenous groups on the edge of starvation and the Carolina colony considerably weakened. As a result, even wealthy rice planters felt fragile and threatened in the war's aftermath as relationships with Indigenous people remained hostile.[3]

By the late 1720s, planters increasingly relied upon enslaved African laborers, and only those planters wealthy enough to afford large numbers of bondspeople found themselves able to compete in the thriving rice market. In consequence, less affluent planters left the lowcountry tidewater region, and dominant planters added more land and laborers to their plantations, creating a colony in which enslaved people largely of African descent outnumbered Europeans. This circumstance troubled planters afraid of a revolt. Finally, Spanish claims to Carolina, along with a strengthening French presence in the Mississippi Delta region, raised planters' concerns about imperial competition for land. The French appeared to have better relations with Indigenous people than British colonists did, and rumors abounded that the Spanish in Florida offered freedom to bondspeople who escaped from British plantations and fled south. All of these conditions meant that South Carolina colonists feared attack—by Indigenous groups, by enslaved Africans, and by European rivals.[4]

In London, a group of philanthropists considered financing a new colony to the south of Carolina. These Trustees hoped that the region's warm climate would allow colonists to produce valuable commodities such as silk and wine. Previous imperial designs had also imagined warm regions of the Americas as ideal places for these crops, but as colonists realized that tobacco, sugar, and rice produced significant profits within a relatively short time span, they rapidly dedicated most of the land they took from Indigenous people to these latter commodities. The Trustees envisioned a different scenario. In their estimation, Britain could not provide enough work for all its residents, and many otherwise capable laborers did not contribute enough to the economy or to national prosperity. These people, the Trustees believed, could become productive laborers if given the right encouragement. A new colony—called Georgia, after the king—could offer just such an opportunity. The Trustees, Parliament, and private investors would supply the capital necessary for establishing Georgia and sustaining its initial residents for a few years, enough to allow time for clearing land, planting vines and mulberry trees for silkworms, and launching wine and silk production.[5]

Establishing a colony south of Carolina could help allay Carolinians' fears. The Trustees were determined that the Georgia colonists should form friendly relationships with local Indigenous people, in part to offset the deep distrust sown by their northern neighbors in recent years. In addition, good relations with Indigenous people would be crucial if the British wanted to dominate their Spanish and French rivals in the region. Most importantly, the Trustees would strongly discourage African slavery in Georgia. In part, they thought this policy would help Carolina planters who repeatedly complained of enslaved people deserting for Florida. A colony inhabited solely by white and Indigenous people in between South Carolina and Florida meant that fleeing Black people could be caught and returned to Carolina plantations.[6]

In addition, many of the Trustees feared that the presence of enslaved African laborers would undercut the purpose of the new colony. The Trustees believed their plan would benefit Britain by instilling a strong work ethic in "unproductive" members of society. Marketing their plan to Parliament, the Trustees emphasized the employment opportunities Georgia would afford Britons, who would produce highly valued trade goods. As the vast majority of the colony's finances came from Parliamentary aid, there was no reason for colonists—many of whose travels and land would be provided or subsidized—to accumulate personal wealth. In the Trustees' view, slaveholding planters in South Carolina and Virginia relied too heavily upon enslaved laborers, whose efforts only enriched already ostentatiously wealthy planters. For the Trustees, it was essential that colonists exert their own labor upon the soil, as this process would impress upon them the value of hard work.[7]

Crucially, the Trustees, set to make a substantial investment in a new colony, did not see the climate as an obstacle to their plan. They were no doubt aware of the various types of climatic rhetoric and reputations of warm climates in circulation at the time, but they did not automatically fear the effects of the lowcountry climate upon British bodies. It is true that to avoid competing with Carolina planters the Trustees did not prioritize (though nor did they prohibit) rice production, the lowcountry crop most associated with slave labor in the early eighteenth century. But they did expect European settlers to clear dense forests, as well as to plant and harvest crops. There was enough affirmative evidence from the previous century of English habitation in warm places for the Trustees to believe that Georgia's climate would not prevent white people from laboring.

The image that the Trustees circulated to raise support for their cause demonstrated their confidence in the abilities of European laborers. Explaining that funds would give Britain's "poor subjects" a fresh start in Georgia, the Trustees advertised that settlers in the new colony would cultivate plots of land both for their own subsistence and for colonial trade. Although fanciful on many levels, the image accompanying the request for donations emphasized an ideal climate in which white people would coexist peacefully with Indigenous people.

An engraving at the top of the paper depicted over a dozen men working together, nine with lighter skin in European clothing, and five darker-skinned men in loincloths, their well-defined muscles taut as they chopped trees and hauled logs. The best-dressed European man oversaw the harmonious workers in the image from a vantage point that afforded a view of the Savannah River, the fortified town, and orderly plots of cleared land, laid out for miles stretching into the forest. Several boats on the river signified a bustling trade, and the hard-working tree-fellers, log-cutters, sawyers, and carpenters in the engraving had nearly finished a spacious two-story log dwelling. This lush, verdant land was an ideal setting for a colony, the image assured potential subscribers. Thick forests abounded with many different kinds of large, leafy trees, and the Europeans and Indigenous people could easily—and would readily—work together to clear the land and construct impressive buildings under minimal supervision.[8]

Fig. 2.1 This engraving by John Pine appeared at the top of a broadside soliciting investors for the colony of Georgia; one of these broadsides can be found at the National Library of Scotland, GB233/Ch 2634. The image also appeared as the frontispiece for Benjamin Martyn's promotional tract *Some Account of the Designs of the Trustees for Establishing the Colony of Georgia in America* (1732). Image courtesy of the John Carter Brown Library.

The image depicted several palms among the trees, which the engraver imagined might grow naturally in Georgia. Their presence in the engraving signaled a warm, almost tropical, climate. Bearing little resemblance to the cold New England or mid-Atlantic regions of North America, Georgia appeared closer to Britain's West Indian colonies, albeit with apparently snow-capped mountains in the distance, perhaps to reassure would-be contributors that the climate was not actually too hot. There white people would have no trouble with manual labor despite the presence of palm trees. Georgia had, according to the engraving, an ideal climate.[9]

In fact, the Trustees had only a vague sense of Georgia's actual climate. Promotional literature boasted of its paradisiacal nature, some writers pointing to its similarities with the fertile Mediterranean and the silk-producing regions of China. One account, published in 1717 as a proposal for establishing a colony to the south of Carolina, claimed that the land was "the most amiable Country of the Universe." Other promotional accounts expressed a similar exuberance, although the Trustees heard and read little accurate testimony from eyewitness observers. In the early part of the eighteenth century, the Trustees' sense of climate would have been largely latitudinal, though tempered with a sense of other environmental factors. That is, they would have expected Georgia to be warm, perhaps even stiflingly hot in the summer months, but they also believed that features such as mountains, rivers, and trees would mitigate the heat and regulate the climate. Clearing forests would allow air to flow freely through the region, and mountains (in the image, if not in reality) would bring cool breezes into the valley.[10]

Although the image created by a British engraver was imaginary, its portrayal of Georgia's climate was deliberate. The Trustees reproduced the image in their early promotional materials, including a pamphlet attributed to James Oglethorpe. One of the most enthusiastic Trustees, and the only one to ever set foot in Georgia, Oglethorpe encouraged this romanticized notion of Georgia's climate. Aiming to convince supporters that Georgia would work as a colony, Oglethorpe described Georgia as an abundant place, capable of producing many kinds of plants and of sustaining all sorts of animals and people. Ocean breezes provided relief from heat in summer, he explained, and the lowcountry never experienced the frigid temperatures of settlements farther north. The fertile soil could nurture many different products, from flax and hemp to olives, dates, and grapes for wine and raisins.[11] Although the Trustees almost certainly did not believe that Georgia was quite so Edenic as their promotional material claimed, they recognized the value of advertising such an image to attract private and Parliamentary financial support for the venture.[12]

If the Trustees wanted Europeans to thrive in Georgia, their central climatic concern should have been an awareness of the need for a seasoning or adjustment period when the colonists first arrived. Expecting Britons to labor intensely immediately after arrival could result in high rates of illness, a complication with which the Trustees would have to contend. To alleviate the potential hazards of a hot climate to British bodies, travelers and residents of warm colonial climates universally acknowledged the need for a seasoning period upon arrival in the Greater Caribbean region. Bodies would slowly adapt to the unfamiliar environment during this seasoning, either through an initial period of illness or through incremental bodily adjustments. Either way, seasoning was the body's way of realigning its internal humors to match the external environment. This concept was not new at Georgia's founding; scores of people had already been reporting on the seasoning process from other warm climates for many decades. Even some of the promotional pamphlets acknowledged the need for a seasoning period as bodies adapted to the lowcountry environment. As one such pamphlet explained about South Carolina, springtime fevers would affect "new Comers into the Country, which is commonly call'd a Seasoning." After this period, which especially struck those living in damp regions, if people remained temperate and lived on "dry, healthy Land," they tended to stay healthy. New arrivals, then, should expect to allow their bodies some time to adjust.[13]

The Early Years

James Oglethorpe and the first group of Georgia settlers arrived in Yamacraw territory in February of 1733. A small group formed from Yamasee and Lower Creek people, the Yamacraw occupied large amounts of land following the devastation of the Yamasee War. Their leader Tomochichi began a trading relationship with Oglethorpe and allowed the colonists to settle on the bluffs along the Savannah River. The area had easy access to water and was exposed to breezes. Less promisingly, the land surrounding Savannah was covered in abundant forests, and the English and Scottish migrants had no experience cutting down trees. There was not enough time for a seasoning period: Oglethorpe and the Trustees expected the new settlers to begin working immediately. To help the new arrivals, Oglethorpe turned to South Carolina, where he asked slaveholders for the temporary use of enslaved Black laborers to help clear land for a town. Although the Trustees were unwilling to finance a colony of wealthy planters dependent on slavery, they allowed the Georgia settlers to supplement their workforce with enslaved laborers at first.[14]

Labor was difficult. The forest was dense and colonists were unprepared for the work. A month after the colonists' arrival, magistrate Thomas Causton wrote to his wife that the Savannah group consisted of "some Grumbletonians." Despite these grumblings, Causton noted that the Savannah settlers had experienced

"very little Illness" in their first month in the colony, likely due to the settlement's
favorable environment.[15]

Despite Savannah's healthy location, the Trustees soon received their first
complaint. Local merchants responded strongly to the Trustees' discouragement
of slavery in the colony. South Carolina lumber merchant Samuel Eveleigh, for
example, saw his opportunities in Georgia diminish, if not evaporate altogether,
if he could not rely on enslaved laborers. Georgia's lush forests promised great
wealth, but only if Eveleigh could use experienced workers to cut the trees at a
low cost. Framing his complaint as a larger economic problem, Eveleigh tried
to convince the Trustees that their plan to rely on white laborers would ruin
the colony. If the settlers "were to have no Negroes Amongst them," he wrote,
the policy would be at least "a great prejudice" working against the colony and
at most "a means to Overset your Noble design." While praising the Trustees'
intent for a colony encouraging poor Europeans to work, Eveleigh informed
the Trustees that the colony would never generate any wealth without enslaved
laborers. Referencing his own line of business, Eveleigh explained that "persons
that are not used to work" could never harvest trees in Georgia. The problem,
then, was the new arrivals' lack of experience. Settlers unaccustomed to work
would be a significant hindrance for merchants hoping to turn a quick profit.[16]

Eveleigh also took his argument a step further. It would be, he wrote, "very difficult for White people to hoe and tend their Corn in the Hot wether." Eveleigh
wrote to the Trustees in the first week of April 1733, a mere two months after
settlers arrived in Savannah. Corn planting had not yet begun, nor had the hot
weather. Moreover, in South Carolina bondspeople did much of the agricultural
labor in the colony. As a wealthy merchant, Eveleigh would have been unlikely
to have had direct experience to support his claim about the inability of "White
people" to cultivate crops in the heat; instead, he based his argument upon preexisting rhetoric. Eager for his lumber business to prosper, Eveleigh drew upon
familiar climatic tropes in an attempt to persuade the Trustees to allow slavery
in Georgia.[17]

Apart from Eveleigh's criticism, during the colony's early years the Trustees
did not receive significant complaints about the climate. Instead, colonists
expressed other grievances. The first of these was related to land. Migrants who
brought servants with them received two plots of land: a small one in the heart
of what would become Savannah, the settlement's central town, along with a
larger parcel outside of town. The first would be a site for a house and garden,
while the second would become farmland for cultivating both subsistence
crops and, ideally, lucrative crops that the Trustees could use to demonstrate
to Parliament the success of the venture. But this setup caused problems from
the beginning. Although settlers were able to quickly clear their town plots, the
larger, more distant pieces of land posed logistical problems. The land was far

from town and often inaccessible; settler Patrick Tailfer's 500 acres, for example, were many miles from Savannah. This land was so far away, Tailfer explained to the Trustees, that he could not possibly begin to clear or cultivate it. Informing the Trustees that he was "in a manner settled in this town," Tailfer requested a closer piece of land that would be more practical to plant and tend.[18]

(a)   (b)

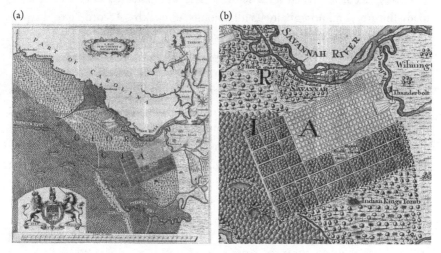

Fig. 2.2 Map of Georgia. Note the smaller town and larger country plots of Savannah in 2.2b, as well as the settlement's proximity to South Carolina in 2.2a. Courtesy of Hargrett Rare Book and Manuscript Library/University of Georgia Libraries.

Those who did manage to clear their land faced additional problems. Some settlers began planting their lots in earnest, eager to take advantage of the land and to prove to the Trustees that they were hard workers. But because people had been assigned particular plots of land before crossing the ocean, and only some of those people cleared and planted after getting to Georgia, the unevenness of the cultivated land aggravated the planters. "Many people who have cleared," Savannah resident John Brownfield informed the Trustees in June of 1737, "complain of their neighbours for not clearing because the vermin & insects bred in uncultivated lands destroy the crops of those who have planted." Furthermore, the trees in uncleared lots provided too much shade for neighboring cornfields, which meant that corn on the edges of the lots could not grow.[19]

Fencing and a lack of roads also aggravated colonists. It took several years for surveyors to measure and allot all the land the Trustees had assigned to settlers, and until they knew the bounds of their land most people did not want to build fences. But without fences to enclose their land and protect it from roaming animals, people found that both domestic and wild animals demolished their crops. "Many have suffered vast losses by their neighbours cattle breaking in & destroying: besides which the wild deer & insects devour abundance," Brownfield explained in another letter. Even those who did manage to raise and harvest crops found they could not bring their grain to town to sell because the province had insufficient roads. In the Trustees' scheme, everyone was supposed to be a small farmer, but without enough people to work on public projects such as building roads, the farmers could not subsist.[20]

Finally, according to several settlers, the abundance of uncultivated land made the area, and potentially its inhabitants, unhealthy. According to the prevailing environmental view of health and disease, healthy places bred healthy people and vice versa. For colonists contending with apparently endless acres of woodland, the trees could be a problem. As several of the settlers pointed out, uncultivated land, including many of their neighbors' lots, abounded with trees that prevented "the free circulation of air," making these places "sickly." "Nothing more conduces to relieve either persons or vegetables than a free current of air," one colonist wrote. But so far, because cultivation was uneven, the "many small improvements made are butt out of a surrounding forrest which admitting no avenues of air the health of the inhabitants is impair'd and the hopes of the labourer disappointed." The stagnant air surrounding cleared plots of land could endanger the health of colonists and servants.[21]

In addition to complaints about land, servants—or the lack thereof—caused the second main grievance for Savannah settlers. Patrick Tailfer, who had planned to travel to Georgia with eighteen servants in tow, lost thirteen of them even before departing Britain. "Having only three men a boy & woman servant left" upon arrival in Savannah, Tailfer felt he could not clear and settle his land with such a small labor force. He would have to wait for more servants to arrive from England. In the meantime, he rented a house in Savannah and set up practice as a physician.[22]

Other Georgia settlers also had trouble with servants. Francis Bathurst reported that he liked Georgia a great deal but wished the Trustees would send him two or three more servants, having lost one of his to "ye scurveys and a dropsie" and the other "of a dropsie and an ulcer in his leg" not long after arrival. Noble Jones complained to Oglethorpe that he had "had bad luck with servants," as they were constantly falling ill, conspiring to rob him, or running away. Of the two he had recaptured, he was "forc't to keep one of em with a chain on his leg" to prevent him from running off again. John Brownfield also lost servants: one drowned in the river, and the other stabbed Brownfield with a sword. Although Brownfield survived the attack, the servant died in prison.[23]

The Trustees continued to receive complaints against servants: they refused to work, or ran away, or spent too much time languishing in bed out of illness, laziness, or both. Still others were "corrupted": Samuel Holmes, a bricklayer, found that his servants had been "corupted by sum evill persons," causing him great expense as well as the loss of both of them; he asked the Trustees to send him a few more so that he could instruct them in the art of bricklaying. Even the Trustees' Georgia secretary William Stephens, who had been dispatched to Savannah to send back accurate reports from the colony, had bad luck with servants. In January of 1738 he thanked the Trustees for sending over new servants because the ones he had kept falling ill. If their illness was a "seasoning" that would "happily preserve 'em when the heats come," the period of sickness would be worthwhile. But eight months later he was frustrated. Once his servants had recovered, he found they had "grown so false and lazy, through the poisonous Influence of other idle Rascals," that they were no longer worth their labor. Nearly everyone, as it turned out, reported challenges keeping servants.[24]

Oglethorpe noted that the freeholding settlers themselves were no better. Early on, in the summer of 1733, he informed the Trustees that he had dismissed the enslaved "Negroes who Sawed for us" who had come temporarily from South Carolina, because he found their presence sapped the work ethic of the colonists. He also reported a troubling tendency among the colonists to drink too much rum, which he believed led to rampant illness. (In later years, Oglethorpe repeatedly denounced the evil consequences of rum consumption, alleging that it caused sickness that would be unfairly blamed on Georgia's hot climate.) He assured the Trustees that "by Degrees" he had "brought the People to Discipline," but that he could not "revive the Spirit of Labour." The colonists were proving reluctant to perform the labor the Trustees had imagined they eagerly would. The bulk of Georgia colonists' early complaints, then, addressed problems with land and with labor—not with the climate. Both servants and freeholders proved to be less industrious than the Trustees had hoped, and their lack of industry contributed to the unevenness of cultivated land, further discouraging those who did work.[25]

In response, the Trustees amended the charter to include a firm prohibition on African slavery. Previously, Georgia settlers could not own enslaved laborers themselves, but could borrow them from South Carolina to assist with various tasks. After seeing the effect they had on the Georgia colonists' work habits, the Trustees explicitly banned the importation, sale, or barter of "any Black or Blacks Negroe or Negroes" from the colony. Notably, the act was silent on enslaved Indigenous people. The Trustees were apparently more concerned with the various dangers they thought enslaved Black people posed to the colony. In addition to jeopardizing the work ethic of white people, these dangers included the possibility of "insurrections tumults and rebellions of such slaves and negroes." Racial prejudice likely also played a role; ideas about race were still fluid among Euro-Americans, just as they were among Indigenous people in the South at this time, but white people often held anti-Black sentiments.[26]

Wealthy Virginia planter William Byrd wrote to the Trustees congratulating them on the prohibition. While he expressed discomfort with the "unchristian

Traffick of makeing Merchandize of Our Fellow Creatures," Byrd's letter revealed
the racist assumptions that lay behind his concern. "Negros," he wrote, became
"insolent," even "troublesome and dangerous" in large groups, leading planters
to "the necessity of being severe." Most significantly for the Trustees, Byrd wrote
that the very presence of enslaved Black people "blow up the pride, and ruin the
Industry of our White People, who . . . detest work for fear it shoud (*sic*) make
them look like Slaves." Byrd maintained that enslaved people were responsible
for violence in both directions: they might instigate Black violence against white
people and, conversely, provoke white violence against enslaved Black people.
While the slaveholder Byrd professed to dislike slavery, he also demonstrated
an antipathy for Blackness and assumed that the Trustees shared his opinion.
The Trustees would have noted Byrd's claim that the presence of enslaved Black
laborers caused "Idleness" among whites.[27]

If Georgia was to have no enslaved Black laborers, the white settlers demanded
that the Trustees send over more servants. Yet despite recruitment efforts, the
shortage of servants appeared to be a chronic problem. "We are in great want
of servants," Oglethorpe wrote in 1736. If the Trustees could send several hundred to the colony, "there are persons enough here, & to the south, who [would]
be glad to purchase [them] immediately." When the Trustees did send new
servants, some colonists continued to complain. Even servants who proved to
be hard workers, these colonists wrote, were too expensive to maintain.[28]

Labor was not cheap, and the inhabitants of Savannah felt this to be a particular sore spot given the abundance of enslaved laborers across the river in
South Carolina. Merchant Samuel Eveleigh, who spent the summer of 1735
in Georgia despite his misgivings about white workers, complained about
the cost of labor there. "I found the lumber to cost me (being cutt by white
people) four times as much" as it would have cost in South Carolina, he informed the Trustees' London secretary Benjamin Martyn. In another letter,
he wrote to an acquaintance that he had procured 70 tons of live oak timber
from Georgia. The timber, though, "was cut by white people and has cost me
a great deal of money," he wrote. If the wood turned out to be good quality,
Eveleigh continued, "I shall for the future employ Negroes," which would be
"a great deal cheaper." Eveleigh's letters to his friend suggest that he intended to
directly flout the slavery prohibition by using enslaved loggers in Georgia for
the economic benefit. Notably, his letters reveal that in his experience white
people could labor in Georgia, but demanded more money than Eveleigh
wanted to pay.[29]

The only climatic complaint the settlers made in the early years was about
the lack of a seasoning period. In 1735 the first organized faction of disgruntled settlers, led by Patrick Tailfer, sent a letter to the Trustees demanding to
use enslaved Black laborers. "We all having Land, in your Colony of Georgia,"

this group of Malcontents wrote in early summer, "and having come here chiefly with a Design to Settle upon and improve our Land, find that it is next to an impossibility to do it without the Use of Negroes." They offered two main reasons to support this complaint. "In the first place, most part of our white Servants not being used to so hot a Climate can't bear the Scorching Rays of the Sun in the Summer when they are at Work in the Woods, without falling into Distempers which render them useless for almost one half of the Year," they wrote. Without a seasoning period, the servants were not yet "used to so hot a Climate" and could not work to their full capacity. "Secondly, There is a great Deal of Difference betwixt the Expence of white Servants & of Negroes." This second point, actually, was the main one: the letter went on to detail all of the costs associated with European servants in contrast to enslaved Africans. Servants, the Malcontents argued, required more expensive food, drink, and clothing than did slaves. After such an investment, even the servants who did not run away or die before their indentures expired only stayed for a short time.[30]

The two grievances in this letter became the main sticking points in the dispute over slavery between the Malcontents and the Trustees. The first point underscored the difficulty of relying on unseasoned workers. The Trustees wanted a healthy and industrious colony, but how could Europeans perform the intensive manual labor required of a new colony if their bodies had not yet adjusted to the environment? As Savannah resident Hugh Anderson wrote to the Trustees, "It will easily be believed that a removall from Brittain to so southern a latitude must very sensibly affect the constitution." The vastly different environments would require bodily adjustment, as the Trustees must recognize.[31]

The climate itself, then, was not the problem. The Malcontents' early letters did not assert that white people could never work in Georgia's climate; they merely argued that freshly arrived European bodies had had insufficient time to adjust to the new climate. The people were not used to either the heat or to manual labor, nor did they have farming skills. Yet with the prohibition on Black slavery, the Trustees expected Europeans to work immediately upon arrival. This expectation aggravated prospective farmers in Georgia and increased their demands for slaves.[32]

The second point reflected the Malcontents' frustration over the hardships of keeping and the economic difficulties of caring for servants. The freeholders had received no provisions for their servants despite their expectations to the contrary, they wrote. They were able and willing, they contended, to cultivate their grants of land according to the Georgia plan. But with their plots of land so far away, and with servants so problematic—constantly running away, and costing so much when they stayed—the settler-colonists were growing increasingly frustrated.[33]

Georgia could, in time, become the exceptionally healthy place promised in the promotional literature. But to achieve the robust, flourishing colony the Trustees envisioned, many of the settlers felt they faced a paradox. They needed to clear land to plant crops, but they also needed to give their bodies time to adjust to the new environment. Servants who worked too intensively with no seasoning period fell ill, and those who allowed their bodies time to adapt left their land uncultivated and had to depend on the generosity of the Trustees for provisions. The early use of some of South Carolina's bondspeople seemed to confirm the Trustees' fears of laziness in Georgia's colonists, but without seasoned laborers to clear the land, Savannah's settlers felt unequal to the task. Fantasies of Indigenous people working freely and harmoniously with Europeans fizzled almost as soon as settlers arrived in Savannah, and the colonists who were left to clear land, plant fields, and build homes for themselves were running out of patience. They began petitioning the Trustees in earnest, pleading for more European servants or the ability to purchase enslaved Africans.

Contrasting Evidence

The Trustees considered the Malcontents' economic and climatic complaints separately. They were entirely unsympathetic to the economic arguments, quickly dismissing settlers' grievances about the relative costs of servants versus slaves. They had not founded the colony in order to enrich individuals; rather they intended their philanthropy to teach the values of hard work and to boost the economy of the British Empire. Individual profits, then, held no interest for the Trustees. In fact, their policies on landholding reflected those values: land in Georgia could only be passed to a male heir. The Trustees wanted to prevent the merging of large properties through marriage, which would consolidate wealth in the hands of a few people, as it did in South Carolina. This policy was unpopular with settlers, especially among those without male heirs who saw no reason to clear and cultivate land if their daughters could not inherit it. But the Trustees were determined that their philanthropic plan should help the "worthy poor," and they remained wary of mirroring South Carolina's elitist structure. Economic arguments in favor of slavery, then, failed to move the Trustees.

The climate, though, was a different issue. Concern for the colonists' health—and for Georgia's subsequent reputation—interested the Trustees a great deal. Was Georgia in fact cultivable by white people? The Trustees sought assurance that it was: they could grant the need for a seasoning period if most Europeans would survive the initial bodily adjustment and prove capable of labor as a result. To continue with the Georgia project, the Trustees tried to obtain accurate information about the lowcountry climate's effect on white bodies.

Reassuringly, some settlers sent positive reports about their health back to Britain. "I should chearfully spend the remainder of my days here, being, I think, a very healthy climate, and agreeing the best with my constitution of any that I ever breathed in," wrote one British colonist. Private correspondence reinforced reports like these. As one settler wrote to his mother in the fall of 1736, "the country seems to agree with me very well." A Scottish merchant in Savannah informed his uncle in February 1739 that he was "well & healthe," and in late July of the same year he confirmed his earlier report. "I and familie keeps there health," he wrote, "only Robt had a small tutch of the fever & ague." These letters reflected settlers' experiences: some people had little trouble adjusting to the lowcountry warmth.[34]

Still, the Malcontents' grumblings intensified. In late 1738, they sent the Trustees a petition signed by 117 inhabitants of Savannah. Among other things, most notably a relief of restrictions on land tenure, the petitioners demanded the right to hold enslaved African laborers in Georgia. In part, the petitioners grounded their demands in financial arguments. Georgians could never prosper, the Malcontents asserted, because South Carolinians had cheaper labor and would thus "always ruin the market." As the colony's recorder Thomas Christie had explained earlier, Carolina planters used enslaved people to produce voluminous amounts of rice, which the planters then sold for low prices. "They will always undersell us," he wrote, so "we need not sow any." Workers' bodies were also key. While earlier letters had emphasized the lack of a seasoning period, advocates of slavery soon dropped the seasoning argument in favor of more starkly worded language. White people, the petitioners claimed, simply could not perform manual labor in Georgia's climate.[35]

Merchant Samuel Eveleigh had earlier complained that the prohibition on people of African descent in Georgia was a great loss of potential income for the colony. "I observed whilst at Georgia great quantitys of choice good land for rice," he wrote to the Trustees, "and am possitive that, that commodity can't (in any great quantity's) be produced by white people, because the work is too laborious, the heat very intent, and the whites can't work in the wett at that season of the year as Negroes do to weed the rice." Bolstered by Eveleigh's suppositions and rhetoric, the Malcontents began including these arguments in their petitions. Assumptions about bodily difference between Africans and Europeans, which had previously been marginal to the Malcontents' complaints, became central to their case.[36]

In December of 1740 the Malcontents prepared another petition, this one signed by a number of former servants in Georgia. The petitioners had come to Georgia, they claimed, believing that "the Lands were so fertile We should be able to make a Comfortable Living by the Labour of White Men only." But they found "the heats in Summer" to be "so Excessive" that vast numbers of people died. The dead included "free men as well as servants, of Distempers Contracted by the Laborious Work" they were "forced to go through in their Endeavours to raise a little Corn." The Malcontents had implored the Trustees for slaves, they wrote, and in the meantime believed the land would become healthier as it was cleared, but all to no avail. No ships would trade in Savannah because merchants could obtain every item for less money in Charleston, and still the petitioners suffered in vain.[37]

The petitioners tried to convince the Trustees that they were not purely profit-seeking in their insistence on the need for enslaved Black labor. "Consider the difference of the Climate," they urged. "Think how unfit a British Constitution is to undergo hard labour in a country twenty-three degrees to the South of England." Summer heat caused the servants to sweat so much that it sapped all strength from their weakened bodies. "No Englishman can work in the field without endangering his life," the erstwhile servants insisted. The servants and other Malcontents made these claims, of course, despite having survived their own time in the fields. Still, they insisted that they had been in grave danger through years of work. They implored the Trustees to imagine "How Shocking must it be even to a person of the least humanity to See his own Countryman, perhaps his own Townsman Labouring in the Corn or Rice field, Broiling in the Sun, Pale and Fainting under the Excessive heat." The situation was dire: "Instances there has been of their dieing on the very Spot." On the other hand, the petitioners assured the Trustees that Black people enjoyed such labor. "The Negroes in the same fields . . . go through their Work with pleasure," the petitioners wrote; indeed, "their Spirits are at the Highest" during the strongest heat in the middle of the day.[38]

The petitioners, then, pursued several angles in an attempt to persuade the Trustees that without enslaved Black laborers, the settlers' very lives were at stake. They compared their bodies to robust enslaved Black people who worked in the sun "with pleasure." In contrast, their frail English bodies apparently dropped dead in the fields. The Malcontents included imagery calculated to appeal to the Trustees' knowledge of climatic tropes. Readers could well imagine how poorly a British body would be prepared for a dangerously hot and sunny place. Surely the Trustees could sympathize with the plight of their "own Countryman" laboring in fields under the broiling sun, as opposed to the foreign Africans, who "welcomed" the sun. Most of all, the Malcontents stressed the authority of experience in their appeal to the Trustees. "It is Experience," they wrote, "Seven long years Experience that has confirmed us of the Impossibility of White men being able to Work here and live." Here the petitioners appealed to the Trustees' weak spot: other than Oglethorpe, none of the Trustees had ever been to Georgia, and they continuously sought to ascertain the truth about the climate. This was exactly the kind of argument calculated to appeal to the Trustees.[39]

Had Georgia colonists been united in their demands, the Trustees might have been inclined to believe the climatic arguments. But the Trustees received many different reports, several of which contained conflicting information. Perhaps the most persuasive of these came from the Salzburgers, a group of German-speaking Protestants living in Ebenezer, a settlement 25 miles upriver from Savannah.[40]

In December 1740, John Martin Bolzius, the leader of the Salzburger community, wrote to Harman Verelst, the Trustees' accountant, requesting funds to support the construction of new rice and corn mills at Ebenezer. The Salzburgers had been in the area since 1734, and each year they produced ample harvests of corn, peas, rice, and potatoes. Like the Trustees, the tight-knit Salzburger community opposed slavery because they believed it discouraged free people from working. They may well also have held prejudices against non-whites and, like William Byrd, feared the potential violence they associated with enslaved Africans. The Stono Rebellion in South Carolina in September 1739 would have confirmed any misgivings the Salzburgers held about African slavery, but even before that, they opposed introducing slavery into the colony. Hearing of the Malcontents' petitions, the Salzburgers voiced their opposition, eager to explain that Georgia's climate in fact posed no obstacle to white labor. "Tho 'tis here a hotter Season than our native Country," the Salzburgers wrote to Oglethorpe in March 1739, "it is not so extreamly hot as we were told in the first Time of our Arrival." They had adapted their customs and working hours to the climate, along with their bodies. "Since we have been now used to the country," the Salzburgers continued, "we find it tolerable, and for working People very convenient, setting themselves to work early in the Morning till Ten o'Clock, and in the Afternoon from Three to Sun-set." During the strongest heat in the middle of the day, people took care of "Business at Home." With some small adjustments, then, the Salzburgers found themselves able to labor productively in Georgia.[41]

Bolzius also wrote to Verelst and the Trustees, assuring them of the same thing. After five years in Georgia, Bolzius explained, the Salzburgers knew "what wholesome, fruitful . . . & profitable climate this country is" when worked by "industrious honest people." The Salzburgers found that farming in Georgia was not only possible for Europeans; it could even be profitable. A fourth transport of Salzburgers was on its way, and Bolzius expressed his certainty that the new arrivals would like the place. "They will be here as well satisfy'd, as we are," he wrote, "having not the least reason now, to make any complaint about the hot season of the countrey, being not so very hot, as idle & delicate people endeavour to persuade themselves & others." He implored the Trustees not to allow slavery in the colony because "the consequences of it would be very bad & the ruin of poor labourers." Instead, "white people, if industrious," he believed "are capable enough to plant here every sort of countrey-grain without hurting

their health in the summer season, of which is witness my whole congregation."
For Bolzius, the Malcontents were simply lazy. Those "idle & delicate people"
should have no reason to complain of the climate, he wrote, and the good health
of the Salzburgers, combined with their impressive harvests, should serve as
ample proof.[42]

As news of the pro- and anti-slavery petitions spread, a group of Highland
Scots living in Darien, Georgia, also petitioned the Trustees not to allow slavery
in the colony. Slaves, they believed, were an unnecessary luxury that would
bankrupt small farmers. "We are not rich," the settlers wrote, "and becoming
Debtors for Slaves, in Case of their running away or dying, would inevitably
ruin the poor Master, and he become a greater Slave to the Negroe-Merchant,
than the Slave he bought could be to him." They would farm the land themselves, they claimed. "We are laborious, and know a white Man may be, by the
Year, more usefully employed than a Negroe." Here they made an economic
argument to counteract that of the Malcontents. Slaves were expensive, and
risking a bondsperson "running away or dying" could turn slaveholders into
debtors. They also hit upon an issue that would resurface in later correspondence the Trustees received: the potential power and stronghold of a slave merchant in the colony.[43]

Hearing of the Darien counter-petition, the Malcontents complained
that Oglethorpe had bribed the Darien settlers, promising them money and
cattle if they signed the petition against slavery. Whether or not this was
the case, Scottish migrants did not feel constitutionally unable to labor in
Georgia's climate. The soldiers at Frederica on St. Simon's Island, for example, provided testimony corroborating the Salzburgers' claims about
white peoples' ability to work the land in Georgia. Captain Hugh Mackay,
who had commanded a group of seventeen servants for two years, swore that
in that time "the Said Servants work'd very hard, and that they never lay by
in Summer by reason of the heat of the weather." The previous summer, he
continued, the servants had worked "in the open air and Sun, in falling trees,
cross cutting and Splitting timber, and carrying it on their Shoulders when
Split from the Woods to the Camp." Mackay testified that this labor "did
not occasion any illness among them."[44] Lieutenant Raymond Demare, who
oversaw a regiment of soldiers in the summer of 1738, told the recorder that
the soldiers worked "in the Sun & Air" clearing land, hauling materials, and
building huts. "During all the Said term, the Men continued very healthy,"
Demare reported, adding that he "never knew any man desire to be excused
from labour on account of the heat." And Lieutenant George Dunbar
explained that the soldiers under his command worked during the morning,
had a break at midday, and resumed work again in the afternoon hours. He
had never heard anyone make "the Heat a Pretence for not Working." Just as

the Salzburger farmers had timed their labor to work around the heat of the day, so were the Highland soldiers able to clear forested land and perform physical labor despite Georgia's heat.[45]

According to an overwhelming number of letters coming from Georgia, the chief drawback of European labor lay not in its impossibility but in its exorbitant cost. All three of these witnesses, along with others, testified that Europeans could indeed work the land in Georgia, even in the heat of the summer. Dunbar, for example, testified that even though European labor was possible, "in the Negroe Colonies the hire of white men is dearer than that of Negroes." In South Carolina, he explained, "white Ship Carpenters & caulkers have about one third more wages than a Negroe of the same trade & occupation." Dunbar found that other trades also had the same difference in pay. In this regard, then, the Malcontents were not alone. Several people found economic arguments to be the strongest reason for allowing slavery in the colony. Still, as the Darien and Salzburger settlers pointed out, the long-term economic effects of slave societies could be even more devastating to the small farmer than the initial years of struggle without adequate labor forces or the relatively high costs of employing servants. But unlike the Malcontents, the counter-petitioners unilaterally agreed that the warm climate was not a problem for industrious people willing to work.[46]

Rumors of climatic dangers, though, also circulated locally in Georgia. One colonist reported that he considered planting rice but was discouraged by neighbors' warnings. In Carolina, he wrote, "the Negroes" were "the only proper planters" for growing rice because "whenever white people are employed in that way of working, they die like fflies." The Salzburgers dismissed these rumors succinctly. "We [were] told by several people after our arrival that it proves quite impossible and Dangerous for White People to plant and Manufacture any Rice, being a work only for Negroes, not for European people," they wrote to the Trustees in a letter pleading to keep the ban on slavery. "But having Experience of the Congregation we laugh at such a Tale seeing that several people of us have had in last Harvest a greater Crop of Rice, than they wanted for their own Consumption." Despite Eveleigh's conviction that white people could not possibly handle rice production, the Salzburgers quietly went about the work of sowing, and later harvesting, many types of grain, rice included. By 1740, the Salzburgers were hard at work building a stamping-mill to process their rice, a sign that they had had several good harvests and expected such harvests to continue. The ability of the Salzburgers to cultivate rice undermined some of the most ardent Malcontent complaints.[47]

In the following years the Salzburgers grew plenty of rice and had no problems harvesting it. In 1742, for example, they produced 733 bushels of rice, along with over 3,000 bushels of corn and several hundred more of peas and potatoes. Other people in Georgia also experimented with growing rice. Isaac Nuñez Henriquez produced fifteen bushels of rice on his garden lot in Savannah in 1736, and nine on his farm lot two years later. In 1748, Bartholomew Londerbukler wrote to the Trustees requesting servants to help harvest the rice, corn, and potatoes he had planted. Even Patrick Tailfer's town lot proved to be a fertile one: in 1738, he had leased his land to Patrick Graham, who apparently was able to produce 100 bushels of rice.[48]

Still, incentive to plant rice remained low. Some may have been convinced by the repeated claims of South Carolinians that they should not attempt it; others had been cowed by Carolinians' threats to potential competitors. In August 1740, the Trustees' Savannah secretary William Stephens wrote in his journal that he had received an unexpected visit from some South Carolinians. He showed them around Savannah as they conversed about the town's condition, and Stephens agreed with the men that Georgians should not plant rice because the market was already glutted. The Carolinians may have visited Stephens expressly for that purpose; a few months later several people provided statements under oath in Savannah's court on the condition of Georgia. Their testimony revealed a reluctance to enter Carolina's market. "It is not any Business of this Colony, nor any Benefit to the Trade of England, to interfere with what other English Plantations have produced, such as Rice," one person proclaimed. In their efforts to discourage competition in the market, the Carolina planters had effectively dissuaded many of the Georgia settlers from even attempting to plant rice.[49]

As the conflicts over rice production show, climatic rhetoric and skepticism about white peoples' ability to labor in hot climates were tied to economics in multiple ways. In addition to economic arguments for slavery masquerading as climatic concerns, colonists felt local pressure not to produce particular crops. Although the Trustees initially hoped Savannah would benefit from its proximity to Charleston, according to Oglethorpe this location turned out to be a disadvantage. Writing in response to the Malcontents' petition, Oglethorpe assured the Trustees that plenty of settlers in Georgia had no desire for slaves—that, in fact, they specifically requested that the Trustees uphold the prohibition. One of the Trustees, the Earl of Egmont, kept a journal in which he described a letter Oglethorpe had sent in January 1739. The "idleness of the town of Savannah," Oglethorpe informed the Trustees, "is chiefly owing to their seeing Negroes in S. Carolina." Residents of places farther removed— Darien, Frederica, and Ebenezer—cultivated several different crops with a measure of success in the Georgia climate, and Oglethorpe believed these places' distance from Charleston partially accounted for their settlers' industrious habits.[50]

Scheming for Slavery

As it turned out, some of the Malcontents had ulterior motives in campaigning for slavery. According to Oglethorpe, Savannah settlers did not necessarily want slaves, but signed the Malcontents' petitions for other reasons. The Trustees had recently ousted their storekeeper Thomas Causton from the colony, and Causton had a habit of handing out special favors to particular colonists. Oglethorpe believed that some people, annoyed at their loss of these favors, had signed the petitions in retaliation. Several settlers had also run out of money, and the petitions—which demanded both permission for slavery and settlers' rights to hold the titles to their land—could provide colonists with an economic boost. If the Trustees granted titles, settlers would hold real property. But most dangerous of all, Oglethorpe explained, several people signed because Savannah resident Robert Williams had family ties to the slave trade and sought to benefit personally by introducing slavery into the colony. According to Oglethorpe, Williams had promised several Savannah residents "to let them have Negroes, if they could sell or morgage their lands to him for them, which proved a bait for all those to sign the Representation for Negroes." William Stephens sent a separate letter to the Trustees stating the same thing: the Georgia residents' requests for holding their land in fee simple were bound up with their demands for slaves, because if they could own the titles to their land, they could use them as credit to acquire slaves. Robert Williams "was engaged in partnership with others who dealt in Negroes," Stephens explained, and was one of the two "chief Fabricators" of the petition. The other was Williams's brother-in-law, Malcontent leader Patrick Tailfer.[51]

The Trustees received several pieces of information suggesting these two Malcontents had ulterior motives for their petitions in favor of slavery. A number of letters from Savannah, as well as some Georgia residents' visits to London, drew the Trustees' attention to Robert Williams's connections to the slave trade. Colonel Cochran and Captain Thompson informed the Earl of Egmont in person that Williams "was urgent for Negroes because he trafficks in them." Robert Howes, onetime clerk of Savannah, told Egmont that Williams, "being a Merchant," had "a private Interest of his own" in instigating the colonists' desires for slaves.[52] Oglethorpe explained to the Trustees that having refused "to confirm a certificate" in Robert Williams's favor, he had provoked Williams's fury:

> Mr. Williams is very angry and hath got the poor people of Savannah, many of whom are deeply in debt to him, to sign the petition for Negroes which affirms that white men cannot work in this Province. This assertion I can disprove by hundreds of witnesses, all the Saltzburghers,

the people at Darien, many at Frederica and Savannah and all the industrious in the Province. The idle ones are indeed for Negroes[.] If
the Petition is countenanced, the Province is ruined. Mr. Williams and
Doctor [Tailfer] will buy most of the Lands at Savannah with Debts due
to them and the Inhabitants must go off and be succeeded by Negroes.
Yet the very debtors have been weak enough to sign their Desire of
Leave to sell.[53]

Williams and Tailfer, then, planned to cash in on debts owed to them, buy
up settlers' land, consolidate smaller plots into massive plantations, and use
enslaved laborers to work the land. Oglethorpe later elaborated on Tailfer's role
in the scheme: as Savannah's main surgeon, he and Williams, who had apparently begun selling rum, "had almost all the town of Savannah indebted to them
for Physick and Rum." The two used this debt to convince—or rather coerce—
Savannah's residents to sign the petition. If Williams and Tailfer had their way,
Georgia would transform into an extension of South Carolina.[54]

William Stephens corroborated Oglethorpe's report. According to Stephens,
Robert Williams was "in partnership with his brother & others at St. Kitts &
Bristol, who made much in importing Negroes into the West Indies." Tailfer had
made money in part by hiring out his servants, and in part through his practice
as a physician, and he and Williams conspired to add to that wealth. Through his
family connections, Williams would provide Savannah residents with slaves, but
knowing most people did not have the money to pay for them, he would take
the titles to their land as payment. To do this, Williams and Tailfer needed to
convince the Trustees to give people the titles to their lands and to allow slavery
in the colony. After their repeated economic arguments in favor of slavery failed,
Tailfer and Williams had begun to emphasize the climate argument.[55]

By then the Malcontents had gained considerable traction in the colony, and
their repeated public complaints, as well as their tactics, could be intimidating.
They solicited supporting testimony from residents of Savannah, which they
sent to the Trustees as evidence of colonists' desire for enslaved laborers. George
Philip, a young Scottish merchant in Savannah, provided one of these public
testimonials. He claimed that he had heard from some Darien residents who
had signed the earlier petition against slavery that they regretted their decision,
"it being contrary to the *true* Interest of themselves and the whole Country."
According to Philip, the province in general was languishing, and even "the most
industrious" settlers found that their harvests did "*not* answer the Expence of
a *White-man's Labour*." Philip had traveled to Savannah to set up a business in
partnership with his uncle, who was a merchant in Edinburgh. His public stance
was thus decidedly in favor of slavery, because if residents prospered, Philip
would too.[56]

Private documents, however, also reveal Philip's knowledge of Robert Williams's influence and connections. Not long after the Malcontents submitted their first petition, Philip wrote to his uncle to tell him about it. "There is a petition made [that] goes home with a gentilman who brought to this colloney some £1000 with him," he wrote. "He is determined to spend money upon it," Philip added, "if the Trustees will not grant to fullfill the petition, to cary it to the Board of Tread (*sic*), if not then to the King in Councill." This person, in other words, left Georgia for London with a written demand for slavery. He hoped to persuade the Trustees in person, but if that did not work then he would go over their heads. The "gentilman," Philip wrote, had "very good friends at home he is in partnership with some people at St. Christophers [St. Kitts] and is as great dealers as in that Iland, his name Robert Williams." Philip himself favored the petition both because he hoped the Trustees would lift restrictions on trade if they sanctioned the petition, and because he believed access to slaves would bolster Savannah's economy, allowing his own business to thrive. Many of the landholders in Georgia, he added, were beginning to abandon their efforts at cultivation because they could not hold the titles to their land. "The people will thro up all there improvements, if they do not get a free title to there lands," he explained. Philip's private correspondence demonstrated both his knowledge of the scheme and his personal economic reasons for supporting the petition for slavery. Nowhere did climate, or the inability of white people to labor in Georgia, figure into the desire for slaves.[57]

Although the Trustees never saw Philip's letters to his uncle, their existence suggests that Williams's motives were no secret in Savannah. Moreover, one of the Malcontents' chief supporters had himself inadvertently given the Trustees reason to doubt the accuracy of the Malcontents' claims. Thomas Stephens, who enraged his father Secretary William Stephens by publicly championing the Malcontents' cause, informed the Trustees that he needed to travel from Georgia to England because he was ill. The Trustees had sent Thomas out to assist his father but allowed him leave to return home. Once in London Thomas confessed the real reason for his visit. "It was not ill health that brought him from Georgia," Egmont fumed in his diary, "but resentment [against] Col. Oglethorpe and Mr. Tho. Jones, and to overturn the Constitution of the Province." Egmont was unimpressed with the "hot headed conceited & malicious Mr. Tho. Stephens" and refuted all of Stephens's arguments with simple logic. "I told him, if the Colony is so poor and distrest as he represented, the Inhabitants would not be able to buy or borrow Negroes, if allow'd to have them." Egmont did not yet know of Williams and Tailfer's scheme to help settlers purchase bondspeople through loans underwritten by mortgages on their land, and Stephens, if he was aware of the plan, did not enlighten Egmont. But if Stephens hoped to convey that the Georgia climate was dangerous to European bodies, he did himself no favors in his trip. "His pretence for coming to England was sickness, but it soon appeard his errant was of another sort," wrote Egmont. Stephens's claim of sickness— and his need to travel to England to alleviate it—backfired as the Trustees discovered that he was not unhealthy after all. This measure of deceit could not have helped the Malcontents' complaints about Georgia's unhealthy climate.[58]

With enough evidence from Oglethorpe and other residents of Savannah to fuel their suspicions of Williams, the Trustees dug in their heels on the question of African slavery. They wanted to increase Savannah's population and turn Georgia into a thriving colony, but not by allowing it to become a slave society. Condoning African slavery would open a path for wealthy merchants like Robert Williams to take control of the colony, making it into a replica of other Atlantic plantation economies and the antithesis of the Trustees' design. Their refusal to give in to the Malcontents' demands eventually drove most of those Malcontents away; in the fall of 1740 Tailfer and Williams, along with several others, decamped for South Carolina.[59]

From there they sought to undermine Georgia's existence by discouraging potential settlers. Led by Patrick Tailfer, in 1741 the Malcontents published a tract, *A True and Historical Narrative of the Colony of Georgia in America*, disparaging the colony and demanding Black slavery. The pamphlet made unequivocal claims about the heavy costs of European labor in contrast with that of enslaved Africans. After railing against the expenses, Tailfer turned to the climate and the difficulties the early settlers had faced:

> The *Felling of Timber* was a Task very unequal to the Strength and Constitution of White Servants, and the *Hoeing the Ground,* they being exposed to the sultry Heat of the Sun, insupportable; and it is well known, that this Labour is one of the hardest upon the Negroes, even though their Constitutions are much stronger than white People, and the Heat no way disagreeable nor hurtful to them; but in us it created *inflammatory Fevers* of various kinds both *continued* and *intermittent, wasting* and *tormenting Fluxes*, most *excruciating Cholicks*, and *Dry-Belly-Achs; Tremors, Vertigoes, Palsies*, and a long Train of *painful* and *lingering nervous Distempers*; which brought on to many a Cessation both from Work and Life[.][60]

The sickness of servants, Tailfer added, proved to be an unsupportable expense for most people—though not in medical costs (because he was the resident physician); instead because "each Servant, generally speaking, cost his Master as much as would have maintained a Negroe for *four* Years." According to Tailfer, then, the upkeep of "White Servants" was significantly costlier than that of enslaved Black laborers, although his calculations neglected to mention initial purchase prices. In a bid for readers' sympathy and to discourage potential settlers, Tailfer cautioned that white servants in Georgia suffered from fevers, fluxes, and other illnesses brought on by clearing trees and tilling soil in the heat.[61]

Unfortunately for the Trustees, the "scurilous pamphlet," as Egmont called it, along with substantial Malcontent pressure, appeared to be effective. In October 1741, Captain Thompson from Savannah informed Egmont that several of the Malcontents, "do yet tho absent all they can to discourage any man from labouring and cultivating their land, lest they should be examples that Men can live and support themselves without Negroes." By exerting various pressures, the Malcontents appeared determined to ruin the colony of Georgia if they could not have their way, and anyone farming successfully would undermine their arguments.[62]

The frustrated Trustees responded by publishing their own pamphlet. Endeavoring to "lay the naked Truth" before the public, *An Impartial Enquiry into the State and Utility of the Province of Georgia* identified five chief objections to the colony's situation. The first of these complaints, and possibly the one that most frustrated the Trustees, related to the supposed unhealthiness of the climate. "The Reverse of this has been found by the People," explained Benjamin Martyn, who authored the pamphlet. Settlers had remained healthy even in the colony's early days, "and this was the Time of Trial. No general Illness has at any Time prevailed there (even when *South Carolina* has suffered by them) unless when Rum and other spirituous Liquors have stolen into the Province." Martyn conceded that during one year "many of the People" had died, but he attributed their deaths to excessive drinking, which "they confess'd at their Deaths." As for the claims that Georgia's climate induced fluxes, Martyn wrote:

> The Flux is a Distemper to which new Comers in most Countries are liable, and some of the People in *Georgia* had it. But it was chiefly owing to the Want of Reflection, how requisite it is for Men to regulate their Diet and Manner of Living, in a different Way in the Latitude of 31, from that which they were accustom'd to in the Latitude of 51[.][63]

In other words, people often experienced fluxes when they changed countries and climates, particularly if they neglected to adjust their habits and their diets. The flux was a form of seasoning and therefore to be expected. It was not, Martyn stressed, a function of Georgia's climate nor was it particular to Georgia. Martyn pointed to the success of the Salzburgers and the Highlanders at Darien, arguing that people "accustom'd to Hardship, and Labour" had no trouble cultivating provisions in Georgia. As for the economic calculations of servant versus slave labor, Martyn suggested an adjustment. "The Value of an unseasoned Negroe's

Life," he wrote, "cannot be computed at more than seven Years Purchase." The Malcontents' calculations were incomplete.[64]

Here Martyn drew attention to a common belief that the Malcontents had ignored altogether in their arguments: an unseasoned person arriving from Africa would need to undergo the same seasoning process as someone arriving from Europe. Yet the Malcontents conveniently ignored this in their petitions. Perhaps some of the petitioners believed they would acquire enslaved people from South Carolina, either those who had already been seasoned to the climate or (even better) those who had been born there. But Robert Williams, for one, had no such designs. His business plan relied upon working with his brother in St. Christopher who, as one Savannah resident explained, "carried on a Trade to Guinea for Negroe Slaves." Someone coming from Africa, though, would be unseasoned to Georgia's climate. The Malcontents based their comparisons on South Carolina's situation, although many enslaved laborers there had been born in the lowcountry. Such would not be the case in Georgia.[65]

The Trustees hoped to silence the Malcontents with their pamphlet and to dispel arguments that divided the Georgia populace. But they could not undo the significant damage the Malcontents had inflicted upon the colony. Throughout the 1740s the Malcontents kept chipping away at the Trustees' resolve, and the Trustees, to their dismay, saw Savannah's population dwindle as "idle" settlers left for slaveholding South Carolina. By the end of the decade Georgia was languishing. John Dobell, a supporter of the Trustees, wrote from Charleston of the dire situation. The Malcontents were "unpeopling Georgia very swiftly," he despaired, "discouraging" some potential settlers and "driving away" other "worthy" planters. Dobell explained the familiar situation. The "single objection . . . against the cultivation of lands in this place or in Georgia by white people is the heat of the weather," he wrote. But "the white people in Georgia who have or do cultivate land, generally, make no such complaint." These people were "very industrious" and never complained about "the heat of the climate" at all, Dobell continued, and the substantial number of these industrious farmers were "sufficient proofs" that "white people are able to live prosperously by their cultivation of lands without the use of Negroes." Despite this ample evidence, the Malcontents were relentless and Georgia's population exodus was undeniable. "Thus," wrote Dobell, "the colony is as it were on fire," and unless some drastic changes occurred "it must inevitably perish." The Trustees, loath as they were to condone slavery in Georgia, also heard that settlers were increasingly flouting the ban. With very few anti-slavery holdouts left in the colony, and with others openly keeping bondspeople, in 1750 the Trustees ultimately sanctioned slavery in Georgia. A couple of years later, Parliament revoked the Trustees' charter. After overseeing a struggling colony for two decades, the Trustees relinquished control of Georgia, which became a royal colony.[66]

The Health of the Colony

A variety of factors contributed to the eventual reversal of the Trustees' policy and the transition to slavery in Georgia. Savannah's proximity to a colony where slavery was entrenched hurt Georgia's chances, and the lack of farming skills among its residents did not help. Endemic problems with servants running away or falling ill because they had had insufficient time to become seasoned to the climate frustrated many potential planters. The vermin, insects, and trees of un-cultivated land thwarted those who had worked to clear their own plots, as did the lack of industry on the part of their neighbors. Ultimately, the Malcontents felt frustrated by the Trustees' policies, which limited great wealth, while Carolina planters prospered across the river. Although the Trustees never in-tended Georgia to be a profit-driven colony, the early colonists felt shunted from the surrounding market economy. But after the Trustees turned a deaf ear to economic-based pleas, the Malcontents pursued the climatic argument, hoping that would sway the Trustees and the members of Parliament who oversaw the colony's charter.[67]

By emphasizing the climate argument, the Malcontents made a calcu-lated choice. Although the Trustees were unconvinced by the Malcontents' complaints, the disgruntled settlers publicized their supposed suffering because they hoped to win popular sympathy, and they were familiar with existing cli-matic rhetoric. Moreover, the Trustees, having never experienced the colony for themselves, could not entirely disregard negative reports. And several of Georgia's residents were happy to capitalize on the preconceptions Britons held about warm climates across the Atlantic. Despite various "improvement" projects English settlers undertook in the Americas during the seventeenth cen-tury and into the eighteenth, the settlers could not significantly change the envi-ronment. They might have been able to make it somewhat healthier by clearing brush and draining swampland, but Savannah lay in a semitropical region that, for the English, would always be a warm climate. The Malcontents' resort to the climate argument, then, was a strategic move aimed at convincing the Trustees of the need for slavery after their other arguments failed.[68]

Despite the dramatic reports of illness the Malcontents described in their pamphlet, Georgia did not appear to be an exceptionally unhealthy place in its early years. William Stephens kept careful note of sickness in the colony, so the Trustees had a fairly reliable record of local illnesses. Although his journals may have been intended to pacify the Trustees, his characterizations of health and illness are nevertheless instructive. During the 1730s and 1740s, Stephens wrote of fevers and agues affecting Savannah. These ailments, according to Stephens, resulted from "great vicissitude of weather"; "thick, unwholesome Air, and sultry

Heat"; "heavy rains"; and "the Peoples Unwariness in taking cold when they are Hot." This combination of environmental conditions and incautious behavior was consistent with medical thinking at the time. Although during the first half of the eighteenth century diagnoses of particular diseases, such as yellow fever, were inconsistent at best, there were no recorded outbreaks of specific diseases in Georgia during the Trusteeship. Charleston, on the other hand, experienced a number of notable diseases during the same period. Stephens wrote of an outbreak of smallpox in August 1738, which "carr[ied] off a great Number of People, both White and Black." The unfortunate town had barely recovered when Stephens heard of "a new Distemper . . . spreading itself among them, which was thought epidemical if not contagious." The following September Stephens received word of "a very terrible Calamity of Sickness" in Charleston, "which proved exceeding mortal, great Numbers dying weekly, and it is termed a contagious, malignant Fever." The next fall, while Savannah residents experienced "Fluxes, dry Gripes, lingering Fevers, &c.," word arrived from Charleston "of a dangerous Distemper raging there, which they call the yellow Fever, from the Corpse immediately so changing, after Death." The fever, Stephens wrote, "proved most fatal to new Comers." Unlike Charleston, which experienced several serious disease outbreaks in the late 1730s and early 1740s, Georgia inhabitants suffered from relatively common fluxes and fevers.[69]

There are two significant factors in these accounts of illness. First, Stephens did not differentiate between diseases affecting African and European populations; instead, "distempers," such as smallpox, appeared to affect "both White and Black" residents of Charleston. At least according to Stephens's notes, skin color did not seem to determine susceptibility to illness. Stephens did not note the health of Indigenous people, suggesting that their numbers in Charleston were minimal or that they were left off of records. Second, the variable Stephens did mention was, in effect, seasoning—the yellow fever outbreak of 1740 hit "new Comers" the hardest. New arrivals, or those unseasoned to the climate, proved most vulnerable to illness. This interpretation was entirely consistent with medical thinking of the time. For most colonists in the Anglo-Atlantic world, the significant health difference between people lay in whether or not they were seasoned to a particular climate. The fluxes and fevers Stephens described also fit with ideas of seasoning; many physicians and colonists thought that people would become seasoned to a place after experiencing a period of ill health.

Although fevers could be "continued" or "intermittent," eighteenth-century inhabitants of the Greater Caribbean did not ascribe the causes of these fevers to genetic traits. Instead, they blamed them in general on environmental conditions. Both physicians and other observers noted that unseasoned people, or "strangers," were by far the most likely to become ill. In another journal entry, for example, William Stephens noted that although soldiers in Florida had "grown very sickly," their illness was "a Sort of Ague and Fever with regular Intermission . . . such as is pretty common in these Parts, at certain Seasons, especially among fresh People from Europe, and is usually termed a Seasoning." Descriptions of illness consistently mentioned the susceptibility of strangers and of "fresh" arrivals.[70]

Prevailing interpretations among white people of who was most likely to fall ill consistently differentiated between inhabitants and strangers and not, as the Malcontents insisted, between Black and white people. Rather than ascribing differences in disease susceptibility to people's origins or physiology, eighteenth-century observers more frequently attributed these differences to seasoning and bodily adjustment to the environment. All people were much more likely to become ill if they had recently arrived from a distant place, and all people needed to be seasoned to the local climate.[71]

Although surely the Malcontents were familiar with these commonly held notions, it served their purposes better to claim differences between Africans and Europeans. The Malcontents also built upon a sprinkling of local climatic arguments, most notably Samuel Eveleigh's. Although Eveleigh argued that white people were constitutionally unable to labor in rice fields, he made these claims before the Salzburgers and other Georgia residents managed to successfully cultivate rice. In addition, he based them on his experience in South Carolina, a society in which Black slavery was entrenched and where white people did not physically work to produce rice. In Georgia, the Salzburgers grew rice successfully for a while, but felt pressure from South Carolina to branch out; still, they cultivated a number of grains with their own labor. A few other Savannah residents grew rice for a brief period but were discouraged by Carolina's lower prices.[72]

White labor in a warm climate, then, was not itself the problem. Instead, the Malcontents' climatic arguments were simply an abuse of the Trustees' preconceptions of warm climates. With no people of African descent in Georgia under the Trustees (or at least none officially), it is impossible to know the exact measures of disease susceptibility among European and African populations. Even though the Malcontents complained about the climate, there is little evidence to show that the Malcontents actually believed that the Georgia climate necessitated Black labor. On the other hand, there is plenty of evidence to suggest that Tailfer and Williams had personal interests in bringing slavery to Georgia and that both men held enough power in the colony to entice settlers to sign petitions that may not have reflected their true beliefs. In addition, despite their claims that Black people worked under the hot sun "with pleasure," the Malcontents had no evidence to show that Black people did not also suffer from the "fevers," "fluxes," and other "distempers" that they claimed afflicted white people. Instead, their arguments exemplified environmental racism.[73]

Tailfer and Williams wanted to introduce slavery from the beginning of their time in Georgia, if not sooner. When complaining about financial discrepancies between servants and slaves proved unsuccessful, the two combined those complaints with the inability of unseasoned servants to work the land. Only after that too yielded no consent from the Trustees did the Malcontents begin to argue that white people were physically incapable of laboring in Georgia.

Historians have treated Georgia as an anomaly, a strange blip in the history of Anglo-Atlantic plantation societies. To observers at the time, the decision to legalize African slavery in Georgia would have seemed proof that white people could not labor in the heat. Although people's experiences in Georgia under the Trustees did not confirm speculation about the inability of white people to work in a hot climate, the Malcontents' persistent arguments expanded this myth. The argument–not borne out by experience–that white people were constitutionally unable to labor in a hot climate perpetuated and justified racial slavery across the Greater Caribbean. Despite evidence to the contrary, a handful of Georgia colonists manipulated climatic rhetoric to suit their economic purposes. But from the outside, the story seemed to confirm that a large swath of the Americas, including the lowcountry and the Caribbean, was simply too hot for white people to work the land themselves.

"An Excellent & Healthfull Situation"

Colonial Patterns of Settlement

With the legalization of African slavery in Georgia, white planters began to take advantage of the lowcountry's swampy lands for rice cultivation. Rice grew best in wet ground, covered with a shallow layer of standing water. As a result, the enslaved laborers who created and tended the rice fields of the lowcountry constructed unhealthy environments where they then had to live and work. As one white writer explained, the water necessary for rice cultivation made the region "very sickly," especially during the summer. Enslaved laborers were "turned out to work in the Rice Swamps, half leg deep in water, which brings on pleurisies and peripneumonies, and destroys numbers of them." Another visitor traveling through the region noted that the "rice dams, and swamps" held "a great quantity of stagnated water in summer." This water, he wrote, was responsible for "fall fevers and agues, dry gripes, and other disorders, which are often fatal to the lower set of people, as well white as black." Others explained that wealthy planters escaped to their town homes during "the sickly seasons" in order to avoid the "stagnating Water" in the rice fields.[1]

These comments reveal a great deal about eighteenth-century plantation environments. These white writers observed Black people becoming sick and dying on plantations and attributed their ill health to the local environment. Unlike wealthy planters who left their country estates during summer and fall to live in healthier places, "the lower set of people," both Black and white, had no choice but to remain on plantations where they fell ill and sometimes died. It is essential that white observers noted that environmental conditions on plantations made Black inhabitants ill. The fact that plantation environments, such as swampy lowcountry rice fields, caused significant illness among the enslaved undermines any arguments that Black people were especially suited to labor in these environments. Instead, both Black and white laborers fell victim to fatal illnesses, which observers attributed to the environment. These

The Nature of Slavery. Katherine Johnston, Oxford University Press. © Oxford University Press 2022.
DOI: 10.1093/oso/9780197514603.003.0004

observers differentiated between healthy and unhealthy places but did not consider Black bodies to be healthier than white bodies in dangerous environmental conditions.

The prevailing rhetoric that portrayed hot climates as universally dangerous to Britons and healthier for Africans obscured significant nuance in the ways colonial inhabitants actually thought and wrote about differences among various places. In the lowcountry, for example, some spaces could be healthy, while others could be remarkably less so, even dangerously unhealthy, for all bodies. The same was true of the Caribbean. For settler-colonists who lived in these places, climatic nuance—a sense of microclimates dependent upon a region's elevation, proximity to stagnant or moving water, and air flow, among other variables—was essential to determining which places were healthy or unhealthy. Colonists considered a region's microclimates a critical factor in constructing homes, towns, hospitals, and soldiers' barracks. In situating each of these spaces, settlers, planters, physicians, and others tried to take advantage of a region's natural environmental features to promote good health. The extent to which colonists took differences in local environments into account as they built or rebuilt both public and private spaces in Greater Caribbean colonies belied monolithic statements about hot climates in general.

Examining patterns of settlement within these colonies demonstrates the vital importance of place to eighteenth-century settler-colonists. Colonists made substantial efforts to create and use spaces that protected their health. Moreover, planters believed that the same places and environmental conditions conducive to their own health would preserve the health of enslaved Black laborers, just as they recognized that unhealthy environments endangered all bodies. Letters from planters and plantation managers show a marked similarity in their perceptions of Africans' and Europeans' bodily reactions to weather and to local environments. While not every single body reacted to environmental conditions in exactly the same way, on a large scale, all bodies benefited from the same environmental management projects, such as clearing wooded areas, and suffered from others, such as creating rice fields. Colonial officials considered how the local environment would impact bodily health in the construction of towns and cities, and planters took these same factors into account when laying out a plantation's living quarters and medical facilities. Finally, military officers also thought about local environmental conditions when trying to preserve the health of British troops in the West Indies, a group with a notoriously high death rate. In all of these cases, inhabitants of the Greater Caribbean were highly attuned to the variability of environmental conditions across even the smallest of areas, and these perceived differences shaped colonial spaces.

Lowcountry Locations

When the Lords Proprietors established the colony of Carolina in the late seventeenth century, they thought that finding a healthy place for the capital could determine the colony's success. Both settlers and the Lords Proprietors, who held the colony's charter, wanted to locate the capital of Charles Towne in a strategic spot. Easy access to the ocean was essential, although colonists also sought a protected bay, ideally slightly upriver from the open sea. After a short-lived settlement in the 1660s, a determined group of colonists arrived on the Carolina coast in 1670 and staked out a place for a permanent capital.[2]

As the group considered the layout of the future colony, Lord Anthony Ashley Cooper, Earl of Shaftesbury and Carolina's foremost Proprietor, wrote to the group's leader Sir John Yeamans with detailed instructions for settling a town. "Let me recomend to you," Shaftesbury wrote, "to chuse such a place as may [be] healthyest & seated upon ye highest ground." From what Shaftesbury gathered of the settlers' descriptions, their temporary settlement was "so moorish [marshy] that it must needs be unhealthy," a disadvantage certain to doom the fledgling colony. Four months later, a colonist informed Shaftesbury that the group had settled upon a location for Charles Towne. The spot, the colonist assured Shaftesbury, "must of necessity be very healthy being free from any noisome vapours, and all the summer long refreshed with continued coole breathings from the sea." The colonists had chosen a site along the Kiawah River (which they renamed the Ashley), further upriver from their initial settlement but still close enough to benefit from sea breezes.[3]

But after several summers and autumns, increasing numbers of people in the settlement suffered from fevers and agues, and prevailing opinions about the healthiness of Charles Towne's location began to change. Concerned about the colony's survival, the Lords Proprietors ordered the inhabitants of Carolina to settle new towns further upriver and to move Charles Towne to a healthier location. Only a few years after establishing the first settlement on Shaftesbury's instructions, in 1678 the colonists moved the town to a different spot across the river, just a few miles away. The new location, Oyster Point, proved to have better air circulation and settlers seemed healthier. With these advantages, the colony's chances of survival increased both because the settler-colonists already there would be more likely to survive and because a healthier reputation would be more likely to attract new settlers. The movement of the Carolina colonists from a rudimentary town which appeared healthy until circumstances indicated otherwise demonstrates the importance they attached to settling in a healthy place. To those financing the colony, the settlers' health was crucial to the colony's success.[4]

Half a century later, James Oglethorpe consulted with local Yamacraw leader Tomochichi about the best place for a settlement. Tomochichi suggested "a healthy situation about ten miles from the sea" upon which to build the town of Savannah. "The landskip is very agreeable," Oglethorpe informed the Trustees, and the following month a visitor from Charleston noted the location's "beautiful prospect" as "a wholesome place, for a town or city." Far from fortunate happenstance and in addition to Tomochichi's sound advice, Oglethorpe had planned carefully for Georgia. In Oglethorpe's view, anyone constructing a town should "consult the wholesomeness of the Air and Waters" and choose "a healthy situation" far from marshes so as to avoid their noxious exhalations. Savannah's town plan famously incorporated open squares with green spaces designed for airing out the city so that residents would never be far from fresh air. By insisting on the town's healthy location and layout, Oglethorpe hoped to strengthen the colony as well as the empire.[5]

In the seventeenth and eighteenth centuries, both physicians and lay-people believed that all places could be characterized according to varying degrees of healthfulness. Certain factors would determine the relative health of a place: most people believed that fresh air and water signified a healthy spot, while marshy, lowland areas bred miasmas, a term for a type of noxious air that physicians believed caused disease. Settlers in the Americas often took steps to "improve" the healthiness of colonial landscapes by draining swamps, cutting down trees, and cultivating the land. Several colonists believed that their improvement schemes went beyond the immediate environment and claimed that they were actually changing the climate. But even given the serious efforts to tame or improve the land, European inhabitants of the Americas recognized the limits of their abilities. Residents of Britain's tropical and semitropical American colonies noted the direction and timing of air currents, rainfall and moisture in the air, changes in temperature, and seasonal weather patterns so that they could choose the healthiest spots for building homes and for encouraging future migration. From Carolina in the 1670s through Dominica in the 1760s, whenever these climatic nuances involved the placement of colonial capitals, colonists as well as officials in London gave serious thought to arguments about the relative health of various places.[6]

Kingston, Jamaica, 1754

Locating the capital of a new colony, as in Carolina and Georgia, took careful consideration as well as luck. The situation looked slightly different, however, in an existing colony. The debate over the location of Jamaica's capital during the 1750s demonstrates the extent to which both settlers and colonial officials took health—and a place's reputation for health—seriously. For those with personal, financial, or political stakes, health mattered.

The controversy began in Kingston. The burgeoning town was not far from the once flourishing, but by then largely ruined, Port Royal. In the decades following the earthquake of 1692, a series of disasters—a fire and two hurricanes—had repeatedly devastated the port, and by mid-century Jamaican merchants had all but given up on the narrow spit of sand. They settled instead across the bay in Kingston, which lay nestled in the lowlands on the water. With hills rising sharply to the east and uplands to the north, what had once been a forested area sloping from the Liguanea plain to the sea was rapidly developing into a bustling port city. By mid-century, Kingston's residents felt that its status as the island's major seaport and as a central hub for colonial merchants merited recognition. To this end, a group of merchants asked the colony's new governor, Admiral Charles Knowles, to consider moving the capital from Spanish Town to Kingston. Spanish Town, or St. Jago de la Vega, had been inherited from Spanish control of the island a century earlier. It lay north and west of Kingston, some twelve miles or so into the uplands. The merchants argued that Kingston would make a better site for colonial activity: it had the largest population flow on the island because nearly everyone who arrived in Jamaica sailed into Kingston's harbor. It also had a more urban layout than Spanish Town, with its buildings situated close together and its streets laid out in a grid. Already the economic center of the colony, merchants and residents argued, Kingston should also be the political center.[7]

Knowles seized upon the opportunity to distinguish himself amongst his new constituents. Eschewing the traditional governor's home, Knowles spent much of his time in Kingston already and was eager for an official excuse to live there full time. Writing to the Board of Trade in London, Knowles pitched the merchants' idea, explaining that both trade and convenience made Kingston the most sensible place to locate the capital. Residents of Spanish Town did not want to lose the seat of government, so they too sent petitions to the governor and to the Board of Trade. Preoccupied with more pressing domestic and foreign affairs, the British government did not give these petitions much consideration until Knowles took matters into his own hands and declared Kingston the new capital. This bold move on the part of the new governor prompted the Board of Trade to conduct an inquiry. Hoping to determine whether moving the seat of government from Spanish Town to Kingston would be "for the general interest for the island of Jamaica the trade thereof and the Mother Country," the Board posed a number of questions to residents of both towns and the surrounding areas. Drawing on the arguments presented in the petitions, the Board asked which of the towns would be the best location for trade and which would better protect the colony's papers and records from potential invaders. Notably, the Board also asked which of the two places had the healthier climate.[8]

The local climate of each place and the relative healthiness of the two towns concerned the Board a great deal. Officials in London well knew the importance of a colony's reputation, particularly in the case of Jamaica. Although it had been sixty years since the Port Royal earthquake and a full century since the Western Design, Jamaica's reputation in Britain was dubious, if not dreadful. A poor reputation could dissuade both servants and other settlers from flocking to the colony, and if British officials wanted to hold onto their colonies, they needed to populate those places, particularly with white people able to bear arms. The recent fiasco with Georgia, in which the Malcontents had deliberately represented the climate as dangerous to Europeans in order to introduce racial slavery, had not helped the reputation of colonies in warm climates, and the British government was eager to encourage white settlement. Members of the Board of Trade, then, had a distinct interest in making Jamaica attractive enough to draw a colonial population and strengthen the economy. But distance between London and the West Indies and a lack of personal experience among British officials complicated matters. Both colonists and colonial officials could be unreliable narrators; colonial governors complained about the West Indian climate with some regularity and sometimes did so in order to bargain for more money or a better position. In the case of Georgia, the Trustees had a hard time determining which climatic complaints were genuine and which were tools of manipulation. A history of colonial inhabitants portraying the Greater Caribbean climate as more dangerous than they actually found it made it difficult for officials in London to separate individual economic motivations from policies beneficial to broader colonial interests.

In the Jamaica debate, the petitioners from both Kingston and Spanish Town recognized that health played an important role in the dispute over the island's capital. In the merchants' petition to London, they argued that Jamaica had suffered a declining state of trade in recent years. They attributed this decline largely to the fact that merchants on incoming ships were required to visit the governor at his official residence in Spanish Town. Not only did this journey of twelve miles over hilly roads constitute a considerable expense, they argued, it also endangered their lives. Merchants faced "the Risque of their health & lives which are too often lost thro' the violent heat of the climate by their journeys to and from St. Jago de la Vega," the petitioners wrote. The merchants included the health risk in their petition presumably to persuade the Board of Trade.[9]

Several members of the Jamaica Assembly agreed. They argued that Spanish Town's location inconvenienced residents of Jamaica as well as traveling merchants; anyone who needed to appear before the court was forced to travel to the capital. This journey deterred people, as "many of the prosecutors, & their witnesses, thrô the inclemency of the weather, & the heat of the climate, did lose their lives" so that "some chose to lose their debts, rather than run such risques." Residents of St. Andrews parish, which encompassed Kingston, expressed their concern for the "risque of the healths and lives" of anyone traveling to Spanish Town from Kingston. Both merchants and residents tried to impress upon colonial officials the idea that traveling posed such a danger that people would simply forego the journey and trade would suffer as a result.[10]

Advocates for Spanish Town, though, believed that they had the stronger footing when it came to arguing about health. In their own petition, they argued that "the said Town of Saint Jago de la Vega is one of the most healthy Places in America," so it should doubtless serve as the capital of the colony. Kingston, on the other hand, was "one of the most unhealthy Towns in the Kings Dominions." People often died there who "might have lived long in any other more healthy place." As everyone knew, they wrote, Spanish Town's reputation for health far exceeded Kingston's.[11]

The Kingston petitioners admitted that Spanish Town had a better reputation for health but emphasized that Kingston's reputation differed from reality. Claims about Kingston's poor health, advocates wrote in a counter-petition, were "stale and worn out." "It must be owned," they wrote, "that it was sickly for some few years, as most new settlements commonly are in this part of the world, especially such as are just cleared of the woods, as Kingston was." But they claimed that the town had overcome its sickliness as the newly cleared ground had exhaled all of its harmful vapors. Other reports of sickness in Kingston, they argued, had likely resulted from the after-effects of the Port Royal earthquake, fire, and hurricanes, which left people without adequate shelter and food. Although the illnesses in Kingston that followed these disasters "brought a disreputation on the place," in recent years the settlement had been "as healthy as any part of the West Indies." Considering the size of the population, they wrote, "few have dyed there," and those who had were mostly "transient persons & seamen," many of whom brought illness and death upon themselves "by debauches." According to the Kingston petitioners, then, reports of sickness could be easily explained away. The settlement was unhealthy at first because, as everyone knew, newly cleared land exuded dangerous miasmas. Illnesses since the area had been cleared were either circumstantial—the result of various disasters, and not of local environmental conditions—or else behavioral, in the case of drunken sailors.[12]

Spanish Town's petitioners proved just as eager to refute the claims against the dangers of the trek to their town, arguing that they found "not the least Danger from the nature of the Climate or Inclemency of the Air in going from Kingston to Saint Jago de la Vega and back again." In fact, they wrote, the journey was "one of the Pleasantest passages and most salubrious that any country affords." Just in case the colonial officials in Britain remained doubtful and chose to believe the Kingston merchants instead, the petitioners pointed out that three quarters of Jamaica's inhabitants lived in places that required a trip through or near Spanish Town to reach Kingston to conduct business. All those people, then, would need to "undergo the Hazard of the Passage from Saint Jago de la Vega to that Town [Kingston] and back again which is represented (but without the least Formation in fact) by the Inhabitants thereof to be so Dreadfull and Dangerous to the Lives and healths of the Merchants." In other words, the twelve-mile-long passage between the two towns was not at all dangerous. But if it was as bad as Kingston's petitioners made it out to be, then most of the residents of Jamaica would be subjected to that danger if they had to go as far as Kingston to conduct their official business.[13]

Both sides, then, hedged their bets: Kingston's proponents argued that the journey between the towns caused illness, and while they acknowledged that their city used to be unhealthy, they maintained that by the 1750s it suffered only from a lingering reputation. Spanish Town's petitioners had less trouble presenting their town as the healthier of the two, instead making a convoluted argument about the unhealthiness of the trip between the places. Inhabitants of each town tried to argue that, for reasons of health, the colonial capital should be situated in their particular locale. Notably, in both cases advocates did not explicitly mention the health of Black bodies, so presumably their argument was that their town was healthy either for white bodies or for all bodies. Because many of the people who traveled to these towns on official business were white, the arguments on both sides had embedded assumptions that these would be healthy places for white people.

The Board of Trade took the health claims seriously. Gaining and then maintaining some reputation of good health in such a disreputable place could do a great deal to encourage future British settlement on the island, which would bolster the strength of the imperial power. With this aim in mind, officials in Britain called on physicians with experience in the two towns to submit their opinions about each place so that the government could make an informed decision.

One physician testified that in his twelve years' residence on the island, he found that Spanish Town "was always a healthy" place, while Kingston's "natural situation" had "a great deal of stagnated water," making it unhealthy. During the rainy seasons, he continued, "there is a sickness all over the country," although it was worse at Kingston, in part because of "a moras (*sic*) on the west where the water is stagnated." Spanish Town, on the other hand, was built "on an eminence near a fine running river." Spanish Town's situation, close to mountains and moving water, made it a healthier place than a low-lying area with stagnant water. The marsh to Kingston's west would produce miasmas, and, depending on the direction of the winds, could bring disease-ridden air to the low-lying town. In fact, the doctor continued, "a great many" Kingston residents left the city to recover their health on a regular basis. He could not say the same for Spanish Town, which was, in his opinion, the better place for Jamaica's seat of government.[14]

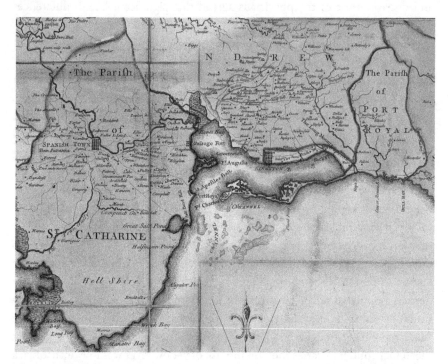

Fig. 3.1 Two separate 1763 maps have been digitally merged to create this map including Kingston and Spanish Town. Spanish Town is shown on the left, in St. Catharine's Parish, with Kingston at the north end of the harbor and the marsh in the upper middle of the image. Both original maps created by Thomas Craskell and published in London. Courtesy of the John Carter Brown Library, Acc. C-6514; Shelf En763 (1) and C-6515; Shelf En763 (3). Map digitally created by Leslie Tobias-Olsen.

In contrast, some of the physicians who spoke in favor of Kingston argued that the prevailing winds actually blew the swamp's vapors away from the town, so that miasmas did not affect most of the residents. "I can't pretend to say that stagnated water affect the town of Kins," one claimed. "The breezes generally carry the vapour from the town about two mile from the town." Another agreed on the direction of the winds, saying, "I know no moras that blows towards Kinstown but towards the mountains." A third argued that "In a morning or evening there are stenches but they don't affect Kinstown but to the west. Spanish Town lies west of these stenches but at some distance." According to these doctors, any miasmas or vapors produced by this marsh blew away from

Kingston rather than toward it. The physician who admitted that stenches—a sure sign of miasmas—affected Kingston dismissed concerns by arguing that these smells only appeared in the morning and the evening, and only in the western part of the town. Situating the government farther east and downtown, therefore, would not be a health hazard. Based on their experiences with health and disease, most of the physicians agreed that significant health differences existed between the two places.[15]

Several other doctors admitted that they found Kingston unhealthy, but the cause, they supposed, lay not so much in the town's physical situation but rather in its position as a port city. There were "more illnesses at Kinstown than Spanish Town," one physician reported, "from the greater number of strangers that first come to Kins." Another agreed: "The strangers being more numerous at Kinstown there are more who have the yellow fever." These comments reflected the common assumption that yellow fever was a "stranger's disease," affecting not seasoned inhabitants of the island, either Black or white, but new arrivals, especially the young and healthy. Others agreed, arguing that moving the courts to Kingston would oblige people to travel "from their distant country habitations" to "a place unwholesome by the scituation, ill furnished with water & subject to infectious distempers brought ashore by the great Resort of Guinea Ships to the Harbour." West Indian residents commonly believed that slave ships, also known as Guinea ships, brought yellow fever with them, which flourished in densely populated areas. Jamaica's population was overwhelmingly African in origin by the middle of the eighteenth century. Significantly, the high ratio of Black to white, estimated at about 10 to 1 a decade before the debate, did not mean that contemporaries thought the risk of yellow fever was low or that Black people were not susceptible. Instead, they wrote that yellow fever arrived on ships coming from Africa—an observation that signaled no sense of African immunity to yellow fever. Immune people would not carry the fever.[16]

If, as another physician argued, "where ever ships come they bring the yellow fever & small pox," Kingston's layout, with houses built in close proximity to one another, provided an easier conduit for the spread of disease than did Spanish Town's. Another doctor agreed, arguing that the situation of Kingston's buildings made the city "one of the most unhealthy." The same arguments, then, that proponents of Kingston used to advocate for the town—its urban layout and considerable population flow as the island's main harbor—could be used against the city. In contrast to the "fine air about Spa[nish Town]," to quote another physician, Kingston harbored disease. The number of people in Kingston meant that disease would easily spread from the ships through newcomers to the population at large.[17]

But the physicians' testimony did not settle the matter. The proposal divided the island. Even those who tried to remain neutral realized that they would have to choose sides in what was, in one person's words, "the most equal struggle that ever was in the country." The Assembly heard complaints from people in Spanish Town who made their living renting out rooms to visitors to the capital, as well as from planters who argued that enslaved people in the surrounding parishes of St. Catherine, St. John, St. Dorothy, and St. Thomas in the Vale "would entirely lose a market for their provisions" should Spanish Town lose the seat of government. Enslaved people often sold home-grown provisions at a market in Spanish Town, and visitors to the capital comprised their main clientele. Without visitors, the enslaved people would not have enough customers. The planters warned that this loss of a market could have "evil consequences" for "the island in general," in essence implying that the removal would incite such anger on the part of enslaved people that they might revolt. Meanwhile, merchants and other businesspeople showed strong support for Kingston, rallying no small force of allies from Liverpool, Bristol, Lancaster, Philadelphia, and New York to their cause.[18]

The Board had a difficult proposal to consider. Kingston did indeed function as the economic center of the island, but, located right on the harbor, its position left it more exposed to the same natural disasters that had devastated Port Royal. Spanish Town, on the other hand, because of its elevated position further inland, would be unlikely to fall into the ocean in an earthquake or hurricane. But its location, farther from the harbor, made it accessible only by overland roads, which could sometimes be difficult to traverse. The testimony by the physicians, while far from conclusive or unanimous, raised an important point. Would it be worth the convenience of governing from Kingston, given the risk of disease? The Board received scores of petitions and letters insisting that it was not. Complicating matters further, Governor Knowles acted without direction from the Board and, at times, without informing its members of his actions.[19]

In the end the Board of Trade, deciding that Knowles had overstepped his authority by declaring Kingston the new capital, moved the seat of government back to Spanish Town, despite continued protests from local merchants. As conciliatory gestures, the Board also decided that ship masters did not have to travel to Spanish Town upon arrival in Jamaica and that the governor could live wherever he wanted. Frustrated with Knowles's insubordination, however, the Board of Trade removed him from his position.[20]

The Board's decision demonstrated that economic concerns did not always constitute the primary consideration in determining the shape of the empire. The extensive investigation conducted by the Board, and the entire debate, which lasted for several years, focused to a large extent on both the natural and the built environment of the two neighboring towns and the effects of the environment on bodily health. The breezes, direction of the winds, location of standing water, and the layout of the buildings all created significant differences between the local climates of the two towns. Not a single person who testified seemed surprised that these two towns, roughly twelve miles apart, would have different environments or degrees of health. And nobody thought it strange that in considering the location for the seat of government in Jamaica, physicians would be called upon to describe the local environments and to help determine which was the healthier place. The environment held enormous importance in determining the use of any given space, and the Board of Trade considered information about the relative health of different places essential in deciding the future of the colony.

The 1750s debate in Jamaica brought concerns about health and place to a public stage. In Jamaica, the issue divided the island, and in London colonial officials found themselves poring over testimonials from residents, physicians, and tradespeople with various opinions on the matter. The debate illustrates the enormous importance colonial settlers and officials placed on the health—and reputation for health—of particular areas and the ways in which the perceived health of places determined patterns of settlement. Colonial officials in Britain often had little or no first-hand experience with the areas they oversaw, but they understood the necessity of cultivating a favorable reputation of these places if they wanted to encourage future settlers to populate the colonies and strengthen the empire.

Moreover, the debate showcased large groups of white Jamaican residents writing explicitly about how healthy certain places were. Although they did not mention skin color, representatives of each side understood that they were primarily discussing white bodily health in Jamaica. At the same time, their arguments about health applied universally; some places were healthier than others for all bodies, regardless of skin color. For these Jamaican residents of the mid-eighteenth century, environmental conditions were paramount in determining bodily health.

Local Environments

The arguments in the Jamaica debate also illustrate that, far from regarding the West Indies as uniform, colonists and even sometimes officials in London believed that incremental geographic distances could significantly affect people's health. Similarly, British writers of medical manuals and natural histories of the colonies noted environmental nuance as a way of demonstrating that people's health could change over short distances. Physician John Rollo believed that the islands in the West Indies varied "considerably in climate, and in respect of health" from one another, and Edward Long, who spent time on his family's Jamaican plantation before returning to England, noted that significant environmental variation could be found within particular islands. In his *History of Jamaica*, Long gave an extensive account of the types of water, elevation, temperature, and general health of different regional environments across Jamaica. He found the hills "universally healthful," in contrast to the "air of the low grounds," especially land which was "swampy, or not drained." Regarding Kingston, Long wrote that it had "been accused of being an unwholesome spot," particularly the area west of town which was "low and flat, interspersed with lagoons," and "contiguous to marshes." But because Long thought that for "every mile" a person traveled in Jamaica there was "a sensible change" in temperature, he advised anyone uncomfortable in Kingston to simply travel a few miles into the hills, where the air was cool and refreshing.[21]

Long's voluminous *History* gave detailed accounts of microclimates on the island, along with advice about where a person could seek out a healthy place. "From this variety of climate it must appear," he announced, "that heat and cold are here entirely local and relative; depending on situation." Elevation, proximity to hills, and air flow all determined a place's environment, Long wrote. "This shews the absurdity," he concluded, "of conveying an idea of the climate of any country in general, by a description which is only applicable to certain parts of it." In other words, the very idea of a "Jamaican climate," let alone a West Indian or a tropical one, was insufficient. Too many variations existed, so many as to make the idea of generalizing among them impossible.[22]

Perceived differences in health among various places resulted in large part from naturally occurring features and conditions of the landscape, but human intervention also played a role. For example, settler-colonists altered local environments in part by cutting down trees because they believed that woods prevented fresh air from flowing into an area. According to prevailing theories, tree branches trapped miasmatic air and endangered the health of residents, so cutting down trees was a good way to make a place healthier. In South Carolina, for example, physician George Millegan Johnston noted Charleston's lack of trees approvingly. Diseases in town, he wrote in 1763, were "proportionably less frequent, and milder than in the Country; for here we are pretty clear of Trees." Johnston credited the town's healthiness with the circulation of fresh air from the sea, enabled by the lack of trees. Settlers elsewhere in Carolina expressed similar opinions. Planter Robert Duff believed that the land around his plantation would become "more healthy & agreeable" as it was cleared, and planter George Ogilvie explained to his sister that his residence would become both prettier and healthier as he cleared the trees away.[23]

In the West Indies Governor Campbell Dalrymple reported in 1763 that much of Dominica, over which the British had recently gained control, was "very unhealthy & subject to fevers & agues." He thought "this evil" would "be in a great measure removed when the country is cleared; as those parts already cleared are by many degrees the most healthy." The following decade another report noted that Tobago's climate was "rather Hott, owing to the want of a free circulation of air occasioned by the standing of the woods between the several plantations now settling." Still, the inhabitants did not seem to mind, "well knowing that when once the island is tolerably clear of wood they will enjoy the healthiest climate in the West Indies." For these observers, the formula was straightforward: cleared land would be healthier land.[24]

In other cases, planters believed that their environmental management projects ended up making areas less healthy. This was particularly true of the rice fields of the lowcountry, which contemporaries recognized as being unhealthy for both Black and white populations. Eighteenth-century engineer and surveyor William Gerard de Brahm even lamented that Georgians had removed trees to create rice plantations. Savannah, he wrote, was "a very healthy place" for the first three decades of colonial settlement. Noting that South Carolinians used to travel to Georgia to recover their health, de Brahm attributed the disparities between the two places to the forests surrounding Savannah. According to de Brahm, although Savannah had swamps and marshes nearby, trees attracted vapors rising from the swamps, and the poisonous air then disappeared "on the road of the wind." De Brahm was unusual in his belief that trees made a place healthy, but he agreed that rice fields were the unhealthiest environments. In his explanation, once the residents of Savannah cut down the surrounding trees and converted the lands into rice fields, the miasmatic air had nowhere else to go and filled "all the streets and houses." Savannah's disease environment then became like South Carolina's. Planters had deliberately created swampland to grow rice, and stagnant water produced unhealthy conditions. In their efforts to alter the environment for planting purposes, planters had forced enslaved laborers to construct unhealthy environments.[25]

Cleared land also caused problems, and planters in the West Indies found that turning forests into fields had unwelcome environmental consequences. As colonists actively sought to clear land of woods to plant crops and create healthier environments, they began to notice that their actions contributed to drought conditions on the islands. In St. Vincent, for example, planter John Farquharson wrote to his family in Scotland describing a plot of land he hoped to sell. The soil, he explained, was "excellent," but "for some time to come the air will be humid and the climate wet—when the lands are cleared that will of course cease to be the case in a great degree." Farquharson's letter implied that trees made the local environment wet and humid, and that those conditions would change if the trees were gone. In addition, Farquharson believed that trees actually caused rainfall. Explaining the phenomenon in St. Vincent, Farquharson wrote that the island's mountainous interior was "mostly covered with impenetrable woods—the lofty tops of these attract the clouds and give us abundance of rain." According to this view, treetops "attracted" rainclouds that watered the island. For planters wanting to irrigate cropland, rain was a valuable resource. "We reckon it particularly fortunate that in this island there falls, in all seasons of the year, a sufficient quantity of rain to keep the young plants healthy and to give us eternal verdure," Farquharson informed his family. In some of the more cultivated islands, he wrote, "this is not the case. Some of these suffer extremely from dry weather. In Antigua, for instance, and St. Kitts the sugar crop will this year be so scanty that the planters there will be badly off." Planters in the West Indies depended on rain to irrigate crops. For this reason, even if trees endangered human health and took up valuable planting land, planters acknowledged that some forested land should be preserved to ensure that existing crops could thrive.[26]

Although planters recognized the need for rainfall, they were reluctant to relinquish their own cropland in favor of trees. To combat this problem, sometimes colonial legislatures acted to prevent drought. In St. Vincent, just after Farquharson wrote, the legislature voted on a bill to protect a piece of forested land in the parish of St. George known as the King's Hill. According to the bill, the existing trees in the area helped many surrounding planters because they "attract[ed] the Clouds and Rain." Residents had been taking trees from the plot of land, which the bill declared "highly injurious" to local planters because fewer trees meant less rain. The "Timber and other Trees and Wood growing, or that may grow" on the King's Hill, the bill proclaimed, would be "hereby reserved and appropriated for the Purpose of attracting the Clouds and Rain." The assembly and council ordered a survey of the property and directed planters whose land bordered the King's Hill to plant hedges delineating their property and to maintain this boundary marker or else face a stiff penalty. Anyone caught taking wood from the hill, or attempting to clear, plant, or cultivate it, would be fined for the offense. The government of St. Vincent did not want to risk creating drought conditions on the island and acted upon the conviction that trees caused rainfall.[27]

Private writings from colonists and other observers, published texts by physicians, historians, and cartographers, official reports from colonial governors and military officers, and legislative policy all demonstrate eighteenth-century understandings of environments as both locally variable and subject to change. As Edward Long wrote, it would be an "absurdity" to try to gauge a general sense of the West Indian climate from a description of just one place or even a few places. Many different factors influenced a place's local environment, from the presence of trees to the direction and strength of breezes and proximity to running or stagnant water. Colonial attempts to change the environment, especially by cutting down trees or flooding rice fields, could have unforeseen consequences, such as creating dry conditions or noticeably dangerous disease environments. Those with the means to do so could choose healthy locations; as one former resident of the West Indies put it, "a West India climate may be suspected to be dangerous" to visitors, but with the "liberty of choosing the place of residence, it will be found not at all inconvenient or disagreeable." Overall, though, writings from a variety of people demonstrate widespread beliefs that environments and related health conditions varied significantly among places across the Greater Caribbean.[28]

Plantation Spaces

With this knowledge in hand, planters and other colonists sought to protect their own bodies. As colonists created settlements and constructed homes, they tried to pay attention to environmental nuances so that they could choose healthy places in which to live. In addition, during the latter decades of the eighteenth century, rumors of a strengthening abolitionist movement in Britain began to threaten the continuance of the Atlantic slave trade. Combating abolitionist claims of slaveholders' abysmal treatment of the enslaved, along with a potential shortage of future laborers, planters took steps to protect the bodies of existing enslaved laborers from illness. These included seeking healthy places for enslaved people. In selecting such places, colonists and planters saw no differences between Black and white bodily health and believed that particular environmental conditions would affect all bodies in the same way. Planters tried to find the best and healthiest spaces on their plantations upon which to build their own homes, and they also tried to choose healthy spots to construct cabins for enslaved laborers.

Samuel Martin of Antigua, for example, wrote to his son in England in 1775, assuring him that his plantation lay on a healthy tract of land. "You seem to be apprehensive," he wrote, "that the sand pits . . . may, by being fill'd with stagnated water, be injurious to the health of the inhabitants of my plantation." Because Antigua lacked abundant sources of fresh water, planters often dug pits to collect rainwater for the people, animals, and crops on the plantations. But these pits collected standing water, which many people believed could produce noxious vapors injurious to health. "You may be easy when I assure you," Martin informed his son, "that those pits are at the North side of my plantation from whence the exhalations can never pass to my dwelling, or the negro houses." So situated, out of the way of any potentially dangerous miasmas, the living spaces on the plantation could sustain the health of their inhabitants.[29]

Martin paid particular attention to the situation of the slave cabins on his plantation, explaining in his popular planting manual, *An Essay on Plantership*, the necessity of selecting "airy, dry situations for their houses." To preserve the "strength, and the longevity of negroes," he wrote that planters should ensure that cabins for enslaved laborers were "perfectly water-tight" because "the inclemencies of weather generate the most malignant diseases." Choosing a healthy location over an unhealthy one for bondspeoples' homes cost little to nothing but would reap significant benefits for the planter who would have a healthier, longer-working group of laborers.[30]

In Jamaica, planter Simon Taylor wrote to a friend emphasizing the need to situate enslaved peoples' lodgings carefully. Taylor gave advice about purchasing new laborers and about how to care for them. "Buying Negroes is a lottery," he wrote, "sometimes a person in buying a lott of ten or 12 will lose the greatest part of them or the whole within the first three years." To increase the chances of their survival, Taylor informed his friend, "a great deal depends on . . . the situation of their houses." Similarly, Edward Long believed that in the Jamaican parish of St. Thomas in the East, the unhealthy air of coastal lowlands had detrimental effects on enslaved inhabitants. "The Negroes on the plantations which border on Plantain Garden River are subject to frequent mortalities," he wrote, "especially if their huts are placed on the levels, which are damp, and annoyed by constant exhalations." In contrast, those who lived in the island's interior benefitted from the "exceedingly healthful" climate of the region. Long knew the climate was healthy, he wrote, because of "the good appearance and longevity of those persons, Whites or Negroes," who lived in the area. Several years later, in 1787, Taylor advised a friend against sending newly arrived enslaved laborers to a specific location. "The Penn near Spanish Town," he explained, "is not healthy in the latter end of the year, being so much in the draft of the river." Instead, Taylor advised his friend to rent that particular parcel of land out to someone else and to keep his own enslaved laborers in a healthier place. In all of these cases, planters believed that both Black and white inhabitants of the Caribbean benefited and suffered from the same environmental conditions.[31]

Planters and other colonists also tried to build their own homes with the local environment in mind. Edward Long, for example, believed that houses in warm climates "should be placed on sufficiently-dry and elevated spots, far from swamps or morass, and where there is a free circulation of air." Homes should be kept away from "all low, unventilated situations," which "in this part of the world" he thought "most unwholesome." Planter Joshua Steele, who moved from England to Barbados in 1780, agreed. The ocean breezes he felt on his property, he wrote, made his estate "the finest climate in the world." And in 1788 physician John Hunter, who published a tract based on his experience in the army in Jamaica, informed his readers that "the inhabitants [of Jamaica] never set down their houses in such [marshy vaporous] bottoms, but constantly make choice of a lofty situation." Elevation and proximity to ocean breezes made a place particularly healthful.[32]

Residents not only elevated their houses, but also ensured a constant flow of air through the buildings, a measure of which Hunter approved. "Every house in the country is constructed so, as to give as free admission to the air as possible," he wrote. Lowcountry residents, too, incorporated features in their homes to moderate the temperature and encourage fresh air. In his trip through the lowcountry colonies in the 1760s, John Bartram noted the number of houses with wraparound sleeping porches. "Ye inhabitants of both Carolinas & Georgia generally builds piazzas at one or more sides of their houses which is very commodious in these hot climates," he wrote. "They screen off ye violent scorching sunshine & draws ye breeze finely." By selecting places away from stagnant water, and by encouraging a flow of fresh air, inhabitants of the colonies could try to protect bodily health.[33]

Planters and managers demonstrated a similar concern for the placement and construction of plantation hospitals, also known as hot houses. These buildings housed sick enslaved laborers, and because physicians believed that heat intensified the noxious effects of foul-smelling or bad air, allowing for air circulation in hospitals was particularly important. Especially after Parliamentary discussions about the abolition of the slave trade reached the West Indies in the mid-1780s, planters, conscious that they might face an impending end to their labor supply, sought to preserve the lives of laborers with increased vigor. Slaveholders also sought to defend the institution of slavery against accusations that they provided atrocious medical care for enslaved laborers. Abolitionists argued that the high death rates enslaved people suffered on plantations proved that slaveholders neglected sick laborers, and they used this evidence to call for an end to slavery.[34]

Letters from planters around this time show careful attention to the location and layout of hot houses, as well as increased medical care on their plantations. In 1788, Samuel Cary of Grenada wrote to absentee owner Charles Spooner about moving the hot house on his plantation "to a more healthy situation." The building needed repairing anyway, Cary added, so with Spooner's approval he would demolish the old one and build a new one in a healthier place. A couple of years later, Simon Taylor of Jamaica informed Chaloner Arcedeckne, whose properties Taylor managed, that one of his plantations was in desperate need of a new hot house. "We must build the Hott House, the present one is exceeding bad," he wrote. Location mattered; it should be built "upon a dry place, near water, where it can be kept clean, and [where] we can use the warm bath." The new hospital would have several different rooms, including one for men, another for women, a third, separate one for venereal patients, one for "the black doctor," and another for bathing. "All filth will be discharged into running water," he added, "so there will be no risk of infection." As both managers explained, the location of the hospital was important to maintaining the health and working ability of enslaved laborers.[35]

Joseph Foster Barham's manager in Jamaica also recognized the need to move the plantation hospital to a healthier spot. He wrote to Barham that he had "long had a wish of removing the hospital to a spot very near the great House on account of its healthy air & superiority over the present one which is actually in a swamp." The old building's location made its occupants too vulnerable to illness from the wet, marshy surroundings. The plantation house, on the other hand, was well situated in a healthy place, and the manager thought it best to move the hot house close by to protect the health of sick enslaved laborers. Similarly, Charles Gordon Gray, who managed his family's estate in Jamaica, informed his father of the need for a new hospital. "I have considered our Hospital to be very badly situated," he wrote, "and I have been recommended by the Medical Man to remove it. I shall do so and bring it to the top of the Hill." Gray's father thought that building an entirely new hospital was an exorbitant expense, and Gray repeatedly tried to justify the cost to his father. "The Expences about the Works & the Buildings were absolutely necessary," he wrote. "A new Hospital had been long wanted, I delayed it 'til 'twas evident the Health of the Negroes were of more value." The following winter, he tried again to persuade his father of the long-term value of the investment. "The Cause why such heavy expences have been incurr'd were of the first consequence. A new Hospital was absolutely necessary, the old one was not a fit place for a sick Negroe," he wrote. Gray stood firm: in his mind, moving the hospital to a healthier location was essential for preserving the health of the plantation's enslaved laborers. Black bodies would respond no better to marshy areas than would white bodies, and to sustain everyone's health, living quarters should be constructed in the healthiest places on plantations.[36]

Plantation hospitals were often cramped, uncomfortable places; some were purposely miserable to deter enslaved laborers from "feigning illness." They also sometimes functioned as places of imprisonment on plantations, and both the military and public hospitals constructed in eighteenth-century Jamaica served similar functions. Scholars have also pointed out that designing hospitals to confine people and to prevent desertion and drunkenness meant that medical concerns came last. As a result, hospitals in Jamaica—whether for the military or the enslaved—were often better conduits of sickness than they were places of recovery and recuperation. In the late eighteenth century, though, planters began to rethink their plantation hospitals as they responded to an increased need to preserve the lives of enslaved laborers.[37]

Finally, many of the same health concerns that motivated planters to construct homes and plantation hospitals in particular locations prompted military officers and physicians to think critically about the placement of colonial troops.

As British soldiers scouted Caribbean islands at the end of the Seven Years War, for example, officers carefully considered the healthiest locations for soldiers' barracks. In Dominica, Governor Campbell Dalrymple found the existing capital, Roseau, "so deficient in every necessary, for health" and other factors that he "resolve'd on establishing ourselves in a bay about a mile to the southward of it," where he hoped "all these defects will be remedy'd." He ordered the British troops in Dominica to leave Roseau for a neighboring town, Loubiere, which he believed had better quality air and water. In St. Vincent, the governor described a number of different towns, offering his opinion as to their relative health and suitability for housing troops. He found Waslabau Bay "so sickly, that the people who have attempted to settle there, have either died or been obliged to leave it for want of health." He thought it best to remove the troops stationed there to barracks elsewhere on the island, choosing another town which he found "very healthy." And in Tobago, acting Governor Robert Melville "fixed on a very commodious place for a first town settlement" which had "a river of wholesome water running into it." He thought an adjoining piece of land would be "an excellent & healthfull situation for the placing of his Majesty's troops." Running water and exposure to sea breezes would protect the health of soldiers and of future residents.[38]

In cases where officers found existing barracks, they inspected the quarters carefully, reporting on the varying health conditions they found. In Grenada, the governor encountered several different places with soldiers' barracks. One of these places, Santeur, had its barracks built on the side of a hill, "perfectly exposed to the trade wind." "With respect to health," the governor wrote, the area appeared "to have every advantage." On the other hand, another place lay "in the middle of a swamp," which, of course, made it "extreamly unhealthy." The governor found this settlement, Marquis, sparsely inhabited, and the faces of the residents confirmed his suspicions of the place's ill health. "The complexions of the inhabitants are wan and sallow," he wrote, "and denote the fever in every feature." Although the government initially sent soldiers to both towns to occupy the existing barracks, after a short time the governor moved the soldiers in Marquis to Santeur "after losing a number of men."[39]

Military physicians insisted upon the thoughtful placement of barracks and hospitals to protect soldiers' health. As physician John Hunter pointed out, "what has the greatest influence, of all the circumstances that affect the health of soldiers in those climates, is the kind of quarters in which they are placed." In Jamaica he thought Spanish Town was better than Kingston, though neither compared to the healthiest places, which consisted of "dry sand-banks, surrounded either wholly, or in part, by the sea, and out of the reach of noxious winds blowing from swamps and marshes; and elevated stations in the mountains." Hunter's fellow physicians agreed. Robert Jackson noted that soldiers who camped downwind of marshes fell ill, while those who did not remained much healthier. The conclusion was obvious, he wrote: "instead of exposing encampments to streams of air, which blow from rivers or swamps, it ought to be our principal business to guard against those noxious effluvia" by building barracks out of the way of noxious air. "So great is the importance of preserving the health of an army in the field," he continued, "that the choice of encampments ought to be made a subject of particular enquiry." During the eighteenth century, as military postings in the West Indies held a reputation as probable death sentences for British soldiers, military physicians placed great importance on the location of soldiers' living quarters. For the most part, these soldiers were European by birth, but sometimes enslaved and free Afro-Caribbean men also served in the British armed forces. Either way, physicians believed that building barracks in healthy spots could preserve the health and lives of large numbers of men who otherwise sickened and died. But an imperial army more concerned with expedient military strategy than with the health of its members did not always attend to these physicians' concerns, and powerful planters eager to have troops close by to deter slave insurrections managed to keep barracks in unhealthy lowland locations.[40]

This neglect of colonial soldiers' health rankled observers in the islands. Edward Long expressed frustration that the military did not take all possible precautions to preserve its members' health. When soldiers constructed barracks "in very improper situations; near swamps, the oozy banks of rivers, and stinking lagoon waters," he wrote, healthy troops fell ill in strikingly high numbers. In the parish of St. Elizabeth, for example, a company of the 66th regiment was "attacked with putrid fevers and dysenteries, so fatal to them," that in a single year, 1764, they lost "no less than one hundred and two men." The 36th regiment, on the other hand, whose soldiers had arrived in Jamaica at the same time but stayed on higher ground, lost only thirty men in the same year. The "ravage" of the 66th regiment, Long explained, "is to be ascribed to no other cause than the exhalations reeking from the marshy soil around them," which "imparted an evil disposition to the atmosphere" in the swampy coastal lands surrounding the barracks. The evidence spoke for itself. Troops, especially those newly arrived in the islands, should only be stationed in healthy spots, away from "swampy places."[41]

Experienced soldiers agreed that the choice of housing was essential to preserving health in the West Indies. In 1781, Lord George Germain, who had been active in the British military for many years and who had served in several wars, wrote from London to John Dalling, the governor of Jamaica at the time. British soldiers in the West Indies were falling fast, and Germain expressed concern about their health, attributing the rate of illness in large part to the situation of their housing. "The greatness of the mortality among the troops & the continuance of the sickness," he wrote, "afford but too melancholy proofs of the unhealthiness of the situation of the barracks in which they are quartered." Germain thought it "inhuman" of the British government to send soldiers to Jamaica, "only to arrive & die," and urged Dalling to convince the Jamaica assembly to pass a measure for the construction of new barracks. "If the calamity can be avoided by removing the barracks to other parts of the island," Germain instructed, "it surely is incumbent on the assembly to dispose of the present buildings & employ the money in erecting others where the troops may be expected to live." Dalling agreed, requesting funds to purchase land on which to build new barracks, writing that the island would never be "in a state of safety, till the Barracks are erected in the proper places, as no force can be considered as a preservation unless a tolerable share of Health can be established." In both Germain's and Dalling's assessments, British troops in Jamaica were falling ill at astounding rates, and both men blamed the unhealthy situation of the barracks. Their experiences had led them to believe that building housing in a healthy place would significantly improve the health of the troops, enabling them to better defend the island.[42]

In each of these cases, military officers tried to find the healthiest locations, both for soldiers' barracks and for towns. Local environments could mean the difference between life and death for soldiers, and between thriving towns and those where the inhabitants were so sickly that they displayed "the fever in every feature." In many situations, selecting a healthy place was essential to the survival of individuals and sometimes of towns or even colonies. For a British government attempting to expand its colonial holdings, healthy places and healthy people were essential. Moreover, as some of these observers expressed, being in a hot climate like that of the West Indies, even for active soldiers, was not a death sentence in and of itself. Rather, some places were healthier than others. If barracks were well ventilated and located in elevated, airy spaces, the mortality rate among soldiers would probably drop significantly.

Unfortunately for soldiers, military hospitals were often in unhealthy places, and it could take a great deal of work to move them. But sometimes officials in London could be persuaded, as was the case with Greenwich Hospital, a military hospital built near Kingston in the 1740s. Recalling the old hospital, naval physician James Lind wrote that despite being "commodious and excellent," the building had been constructed "near a marsh, upon a most unhealthy spot of ground." Because of the hospital's "unhealthy situation," Lind wrote, "when a patient was sent thither, with only a gentle or intermitting fever, this mild indisposition was apt to be changed either into a malignant fever, a bloody flux, or some other mortal distemper." These ailments, Lind explained, clearly proceeded from the hospital's situation. Happily, British officials heeded the advice of correspondents in Jamaica who complained about the unhealthy location and its consequences for patients' health. With mortality rates soaring, and with "the cause of it so obvious," the military abandoned the hospital and built a new one "in a better air," where the mortality rate dropped sharply.[43]

Lind did not explain how the British government became persuaded that a new hospital should be financed and built in Jamaica. But in what later proved to be an ironic twist to the Kingston/Spanish Town debate of the 1750s, the person who advocated most vociferously for the new hospital was none other than Rear Admiral Charles Knowles, the future Governor of Jamaica. In 1748, Knowles had been on a ship stationed near Kingston. Along with some fellow officers, Knowles sent a letter to the Lords Commissioners of the Admiralty assessing the health of the area, with particular attention to the situation of Greenwich Hospital, located just west of Kingston. In the letter, Knowles stated in no uncertain terms that he found it "next to an impossibility to remedy the unwholsomeness" of "the unhealthy situation of the Hospital at New Greenwich." The hospital was "surrounded with morasses from whence constantly arises a noxious vapour which in the daytime is exhaled in great quantitys." Physicians found this vapor "very prejudicial to the sick who become faint and languid," Knowles explained, and the resulting "fevers & colds" which were "the natural consequences" of such vapors affected even "the most robust and most healthy" of men, let alone "sick folks or men just upon the recovery." Even Marines who had "only been sent ashoar as Guards to the Hospital" ended up dying "within a few days after being upon duty," Knowles wrote, concluding that the hospital was "rather a hurt to the service than a relief." Instead, Knowles strongly suggested that the military build a new hospital at Port Royal, which he found to be "the most healthful" place "in all the Island for lodging sick seamen." He himself felt healthier in Port Royal than he did anywhere else in Jamaica, and he pointed out that many local residents went there for the restoration of their health.[44]

Seven years after Knowles's report, amid heated debate between Kingston and Spanish Town, the Lords Commissioners of the Admiralty sent a copy of this letter to the Lords Commissioners for Trade and Plantations as proof of "the unhealthiness of the town of Kingston," confirmed by none other than Governor Knowles himself. Knowles, who sided with the merchants advocating for Kingston, had written a scathing report of a nearby hospital less than a decade earlier. How, then, could the Lords Commissioners take his position seriously? It was true that the old hospital was not in downtown Kingston. But the morass that Knowles blamed for New Greenwich's unhealthiness was the same tract of marshland as the one that physicians blamed for the unhealthy vapors in Kingston in their testimony. In the debate with Spanish Town, Knowles's apparent disregard for the concerns about Kingston's unhealthy environment rang false in light of his earlier report. The Board of Trade concluded that Knowles had been influenced by the merchants and displayed too little concern for the health of the residents of Jamaica.[45]

Perhaps Knowles's letter undermining his own case for Kingston played a part in the Board's decision to keep the capital in Spanish Town. Perhaps the Board was swayed by the climatic arguments or by the protests of people unhappy with the potential new arrangement. Or perhaps it had other motivations altogether. But as the debate and other evidence about the location of towns, homes, and other buildings showed, both the Board of Trade and colonial residents took the health of a place seriously.[46]

* * *

Rather than thinking of the tropical and semi-tropical Atlantic colonies as one hot region, unhealthy for British bodies, residents of these places held a nuanced and complex understanding of the local climate. Some areas were indeed unhealthy, but these places had the same types of climatic features that made any area of the world dangerous, such as standing water and miasmas. But inhabitants of the lowcountry and, especially, the Caribbean, stressed the variability of climate across short distances and insisted that several of these microclimatic regions were healthy places where residents could expect to enjoy long and fruitful lives. By the second half of the eighteenth century, several texts detailing the variability of climate and health in the tropics had appeared in print. These texts noted significant differences between healthy and unhealthy environments in the Greater Caribbean, challenging the region's established reputation as uniformly unhealthy.[47]

In fact, settler-colonists in the British West Indies and the lowcountry considered the preservation of health to be crucial to the construction of Atlantic colonies. Convictions about the variability of regional climate over short distances influenced the placement of colonial capitals and other towns. Considerations of climate and health affected the makeup of empire at every level—from the construction of private homes, to hospitals, to places of trade and government. The health of a place could be measured on a general, universal level: some places were healthy for everyone, while damp, marshy spots bred disease for all bodies. The debate over the placement of Jamaica's capital illustrates the fervency with which people sometimes argued in favor of or against certain places, while evidence from personal correspondence demonstrates both the persistence and consistency of health concerns from a macroscopic to an individual level.

Crucially, planters believed that neither African nor European bodies naturally suited the Greater Caribbean climate, but both could potentially thrive in healthy places within that environment, just as both could suffer from unhealthy conditions. According to Edward Long, in Jamaica, "the settlers who live nearest the central region of the island, and their Negroes, are as healthy as a like number in any given part of Great Britain." In addition to both Black and white residents enjoying good health in central Jamaica, Long's comment implied that Africans would also be healthy in Britain. Long based differences of health, then, on place rather than on skin color. Similarly, planter and natural historian William Beckford explained that the "alternations of stifling heat and trembling cold" in the West Indies were sometimes "prejudicial to the health of the white people, and inimical to the constitutions of the negroes." Here, significant variations in temperature afflicted both Black and white bodies; neither would do well in such a variable environment.[48]

These comments are consistent with the observations of lowcountry visitors who wrote of the region's "sickly" rice plantations. White observers noted that stagnant water caused fatal illnesses among "the lower set of people, as well white as black" in the lowcountry. These regions were no healthier for Black people than they were for white people. Instead, both suffered from the unhealthiness of the place. At the same time, dangerous environments did not actually prevent white people from working. The same writer who noted that enslaved laborers forced to stand "half leg deep" in water died in large numbers explained that "many of the poor White people in Carolina and Georgia raise grain without the assistance of Negroes." Moreover, he wrote that the "White Creoles" who produced crops in Anguilla, Tortola, and Barbados "prove that White men can cultivate lands in a tropical climate." The fact that contemporaries recognized the universal unhealthiness of rice swamps belies planters' later arguments about white people's supposedly singular inability to remain healthy in these places. It was a matter of wealth and social structures, not skin color, that determined who labored on rice plantations and who did not.[49]

In theory, colonists' understandings of environmental nuance could have worked to preserve their own health as well as that of enslaved laborers. They knew which environmental conditions were likely to encourage good health and which were likely to induce illness. In practice, however, slaveholders consistently placed enslaved laborers in hazardous environments. Although some slaveholders wrote about their desire to preserve the health of enslaved laborers by locating an estate's hospital or hot house in a healthy spot, or by situating enslaved people's cabins away from marshy areas, these measures only went so far. Beyond these small gestures, planters failed to protect the health of enslaved laborers. They did not provide them with homes that sealed out water so that they would not be exposed to the damp air that colonists considered unhealthy. And they deliberately placed Black bodies in dangerous environments. Planters measured the lives of the enslaved against the possibility of a lucrative harvest. Ultimately, colonists did not consider large groups of Black or white bodies to be fundamentally different from one another; the same environmental conditions would be healthy or unhealthy for everyone. Instead, they simply chose to place Black bodies in environments that endangered their health and their lives.

Atlantic Bodies

Health, Seasoning, and Race

Early in the spring of 1788, absentee planter Chaloner Arcedeckne received a letter from his friend and longtime manager of his Jamaican properties, Simon Taylor. "I will buy for you the first good gang of seasoned Negroes I know of," Taylor wrote. Several weeks later Taylor reported success. In addition to purchasing some "new Negroes" for one of Arcedeckne's properties, he had also "bought 33 seasoned ones" for another. The laborers had "been seasoned near the place," Taylor added, "and will I am hopefull by and by establish there a good gang." By the time he wrote, Taylor had been managing Arcedeckne's plantations for decades. He routinely kept his friend and employer abreast of the condition of his properties, a large sugar estate and a livestock pen, including their annual crops, the weather, and the health of the enslaved laborers. While the letters in 1788 followed this usual pattern, they also demonstrated Taylor's outrage and anxiety over the political situation regarding abolition in Britain. In the same letter informing Arcedeckne that he would look for a "gang of seasoned Negroes," Taylor wrote of his "hope that the humanity" of abolitionists would "extend itself to the colonists" who might be "stripped of their property." Taylor both defended the living conditions of bondsmen in the West Indies and warned that, if the British transatlantic trade came to an end, "the manufacturers of goods for the African and West Indian trades must starve, and turn thieves." Months later, shortly after Taylor had "bought 33 seasoned" laborers for Arcedeckne, he once again despaired at the political situation unfolding in Britain. Abolition of the transatlantic slave trade, Taylor wrote, would "be the same as giving up the colonies all together, for it is absolutely impossible for them to exist without it." For Taylor, abolishing the trade would pose an existential threat to Britain's colonies.[1]

That same spring, Arcedeckne also received a letter from physician William Wright, who had recently returned to Edinburgh after twenty-five years in the

The Nature of Slavery. Katherine Johnston, Oxford University Press. © Oxford University Press 2022.
DOI: 10.1093/oso/9780197514603.003.0005

West Indies. Like Taylor, Wright asserted that the existence of plantation colonies depended on the slave trade. In the sugar islands, Wright wrote, "The Negroe from Africa, and their progeny are in a climate perfectly suited to their constitution." According to Wright, this climatic suitability meant that Africans and their descendants were ideal laborers for the West Indies. Although labor on a sugar plantation was notoriously difficult, Wright assured Arcedeckne that enslaved people performed this work "easily in a climate suitable to [their] constitution." In fact, Wright wrote that enslaved people thrived in Jamaica. In that "happy island," he wrote, "the Negroe wallows in provisions every way calculated to make him healthy, robust, and opulent." In contrast, should the transatlantic slave trade end, Wright explained that the islands would be devoid of laborers because "It is utterly impossible to cultivate West India Estates with White People. They can bear but little labour much less fatigue in so warm a country."[2]

On one hand, Wright's claims about laborers are unsurprising. Slaveholders' escalating alarm at abolitionists' attempts to end the trade provoked similar claims from planters all over the Caribbean. Wright's letter, in fact, was intended to serve as evidence for a committee investigating the slave trade. Wright drew clear divisions between "happy, robust, and opulent" enslaved Black laborers working "easily" in sugar fields in a climate "perfectly suited to their constitution" and white people who could "bear but little labour" because, implicitly, they did not suit the climate. On the other hand, these claims and the divisions in Wright's letter provide a startling contrast to both Black and white people's experiences of the West Indies. It is obvious that bondspeople were neither happy, robust, nor opulent in their enslavement. Less obvious are the ways in which Wright's claims departed from eighteenth-century settler-colonists' understandings of climates, environments, and bodily difference.

Colonists did not consider suitability to particular climates to be a matter of race or skin color. In the 1770s, for example, a white plantation manager in Jamaica wrote of his hesitancy to return to Britain because he and his wife found their bodies "so well suited" to the West Indian climate. He was not alone; letter after letter from white residents describes their bodily suitability for plantation colonies. Most white letter writers did not, of course, tend to perform difficult labor on plantations, and it would not occur to them that their comments on their bodies' fitness for warm places would indicate a proclivity to labor. If pressed, these white writers might have said that they could live comfortably in warm places, but they would have been horrified at the suggestion that they do physical work. The reasons that most white people did not participate in hard labor in the Caribbean were more social than climatic, however: white people had constructed a hierarchical system based upon skin color. In this system, white planters forced and expected Black people to perform difficult labor, especially in dangerous environments. Because this social structure based upon racial prejudice often exempted white people from difficult labor, Wright had no basis for comparison between Black and white ability to labor. Yet it is significant that, when not faced with threats to the transatlantic slave trade, many white residents of the Greater Caribbean wrote about how well their bodies suited the climate. Thus, they did not consider suitability to the climate to be divided along racial lines.[3]

The ability to labor was predicated on a body's ability to be healthy, and both planters and physicians considered local environmental conditions, not skin color, as the primary determinant in people's health. Writings from colonists demonstrate a belief that weather and local environmental nuances affected all bodies in the same way. Both Black and white bodies would fall ill under particular environmental conditions, and all bodies would benefit from other conditions. The supposedly clear distinctions between Black and white bodies that Wright laid out had no precedent in eighteenth-century medical practice or experience.

In addition, Taylor wrote about finding "seasoned Negroes" to cultivate Arcedeckne's property. Seasoning, or bodily adjustment to an unfamiliar environment, was the most important concept relative to bodily health in the eighteenth-century colonial Atlantic. Those who arrived in a new place experienced changes in their bodies as they adapted to different temperatures, humidity levels, breezes, and other environmental features. These adaptations were semi-permanent; that is, bodies remained in their seasoned states as long as they lived in a particular place, and if people moved again, including returning to a previous home, they would have to be re-seasoned. While historians have written about this seasoning process for Europeans crossing the Atlantic, they have tended to interpret African seasoning differently. Rather than considering African seasoning as bodily adaptation to the climate, most historians explain the seasoning process for Africans as an adjustment to the severe work regime enforced on plantations. Planters, though, understood the process of seasoning enslaved laborers as twofold. Newly arrived Africans would have to become seasoned to plantation work, but both slaveholders and physicians recognized that African bodies, like European transplants, would have to be seasoned to environmental differences as well. Although scholars have portrayed seasoning as distinctive, discrete processes for African and European populations, planters did not conceive of it in such divisive terms: all bodies arriving in the West Indies or the lowcountry would need to acclimate to the different environment, whether or not they labored. Contrary to Wright's assertion, most experienced planters did not believe that Africans were "perfectly suited" to West Indian environments.[4]

Seasoning played a crucial role in colonial conceptions of health, and whether or not a native African had been seasoned to the climate in the Americas mattered a great deal to planters. These bodily changes had monetary value. Even absentee planters living in Britain recognized that newly arrived Africans needed to be seasoned to the local environment, and price differences of bondspeople reflected this knowledge. Planters paid more for seasoned enslaved laborers than for unseasoned people. But this distinction obscured essential local variations in environment; for colonial residents, seasoning itself was highly specific and dependent on place. Taylor wrote that the enslaved laborers he purchased had "been seasoned near the place," an indication that their health would not suffer unduly on their new plantation. This location mattered. Those who had been seasoned elsewhere, even if only a few miles away, would be suited instead to a different set of environmental conditions. This strong sense of localism meant that enslaved people held different economic values from one another, as well as to different slaveholders, depending on where a particular plantation was located and where a person had been seasoned. As Taylor noted, the laborers he purchased for Arcedeckne would be a wise investment because they had been seasoned close to Arcedeckne's property. Bondspeople seasoned farther afield could easily hold less value for Arcedeckne because their bodies would have adapted to a potentially different environment. Thus, the same person held variable values for different planters, a factor that contributed to complex economic calculations surrounding enslaved people's health.[5]

Finally, the emphasis colonists placed on seasoning, or this process of bodily alteration, demonstrates the fluidity of concepts of bodily difference during the eighteenth century. Seasoning was an essential process: as colonists understood it, after residence in plantation colonies, Europeans no longer suited Europe and Africans no longer suited Africa; the bodies of both changed fundamentally during seasoning. In the colonial Greater Caribbean, seasoning signified a change in a person's body that was directly linked to a change in identity. Later binary claims about Africans' and Europeans' physical differences obscure a much richer, more complex set of notions that guided eighteenth-century colonial physicians and planters. Examining these notions about health demonstrates the extent to which arguments such as Wright's departed from planters' and slaveholders' conceptions of bodies. Planters' and physicians' understandings of bodily health were essential to arguments about different bodies' abilities to labor. Ultimately, European and Euro-American notions of bodily health were complex, but they were not based upon race.[6]

Health and Environment

For eighteenth-century physicians, supporting bodily health required maintaining a careful balance between internal humors and external elements, as well as sustaining a flow within the body itself. In healthy bodies, intake and output equalized one another, and the internal bodily workings calibrated to changes in the external environment. Historians investigating the specifics of health care and medical practice in the Atlantic world have shown the ways in which European physicians sought curative plants and other materials, as well as medicinal knowledge, from Indigenous peoples in the Americas. Scholars have also argued that Euro-Caribbean and Euro-American physicians changed their approaches to medicine as a result of contact with African and Indigenous populations and as a consequence of prolonged residence in different climates. On a basic level, physicians' writings and private letters from planters and plantation managers demonstrate three core beliefs about bodily health. First, planters and physicians thought that wet places and weather caused illness, while dry conditions could help heal sick bodies. Second, unhealthy bodies often benefitted from a change of air, which sometimes required a local or a long-distance move. And third, all bodies had individual constitutions, which determined particular bodily responses to specific environmental conditions.[7]

In plantation correspondence, managers consistently equated wet weather with illness. On one Jamaican plantation, the manager reported in May 1766 that the enslaved laborers had "been very sickly," with "seldom less than twenty in our hot house daily." The "complaints," he added, resulted from "the excessive rains," and as the weather began to clear, the population became "more healthy." In July 1787, another manager noted that enslaved laborers had been "very sickly" with "violent fevers and colds" because of two months of "violent and continued rain," and a few years later a third manager reported that the "weather continues very wet indeed . . . the Negroes are now very sickly." A resident planter later noted the same pattern in a letter to his father, writing one September that the plantation laborers had suffered "much sickness," especially "fevers from the continual rains." The reverse was also true, as managers correlated dry weather with improved health.[8]

Physicians confirmed this assessment. In his 1788 medical treatise, John Hunter explained that "noxious exhalations from wet, low, and marshy grounds" combined with heat caused fevers. Similarly, physician Robert Jackson wrote in 1791 that "fevers of the intermitting and remitting kind, owe their origin to exhalations from swampy and moist grounds," especially in hot places. Yet another physician announced in 1797 that "it is a fact universally admitted, that moisture is the chief predisposing cause to almost every malady," and a fourth cautioned planters that enslaved laborers "should be exposed to the wet as little as possible" in order to keep them healthy. If people were too exposed to moisture, the consequences could be disastrous. Such was the case in 1771, when physician William Sandiford wrote of "a putrid remitting Fever" that struck "many Patients, white as well as black" in Barbados. All those afflicted, Sandiford noted, lived in swampy places with dense tree cover "surrounded with Water," leading Sandiford to conclude that the illness arose from the marshy woodlands. Also in Barbados, physician William Hillary wrote that a particularly rainy summer led to an epidemic of dysentery. The illness affected "many both white and black People, but especially the latter," because they had less protection from the rain. According to these physicians, both Black and white populations were vulnerable to the dangers of wet weather, with no difference aside from their relative exposure.[9]

Believing that most illnesses had environmental causes, physicians and planters often attempted environmental cures. In addition to traditional medical practices such as bloodletting, blistering, and inducing purging, doctors often recommended a change of air. Because bodies responded to their environments, a different location might help readjust the body and bring about a return to good health. Planters tried to follow this advice, both for their own families and sometimes for enslaved laborers. In Grenada, for example, plantation manager Samuel Cary reported in 1788 that the carpenter who worked on the estate was "very weak and low," so had gone to "the North side for change of air." In Jamaica, planter Charles Gordon Gray fretted late one summer because several enslaved people on his plantation were ill. "Of late we have had more rains there than sufficient," he wrote to his father, "which has I am sorry to say been the cause of much sickness." The illness, "an intermittant [fever] with ague," caused "great debility" among its victims. In his attempt to restore them to health, Gray wrote, "I have at this moment one here, one at Moor Park, and another at the Bay for change of air, all my best People." When the enslaved gardener on Thomas Pinckney's South Carolina property fell ill in 1789, Pinckney made plans to "send him down in the schooner" to his sister's home, where the air was different. Also in South Carolina, plantation manager William Page received extensive instructions from his employer, Pierce Butler, regarding the health of enslaved laborers on the plantation. "[W]hen any of the negroes at the rice island [plantation] are taken ill," Butler directed in 1798, "remove them to Hampton 'till they are quite [recovered]; change of air from fresh water to salt has often a great effect." Although plantation managers did not, as a matter of course, move enslaved laborers for a change of air every time someone fell ill, these letters and others like them demonstrate that sometimes planters who particularly valued certain laborers would move them short distances to recover from an illness.[10]

White people received the same advice about the importance of moving location for health reasons. In Antigua, George Ottley wrote that his wife had "been lately so much indisposed" that "she was advised by the Doctors to change the air for a short time without delay." Ottley accompanied her from Antigua to Barbuda, "which is a very short distance from this, & a place noted for the salubrity of its air." In Jamaica, Grace Campbell traveled from her family's plantation to Kingston and found the difference in her health striking. Although she had heard reports of the town's unhealthiness, she wrote to her father, "I believe it to be the most healthy spot in the island—it agrees so well with me." When Samuel Cary's family fell ill in the fall of 1785, he sent them to "the North side [of Grenada] where it is healthy." And when Sam Rogers arrived in Antigua at the end of March 1769, "extremely ill and weak," his relative Samuel Martin tried to nurse him back to health. Martin first placed Rogers in the home of a neighboring doctor, but as his recovery seemed slow, after a couple of weeks he moved Rogers to a plantation a few miles away in the hopes that the "change of air" would better suit his constitution and bring about his recovery.[11]

If a local move proved insufficient to restore someone to health, a longer-distance journey might work. In Jamaica, plantation manager John Graham expressed concern over a sick enslaved person on one of Joseph Foster Barham's plantations in 1792. Cupid, the man in question, had been "for some time past in a bad state of health" with an illness that had progressed from his head to his lungs. Concerned about Cupid's declining health, Graham consulted the doctors. They advised him to send Cupid on a ship to North America as soon as possible and, in the meantime, to send him to another parish. Graham did so, but the local change of air seemed not to have helped. Graham feared Cupid might die. Should that happen, Graham informed Barham, "you will sustain the loss of one of the very best of slaves." But Graham reported that he was taking no chances with Jackie, another enslaved laborer who showed similar symptoms. He would send Jackie directly to North America, on a fleet set to sail in three weeks' time. "The Doctors advise and think the Negroe will be much benefited by the voyage," Graham wrote. A few weeks later, Graham wrote again, to say that in spite of "every attention," Cupid had died. Jackie, though, was on a ship, and Graham hoped the trip would restore him. Unfortunately, even a significant change of air proved insufficient to save Jackie, and several months later, Graham wrote again to report the sad news. "I am truly sorry to acquaint with the loss of your negroe Jackie," he wrote, who, after getting "considerably better" from the "change of air," died in North America. Although neither Cupid nor Jackie survived, it is notable that physicians advised a change of air for the benefit of their health, and that this entailed a trip to North America, where the air was cooler than that in Jamaica.[12]

Also in Jamaica, Doctor James Chisholme related the curious case of a twenty-eight-year-old man, one of Chisholme's "Negro servants." The man, a bricklayer, had been "seized with a violent pleurisy" and fever after several days of "hard drinking, and dancing in the open air" in December 1787. Attempting to cure the bricklayer's illness, Chisholme subjected him to a grueling but common treatment: he blistered the sick man's skin in several places and, in others, made incisions to drain blood from his body. When this treatment proved insufficient,

Chisholme moved the bricklayer out of his home and into Chisholme's, where he could keep a close watch over the sick man. But after two months of nursing the man had not improved, so Chisholme sent him twenty miles overland to the nearest harbor with instructions to board the first small vessel sailing from the port. The man complied and spent roughly the next six weeks at sea, purportedly for the beneficial effects of the sea air. Unfortunately, he fell seasick almost as soon as he boarded the ship. Unable to stand the motion on deck, he spent the entire voyage in the ship's hold, "lying on the top of the cargo, where the air is necessarily very bad." He ate only powdered "ship biscuit" mixed with water as the vessel slowly made its way along Jamaica's coastline. Upon landing again, the bricklayer appeared to be even closer to death than when he began the voyage. He stayed for several days at port as Chisholme sent a chaise to collect him. When the man returned four days later, Chisholme noted that he was in astonishingly good spirits "and seemed convinced he would recover." After three months' convalescence and a diet of milk, rice, and broth, the man recovered entirely, with no more pulmonary complaints.[13]

Chisholme confessed his bafflement over the case: instead of benefitting from the healthy ocean air, the seasick bricklayer spent weeks breathing the stifling air below deck. The rest of the case was not unusual in most respects; Chisholme presumed that the bricklayer had become ill because drinking and dancing had weakened his body and rendered it more vulnerable to environmental forces, particularly to dangerous night air. Treatments such as blistering, bleeding, and purging, as well as exposure to different environments, especially healthy sea air, were meant to correct those imbalances or blockages. For this reason, Chisholme sent the bricklayer in search of healthier air to cure his body. For Chisholme, the case stood out because of the man's inexplicable recovery. The case stands out historically because of the unusual attentions given to an enslaved person, even if his name goes unmentioned.

It almost goes without saying that the bricklayer was an exception, along with Cupid and Jackie, the carpenter on the estate that Samuel Cary managed, the gardener in South Carolina, and perhaps some of the laborers on Charles Gordon Gray's and Pierce Butler's plantations. Most slaveholders did not go to the trouble of relocating sick enslaved laborers. But these cases demonstrate that planters did not think of health or recovery in racial terms. According to Chisholme's letter, he had no reason to believe the bricklayer's condition had anything to do with his skin color. Chisholme's theory about the cause of the man's illness aligned with both physicians' and planters' understandings of environmental and behavioral reasons for ill health. The case reflects the widespread belief in the power of the environment to influence people's bodies, as well as the lack of racial distinction in physicians' diagnoses and treatment of patients. Regardless of whether or not people—enslaved, free, African, or European—could attend to their health on an individual basis, planters and physicians believed that illnesses had environmental causes, and one way to treat these illnesses was by relocation. In this understanding, bodily health was tied to place rather than to race.

On another level, individual bodies responded differently to various environments because all people had particular bodily constitutions. Chisholme's puzzlement demonstrates the significant degree of uncertainty that physicians faced in diagnosing and treating various maladies during the eighteenth century. This uncertainty existed in large part because doctors believed that treatment depended upon an individual's often unknown and unpredictable bodily constitution. For physicians, bodies suited different types of environments, and the conditions that created good health in one person might not do so for another. But these differences were individual, not racial, and medical practitioners recognized the importance of these differences in treating sick patients. As one physician explained, "Without a particular Knowledge of" people's constitutions, physicians could not expect "any tolerable Success" in treating a patient. "It ought therefore to be one chief Care of Physicians, to enquire into the peculiar Constitution of each Patient," he explained. Other doctors agreed. In William Hillary's treatise on Barbados, he noted that "different Constitutions . . . require different Methods of Cure." Yet while some physicians understood a few of their patients' bodily constitutions, most people's internal bodies remained a mystery. This uncertainty left a portion of treatment up to chance—perhaps a physician would guess a person's constitution accurately and a remedy would work, but chances were equally good that the unknown nature of an individual body would render treatment ineffective. Although physicians frequently prescribed travel over various distances, hoping that the treatment would result in the restoration of a person's health, both medical practitioners and others viewed health as dependent upon a person's individual bodily makeup and its response to the environment.[14]

Letter after letter reveals keen attention to the differences among individual bodies for Europeans and Euro-Americans. In 1791, James Stormonth of Scotland explained to his sister Margaret that a friend who had originally intended to return from the West Indies had changed his mind because "he finds a warm climate agrees best with his constitution." Around the same time, George Brissett wrote from Jamaica that he planned to visit England because his constitution "absolutely require[d] a change of climate," but his mother had planned a similar trip and he feared that "the cold weather will not altogether agree with her constitution." Although Samuel Martin found that Antigua's climate suited his constitution, his son Josiah, who was born on the island, never felt healthy there and ultimately moved to North America, where he finally experienced "perfect health." In these cases, letter writers demonstrated their understandings that different bodies suited different climates. Just as local climates differed from one another, individuals had different bodily constitutions that determined the healthiest or best place for their bodies.[15]

Taken together, published and private sources show planters', managers', and physicians' understandings of bodily health and illness on plantations. According to their writings, rainy weather caused illness, and sick bodies that would not heal would benefit from a change of air. In addition, knowledge of a person's bodily constitution could help determine the particular kind of air that would suit that person. Most importantly, race did not enter into these calculations around health. Black and white populations were both susceptible to the same environmental dangers on Greater Caribbean plantations, and both responded to the same methods of treatment. In these writings, bodily health was environmental, not racial.

Seasoning and Location

This environmental view of bodily health prioritized seasoning. Planters and physicians agreed that seasoning Africans to plantations in the Americas took time, and that it was a highly local process. Writing from Jamaica to his father, John Stirling explained, "tho' you have given me liberty to purchase negroes immediately their effect will not be felt for 3 years, as they are never reckoned properly seasoned until that time." Similarly, Simon Taylor warned a friend who wished to become a planter that "no great dependance can be laid on the labour of new Negroes for the first three years untill they are seasoned to the country." Because of this time, planters sometimes preferred locally born laborers. Visiting Samuel Martin's plantation in Antigua, for instance, the Scottish traveler Janet Schaw noted that enslaved laborers "born on the spot and used to the Climate, are by far the most valuable" because they did not fall ill or die nearly as often as newly arrived Africans did.[16]

Underscoring the local nature of seasoning, planters considered that bondsmen and women born in the Americas suited their local climate but would need to be seasoned if moved elsewhere. As physician James Grainger explained, "A gang of Creole Negroes, being transported from the place of their birth to another island, most commonly undergo a seasoning." Grainger advised planters to ensure adequate clothing and familiar food for transplanted laborers, including creoles, or those born in the Americas. Enslaved people "who are accustomed to one island," wrote Grainger, "run no small risque of their lives when transported to another." Moving people even on a small scale was dangerous because local environments differed so much from one another. On a still more localized level, Grainger wrote, "slaves carried from one plantation to another, though on the same island, are apt for some time to droop and be sickly." Moving from island to island, or even plantation to plantation on the same island, could cause bodies to have to adjust to local environmental conditions. Planters who transported laborers any significant distance risked causing illness, or at the very least losing valuable labor time, as they waited for bodies to adapt. For planters who tended to value maximizing profits above all else, understanding the seasoning process could make a difference in their approach to purchasing or moving enslaved laborers.[17]

Financial calculations were both integral to the process of buying enslaved plantation laborers and specific to the plantation's location. In the mid-1780s, for example, absentee planter Charles Spooner instructed his plantation manager Samuel Cary to purchase a group of enslaved laborers for Spooner's plantation in Grenada. Spooner preferred laborers seasoned to the West Indies, he explained, because he calculated that the lower cost of newly arrived Africans was not worth the risk of seasoning them. "It is to no purpose to buy them out of a ship," he wrote, because "one third, if not one half are lost in the seasoning." Too many Africans would fall ill or die as they changed climate, Spooner believed, but those already living in the West Indies would be healthier.[18]

In Grenada, Samuel Cary tried to locate such a group, but had trouble doing so. Although there was a group of enslaved laborers for sale in Antigua, Cary explained that Grenada was far too wet for those who had been seasoned to the drier Antiguan environment. He briefly harbored hopes about a group of laborers from St. Vincent as he thought the environment there more closely approximated Grenada's, but the sale fell through. After a further search with no apparent prospects, Cary informed Spooner that the laborers from Antigua appeared to be the only option. Still, he stressed his reluctance to acquire them as Antigua was too dry to hope for a smooth transition to Grenada. The Antiguans, he wrote, "will run as great risque in seasoning, as New Negroes." In other words, considering the climate of Antigua, the laborers might as well be arriving from Africa. It made no sense, then, for Spooner to spend more money on seasoned laborers who would have to be seasoned all over again. If no locally seasoned laborers could be found, Cary strongly recommended buying Africans instead because they would cost less money and require the same amount of seasoning.[19]

Other plantation managers held similar beliefs. One planter in Jamaica informed his father that he had no desire to buy a group of laborers from an acquaintance, in large part because "removing them so far up the country they require nearly the same seasoning as a New Negroe from the ship; the climate differing so much here from Montego Bay." Another thought that "the transfer of slaves from one Estate to another" in Jamaica was "sometimes precarious" because the two places might have different temperatures. A third expressed opinions along the same lines as Samuel Cary. James Kerr, who managed Hugh Hall's Jamaica plantation, advised Hall to purchase newly arrived Africans for economic reasons. Seasoned enslaved laborers cost more, "and if they are from a Distant part of the Island they are very little easier season'd than New Negroes," he explained. Planters and managers, especially those who lived in the colonies, held highly localized concepts of seasoning. Because environmental conditions differed from island to island, and even within the same island, it was important for planters and managers looking for seasoned laborers to find some living close by or in a similar environment. Newly arrived Africans would have to be seasoned to Jamaica, and several of them would likely die in the process. But so too would enslaved laborers from a different island or from a different part of the same island. Because the largest price differential was between seasoned and unseasoned laborers, it only made financial sense for planters wanting seasoned laborers to purchase those who had been seasoned locally.[20]

These concerns were fairly common among managers throughout the eighteenth century and into the nineteenth, even after Britain officially ended its participation in the slave trade. Joseph Foster Barham Jr., an absentee planter with two plantations in Jamaica, received a letter from his managers discouraging him from purchasing enslaved laborers in Saint Ann parish for his plantation in Westmoreland in 1813. The environment in Saint Ann, wrote Barham's managers, was entirely different from that of Westmoreland, and moving laborers from one place to the other might have "serious consequences." If they found a similar group for sale closer to Barham's plantation, the managers added, they would make the purchase. On another occasion, when Barham suggested moving laborers from his plantation in Westmoreland to the other one in the neighboring parish of Saint Elizabeth, his manager dissuaded him. "I do not think the Negroes could be removed from Mesopotamia [the Westmoreland plantation] to the Island [the Saint Elizabeth plantation] without great risk," the manager wrote. "Neither do I suppose that those Negroes that are advanced in life would be able to withstand the change of climate." Managers assessed the risk of moving enslaved laborers as both physical and social. Seasoning and bodily health were often the central concerns; as Barham's manager noted, older enslaved laborers would have a hard time adjusting to the change of environment from one part of Jamaica to another. From a social perspective, enslaved people often formed connections, including marriages, with people nearby and visited one another's plantations. Separating family members by large distances caused higher rates of desertion by enslaved laborers who ran away to visit loved ones. For these reasons, managers often found it disadvantageous to move large numbers of people long distances.[21]

Conversely, when managers encountered enslaved people for sale from similar climates, they took advantage of the opportunity. In 1789, Charles Rowe, who managed Barham's Island plantation, wrote that he had heard of a group of laborers for sale, and prospects looked good: "being for many years inured to a mountain clime a good deal similar to that of the Island [plantation]," he wrote, "induces me to believe they would . . . suit better than most others to be obtained." The previous decade, Simon Taylor wrote to Chaloner Arcedeckne informing him that a neighboring planter wanted to sell Arcedeckne his enslaved laborers. Taylor thought this sale would be a particularly good match for Arcedeckne because of the proximity of the two plantations. Because the laborers had been seasoned on an adjoining plantation, they would not have to be re-seasoned, and potential survival rates would be high. In both cases, managers recognized the importance of climatic similarity. They thought that more enslaved laborers would survive a transition that did not require a re-seasoning, and they looked for people whose bodies were already accustomed to the same or a similar environment.[22]

Seasoning, then, was a local process, dependent on an area's specific climatic and environmental attributes. Moreover, planters universally acknowledged the need for seasoning Africans. None of them believed that any part of Africa would produce people whose bodies naturally suited the West Indies. And as slaveholders' calculations show, the location of seasoning changed enslaved people's values for potential purchasers. Taken together, this evidence demonstrates planters' clear understandings that people's bodies necessarily changed as they moved locations and that these changes were essential to performing plantation labor. The climate in the Americas was not "perfectly suited" to African constitutions, as physician William Wright asserted in response to the specter of abolition of the transatlantic slave trade, because Africans had to undergo a multi-year seasoning process upon arrival, and many of them died during this process. Moreover, planters and managers made calculated choices as to which people to purchase based upon place. This indicates a belief that a West Indian or Greater Caribbean climate was far too generalized of a term; people's bodies only suited particular places, and Africans did not suit plantations in the Americas without undergoing a rigorous process.

Seasoning and Identity

The other essential aspect of seasoning was the notion that it changed bodies. Although neither Africans nor Europeans naturally suited American climates, eighteenth-century settler-colonists believed that both could—and did—undergo seasoning upon arrival and that both experienced significant bodily changes as they did so. But seasoning was also about more than health; it represented changes in a person's identity. A seasoned person could become, for example, less Angolan or British and more Jamaican or American, and any children born in the Americas of non-Indigenous descent bore a creole identity.

Tellingly, in eighteenth-century parlance the word "creole" described someone
with parents from Africa, Europe, or both. It did not distinguish among them.
Seasoning marked the beginning of creolization, as environments shaped bodies
both in health and in identity.[23]

"No one comes hither without a seasoning," wrote Beville Granville shortly
after his journey from England to Barbados in 1703. "I have had mine," he added,
as he explained that he had suffered from a "wholsome" sickness that had left his
body better suited to the local climate. Several decades later Robert Hamilton
suffered from "a very severe fever" after he moved from Scotland to Jamaica in
1736. He hoped the illness had been a "thorough seasoning," and would leave
him healthy and adapted to Jamaica. Still later in the century John Pinney traveled from Britain to Nevis, writing, "I have had what they call a seasoning, & am
but just recover'd." After a few months of good health, Pinney felt confident. "I
shall enjoy my health here," he assured a friend, because the seasoning sickness
had adjusted his body to the unfamiliar environment. All three of these travelers
believed that a period of illness had served as a seasoning for them, and that
upon recovery, their bodies suited the climate of their new homes.[24]

Medical manuals for travelers specified that the seasoning process would either involve a gradual bodily adjustment over a period of years or else would
occur through "repeated attacks of sickness," as the physician James Lind wrote.
Either way, Europeans who traveled to the tropics would experience "some
change and alteration" in their bodies. Moreover, seasoning signified a deep and
enduring change. Lind stressed the permanence of seasoning, explaining that
settlers would have to undergo the process in reverse should they choose to return "home." Many seasoned travelers, he wrote, "dreading what they may be
exposed to suffer from a change of climate, choose rather to spend the remainder
of their lives abroad, than to return to their native country." Travelers' accounts
corroborate Lind's explanations, as many seasoned settlers expressed trepidation at the idea of returning to their native lands.[25]

William Smalling, who managed plantations in Jamaica for absentee owner
Joseph Foster Barham, was reluctant to leave the island in 1771. "I should be
glad to see my old friends again," he wrote as he considered a return to England.
But he feared the change of climate might prove damaging for both himself and
his wife, both of whose constitutions were "so well suited" to the Jamaican climate. For the next few years, Smalling continued to put off the trip. "I much
question if England would agree so well with me," he mused the following year.
"Mrs. Smalling as well as myself has been upon the whole much better here than
in England." In 1774 he repeated his concerns. "Perhaps the climate of England
may not agree with us," he informed Barham. If either of the Smallings fell ill
upon landing in London, he continued, they would return immediately to
Jamaica. Similarly, when a friend of planter Charles Gordon Gray left Jamaica

for Europe, Gray expected his imminent return. "I should not be at all surprised to see him back again," he confided to his father, "the English Climate after so many years residence here does not suit his Constitution." These letters express genuine anxieties that a cold place would make residents of the West Indies ill. Although people may have been born in Britain, years in a different climate had changed them.[26]

Other West Indian residents felt a similar ambivalence. Wanting to return to Britain after many years away, they worried that the change of climate might be too great a shock for their bodies. George Barclay, a native of northern Scotland, planned to return to Britain in 1739 after many years in Jamaica. He would visit London on the way home, he wrote to a friend, but was "undetermin'd whether to fix there or in Scotland" as he was "under some apprehensions that so cold a climate as that of Aberdeen will not be agreeable to one of my age after having liv'd so many years in the West Indies." Extended residence in a place changed people's bodies. As these letters attest, Britons who had lived for some time in the Caribbean had grown accustomed to the climate and found that it suited them.[27]

Some planters decided that their bodies were so permanently suited to the Caribbean that they were unable even to visit Britain. Much as he longed to see friends and relatives in England, Simon Taylor feared the effects of cold air upon his body. "I should dread a winter," he wrote to Arcedeckne, "which I hardly can think but must be too severe a tryal to a constitution, that has been sun drying 30 years in the Torrid Zone." Although Taylor traveled to England a few summers after writing, he never again returned. Several years later he wrote to his brother to tell him he would stay in Jamaica permanently. "It is highly improbable that I shall ever leave this country," he wrote. "I am persuaded that a voyage to Europe would hasten my end for I really could not bear the cold nor the vicissitudes of the British climate." And Samuel Martin found that after many years in Antigua, northern climates no longer agreed with him. His children lived in Britain and in North America, but each time he visited them, intending to stay permanently, the rheumatism that plagued his joints in New York and the cough that racked his body in England left him convinced that the rest of his life would be "miserable" if he did not return to Antigua for good. As he told Janet Schaw, who visited him from Scotland, he had become "so absolute an exotick" that, in spite of being kept "in a greenhouse" in England, his body was unable to stand the cold, and he returned to Antigua to preserve his health and life.[28]

All these letters, and many others like them, expressed Euro-Caribbean residents' deep conflicts with their predicament. Britons traveling to an unfamiliar climate, unsure of how their bodies would react but uneasy at the possibility of illness, would be relieved to have experienced a seasoning. Once acclimatized, these migrants would feel more certain of their bodies' suitability for the Caribbean climate. Nevertheless, many did not intend to stay for the rest of their lives, and having grown older in the warmer weather, they dreaded another climatic change that might no longer agree with their bodies. Returning to Britain, then, caused them serious concern.

Seasoning and bodily adjustment to the West Indian climate had significant implications. Having undergone a seasoning, British migrants' bodies suited their adopted environments. In a sense, this change in bodily suitability signified a more fundamental change: a person was no longer a Briton, but a West Indian, with a body attuned to the Caribbean environment. Martin believed he had become "an exotick," unable to live anywhere cold. His letters to his son Samuel from the previous several decades had expressed a desire to relocate to Britain, and over the years he asked Samuel for leads on places in Shrewsbury, Shropshire, Southampton, Richmond, and the Isle of Wight. Finding nothing suitable, and troubled with a persistent cough on his visits to England, Martin tried living with his son Josiah in the mid-Atlantic colonies, hoping to purchase land in Pennsylvania. After suffering through a Long Island winter, Martin changed his mind. By the time he met the Scottish traveler Janet Schaw in the mid-1770s, Martin admitted that Antigua was the only place he felt healthy. The last time he returned home to the Caribbean, he wrote to Samuel that as his ship neared the island, his perpetual cough vanished and his health quickly returned. Unable to become seasoned to cold places, Martin's body, and thus a part of his identity, was Antiguan.[29]

Climatic Characteristics

After visiting Samuel Martin's Antigua plantation in 1774, Schaw continued her tour of the West Indies and North America before returning home. As she traveled from the Caribbean to the Carolinas, Schaw noted stark differences between people's appearances in the Americas and those in Britain. In North Carolina she was unimpressed by the "sallow complexions and languid eyes" she observed among "the peasantry," as well as with the "wan looks" of a Scottish man she met. The environment, she believed, was the culprit: "this climate," she wrote, had altered the Scot's appearance significantly. Her assessment of Antigua was no better; as she noted in her diary, many former Britons living on the island had "so entirely changed as not to be known." As Schaw's observations suggest, for eighteenth-century Britons, becoming truly seasoned to a place often involved visible bodily changes. According to contemporaries, the environment could change people's bodies both internally and externally. Health and appearances were the most obvious of these changes, although a change of climate could produce other, more subtle changes as well.[30]

For Jamaican planter Edward Long, the issue of people's appearances was particularly troubling. After several years in Jamaica, Long returned to England, where he began work on his three-volume *History of Jamaica*, published in 1774. Long's personal notes, full of crossed-out passages and re-written sentences, show that he put a great deal of thought into what he wrote; none of his comments, even if buried in the text, should be dismissed as oversights. Although historians often characterize Long's text as the ravings of an ardent racist, a close reading of his work displays a wealth of contradictions on the subject of race. The inconsistencies throughout the text reveal Long's deeply conflicted agenda in writing his *History*. He sought to correct European "prejudices" about the effects of the West Indian climate on British bodies, but several passages still described hierarchical distinctions between Europeans and creoles of European origin. Although he insisted that Africans "naturally" suited the West Indian climate, his own experience in Jamaica had shown him that this was not the case. Long cautioned, for example, that "native Africans" who were "unseasoned to the climate" would be "less able than Creoles" to labor in Jamaica. Like other planters, he also noted the local nature of bodily adaptation, explaining, "The removal of Negroes from a dry to a damp situation, from a South side to a North side parish, has often been fatal to many . . . . Even the Creoles do not bear these removals from places where, perhaps, they have resided from the time of their birth." Edward Long too, then, believed that Africans and their descendants had changeable bodies, receptive to environmental influence and responsive to climatic change.[31]

Like many of his contemporaries, though, Long was most concerned with European bodies, and parts of his text explained that European bodies would fundamentally alter in the Caribbean climate. Although Jamaican-born children of Europeans were "in general tall and well-shaped," Long wrote, their eyes differed noticeably from those of their British-born relatives. According to Long, British creoles possessed particularly deep eye sockets, which were set far back in their heads to protect them from the "strong glare of sun-shine." Their sight was "keen and penetrating" and their joints supple. "Although descended from British ancestors," Long noted, creoles were "stamped with these characteristic deviations," which he attributed in large part to the environment. According to both Schaw and Long, then, environmental factors had visible effects on people's bodies. For Long, first generations of children born in the West Indies already looked noticeably different from their parents.[32]

Yet Long understood that his claims about European bodily change might cause alarm or concern for Britons considering travel to the West Indies. It was one thing if Britons thought they might acquire more supple joints or deeper eye sockets; it was an altogether different concern if they believed their skin would blacken under the influence of the sun. Skin color, then, formed an important exception for Long. Although he wrote that "brunettes . . . become browner" after time spent in the West Indian climate, he insisted that "the genuine English breed" retained a "pure and delicate" skin in Jamaica. Contrary to widespread rumors in England, Long insisted, Jamaican-born children of British parentage were not "converted into black-a-moors," nor did they even turn "swarthy" from exposure to the sun. Likewise, Long also declared that "Creole blacks" did not change skin color in the Americas. As evidence, Long offered that the descendants of Africans in northern climates, even after several generations, were "not at all different in colour from those Negroes who are brought directly from Africa" despite continuous time spent in a cold climate. Long concluded that "the dark membrane which communicates that black colour to their skins," unlike other bodily features, was a permanent characteristic.[33]

Long's denials that skin color could change for either Black or white people were deliberate. Having strong family ties to Jamaica himself and having lived on the island for several years, Long wanted to assure his readers that residence in a hot, sunny place would not alter the fair coloring of the "genuine English breed." Britons and their descendants, Long insisted, could live in the West Indies un-blemished and with their essential whiteness—and thus superiority—unthreat-ened. Similarly, creoles of African origin living in northern climates did not, after several generations, whiten. Skin color, a physical characteristic loaded with significance, proved a way for Long to assert his own Britishness.

Still, in Long's view, creole children of British and/or African parentage could and did have some bodily adaptations to the West Indian climate. Writing that Jamaica's climate was "temperate, and even cool, compared with many parts of Guiney," Long explained that as a result "the Creole Blacks have undeniably more acuteness" than native Africans. Meanwhile, creole whites were taller than their European counterparts. In addition, some characteristics of Caribbean inhabitants—white, Black, and brown—even seemed to be approaching one an-other in kind. Long noted that the "supple" joints of white creoles approximated the bodily makeup of Black creoles and that all West Indian natives seemed to have remarkably good teeth. According to Long's writings, both Europeans and Africans would change as a result of living in a different climate, and the bodies of children born there would inherit these adaptations. Long's text, then, even if shot through with racist invectives, still reiterated two essential points: first, that Africans had to be seasoned to the West Indian climate just as Europeans did, and second, that residence in the West Indies fundamentally altered people's bodies, regardless of their origins.[34]

Letters from West Indian travelers reflected some of Long's contentions, while others appeared to offer evidence to the contrary. Ann Appleton Storrow, who left Boston for Jamaica in the 1790s, found her children altered by the change in climate. Her son, she informed her sister, had become "a true sallow faced creole," so transformed that she was sure her sister would no longer recognize him. A few years earlier, Francis Grant wrote that after many years' residence in Jamaica, his Scottish brother and sister were "both much altered in their looks ... the consequence (no doubt) of much sickness & long residence in a hot climate." When Charles Gordon Gray settled in Jamaica, he wrote to his father that he had been tanned by the sun, and James Savage found that after spending time in the West Indies he had become "as black, as a Spaniard." In the 1780s, William Leckie, who had recently arrived in Jamaica from Scotland, assured his brother-in-law Walter Ewing that the effects of the climate on his appearance were better than Ewing had feared. "You ask me if the sun has hurt my complexion or dimmed my eyes," he wrote. "I answer that the sun & climate together had nigh dim'd them effectually." On the contrary, he found that "the sun so far from dimming a person's eyes generally lights up new fires that you in the frozen regions of the North are unacquainted with." These travelers all felt that they had experienced some physical alteration in their faces, skin, or eyes after time spent in the West Indies. Those who exposed themselves to the sun tanned, while Storrow's son became a "true sallow faced creole." Storrow's phrasing suggests that her sister would have been familiar with the idea that creoles possessed particular physical characteristics, an indication of the common belief that living in the Caribbean did indeed change white people's appearances.[35]

Letters explaining these visible changes reveal colonists' strong sense of bodily fluidity. For them, bodies were not fixed entities, suiting only particular places. In addition to visibly apparent changes, planters and other observers thought that the West Indian climate could affect people's bodies internally. One of the most frequent observations was that heat "relaxed" people's bodily fibers; Long believed this, as did Caribbean residents Simon Taylor and Samuel Martin, both of whom lived to an old age in the islands. Taylor, for example, wrote in 1783 that after "near 23 years in a hott climate" his constitution was "exceedingly relaxed indeed, and requires the assistance of a little cold weather to brace it up again." In fact, several West Indians contrasted the relaxation they felt in the heat with the "bracing" effects of colder climates. Walter Tullidelph of Antigua wrote that he hoped to take a trip to Europe to "renew" his constitution and to "brace up" his relaxed bodily fibers. James Walrond, manager of Charles Tudway's plantation in Antigua, attributed his ill health to his "long continued residence in this warm climate." He hoped to spend a winter in North America to "brace & strengthen" his "solids which in all constitutions are constantly relaxed & loose much of their elasticity by so continued a warmth as we live in." Sometimes this relaxation could even be visible. John Mair, who kept a journal in Barbados during the 1770s, wrote of "a supineness and indolence" common to the island's inhabitants that was "visible in both sexes which I attribute to the climate." As the very fibers of their beings "relaxed," Britons feared that they would become too soft and loose, even supine. Indeed, lethargy—on the part of both Blacks and whites—was another bodily characteristic that Britons attributed to creole bodies. To maintain their Britishness, many West Indian residents from time to time found that they needed "a little bracing," usually in the form of cold air which they thought would strengthen and renew their bodies.[36]

At the same time, this supposed relaxation could be beneficial for older people, whose fibers, according to Edward Long and some physicians of the time, tightened naturally. "Old age contracts the fibres; this climate relaxes," wrote Long. "Aged persons on coming hither find themselves renewed as it were in youth," he insisted, as their bodies recharged due to "this atmosphere." In fact, many planters found the heat of the West Indies beneficial for elderly bodies, and some recommended the place as a health resort for English people no longer able to stand cold winters. "This is the finest climate in the world for an old man," wrote John Campbell from Jamaica to his nephew in London. Caleb Dickinson agreed. "Considering the bleak weather in England," he wrote to his wife, Jamaica "is a better climate especially for people in declining years." Samuel Martin urged his son to consider moving from London to Antigua as he grew older, believing that the Antiguan "climate may be more agreeable to the old age when you arrive at that period." Simon Taylor believed that Jamaica was "the best country for old people, as the climate is so much milder than it is in England." He urged his nephew to visit Jamaica to try the effects of the climate. "I really believe that this climate is more congenial to health than any part of Europe to people that have attained the age of 50 and upwards," he wrote. If his nephew, who suffered from gout, was unable to recover in England, he encouraged him to visit Jamaica, as "you can then chuse which you will preferr as best suiting your constitution." All these letter writers believed that older Britons, whose bodies needed loosening, would actually be healthier and better off in the West Indies than in England.[37]

Taken together, these letters demonstrate residents' beliefs about the strong links between climate and bodily change throughout the eighteenth century. At times the connections were visible: Samuel Martin, for example, noticed the difference in people's faces across the Atlantic when he visited New York in 1768. In contrast to the "rosy complexion" he associated with the English countryside, in his travels through North America Martin found hardly "a florid countenance either male, or female." He attributed these looks to people's winter diets of salt meat, as well as to "the violent heat of summer." The physician Alexander Hamilton, who traveled in the North American continent in the 1740s, ascribed the "washed countenances" of Maryland residents to rampant illness in the "sickly, convulsed state." There was little question, then, that climate determined both health and appearance. Hamilton wrote that he could often guess people's origins by their faces, and as private correspondence demonstrates, this contention was not unusual. Whether bodily changes occurred quickly or incrementally, there was widespread acknowledgement that bodies fundamentally altered as people moved from place to place.[38]

On Race

The ability of bodies to change based upon climate—and the necessity of doing so when transported to plantation societies—signified that bodies were not in fixed racial categories. Plantation correspondence reveals a widespread belief that different climates changed people's bodily constitutions, and the process of seasoning suited them for new environments. As a result, Britons who lived in plantation colonies feared they had lost their Britishness and had become colonials or creoles. They also believed that Africans had undergone a similar adaptation, their bodies changing through the seasoning process and altering them fundamentally. Eighteenth-century colonial medical thinking confirmed this: all bodies were susceptible to the same environmental dangers; all were equally likely to fall ill; differences among bodies could be attributed to relative exposure to environmental dangers or to individual constitutional differences; medical treatment or cures involved the same methods regardless of skin color. This is not to say that all people received the same treatment, but rather that physicians believed similar treatments would help whoever was ailing.[39]

In addition, notions of bodily fluidity demonstrate planters' clear beliefs that African bodies did not naturally suit environmental conditions in the West Indies. Instead, managers consistently wrote of the need for seasoning newly arrived enslaved laborers, claiming that the process required sustained care and attention. Even after seasoning, Africans fell ill frequently, and as the bricklayer's case shows, physicians often believed that the cause of illness in Black bodies, along with the appropriate treatment, did not differ from that of white bodies.

Instead, Greater Caribbean residents believed that illness rates were directly related to people's exposure to the elements.[40] As Edward Long explained, "Negroes are in general the first seized with those distempers which become epidemic," especially after significant amounts of rain, because they had "indifferent cloathing" and were exposed "to the inclemencies of weather." In fact, even as Long claimed that the "bodies and constitutions" of African and Afro-Caribbean people "seem peculiarly adapted to a hot climate," he did not indicate that this climatic fitness was innate. On the contrary, he mused, "perhaps, they owe their health not more to this adaptation, than to their mode of living" because Jamaica's "native Whites," provided they remained sober, were "equally healthy and long-lived." By using the phrase "adaptation" to describe Africans' fitness for hot climates, Long revealed a more tempered view of the climate and of humanity than that for which he is most remembered—insisting that "the

White and the Negroe are two distinct species." The extent to which he wrote about the similarities among African and European creole bodies, in particular their "equal" health in relation to the climate, betrays a less rigid and more malleable view of bodily difference than Long himself might have cared to admit.[41]

* * *

At the end of the eighteenth century and into the early nineteenth, ideas about seasoning remained essential to Europeans' understandings of bodily health. When traveler William Hind arrived in Jamaica in 1792, he informed his sisters Mary and Eliza in England that he had fallen ill with a fever, but that "it is what they call a seasoning in this Island." A decade after that, Mary Hind received another letter from Jamaica, this one from her brother-in-law. He had moved to the island from New England in late February with his family and, he assured his sister-in-law, everyone would be "sufficiently inured to the climate before the fall of the year." After the seasoning process, there was no reason to expect poor health because European bodies were entirely capable of adjusting to hot climates.[42]

In addition, slaveholders remained conscious of the dangers of re-seasoning after the body's initial adjustment. Writing to his father about a friend's plantation, Charles Gordon Gray recounted, "His Negroes which were taken from hence have, I hear, suffer'd much by their removal, they appear to me not the same looking People." The process of seasoning altered people, both internally and externally, and seasoning was a highly localized process.[43]

Planters' private letters support a notion that local variations in climate created notable differences among a place's inhabitants, including in Africa. Disparities in health were among the most important of these differences, but visible changes in people's bodies also concerned observers. For planters and physicians, an "African constitution" would have been an enormous generalization masking important variations. Indeed, as James Lind explained in his medical treatise, climatic differences produced significant bodily variations. "The truth is well known to those who trade for slaves on the African coast," he wrote. Enslaved people stolen from Africa differed in character, health, and appearance "according to the nature of the country." Those purchasing enslaved laborers agreed. Planter Bryan Edwards devoted a substantial portion of his natural history of the West Indies to a description of the differences among nearly a dozen types of African bodies, and slaveholders commonly expressed their preferences for enslaved laborers from various regions over others.[44]

At the same time, faced with threats to the slave trade in the last decades of the eighteenth century, planters found themselves mired in contradictions. They made climatic arguments substantiating their dependence on enslaved African laborers even while their private writings showed clear understandings that

Africans did not, in fact, suit the West Indian environment. Countering calls for abolition, planters made public, unwavering assertions in Parliament that only African bodies could labor in hot climates. These planters claimed on the record that African labor was necessary for the cultivation of the West Indies because the climate of the Caribbean naturally suited Africans'—and not Europeans'—bodily constitutions. The testimony of planters and other advocates of slavery reduced a complex picture of health, seasoning, and bodily adjustment to a stark racial division.[45]

Reporting every counterexample from the thousands of planters' letters that survive in archives would add little to the overall picture. Caribbean planters did not always agree on much—their opinions varied as to how and when to plant and harvest particular crops, whether or not to purchase seasoned laborers, how many new laborers to add to a plantation at a time, as well as the origin of these laborers—in short, the workings of a plantation differed according to the experience, attitudes, and whims of a particular planter. But their letters demonstrate universal agreement on the need for seasoning newly arrived Africans to the significantly different West Indian climate. No one would arrive with a body prepared for the local environment, and whether or not a person—European or African—would adjust appropriately was a matter of chance and that person's constitution.

The ideas that planters and physicians observed racial differences in health and that Africans easily adapted to labor in hot climates form the basis of a pervasive historical and historiographical argument about the development of racial slavery on Atlantic plantations. Yet private correspondence reveals that neither the claims about racialized bodies nor those about the natural suitability of the West Indian environment for African bodies reflected the reality that planters lived and observed in the islands.

A Climatic Debate

The Transatlantic Slave Trade in Parliament, 1788-1791

In the midst of a gray London winter, a group of British politicians convened to discuss the future of people living far from the cold, damp stone Houses of Parliament along the Thames. Should these people, the men considered, continue to be captured in Africa, packed into ships' holds below deck, transported across the Atlantic, and sold in Caribbean colonies as slaves? It turned out to be a difficult question for them to answer. The politicians, members of the Committee for Trade and Plantations of the Privy Council, only partially recognized that they were discussing the fate of Africans. Although abolitionists decried the abysmal conditions both aboard slave ships and on West Indian plantations, participants in the hearings on the state of the transatlantic slave trade saw the question at hand as hinging not only on African lives, but also on the fortunes of planters and, thanks to the efforts of anti-abolitionists, on the future of the British economy.

In February 1788, when the Privy Council began to conduct their inquiry on the slave trade, both supporters and opponents of abolition had substantial contingents advocating their causes. Abolitionists drew upon an expanding network of contacts across Britain, while various West India interest groups, particularly in London, Bristol, Liverpool, and Glasgow, coalesced as merchants and absentee planters increasingly joined forces. Both sides published scores of pamphlets to publicize their agendas, abolitionists portraying the slave trade and slavery itself as abhorrent and anti-humanitarian, and the merchant-planter coalitions defending and refuting abolitionists' claims. Although the hearings ostensibly considered only the continuance of the slave trade, and not slavery itself, the evidence both sides mustered to promote their interests exposed an underlying conviction that the institution of slavery was under scrutiny and in danger.[1]

The Nature of Slavery. Katherine Johnston, Oxford University Press. © Oxford University Press 2022.
DOI: 10.1093/oso/9780197514603.003.0006

The Privy Council's investigation proved remarkably thorough. Despite the initial deadline of May, the Council continued its investigation for over a year, soliciting evidence from planters, governors, and governing boards of every Atlantic colony under British rule. Ship captains, sailors, and surgeons familiar with the Middle Passage also gave testimony, as did merchants, slaveholders, and physicians in the West Indies. Some of these witnesses provided oral statements to the Council, while others mailed responses to lengthy questionnaires from the colonies. The colonial respondents reported on enslaved people's home lives, religious practices, diet, and medical care, suggesting a variety of reasons for their apparent lack of fecundity and variable health on plantations. This combined written and oral testimony served as the evidence upon which the Council would base its recommendation for the future of the slave trade in the British Empire.

Although some of their answers differed from one another's, the planters, physicians, and governors who answered the Council's inquiries appeared unified and unwavering on one particular issue. As members of the Council considered that ending the slave trade might necessitate alternative forms of labor in the colonies, they asked about the possibility of European labor on plantations. The responses were unequivocal. Planters pronounced such a proposition "impossible" because Europeans could never "subsist in such a climate." As the Council and Assembly of Grenada put it, "Few white persons not even creoles can bear exposition to the intense sun of this climate, for a few hours with impunity; It would be impossible for them to bear it, for the many hours which those must unavoidably do who undertake to cultivate the soil." The Jamaica representatives explained that "The nature and constitution of an European are not well adapted to retain even life; much less, to support field labour," in the West Indian climate. And the Council of Barbados insisted that "There has been no single instance of an European dedicating himself to any thing like hard labour, or exposing himself to the sun, who has been able to support the heat of this climate; nor do we think it possible." On the question of European labor in the Caribbean, the colonial representatives were united.[2]

The Committee's investigation proved to be only the beginning of a decades-long debate over labor in the British sugar islands. The arguments used in this debate ricocheted across the Atlantic, recurring in similar debates in the United States over slave labor lasting well into the nineteenth century. Historical scholarship analyzing late eighteenth-century abolition debates points to political, economic, and/or social factors instigating this activism. In much of this scholarship, the question of climate figures only marginally, if at all; scholars tend to focus on the causes of abolitionism rather than on the arguments of the slaveholders, and climate was not a driving force for abolition. Moreover, historian Eric Williams's seminal work on abolition dismissed planters' climatic arguments as essentially absurd because they were blatantly false.[3]

But the rhetoric of climate had lasting implications beyond the abolition debates. Although the question of European labor in hot climates began as one small element of the debates, it developed into a substantial point of contention between slavery's advocates and abolitionists. It also exposed a central contradiction of slaveholders' arguments. Planters argued, on the one hand, that Africans naturally suited the West Indian climate while Europeans did not; that sugar cultivation was "light" compared with much of the work that the "laboring poor" performed in Europe; and that Europeans had never labored in the West Indies. At the same time, they attributed the high death rates of newly arrived African captives to the seasoning process and bodily adjustment to the unfamiliar climate; they claimed that Europeans might be able to work as artisans but that they could never handle the arduous labor of sugar cultivation; and they insisted that, if Europeans had ever actually physically labored in the West Indian climate before, they had surely died from such rigor. Despite leaning heavily on the climate argument to deny the possibility of white labor in the islands, planters also insisted that free Black people could not possibly cultivate plantations without coercion. In other words, sugar cultivation was such light labor that it required the use of force and the condition of enslavement; Africans naturally suited the West Indian climate but died as their bodies struggled to adapt to the environment; and Europeans had never labored in the West Indies but certainly perished from exertion if they ever had.

As arguments over the slave trade exploded, abolitionists and defenders of slavery found themselves embroiled in a debate over who was fit to labor in the West Indian climate and under which types of conditions. The uncertain history of labor in hot climates served as a touchstone in these arguments, as did the nature of labor, the environment, and the effects of both on the health of West Indian inhabitants. As the debates over slavery and abolition increased in intensity, advocates for both sides found themselves forced to articulate the precise nature of bodily difference and the ability of people to labor in specific ways in certain places. Meanwhile, prior uncertainties and varied opinions about the effects of hot climates on white bodies developed into a coherent ideology. Both absentee and resident planters, along with merchants and slave traders, many of whom had never shared ideas or principles before, and several of whom had in the past expressed various beliefs about the Caribbean climate, found common ground on the question of white labor on plantations and presented a united front to the Privy Council. These debates demonstrate the ways in which long-simmering but incoherent theories of bodies, climate, and labor solidified into a clear rhetoric justifying Black slavery in the Americas.

Laboring Bodies

Members of the Committee posed several questions about alternative forms of labor, as well as about enslaved people's health on plantations. In many of their publications, abolitionists drew attention to planters' inhumane treatment of enslaved laborers and pointed out that planters had no incentive to care for laborers who could be easily replaced. Ending the slave trade, they argued, would force planters to improve living conditions for enslaved laborers already on plantations and to rely upon reproduction, rather than replacement, as a way of procuring new laborers. At the same time, Council members pressed planters to consider labor alternatives such as machinery or the hiring of free laborers, either Black or white.[4]

One of the first to provide testimony in the Council's hearings, absentee planter Charles Spooner declared that the cultivation of the West Indies by Europeans was "impracticable." The Council persisted. "Could not a white man, who lives very temperately," the inquisitors asked, working "only in the cooler hours of the day" labor in the West Indies? Spooner, who owned several Leeward Island plantations but who lived in Britain, asserted that such a person could not. "The climate would soon wear out his constitution," he explained. European labor in the islands, he added, "appears, in fact, to have been already tried. See Ligon's *History of Barbados.*" Spooner did not elaborate or cite specifics, but some of his contemporaries also referred to Ligon's text as "proof" of their claims. Stephen Fuller, who compiled answers for the Jamaica Council, quoted the inventory of Ligon's plantation assets, including "96 Negroes" and "28 Christian white servants." Fuller also included Ligon's land. The cultivated portion of this land consisted of two hundred acres of sugar cane, seventy acres of provision grounds, thirty planted with tobacco, and five each of ginger and cotton. "From the above account," Fuller wrote, "I am unavoidably led to conclude, that 200 acres in canes, could not be cultivated by 28 white servants." To Fuller, it seemed "perfectly clear" that "the island of Barbados was cultivated by Negro slaves, and not by white people, as have been asserted (I think) without foundation." Absentee planters who wanted to demonstrate that white people could not possibly labor in the Caribbean turned to Ligon's 1657 text as one of the only historical records available.[5]

Fuller and Spooner in fact marshaled Ligon's book to make different arguments. Spooner, who claimed authority based on his Grenada and St. Christopher plantations despite living four thousand miles away, implied in his testimony that Ligon's experience was a test case with dismal results: Europeans had, in the seventeenth century, attempted to work in the West Indies and failed. Fuller, on the other hand, offered a different interpretation. Fuller expressed strong doubts about whether Barbados, as "has been asserted with confidence," could ever actually have been cultivated by white people. He assumed from reading Ligon's inventory that the "Christian white servants" would have cultivated the tobacco, ginger, or cotton on the plantations, but not the sugar, leaving that to enslaved Africans. Yet admitting at the outset that he had never visited Jamaica and only represented it, Fuller hedged his testimony by acknowledging that his answers might be "imperfect, and in some instances possibly erroneous." At the same time, he reminded the Council that the property and livelihoods of most Jamaican planters was at stake in the hearings and urged them not to take "any decisive measures, affecting their property" on the basis of "these very imperfect answers."[6]

Fuller's answers were indeed imperfect and rooted in his own time. He based his assumptions on an understanding of late-eighteenth-century labor hierarchies. By the time Fuller wrote, sugar was cultivated on large plantations entirely by Africans and their descendants, and sugar cane had taken over all of the low-lying land formerly allocated to other crops, ginger, tobacco, and cotton among them. Sugar required the hardest labor and turned the biggest profit for large plantations; most of the land that was not planted with sugar was too steep to support the canes, so planters used it to grow other crops such as coffee instead. Fuller assumed that the social stratification and labor divisions of the late eighteenth century held true for the mid-seventeenth. He also may have assumed that Europeans could perform some types of labor, such as cultivating lighter crops, but not others, such as growing sugar cane.

Edward Long, who contributed to the Jamaica report, wrote an addendum supporting Fuller's contentions. Responding to murmurs that the English islands had indeed at one time been cultivated by servants from the British Isles, Long insisted, "we have no one evidence either historical, traditional, or inductive, to ascertain as a fact, that at any period of time, from the first discovery by Columbus, a single acre of ground, in that part of the world, has ever been labored and planted with the sugar cane by the hands of white men." Pressing further, Long continued, "The notion therefore, that Barbadoes or any other West India island was *first* planted by *white persons*, without the aid of Negroes, or of Indians, is absolutely, and entirely unfounded." Recognizing that settler-colonists in Barbados did not begin using African laborers immediately, Long suggested that they had instead relied on Indigenous peoples during the colony's nascent period. Colonists did import enslaved Indigenous laborers to Barbados, although the numbers in the colony's early years are difficult to discern. Although Long conceded that he based his argument on conjecture, admitting that he could not be certain what would happen to a European who labored in the heat because he had no actual evidence, he nevertheless proclaimed that "an Englishman cannot labour in the field without iminent [*sic*] danger to his life."

Long, then, like Fuller, began by insisting that Europeans could not grow sugar, but then expanded that argument to encompass all types of labor. From one perspective, this leap was neither enormous nor outrageous because sugar was the primary West Indian crop. But by making a comprehensive assertion in absolute terms—white people could not labor in the West Indies—planters opened the door to a variety of challenges to this expansive statement.[7]

In fact, Ligon's accounts did not prove that Europeans had not cultivated sugar, and nowhere in his text did he claim that white people definitively could not labor in the West Indies. Writing in response to Fuller's and Spooner's testimony, abolitionist witness William Dickson, the former secretary to the governor of Barbados, denied the accuracy of their claims. Insisting that he based his observations on personal experience and touting the value of testimony written by someone "who has *resided* among the people he means to describe," Dickson refuted Fuller's assertions. "*That all the lands in Barbadoes originally were, and that part of them still are, cultivated by* WHITES," he wrote, proved slavery's defenders wrong. Barbados was "originally cleared and cultivated by [white] bond-servants," Dickson insisted, and many poor white people still cultivated, "*with their own hands*" plots of land on the island. In a subsequent argument, Dickson used Ligon's text to fuel his exasperation, referring to parts of the text in which Ligon described Europeans cutting down woods and traveling or laboring ten hours a day. Quoting directly from Ligon, he pointed out that these white servants were "put to *very hard labour*." While Fuller had offered his interpretation of Ligon's work, based largely on his own assumptions, Dickson drew attention to passages in which Ligon had explicitly written that white servants performed "very hard labour" on plantations.[8]

Members of the Privy Council were no doubt befuddled by the contradictory testimony they heard. Having published his *History of Jamaica* over a decade earlier, Edward Long had the wealth, experience, and family connections to give him considerable standing as an authority on life in the West Indies and his testimony carried significant weight. He had also lived for a number of years in Jamaica so, unlike Fuller, he had personal experience in the islands. Yet Dickson drew upon his own experience to make reasonable arguments in direct opposition to those of the pro-slavery planters. The Council valued first-hand experience but found it difficult to reconcile Long's and Dickson's contradictory testimonies. Each side also had only limited historical evidence—Richard Ligon's 1657 text—and both argued that this work justified their own accounts. The two interpretations of Ligon's text, and the dual use of his work as historical precedent, revealed the scarcity of hard evidence the Privy Council had at its disposal. Ligon's text was well over a century old, but both the abolitionists and the planter coalition drew upon it as the sole existing "proof" that Europeans either had, or had not, ever labored on West Indian plantations.

History, then, provided insufficient evidence. The Council had more pressing questions in any case and expressed deeper concerns about contemporary workers than the labor regime of the distant past. If planters seemed united in their vehement denial about the ability of white people to labor in the West Indies because their bodily constitutions could not stand the climate, then, the committee wanted to know, how did Black bodies fare? In truth this was a tricky question, and planters recognized it as such. They insisted that white people would become ill, and possibly die, under the labor required for cultivating sugar in the Caribbean climate. Yet to claim that Black people flourished in the West Indies was a difficult stance to take, as many planters well knew. The proof was in the numbers: account books and plantation ledgers showed that enslaved Africans often fell ill on plantations, and almost no labor force was self-sustaining. That is, enslaved women consistently bore fewer children in any given year than the number of bondspeople who died. This net loss, which happened on nearly every plantation each year, meant that the system of slavery depended on the transatlantic slave trade. It simply could not survive without a constant influx of new laborers. But if planters conceded this lack of fertility and their dependence upon fresh captives, they would have to provide a reason for the ill health of the current laborers. And that reason either had to be poor and severe treatment at the hands of slaveholders—something planters were keen to deny—or else unsuitability to the West Indian climate, an admission with the potential to undermine planters' larger claims about the necessity for Black laborers in the first place.[9]

Some planters did admit, without any trace of irony, that environmental conditions contributed to illnesses upon plantations. Charles Spooner listed the climate of the West Indies as one cause of illness among enslaved laborers, and a physician acknowledged the dangers of enslaved workers "laboring during nine hours exposed to the rays of the sun." The Grenada Council believed that enslaved people exposed to the elements, especially through "their labour under an intense sun" and "from that labour being frequently carried on in moist swampy places," were particularly susceptible to dysentery, and the Barbados Council wrote that enslaved people were "more liable to Diseases, from the abundance of Rain" in the autumn months than were free people, either white or Black. The governor of St. Vincent explained that laborers in the West Indies "certainly are more subject to diseases from the vicissitudes of the weather in the rainy season than are labouring people in Europe" and noted that "the creole Negroes or those seasoned to the climate" survived much longer than native Africans. Some planters acknowledged, then, that atmospheric conditions were responsible for fevers, fluxes, and other illnesses and that enslaved laborers suffered more than others because they had the highest level of exposure to the elements. Some also admitted that Africans suffered from the "change of climate" upon arrival in the

West Indies. But lest these admissions become grounds for condemning the institution of slavery, planters hastily offered additional causes for illness, focusing especially on behavior.[10]

   Enslaved people who fell ill, planters claimed, were at fault themselves. According to the testimony, enslaved people brought about their own illnesses through "neglect in not covering their bodies," from "negligent cookery," "improper diet," a "habit of rambling," and, especially, "the imprudent use of spirituous liquors" or "excessive" dancing, drinking, and "acts of sensuality." Spooner blamed enslaved people's illnesses on "drinking new rum, intemperance and running out in the night," and one physician attributed most illnesses to enslaved people's poor provisions and to nighttime travels, which left them "exposed to the noxious night dews." The Grenada Council also implicated people's attendance at "nocturnal assemblies" which exposed them to the night air as a culprit in causing disease, and the governor of Barbados claimed that enslaved people suffered from "the too free use of rum which they steal." Several of these behavioral causes for illness—especially drinking and dancing—echoed concerns raised in earlier planter correspondence about the health of both Blacks and whites. Blaming victims for their own illnesses was nothing new, but it was a convenient way to deflect responsibility from slaveholders. Although planters' neglect created the inadequate clothing and diets which left enslaved people vulnerable to environmental forces, slaveholders tried to turn attention away from these and toward enslaved people's behavior in those environments.[11]

   Even those witnesses who noted the harmful consequences of labor in such climatic conditions downplayed climate as a factor when compared to people's behavior. Blaming behavior seemed the best way for planters to preserve their livelihoods while admitting illness among enslaved populations. Immoral or irresponsible behavior could, according to contemporary medical thought, cause ill health, and it was something that gave planters a moral high ground as they absolved themselves of responsibility for enslaved laborers' health. As the Privy Council had to admit, nocturnal ramblings were beyond planters' immediate control, and therefore they could not be blamed. Planters did not explain that enslaved people tended to visit one another during the night because that was the only time they had to see family members on other plantations, nor did they take responsibility for the lack of nourishment that people suffered, even though at other times they willingly took credit for providing food. Even the rum, which the Barbados governor blamed for illness among enslaved people, could be, according to him, stolen—an accusation that both exculpated planters and underscored the immoral behavior of the enslaved. No one mentioned that planters themselves sometimes handed out rum as an incentive to keep laborers working long hours during the sugar harvest. Instead, by insisting that enslaved people voluntarily exposed themselves to night air and were "negligent" in their food provision and preparation, planters shifted the blame for enslaved laborers' ill health onto the bondspeople themselves.

It was no secret that enslaved Africans in the Caribbean were not, on the whole, a healthy population. Yet according to slaveholders' testimony, Caribbean plantations could only be cultivated by enslaved African laborers. Planters, merchants, and colonial representatives claimed that Europeans' health would never be able to withstand the West Indian climate. Even while making these claims, slaveholders and others admitted that Africans did not "naturally" suit the West Indian climate and that they tended to fall ill when overly exposed to the sun and rain. At the same time, planters chose to sidestep the question of their treatment of the enslaved and instead blamed laborers for their own ill health.

The Council Presses On

The Privy Council was not easily satisfied. Behavioral explanations of illness, although conceivable for adults, did not address the health of enslaved children. If planters blamed enslaved people's illnesses on their behavior, then what about high mortality rates among infants and children? Did the children of enslaved people suffer from any particular disorders or diseases that did not affect free-born children of either Africans or Europeans? And what accounted for the low birth rates on plantations? The Jamaica Council responded that one-third of enslaved infants born on the island died of lockjaw, or tetanus, within nine days after birth. Of the remaining children, half died of worms or yaws before their fifth birthday. In contrast, children "of the white inhabitants" were "in general not liable precisely to the same distempers; such as the yaws, for example, and venereal and other hereditary taints, which unquestionably conduce so much to the mortality observed among the children of the slaves." The Governor of Barbados blamed high infant mortality rates on "great defects in the conduct of mothers," and the Council of Grenada, which included Charles Spooner's friend and manager Samuel Cary among its six members, answered that lockjaw, or the "jaw fall," disproportionately affected enslaved children because of the "pernicious custom" new mothers apparently had "of denying the breast to an infant for many hours" after birth—an answer that again placed the blame for infant deaths squarely on the mothers. Spooner himself referenced physician Benjamin Moseley's 1787 *Treatise on Tropical Diseases* as he speculated about causes for lockjaw, including specific page numbers in his testimony. Moseley, like the planters, cited behavioral causes, writing that the malady could be "attributed either to the intemperance of the mother during pregnancy, or to the irritation of the navel after birth; or to the smoke of the lying-in room, or to the dampness of its situation; or to the carelessly letting in cold air upon the child." Most of these answers kept the blame with enslaved people: if they were not making themselves ill, they were endangering their children, either through "hereditary taints" like venereal disease and yaws, or else through various behaviors, whether intentional or not, that caused tetanus in infants.[12]

By emphasizing the negligence of enslaved people in causing illness, planters sought to exonerate themselves from any accusations of ill treatment. The Council of Barbados, for instance, wrote that although slave populations suffered a negative birthrate, the decrease "cannot be owing to hard labour or ill treatment." Instead, the Council suggested polygamy, "excess," "natural indolence," hurricanes, "carelessness of mothers," a lack of cleanliness, and sometimes "the injudicious situation of their Houses" as causes of low fertility. The Jamaica Council blamed yaws and venereal disease, along with "menstrual obstructions," "promiscuous venery," worms, and a disproportionate number of males to females for low birth rates among enslaved populations. Yet after listing these "great impediments to natural increase," the Council members insisted that, in fact, "many" enslaved children were born in Jamaica. With an air of resignation, they wrote, "if they could get over the locked jaw, smallpox, measles, yaws and worm diseases, a greater proportion of Negro children would be reared in Jamaica, than is usual in Great Britain." As if these contradictory statements were not enough, the Council continued by claiming that, "hereditary taints" aside, enslaved children were actually not more prone to diseases than were children of either European colonial or free Afro-Caribbean populations. Similarly, Charles Spooner, after testifying that lockjaw "carries off, I should suppose near one half of the children of all Negroes whether free or slaves," while "white children are in general free from it," four weeks later amended his testimony. "In speaking of diseases peculiar to the children of Negro slaves," he explained, "I have said that the disease called the jaw fall, is peculiar to black children, but I find it is also common to white children." Once again, the testimony was unclear. According to these responses, high infant mortality rates among the enslaved were either situational or imagined, as planters claimed both that enslaved infants suffered more and that they suffered the same as free Black and white infants.[13]

Both the Jamaica Council's and Spooner's answers reflect the evasive and ambiguous stance planters took in response to the Privy Council's questions. Again they found themselves in a dilemma: to answer that enslaved children suffered more than others from illness might indicate poor treatment, malnutrition, or a lack of humanity on the part of slaveholders. But to deny the substantial rates of illness and disease among enslaved children would, on the one hand, stand in direct defiance to plantation ledgers, and, on the other, provoke an obvious question: why could not Euro-Caribbean creoles, born in the West Indian climate, be suited to labor there? Planters would not begin to entertain this last question. Their answers had to reflect a delicate balance between evoking the difficult conditions of labor in the West Indies and downplaying their own role in exacerbating these conditions.

Only the governor of St. Vincent offered answers that acknowledged both the climatic and the labor difficulties enslaved people endured in the islands. Africans suffered from stomach disorders, he wrote, more than Europeans did, a likely effect of their poor diet. Moreover, the governor reported that enslaved populations fared worse than free Black people because of their inferior food and clothing. Children born into slavery did not survive as often as free children did because they lacked provisions that would enable them to thrive. The governor of St. Vincent was an outlier in his responses because he admitted that the conditions of slavery were less than adequate to support life and health in the islands. The poor diet and scanty clothing with which enslaved people were provided contributed to their ill health on plantations.[14]

The governor also admitted that the climate of the West Indies contributed to enslaved peoples' suffering. "The West Indian climate," he wrote, "is greatly injurious to the constitutions of all children," a factor that impeded the "natural increase" of bondspeople on the island. He also implicated the "constant labour" slaveholders demanded of enslaved women, along with the poor quality of their food, for the lack of population growth on plantations. As enslaved children who survived infancy grew, they continued to feel the effects of the climate. Yet despite his acknowledgement of the effects of demanding labor, insufficient diet, and climate upon enslaved laborers' health, the governor still claimed that enslaved people who were "indolent and lazy" became ill in greater numbers than did their more "industrious" counterparts, who cultivated their own grounds and thereby supplemented the meager food rations provided by slaveholders. His testimony echoed that of the other governors, planters, and council members throughout the West Indies as he insisted that European cultivation of the islands "would be impossible" because white people would be "absolutely unable" to stand the heat.[15]

Still, the governor's apparent defection—admitting the brutal labor conditions enslaved plantation laborers faced—was enough to cause him concern over other planters' reactions. As the governor sent the Privy Council his answers in late spring of 1788, planter John Farquharson, who had helped to compile them, also mailed a copy to his cousin in Scotland. He did so with a caveat: the papers, Farquharson explained to his cousin, were not "of a secret nature"; indeed, they were "the reverse" as they were to go directly into the public record as part of the Privy Council's investigation. Yet "notwithstanding of this," Farquharson pleaded with his cousin not to share the answers with anyone aside from a few "confidential friends." If others should obtain a copy of the answers and interpret them as a condemnation of planters, Farquharson explained, "it would be rather awkward." Farquharson emphasized that, although the answers suggested that improvements to the system of slavery could, and perhaps should, be made, the "many good regulations & restrictions" that "may be proposed for the benefit of the slaves" could be "adopted without any material prejudice to their owners." It is not clear why the Governor and Council of St. Vincent admitted the brutality of slavery. It is possible that, rather than entangle himself in a series of convoluted and contradictory statements as other colonial governors had, the governor of St. Vincent thought that honest testimony might lead to "regulations & restrictions," as Farquharson put it, that would decrease mortality rates of the enslaved.[16]

Farquharson was careful to articulate his own position in his letters. The brutal conditions of slavery could certainly stand to be improved and the negligence of particular slaveholders remedied through regulations. But free labor was not an option: "That an entire Emancipation of the slaves will take place," he wrote, "is an idea, that no person well acquainted with the circumstances of the West Indies can admit for a moment." Should the idea be debated with any seriousness, Farquharson added, "it would be impossible to substitute the means of conducting the business of Estates here." The West Indies as sugar islands would be ruined.[17]

Regarding the West Indian climate, planters appeared to present a clear opinion, at least publicly. Enslaved Black laborers were necessary for the cultivation of the West Indies, in part because white laborers were not an option; they were simply not suited to the heat of the climate. But the reality was far more complex. Despite their insistence that Africans would naturally suit a warm climate, most of the planters acknowledged the difference between Africans and creoles, recognizing that captives arriving from Africa would have to be seasoned to the different climate of the West Indies. They admitted that creoles of African descent lived longer and were healthier than people born in Africa and transported to the islands, a difference owing in large part to the change of climate and the subsequent seasoning African bodies underwent upon transplantation. If, as planters seemed to agree, people born in the West Indies had bodies best suited to the climate, then could European creoles labor on plantations? The proposition, though seemingly a legitimate one, was out of the question. As the Council of Grenada insisted, "not even creoles" of European descent would be able to stand prolonged exposure to the Caribbean sun should they be put to work in the fields.[18]

On the surface, this claim might appear to be one approaching biological racial difference. But planters' answers reveal no such beliefs. The questionnaires had asked whether Africans, either adults or children, suffered from any diseases that did not also afflict Europeans. If planters had believed in biological differences between Black and white people, one of the simplest arguments would have been for them to claim that the two groups suffered from different illnesses. If their bodies had fundamental differences, these disparities could be evident in variable health or sickness. All planters would have had to do would be to emphasize irreconcilable bodily differences by pointing to inherent susceptibilities to illness. But in their fervent attempts to protect the institution of slavery, many planters denied any instances of enslaved people suffering from any particular diseases. Those who did admit that any such differences existed pointed to behavior or occasionally insufficient nutrition as causes. Eager to refute their reputation for poor treatment of their laborers, slaveholders also denied that the children of enslaved people suffered from sickness in disproportionate numbers compared to free Black populations. But it would be a mistake to conclude that planters and other defenders of slavery missed an opportunity to rely on, or blame, biological differences between Black and white bodies for any differences in rates or types of illness. Instead, the evidence is telling: planters simply did not have a notion that any such differences existed. Their answers reflect an attitude directed solely towards protecting their assets and increasing their own wealth.[19]

Perhaps the clearest evidence that planters insisted on slavery for economic reasons, and not because they believed in biological racial difference, can be found in their answers about the potential for free Black labor. If white people could not work because they could not stand the climate, then, the Privy Council wanted to know, what if planters were to free enslaved people and pay them for their labor? Surely this plan would benefit everyone: planters could no longer complain about the high costs of new laborers, or of housing and feeding them, and workers would be more willing to labor if they received payment. Such a plan would prove impossible, planters insisted. The Council of Barbados claimed that free Black people lacked "the proper industry required to cultivate the lands," while the governor responded that they were too "proud and indolent." The Jamaica Council wrote that they were "averse to labour," and planter John Braithwaite doubted "whether without some compulsion they would be induced to work." Elaborating, he explained, "in warm climates the disposition both of whites and blacks is more averse to labor than in colder countries." William Hutchinson of Antigua also pointed out the need for coercion. "Free Negroes," he mused, "seem as little inclined to submit to labour, as white people." Absentee planter James Tobin "never knew a free negro do field labour" and Robert Hibbert agreed that, although "a great number of free negroes and tradesmen" lived in Jamaica, he "never knew free negroes offer to do field labour." Sugar cultivation was such difficult labor that it required the use of force.[20]

Field labor, especially cane holing and harvesting, also had a significant class component. "As to free Negroes," the Council of Grenada explained, "not a single instance ever occurred of a free Negro [doing field work]. The very becoming free, is considered as an exemption from every labour of that nature, and a free coloured person would think himself disgraced by it." As William Beckford argued, "To suppose that the land in Jamaica, or any portion of it, can be worked by the free negroes, or the people of colour, is absurd in the extreme." Enslaved people who became free, he wrote, would refuse to perform field labor, while "the colour of the mulatto, his birth, and education, naturally exclude him from the possible severity of toil." Europeans would be no better. As Alexander Willock of Antigua complained, "The lower whites are so drunken, there is no dependence on them." Physician Samuel Athill clarified the social effects of a system dependent on slavery. "White domestics have so many negroes about them," he told the House, "that they soon become gentlemen," so much so that "they are generally deemed useless." Athill's grievance attested to the tendency of white servants to perceive and join a racial hierarchy, refusing to do the same work that enslaved Black laborers did. Henry Ellis, onetime governor of South Carolina, wrote to the Privy Council expressing his horror at the suggestion that white people work alongside Black people as field laborers on plantations. "To imagine that white people are to be found," he informed the Council, "willing to degrade themselves so far as to work in the field with Negroes, is being very ignorant of men and things." As another witness put it, it was "morally impossible for Europeans to do the necessary field labour." Here, the climate was no longer an issue. Neither free Blacks nor whites would work in the fields because they felt it would degrade them to do so.[21]

These comments hit upon one of the central reasons planters insisted on the need for enslaved Black laborers on West Indian plantations. By the late eighteenth century, plantation labor, and sugar cultivation especially, had become so associated with African slavery that no person would willingly undertake them. Enslavement was a necessary prerequisite for compelling people to labor, and distinctions of class and skin color were bound up with those of a labor hierarchy. The issue at heart, then, was not so much that white bodies would not be able to physically withstand any sort of labor in the heat because, in fact, some of them had done so for centuries. The concern was rather that neither whites nor free Black people would stoop to labor that was so closely tied to slavery as well as to Blackness.[22]

Some planters also openly admitted the economic benefits of slavery for slaveholders. Robert Hibbert, for example, explained that free labor by Europeans, Africans, or creoles would not be economically viable. "A sugar estate, at the present prices," he testified, "could not afford proper food and accommodation for the necessary number" of laborers. William Hutchinson argued that if planters had to pay laborers even as little as one shilling a day, an amount so small, he wrote, that "it cannot be conceived" that either "an European or free Negro . . . would work for," they would give up on their plantations as unprofitable and the source of inevitable financial ruin. Alexander Campbell, who owned plantations in Grenada, explained that "very few whites are employed on the estates, as formerly at Antigua, the wages and expences of a white man, being double that of a black." And Admiral Shuldham testified that the cultivation of the West Indies by Europeans "must be attended with immense expence." All these testifiers pointed out a problem for planters: if they actually had to pay their laborers, even a minimal amount, they would not be quite as wealthy. Whether or not they would actually be "ruined" is debatable, but the point, for all of them, was that with slavery planters enjoyed unpaid laborers.[23]

Private letters from plantation managers earlier in the century also expressed concerns about the high costs of hiring European laborers. Rowland Ash, for example, wrote to Charles Tudway asking him to send "a sober good workman" or "a good country workman" to be a smith on Tudway's estate in Antigua, but warned him not to pay anything approaching the wages of the wheelwright who, in Ash's opinion, demanded far too much money. Over a decade later a different manager wrote to Charles's son Clement, who had inherited the estate, explaining the high turnover rate of servants on the plantation. "Some of them leave the plantations to get better wages elsewhere," the manager reported, "the people in the new islands give such large salaries, that a great many of the best servants have quitted this island, & it is now very difficult to get proper people for the estates." The manager urged Tudway to send out "boys from England," for he believed that it would "very soon be impossible to get white people enough to do the common business of the plantations." Cost, then, was uppermost in planters' and managers' minds, and free white laborers cost too much.[24]

But if planters admitted that saving money was their central concern in maintaining slavery, they had much less of a chance of winning over the House of Commons. Fabulously wealthy planters complaining about the high costs of hiring laborers and insisting that they own workers instead might not make a strong case. To protect themselves and their assets, defenders of slavery continually reverted back to the climate. In climatic arguments, defenders of slavery had the upper hand: unlike members of the Privy Council and even most supporters of abolition, who had never traveled to the West Indies, planters could claim greater experience and knowledge of the Caribbean climate. As with colonial governors in the late seventeenth century and the Malcontents in Georgia, planters understood the power of climatic ideology in Britain and used it to their advantage in the abolition debates.

Simultaneously downplaying the rigors of plantation labor while refusing to consider the possibility of European workers, planters made increasingly outrageous arguments. In his testimony before the House of Commons, Alexander Campbell claimed that, although "the cutting of canes is not very hard, tying them easy," it would be "impossible for Europeans to stand W. India field-work of any kind." Samuel Athill believed that cane cutting was "done with such alacrity and good spirits that it seems trifling," and that it was, in fact, "so easy, that often more than one cane is brought down by a stroke of the bill." Yet "from the excessive heat," he thought Europeans would be "incapable of field labour in the W. Indies." Planter Gilbert Francklyn also claimed that "the labour of a negro" was "slight compared with any field labour in Europe," but that the Caribbean climate made European labor impossible. These testifiers made their statements about the easiness of sugar cultivation without a trace of irony, despite simultaneous testimony explaining that no free person, Black or white, would ever choose to perform such labor.[25]

Advocates of slavery argued that Europeans would never undertake field labor, in part because their bodies would not be able to withstand the climate, and in part because they would not degrade themselves to such an extent. But this left a large and murky zone of other types of manual labor in the West Indies up for debate. What could white people actually do in hot climates? Some witnesses claimed that many of them worked as carpenters, blacksmiths, joiners, coppersmiths, masons, or sawyers, although the degree to which these tradesmen actually labored varied according to the politics of the witnesses. Abolitionist Reverend James Ramsay, for example, argued that "white handycraft men" in the West Indies "have all more laborious employments than ordinary plantation work," including the work required for sugar cultivation. Lieutenant Baker Davison informed the House that it was "well known, that the [European] shipwrights and other tradesmen, in the king's-yard, Port-Royal, often work all day long," and did not seem to suffer particularly from this labor. "White artificers certainly do work at their trades, in the West Indies, without materially hurting their health," he argued. Planters told a different story. Alexander Campbell testified, "White tradesmen there seldom work, in, or out of doors. They direct negro tradesmen how to lay out the work, and do light, nice jobs." Another witness claimed that "Europeans may do carpenter's or other work, under cover." "Whites, in the W. Indies," he explained, "work as plumbers, masons, &c. and many negroes work under their direction." All agreed that Europeans were employed in the Caribbean, but, as with Ligon's text, the interpretation and extent of that work varied with the testifiers' agendas.[26]

Accounts about the use of the plow differed the most wildly. Some planters insisted that it could never be used at all, either on particular islands or in the West Indies in general because the soil was too rocky and the land too steep. Others argued that they had seen it used in Jamaica, but that it could not be relied upon to do all the work of soil preparation and cane cultivation. Many planters did, in fact, use a plow but feared that if they admitted that fact, members of the House might see it as a replacement for human laborers. Samuel Athill testified that when European "Plough-men and boys were brought out to estates where the plough was tried," they "could not stand the labor." Athill claimed that he

"Never knew a black ploughman in Antigua," though another witness stated that in Jamaica the plough was "often worked by negroes." Elaborating, he explained, "When a plough is first used, a white man is mostly employed," but then the plowman trained enslaved people to do the work. Still, economics played a role in this transition because "White ploughmen and tradesmen have very high wages." If the Privy Council had been hoping for a straightforward answer about plowing, its members were disappointed. According to these responses, plows were either used by Blacks, or by whites, or not at all.[27]

Personal correspondence from planters confirms some of this testimony. Edward East, for example, who managed Anna Eliza Elletson's plantations in Jamaica, wrote in the spring of 1776 asking her to "send out a plowman" from Britain "as soon as possible." "It will be best," he wrote, "to get a man that has been used to work horned cattle." Three years later, though, he informed her that she need not send out another plowman as the enslaved laborers on the plantation carried on the work themselves. Maintaining a British plowman, he wrote, would "not be worth the expence," as the enslaved plowmen had mastered the technique. In this case, East's private correspondence confirms accounts of British plowmen training enslaved laborers to do the work over time. Other planters and managers presented different views. In 1789, when the Privy Council's questions about the use of plows reached Jamaican planter Simon Taylor, he hurried to ensure that nothing would threaten his continued use of slaves. "You say a question has been asked about working by Europeans, and how it is managed by Ploughmen," he wrote to Chaloner Arcedeckne in London. "I know of no white ploughing man working by themselves." Although he admitted that "they may indeed for the first day when they go on an Estate hold the plough for half an hour or so, to show the Negroes how to hold it upright," Taylor insisted, "I never saw a plough going in my life held by a white man an hour, neither did I ever know a ploughman keep his health, but have known two or three go mad, having been struck with coup de soleil in the field from having held it for some little time, and it putting their blood in a ferment." In these letters to be shared in public, Taylor portrayed a more extreme version of the labor training: white plowmen demonstrated plowing for "half an hour or so," but could not possibly stand even an hour. Anyone who tried it apparently suffered serious consequences from sun exposure.[28]

Taylor was enraged at the abolition debates and adamant that members of the House of Commons who considered even for a moment the possibility of European labor be entirely silenced. Adding to his earlier answers, Taylor wanted to be certain that he had made his point: "it would be as certain Death," he wrote to Arcedeckne, "to work white people in the field to digg cane holes, and cutt canes, as to turn them off the ladder at Tyburn with a band about their necks with a ship knott and to hang an hour." He could hardly have been more forceful. "At this present time," he concluded, "I know but of three Estates that use the plough constantly and the work is done by Negroes." According to Taylor, then, Arcedeckne should inform the Council of the situation in Jamaica: only a few estates used the plow, and none of these relied on white plowmen.[29]

Yet in other letters—those intended solely for his absentee employer, and not for Parliamentary reports—Taylor gave a more measured account of plowing. A few months after his earlier insistence, Taylor wrote again to Arcedeckne to inform him that the British plowman employed on Arcedeckne's estate had left. Explaining the process of plowing, Taylor wrote that white plowmen generally started "as early in the morning as possible" and worked until nine, at which point they stopped, and then started again at three in the afternoon and worked until dusk. "This partly accounts how ploughmen live," he wrote, "for by this you see they are not out in the sun in the middle of the day." Taylor still believed that British plowmen tended to be unhealthy in the West Indies, but this later letter—not part of the public record—at least acknowledged that they could work.[30]

The discrepancy between Taylor's private correspondence, in which he not only admitted that British plowmen existed, but even explained how they worked, and his statements to the House of Commons exemplifies the extent to which planters tried to protect their own economic interests. Five years after his statements to Parliament, Taylor again wrote to Arcedeckne asking him to send laborers from Britain to Jamaica. "It will be necessary for you to send out a good plough man if you can get one, that has been used to plough with cattle," he wrote. But Arcedeckne should search for prospects carefully. "The people we want," Taylor explained, "are those that have been bred up hardily in the country, on poor meagre fare, been used to work hard, and get up early, therefore we prefer Scotch young lads to any others." Given Taylor's earlier statements, in which he claimed that white plowmen worked "half an hour or so," it would seem an absurd investment to find and send a Scottish laborer to the West Indies to work for a mere half hour.[31]

Other planters expressed similar preferences in their demands for laborers. In 1795, for example, Joseph Foster Barham's manager requested a cooper and a carpenter, along with bookkeepers, for Barham's Jamaica estates. "If they can be procured from Wales, or from the Country part of Scotland, they are to be preferred," he wrote. In fact, much of the correspondence from the eighteenth century demonstrates planters' desires for Scottish laborers or those who would be inured to difficult labor. In this case, the climate seemed less of an issue than did the ability to work under harsh conditions. Planters and managers assumed that people used to one kind of grueling outdoor labor would be able to adapt to plantation life.[32]

Taken together, none of this evidence suggested either that white people could not labor in the West Indies for any biological reason or that Black people were particularly suited for such labor. Instead, low fertility and high infant mortality rates among enslaved populations signaled that the conditions of Caribbean slavery were dangerously unhealthy for Africans. In addition, neither Black nor white people would undertake sugar cultivation unless forced, and social structures equated particular types of work with the condition of enslavement. Finally, in their private correspondence, planters and managers wrote of a different scenario than the one they presented to the Privy Council. Despite their public claims that Europeans could never labor in a tropical climate, letters demonstrate planters' beliefs that Britons used to hard work—such as Scots—could labor on plantations. Planters' concerns lay instead with the high costs of hiring workers and with the greater economic benefits of purchasing them and owning their labor and their bodies.

The Pamphlet Wars Begin

Some abolitionists who testified before Parliament presented withering criticism of slaveholders' arguments in an attempt to showcase the absurdity of their claims. In June 1788, Parliamentary member Henry Beaufoy spoke before the House of Commons in opposition to planters' recent testimony. Appealing to the humanity of his listeners, Beaufoy deliberately used Britons' assumptions about the dangers of hot climates in his speech on the slave trade. "Some of us imagined," he explained of the condition of slave ships, "that when to the burning atmosphere of the torrid zone, is added the suffocating heat of numbers crowded into a narrow space, the suffering must be dreadful." Instead, he added, his tone clearly sarcastic, "we were mistaken . . . the witnesses say that the additional warmth is the very thing which the Africans desire." Pointing out the ridiculousness of the slaveholders' testimony, Beaufoy added, "One would think from the evidence at the bar, and from the arguments of the counsel upon it, that the solid pestilence, the thick contagion, the substantial rotteness of an African ship is congenial to the constitution, and exhilarating to the spirits of a negro." Beaufoy continued, underscoring the inconsistent, irrational, and often ludicrous arguments that slaveholders offered. Given slaveholders' Parliamentary testimony regarding the benevolent treatment of the enslaved, Beaufoy mused, listeners might "almost be tempted to conclude . . . that the fetters on the hands of the Africans, and the irons on their feet, are intended to check the wild expressions of tumultuous and frantick joy, rather than to counteract the gloomy purposes of despair." If Africans so embraced the heat, Beaufoy reasoned, they must relish being stuffed below deck on a slave ship. And if they were so happy and well-treated, why the need to keep them in chains? Beaufoy did not have to work hard to twist slave traders' and planters' own words against them.[33]

Beaufoy published his speech at a London press with abolitionist leanings, ensuring that the abolition debates were not confined to the chambers of Parliament. In fact, writings on the issue stretched across the Atlantic to audiences in North America as presses in Britain and in the United States spewed forth a string of publications on both sides of the debate. Sometimes these publications consisted of summaries or minutes of the debates themselves. At other times they contained impassioned arguments by either slaveholders or abolitionists, often in direct conversation with the ongoing testimony and with one another.[34]

James Ramsay, for example, testified in Parliament and also became engaged in a print battle over the abolition question with an anonymous West Indian planter. In his testimony, which he gave in early June 1788, Ramsay spoke with the authority of two decades of experience in the West Indies as a surgeon and as a clergyman. Pointing out the hypocrisy of planters' claims, he argued that many European artisans, tradesmen, and dockworkers already labored in the West Indies, often outdoors for much of the day. He could think of no physiological reason, he added, why Europeans could not also cultivate the land. This testimony echoed some of Ramsay's earlier arguments. In a 1786 publication, Ramsay had insisted that plantation labor "might be done by *white men*" if they would just "resolve to be sober." As proof, he argued that seventeenth-century Europeans in the West Indies had cut through forested land to begin plantations and that "the clearing of land from wood is *beyond all comparison harder* than the ordinary field work in a sugar plantation." While not everyone agreed with this point of comparison, no one doubted that clearing forested land was arduous work. Although planters might try to persuade Britons otherwise, social and economic factors, not climatic concerns, kept Europeans out of the sugar fields.[35]

Yet Ramsay did concede one point, at least in part. Edward Long had argued that Europeans could not be employed in "cutting down woods, or clearing the ground from trees," without endangering "their health and lives." Pointing to an example of British soldiers falling ill after clearing ground in Dominica, Long cited medical authority James Lind, in claiming that such labor "*has always proved destructive to Europeans in those Climates.*" Ramsay acknowledged that clearing forests was dangerous labor, but, crucially, he pointed out that it proved as dangerous for Africans as it did for Europeans. Both populations suffered equally in such a demanding job, he wrote, so simply arguing that it was a dangerous job for Europeans did not justify the use of African labor.[36]

Writing in response to Ramsay, an anonymous "West India planter" published a defense of African slavery. The author attacked Ramsay, both personally and as an abolitionist, although he did not disagree with Ramsay's characterization of labor in the West Indies. The planter agreed that the "disforesting" of land in the

West Indian climate was dangerous labor for both white and Black bodies. But there his agreement with Ramsay ended. In the first place, he wrote, because most of the land in the West Indies had already been cleared, he predicted that mortality rates would soon drop in accordance with the lessening demand for such labor. And in what may be one of the most blatant admissions of the slaveholder mindset, the author argued that it was beside the point to complain that Africans suffered through hard labor because that was, in effect, their purpose. Labor, he wrote, was "inseparable from the condition of a slave," and such hard labor would doubtless cause infertility and death among enslaved populations. But any attempts to mitigate labor and to avoid its inevitable effects on the body would undermine the entire purpose of the sugar colonies. Abolitionists, he complained, wanted "so great a relaxation of labour as is totally incompatible with the purpose for which negroes are purchased." Any concerns about the harsh conditions of slavery or the inability of enslaved people to reproduce were misplaced, he continued, as though abolitionists completely missed the point of slavery. "Negroes are not, in the first instance, bought for the increase of the species, but for their work," he wrote. "And, if a certain quantity of work be not done, their owners must be ruined; therefore, the condition of slaves being such as necessarily exposes them to accidents conducing to depopulation, we need not be surprised that their numbers do decrease." Enslaved people, in other words, doubtless experienced low birth rates and high death rates because the labor required of them was so demanding and dangerous. But audaciously (if anonymously), the writer explained that such was the condition—and, indeed, the very purpose—of enslavement.[37]

This argument is remarkable for its boldness and for its unapologetic tone. Rather than offer excuses for the inhumane conditions of slavery, as many other planters did, the writer simply argued that it was reasonable to expect enslaved people to be treated with brutality precisely because they were enslaved. Backpedaling slightly, he also threw in some familiar excuses for enslaved women's infertility for good measure. Depopulation resulted from immoral behavior, he explained, as well as from "exposure to the weather" and an imbalance in the numbers of females and males. But the writer's cloak of anonymity allowed him to profess a truth that many other planters were too ashamed or afraid to admit outright: Laboring, not reproducing, was the purpose for which planters purchased enslaved people, and without forced labor, the sugar colonies would not survive.[38]

Ramsay wrote back with a point-by-point refutation of arguments against abolition advanced both by the anonymous author and by slaveholders at large. For Ramsay, humanitarian concerns should not fall by the wayside in the face of economic prospects. He also pointed to the numerous contradictions inherent in the pro-slavery arguments. Aside from the anonymous author of

Considerations, most planters insisted that enslaved laborers were content and received fair treatment at the hands of masters. But how could such people be happy, Ramsay wondered, and yet also be unable to reproduce? Could such claims "be reconciled to common sense?" he asked. "Can it be the cause of truth, which requires such contradictory assertions to establish it?" Ramsay thought not and endeavored to expose the contradictions that ran through planters' testimonials, contesting them one by one.[39]

Both climate and economics figured among the systematic objections Ramsay presented in his text. Taking issue with the claim that Europeans could not labor in the West Indian climate, Ramsay argued that although hard labor would destroy anyone, Black or white, "white men kept from new rum, may, in the morning and evening, perform double the present task of slaves, without suffering from the climate." Indeed, Ramsay continued, "white men" had settled the islands of Barbados, St. Kitts, and Nevis. Citing the historian Robert Robertson, Ramsay explained that seventeenth-century West Indian planters had, in fact, been loath to use enslaved laborers in place of Europeans, lamenting "that England refused to continue to supply them with white servants." In Ramsay's telling, planters had switched to enslaved laborers only when other sources of labor dried up and then only reluctantly. Regardless of the sequence of cause-and-effect, the fact remained that Europeans could, had, and sometimes did labor in the fields. "Poor white men work along with their slaves," Ramsay wrote, a glaring factor that alone disproved slaveholders' assertions about the dangers of the climate for European bodies.[40]

Ramsay did not ignore the social hierarchy dictating labor patterns, acknowledging that "free negroes or mulattos" would refuse to work in the fields on the basis of class difference. Still, he rejected the flimsy climate argument, even using Long's *History of Jamaica* as counter evidence. Long himself, Ramsay explained, had written that Africans took three years to adjust to the West Indian climate and that up to one half of them died during the seasoning process. A three-year adjustment period, both to climate and labor, was proof that Africans did not naturally suit the West Indian climate. Furthermore, the dangers of the seasoning process, along with the startling losses it entailed, seemed to Ramsay to be a highly unprofitable enterprise. He calculated drastic economic losses through the ever-increasing purchase price of enslaved laborers, followed by several years of uncertainty regarding their health and lives. It seemed much more economically viable to Ramsay to hire laborers already present on the island than to keep up a constant importation of captives, many of whom would die in the process of transportation or seasoning.[41]

Perhaps the most notable part of Ramsay's argument lay not in his insistence that Europeans could labor in the heat, but in his assessment of bodily difference. For Ramsay, the supposed ability of Black people to labor in warm climates had nothing to do with any natural or biological traits, but rather with an acquired adaptation. "The negroe," he explained, "is not endued with any powers for enduring heat, but what *habit* would in time impart to a Tartar or Lapland tribe, if settled between the tropicks." In other words, even people from the coldest regions of the earth would, over time, become accustomed to tropical heat. There was no natural difference in bodily ability between Africans and the inhabitants of northernmost Europe; it was merely a matter of time and adjustment to the climate. Both abolitionists and defenders of slavery and the slave trade attempted to win popular support for their cause by publishing their arguments. Taking the case from Parliamentary hearings to a pamphlet war, factions of writers, publishers, and activists sought support through both passion and reason.[42]

The Climate Debate

Ramsay's ardent and radical beliefs regarding the cruelties of slavery placed him on the far end of a spectrum of ideas about abolition, climate, labor, and bodily difference. Not everyone who wrote in favor of abolition was as unorthodox as Ramsay and, indeed, several of those who argued against slavery included in their arguments the same climate theories that slavery's defenders professed. Robert Nickolls, for example, in 1788 published an abolitionist tract in which he argued that it was the very suitability of Africans for warm climates that revealed the horrors of slavery. Hot places were "congenial" to Africans, he wrote, and less so to Europeans; given this climatic circumstance, it was all the more appalling that Africans did not bear many children in the West Indies. Over the course of the eighteenth century, Nickolls speculated, "whites, in a climate less favourable to them, have lost only one half of their original stock, [whereas] the blacks have lost it four or five times over." He could only conclude that these proportions (although he acknowledged their inaccuracy, he believed they were representative) meant that Africans suffered from extreme "mal-treatment" on West Indian plantations.[43]

Planter Gilbert Francklyn seized the opportunity that Nickolls had left open. The following year, Francklyn published a defense of slavery in which he used Nickolls's climatic argument against him. Quoting Nickolls, who admitted Africans' fitness for warm climates, Francklyn argued, "if negroes are not incommoded with the heat," as Nickolls had written, "they are much better adapted to the cultivation of the lands in the West Indies than white people, who certainly are." Granting that illnesses struck enslaved people, Francklyn blamed familiar culprits: rainy weather and bondspeople's own behavior, particularly dancing all night. Still, Francklyn wrote as a landholder dependent upon enslaved labor. "The planter knows too well," he wrote, "the impossibility of inducing white men to attempt supporting the labours of the field, in this part of the world, to consent to the experiment being tried at his expence." Francklyn's bottom line lay in concern for his own property. If abolitionists succeeded and were "willing to run the risque" of attempting to cultivate plantations with European laborers, "the planters will not, I dare say, make any objections to it, but cede their property to be conducted according to any new mode which shall be adopted, on being paid a reasonable price for their property." Francklyn warned his readers that, "Should such proposal be approved of, it may not be improper to state what will, probably, be the amount of the planters claims on the public." In other words, taxpayers should be wary of approving any measure that might induce a planter to demand payment for lost property and labor, as the resultant costs to the public would be significant. Francklyn repeated these arguments in testimony before Parliament a year later. The minutes noted that Francklyn believed "the only practicable" way to cultivate West Indian islands was through "the labour of the negroes." Not surprisingly, Francklyn seemed most concerned with his own economic prospects: "If he had understood the importation of negroes was to be prohibited," the minutes noted, "he would not have bought lands he could make no use of." For Francklyn, the end of the slave trade signaled an end to British prosperity in the West Indies.[44]

At the end of the initial Parliamentary session, the Privy Council announced its recommendation. The Committee members had determined that it was "absolutely impossible to cultivate the West India islands, so as to produce any commodities that would enrich the mother-country, by white labourers. Fatal experience demonstrates the fallacy of such an expectation." European labor would not be economically or socially viable. The Committee seemed persuaded by a handful of sporadic and inconsistent "trials" that appeared to show the impossibility of European bodily health in hot climates. The Committee cited several of these trials in its summation: in 1749, for example, despite legislation that encouraged Britons to settle in the islands, "very few families" relocated, and of those who had, "not a vestige is left." Furthermore, the Committee continued, other European experiments had failed. The Committee cited the French attempt to settle Cayenne, in French Guiana, "by means of white labourers" in 1763 with disastrous results ("twelve thousand miserable people were the victims of this impolitic scheme"). The sieges of Cartagena in 1741 and Havana in 1762 had proven equally fatal to British troops, the Committee reported. And if the climatic evidence against European labor was an insufficient reason to end the trade, the Committee was convinced that the economic consequences of abolition would be enormous. Planters would expect to be compensated for their loss of property, shipbuilders might find themselves out of work, and British merchants, particularly those involved with the sale of colonial products in England or those who made a living selling goods to the colonies, would be economically devastated. As a whole, the Committee explained, Britain would suffer a considerable loss because the value of property in the West Indies contributed to the national wealth of Britain. As property values in the islands would plummet if abolition took place, so too would the overall wealth of the Empire.[45]

Despite this setback, abolitionists refused to retreat. To drum up popular support, many spokesmen for the abolitionist cause continued to publish pamphlets on both sides of the Atlantic. Curiously, abolitionists, more than pro-slavery advocates, drew upon the history of Georgia to bolster their case. In an early contribution to abolitionist literature, in 1774 John Wesley published his *Thoughts Upon Slavery* in both London and Philadelphia. Wesley framed his tract as an imaginary discussion with a defender of slavery. This prototypical defender, according to Wesley, would argue that slaves were "necessary for the cultivation of our islands; inasmuch as white men are not able to labour in hot climates." On the contrary, Wesley explained to his imagined antagonist, "the supposition on which you ground your argument is false. For white men, even *Englishmen*, are well able to labour in hot climates," he wrote, "provided they are temperate, both in meat and drink, and that they inure themselves to it by degrees." Wesley himself had had such experience, he explained. Comparing the summer heat in Georgia to that of the West Indies, Wesley related his experience in 1730s Savannah, when, along with his family, he spent his "spare time" in the burgeoning colony "in felling of trees and clearing of ground, as hard labour as any negro need be employed in." The eight Wesleys, along with forty Germans, engaged "in all manner of labour" in the province. And yet, Wesley wrote, "this was so far from impairing our health, that we all continued perfectly well, while the idle ones all round about us, were swept away as with a pestilence. It is not true therefore that white men are not able to labour, even in hot climates, full as well as black." Wesley's experience in Georgia had convinced him that hard labor in hot climates was entirely possible for whites; it was only "the idle ones" who suffered illnesses and died.[46]

James Ramsay quoted from this portion of Wesley's tract in his own 1786 anti-slavery work, and other abolitionists also took up the cause. William Bell Crafton, for example, published a summation of abolitionists' arguments, including in his pamphlet a call to British residents to boycott West Indian sugar and rum, products both dependent on and directly supportive of the slave trade and slavery. The book appeared in London and in Philadelphia in 1792, but the Philadelphia version contained an additional section: extracts from Trustee Secretary Benjamin Martyn's 1741 report on Georgia. The selections from Martyn's report gave a brief history of Georgia's founding, including the Trustees' reasons for prohibiting African slavery, and continued with accounts of the petitions sent by both the Salzburgers and the Highlanders at Darien in opposition to slavery. The reasons for Crafton's inclusion of the Georgia material were clear. Abolitionists in Philadelphia hoped to draw upon a chapter of American history free from slavery to show not only that the states could exist without slavery, but that such "truly deserving" people as the Salzburgers and Darien petitioners had argued a just and noble cause and could serve as examples for abolitionist societies and slaveholders alike throughout the United States.[47]

Climatic Contradictions

The arguments for and against abolition escalated, as advocates of both sides continued to publish pamphlets and open letters in the late 1780s and early 1790s. Although climatic theories formed only one part of the debate, most slaveholders and abolitionists used the climate in their arguments. Some, like Nickolls and Francklyn, argued that Africans could move seamlessly across the Atlantic to the West Indies with no noticeable change. Others acknowledged or highlighted the change: as one defender of slavery wrote, although Africans were "removed from their native climate," they "exchange it for one by no means unfavourable to their constitutions." Arguments like these tended to stress the greater suitability of Africans over Europeans for warm climates in general rather than deny any difference between Africa and the West Indies. As another writer put it, "the labour of the field, while it soon exhausts every European constitution, has no effect upon that of the Africans."[48]

On the other side, abolitionists listed the "change of climate" that African captives suffered in their transportation to the West Indies as a factor in their high death rates. Several abolitionists accused Edward Long's work, in particular, of being hypocritical and illogical; William Dickson, for example, used direct evidence from Long's 1774 *History of Jamaica* to undermine Long's own testimony. Dickson pointed especially to Long's explanations of the seasoning process, in which Long had explained that Africans had to be seasoned to the West Indies because they did not naturally suit the climate. As for Europeans, Dickson wrote, it was true "That unseasoned Europeans, cannot hold out, for any time, under the heavy labour of felling trees, digging cane-holes, and carrying out dung, in the West Indies." Yet the problem was not that people would be unable to work because they were Europeans; instead, they were merely unseasoned to the climate and unaccustomed to manual labor. Europeans "inured to the common labour of digging and carrying burdens" could "cultivate these lands very well," Dickson explained, because "The constitution of the human body, when brought up to hard labour, soon accommodates itself to this climate." Because all people arriving in the West Indies needed to be seasoned to labor and to the climate, Dickson saw no reason why Europeans could not labor as Africans could. He had personally witnessed white people in Barbados laboring on "rough ground where they are exposed to the scorching sun." Moreover, as other abolitionists pointed out, if Africans had to be seasoned, then they did not naturally suit the West Indian climate. It was seasoning, then, and not a constitutional inability to labor, that determined who could work in the West Indies.[49]

Abolitionists managed to turn the climatic argument against slaveholders, mainly by pointing out gaping holes in slaveholders' claims. If Africans were suited to the climate of the West Indies, why did they consistently fail to bear enough children, and why did they have such high mortality rates? Some witnesses referenced the Carolina lowcountry in support of their arguments. If planters argued that Africans naturally suited hot climates, then they would have to agree that the West Indian islands were hotter than the lowcountry. And no one could safely argue that the lowcountry, with its rice swamps, was in any way healthy land. Yet enslaved people in South Carolina seemed better able to sustain their populations than did bondspeople in the West Indies. Therefore, if the West Indian climate suited Africans even more than the North American climate did, the inability of enslaved women to bear many children must indicate cruel and brutal treatment at the hands of slaveholders.

As the abolitionist movement grew in strength, Parliamentary hearings resumed. Slavery's defenders had pointed to the mortality of British soldiers as evidence of white peoples' bodily frailty in warm climates, and military physicians answered this charge. Physician Robert Jackson, for instance, testified before the House of Commons that "white artificers may, and actually do, work at their trade in the West Indies" and "that Europeans are, with proper caution, equal to the ordinary field labour, without any material injury to health." Jackson claimed that he knew "from personal experience" that Europeans in the West Indies could "safely walk 20, 30, or more miles a day." Asked about the high, and at times staggering, mortality rates of British troops in the Caribbean, Jackson placed the blame entirely on avoidable circumstances: illness resulted, he argued, from the placement of camps "on unhealthy spots," from the "immoderate use of spirituous liquors," and from a general lack of discipline. There were "perhaps" a few "defects in the medical department," Jackson admitted, but under no circumstances should lawmakers assume that the poor health of troops was a result of the climate. Other physicians expressed similar concerns. Writing from St. Lucia, Sir John Moore complained that the troops under his command were "extremely sickly." He implored his superiors in London to send out fresh troops, taking pains to explain that the poor health of the soldiers "will be imputed to the climate, but it in a great measure proceeds from a total want of interior discipline." According to these physicians, behavior and poor choice of location caused illness, not the climate itself.[50]

Meanwhile, the continuation of the hearings provoked a heightened sense of outrage on both sides of the abolition debate as printing houses published a flurry of pamphlets arguing each side's cause. In addition, both planters and abolitionists used natural histories and medical treatises to advance their arguments. Planter William Beckford, for example, published a natural history of Jamaica in 1790. Addressing the issue of land cultivation, Beckford wrote, "That the land in Jamaica can be cultivated by white people, is a suggestion that I know not how to reconcile to common sense or reason." Britons who attempted to work the land would be overcome by the sun's heat, he wrote, and those who claimed that Europeans already cultivated land in the Caribbean were simply mistaken. "Europeans are no farther employed in the cultivation of the land than as gardeners or ploughmen," he wrote, and "To suppose that Europeans could cultivate the land in the islands, or negroes that of England, would be to acknowledge that climate has not any effect upon bodily exertions, [or] upon national distinctions." Beckford painted a terrifying picture of the consequences of British labor in the West Indies: "If the colonies were to be attempted to be cultivated by white people," he warned, "the whole population of Great-Britain would be unequal to the object, and would in the course of a century be melted down and become extinct." For Beckford, the question of colonial labor threatened the survival of Britain itself.[51]

Beckford's dire prophecy may have been extreme, even by the standards of self-interested and economically minded planters. But even as he tried to warn readers of the catastrophic consequences of attempting to cultivate the sugar islands with white laborers, Beckford admitted the difference in climate between Africa and the West Indies. Seeking to exonerate planters, Beckford attributed the high death rates of African captives in part to the "change of climate" they experienced when transported across the Atlantic. Incredibly, before the passage explaining African deaths as an effect of climatic difference, Beckford downplayed the change of climate Britons would experience upon crossing the Atlantic. He assured British readers that the "dread of a seasoning" they might feel at the thought of leaving England for the West Indies was actually worse than the change itself. The "impending terror," he explained, produced "imaginary" illnesses that were due less to a change in climate than they were to "the alarm" travelers felt at the prospect of change. In this telling, Britons traveling to the West Indies died of fear rather than any climatic difference.[52]

Beckford, then, wanted to have it both ways. English people "imagined" that they would suffer from a change of climate by traveling to the West Indies when in fact their only danger lay in their imaginations. At the same time, Africans suffered so much from the change of climate that many of them died from the different environment or from exertions of climatic adaptation. Yet Europeans would never be able to stand the climate of the West Indies should they be required to labor, but for Africans, the climate of the West Indies was "con-genial to their natural feelings." Several West Indian planters performed sim-ilar feats of outright contradiction. After years of publishing natural histories that tried to convince Britons of the benign nature of the Caribbean climate, these same planters had to stress how dangerous that climate actually was to Europeans. Bryan Edwards, apparently without a shade of irony or self-con-sciousness, in 1792 published a book containing first, a poetic ode to Jamaica which praised its "fragrant" woods, "salubrious" hills, and pleasant shady valleys and streams, and second, a copy of a speech against the abolition bill which warned of the "baneful effects" of the island's swamps and the dangers of woodland vapors.[53]

On the other side of the debate, physician Robert Jackson used the publica-tion of his medical treatise to share his opinions on abolition. In 1791, the same year he testified before Parliament, Jackson's medical treatise was published, containing advice for "preserving the health of soldiers in hot climates." Jackson had served for nearly a decade as a physician to British soldiers in Jamaica, his work adding to a small but growing corpus of medical literature for British soldiers in hot climates. At the end of his treatise, Jackson included his stance on the question of climate then being debated in Parliament. In Jackson's opinion, those who claimed that Britons could never survive in hot climates had not the slightest inkling of the truth. "An idea has been long entertained," he wrote, "that the European constitution cannot bear hard labour in the sun, or perform mil-itary exercises with safety, in the hot climates of the West-Indies." As a result, the British government had seen fit to provide soldiers with "people of colour to do the drudgery." Jackson was entirely against this policy, believing that it encouraged laziness on the part of soldiers and that part of the job of any good soldier was to become "inured" over time both to the work and to the climate or environment in which he served. Unless the British government was prepared to let people of color fight in the army, Jackson believed their presence was detri-mental to the military's spirit of discipline.[54]

Moreover, Jackson explained that although it was "common opinion" that "the fatigues of an active campaign in the West-Indies, would be fatal to the health of the troops," this opinion had not been given a "fair trial." Indeed, Jackson wrote, contrary to this belief, "an Englishman is capable of sustaining fatigue in the West-Indies, equally well with the African, or the native of the islands." As proof Jackson recounted a three-day, hundred-mile journey he once made across the island of Jamaica on foot. Such a trip, he argued, was incontrovertible evi-dence "that the European constitution is capable of sustaining common military fatigues in the climate of Jamaica." In Jackson's experience, British soldiers, and therefore any well-trained Britons, were entirely capable of physical exertion in the West Indies.[55]

The Implications of Planters' Arguments

Despite the earnest personal accounts of Robert Jackson and John Wesley describing their own ability to withstand severe physical exertion in the heat, and regardless of the testimony of several other witnesses, in April 1791 the House of Commons voted 163 to 88 to continue the slave trade. No matter how compelling these witnesses' testimony, they could not compete with powerful planters who had far-reaching networks, family connections in Parliament, and a great deal of money. In addition, planters who gave testimony on the condition of slavery in the West Indies had a distinct advantage over all but a few abolitionists: they could imbue their arguments with the authority of lived experience. They could claim to know the conditions of Caribbean plantation life in ways that Britons could not. They also had vested interests in seeing the continuation of the slave trade and the institution of slavery in the sugar islands. Although their responses to the Council's questions differed from one another's in several respects, on one particular point all the planters who testified agreed: they argued that white bodies could not stand hard labor in the tropics. The climate simply would not fit their constitutions. And members of Parliament, the vast majority of whom had never visited the West Indies, were inclined to believe them. Although they may have seen the holes in planters' arguments and been persuaded by the economic aspects of the slave trade more than anything else, Britons had been exposed to rhetoric about the dangerously hot climate of the West Indies for centuries, and the climatic argument remained a powerful one.[56]

Without exception, those with significant financial investments in the West Indies insisted that the islands could never be cultivated by anyone other than enslaved Black laborers. For both social and economic reasons, planters believed that African slavery was necessary for the cultivation of West Indian plantations. Still, they knew the value of climatic rhetoric, and in formulating their arguments planters drew upon centuries of climatic lore that presented hot climates as dangerous and debilitating for northern European bodies. By grounding their pleas for slavery in notions of climatic danger, planters appealed to their fellow Britons' sensibilities. Planters, themselves familiar with stories about the dangers of the West Indian climate, counted on the power of the climate's reputation to bolster their case. Significantly, their arguments revealed no coherent sense of racial difference between Black and white bodies. Several slaveholders acknowledged the dangers of fieldwork on plantations, but, as one person wrote, labor in these conditions was "the purpose for which negroes are purchased." In other words, planters in the West Indies deliberately placed Black bodies in dangerous environments and, in fact, they specifically sought Black laborers for these hazardous spaces. This sustained and systematic behavior exemplified environmental racism.[57]

Despite their resounding defeat in Parliament, abolitionists continued their campaign. Planters may have breathed a short sigh of relief upon hearing the outcome of the House of Commons vote, but abolitionists took the opportunity to gather steam and to widen their circle of influence. While concerns over abolition took a back seat as the French and Haitian Revolutions erupted across the Atlantic, by the turn of the nineteenth century, some planters, taking note of the abolitionists' resurgence, expressed deep concern for the future of sugar plantations. Planters had both insisted upon the climatic dangers for European laborers in the Caribbean and explained to the Privy Council the class and color divide in plantation societies.[58]

They had also propagated and internalized these divisions themselves. For example, managers sometimes wrote to absentee planters informing them that a white acquaintance who had fathered a child with an enslaved plantation laborer wished to purchase the child. These managers nearly always counseled the planter to sell because a lighter-skinned child would be socially unfit for field labor. As one manager in Jamaica explained to his employer, a neighboring man "has offered me two prime slaves for a brown girl and a son of his . . . . The two negroes that I will receive will be able people and capable of doing field work," while the man's son and daughter had never worked. The girl, he wrote, was "nearly white" and thus would only ever do housework, and the boy was "so near white that he will not be of use to the property." Another manager in Antigua advised his employer to consent to the proposed sale of his "girl child by a Mulatto Woman." The child in question, the manager wrote, was "of so fair a complexion, that she can hardly be made anything of but a sempstress." As plantation correspondence made clear, these labor restrictions resulted from social and racial divisions in plantation societies. Climate could not be the issue; many planters pointed out the distinction between enslaved creoles and native Africans, emphasizing that because creoles experienced "no change of climate" they were "of course more highly valued" than Africans. But this high value decreased significantly if they had enough European blood that they looked too light-skinned for field labor; in those cases, the people in question considered themselves exempt, as did everyone else, by virtue of their color. Because of the social classes planters themselves had worked to create, and because of the arguments they spread through pamphlets, by the end of the eighteenth century slaveholders had no alternative labor force. The threat of ending the slave trade signaled the end of an era of planter prosperity built on slavery.[59]

* * *

Although planters had advocated vociferously for African slavery in their testimony, arguing that Europeans would never be able to survive labor in the West Indian climate, their private writings told a much more complicated story. Rather than believing that Africans naturally suited the West Indian climate, planters universally acknowledged the need for a seasoning period, to the climate as well as to labor. They also noted high rates of illness among enslaved people, which they thought was due to climatic conditions. Planters acknowledged that enslaved peoples' exposure to the elements either through field labor or insufficiently insulated homes compounded environmental factors in causing illness. Rather than believing that Europeans could not labor in the West Indies at all, planters reacted to a dwindling supply. As Simon Taylor put it in one letter from 1793, "we cannot gett a sufficiency of white people from England or Scotland." Those who did arrive demanded high wages, which planters proved reluctant to pay.[60]

While combating the climate arguments, some abolitionists laid bare the virulent racism and resolute economic mindset that underlay planters' arguments. Some writers, for instance, argued that, although Europeans had suffered in the past from clearing land in the islands, Africans had not fared any better. By pointing to the similar deadly consequences that both Africans and Europeans faced in clearing land in the West Indies, abolitionists forced planters to admit, as one did anonymously, that they saw Africans as undeserving of the same health considerations as free white people. Yet by the early nineteenth century the outlook for planters reliant on only the darkest-skinned laborers looked increasingly dim. Plantation correspondence reveals slaveholders' growing desperation as prospects for abolition of the trade began to intensify. Planters seemed to have backed themselves into a corner. Arguing, as some did, that it was "absolutely impossible" for the sugar islands to exist without the African slave trade left planters in a difficult position as abolitionist fervor grew on both sides of the Atlantic.[61]

Meanwhile, politicians in the United States followed the Parliamentary hearings closely. The transatlantic slave trade had paused during the Revolution, and only some states had reopened it. Not surprisingly, those states most in favor of maintaining the trade lay in the plantation South. Representatives from these states were anxious to preserve the trade, although they were not as reliant upon it as were West Indian planters because the United States had a significant and self-sustaining population of enslaved Black laborers already. But planters continually wanted more enslaved laborers as they tried to increase their own wealth, and, like their West Indian counterparts, they saw the potential abolition of the trade as a first step toward a more general emancipation. Most importantly, the Parliamentary reports from slaveholders had articulated a rhetoric about climate and labor that Americans could turn to as a shorthand in their defense of racial slavery. While planters' testimony was not the first time this rhetoric appeared, it was the most sustained, vigorous, and unified expression of it, both verbal and written, and it had a lasting impact.

6

The Place of Black Americans

Rhetoric and Race in the Nineteenth Century

In the late eighteenth century, debates over the slave trade solidified a rhetoric of climate and race across the Anglo-Atlantic world. While underlying theories of climate and bodily difference had long been available to slaveholders and others, threats to the slave trade caused planters to draw upon these theories heavily and repeatedly. As they did so, slavery's defenders effectively condensed an imprecise and indefinite sense of bodily difference into a language of race. Planters justifying racial slavery insisted that white bodies could not labor in the heat and that only Black bodies could cultivate lucrative plantation crops. This notion became ingrained in public consciousness on both sides of the Atlantic and established itself as a maxim in the new United States.

From the earliest sessions of Congress at the turn of the 1790s through the aftermath of the Civil War in the 1860s, defenders of slavery repeatedly invoked this tenet of race, climate, and labor to uphold racial slavery in the United States. Slaveholders' demands for laborers held in bondage led them to justify the practice of racial slavery by insisting that Black bodies could endure hot climates and white bodies could not. Although the climatic argument was not the only way that planters defended racial slavery in the American South, it was essential to increasing white convictions of biological bodily differences between Black and white people. The implication of planters' arguments was straightforward: if each body only suited a particular climate, then those bodies must be different internally as well as externally.

During the nineteenth century, the climatic argument emerged repeatedly in a variety of changing political and social contexts in the United States. Slaveholders, politicians, activists, journalists, and others used this argument when it served their interests, often relying on it to do various kinds of symbolic work. Those seeking to maintain slave labor on southern plantations drew upon the climatic argument to warn of economic devastation and a regional, even

The Nature of Slavery. Katherine Johnston, Oxford University Press. © Oxford University Press 2022.
DOI: 10.1093/oso/9780197514603.003.0007

national, collapse of civilization should racial slavery be abolished. According to this narrative, those who supported ending slavery would contribute to the deaths of white people, who would be forced to labor in an inhospitable, deadly climate. In this portrayal, racial slavery was essential to the very foundation of the United States, and without it the nascent nation would fail. Both white and Black Americans also engaged the climatic rhetoric to promote or, alternatively, to resist colonization schemes that called for Black Americans to leave the country. At the same time, Black Americans considering emigration referenced the climatic argument to advertise as well as to cast doubt on potential new homes abroad, most notably those in Canada and the Caribbean. Black Americans' engagement with climatic language in these cases demonstrates its pervasiveness throughout much of the nineteenth century. Whether or not they subscribed to it—and most Black Americans did not—the climatic language was ubiquitous.

In addition, white politicians used the climatic argument to sanction the extension or rejection of slavery. As the U.S. government forcibly appropriated increasing amounts of territory from Indigenous peoples, Congressional debates raged over which of these areas would endorse slaveholding as they became states. Politicians in these cases sometimes represented the rhetoric of climate and slavery as a supposed law of nature. The "great climatic law," as one politician put it, dominated some of the most heated debates over the extension of slavery. By naturalizing theories about climate, labor, and bodies, slaveholders and politicians both supported slavery and promoted ideas of biological race.[1]

Ironically, in the aftermath of the Civil War, those who had relied upon the climatic rhetoric to bolster and safeguard racial slavery found themselves backpedaling, sometimes making entirely contradictory claims. Former slaveholders fearing a labor shortage on their plantations directed their energies toward encouraging white immigrant labor, primarily from western and northern Europe. To do so, they had to deny the climatic rhetoric that had become part of a common parlance. Yet thanks to the efforts of slaveholders, the climatic argument had become an axiom too difficult to dislodge.[2]

At heart, many of these discussions revolved around the central question of the place of Black Americans in the United States. These debates had begun long before the nation's official founding, and from the moment of its inception, white, and sometimes Black, Americans debated the legal, political, social, and physical place of Black people in the country. Some white people maintained that Black people should be enslaved and that they belonged in the American South. Others argued that they did not belong in the United States at all. Black Americans themselves had a voice in these discussions. Some rejected essentialist racialized language about climatic determinism, while others pondered the merits of various climates for their bodies. Overall, they did not reach a consensus on their place in a racist country.

These examples are just some of the ways the climate argument appeared from the late eighteenth through the mid-nineteenth century. Their variety and regularity show the extent to which the climatic rhetoric permeated a general consciousness in America. It was a shortcut, a tool that people used to support a range of causes. Ultimately, a rhetoric that developed in the eighteenth-century Atlantic for a specific purpose affected politics in the United States and shaped the lives of people living there. These episodes demonstrate the pervasiveness, prevalence, and insidiousness of the climatic racial rhetoric in the nation through the Civil War era. Assumptions about climates and bodies surfaced repeatedly during this period, both explicitly and implicitly, in a variety of formats. Examining just some of the ways that people used climatic language to do ideological work shows the deeply ingrained nature of this rhetoric in the United States through much of the nineteenth century.

Georgia Revisited

In March 1790, members of the first United States Congress prepared to answer a petition submitted by Pennsylvania abolitionists. The petitioners had called on Congress to consider abolishing the Atlantic slave trade, and Congress had convened a special committee to answer the petition. The Congressional response encapsulated and foreshadowed the nature of similar debates over the legal place of Black Americans that would play out in Congress and in the country as a whole during the ensuing three quarters of a century. Although most states had not reopened the transatlantic slave trade after its suspension during the American Revolution, the Congressional committee rejected the petition. A clause in the Constitution stated that the government could not prohibit the Atlantic slave trade until 1808 at the earliest, and the committee adhered to that provision. Despite the committee's definitive answer, a handful of legislators grew alarmed that Congress would even bother to respond to the petition at all, fearing that an answer showed a willingness to engage with the issue of slaveholding. In their view, the future of slavery itself could soon be at stake. Ignoring the warnings of some fellow southerners that a passionate defense would only draw unwanted attention to the subject of slavery, Representative William Loughton Smith of South Carolina felt compelled to deliver a lengthy address to his fellow members of Congress defending slavery.

For Smith, any threat to racial slavery was an existential threat to his region and, eventually, to the entire nation. His argument turned on the question of climate. His state, Smith announced, could "only be cultivated by slaves; the climate, the nature of the soil . . . forbid the whites from performing the labor." Continuing the arguments that would prove to be successful in maintaining the slave trade in a Parliamentary vote in Britain the following month, Smith insisted that the institution of slavery was essential to the southern economy. South Carolina had reopened the transatlantic trade, and then closed it again in 1787, and the growing clamor of abolitionists made Smith fear for the future of slavery. If slavery were abolished, he warned, emancipated people would never choose to stay on their plantations to cultivate crops. Therefore, he continued, if emancipation were to take place, "the whole of the low country, all the fertile rice and indigo swamps will be deserted, and become a wilderness." This was a dire prediction; white Americans viewed "wilderness" as the antithesis of civilization. Despite clear evidence of Indigenous people cultivating crops in North America, generations of white settler-colonists justified their appropriation of Indigenous land in part through a model of ownership based on their aggressive cultivation and "improvement" of that land. According to Smith, if slavery were to end, the uncultivated South would become a deserted, wild place symbolizing the downfall of Euro-American sovereignty over the land. Beyond the localized wilderness Smith predicted, the entire U.S. economy would suffer as the "great staple commodities of the South would be annihilated without the labor of slaves." Smith's argument in favor of slavery repeated planters' claims in the concurrent debates across the Atlantic: warm climates necessitated enslaved Black laborers, and without these laborers crop production would evaporate and entire economies would be shattered.[3]

Smith articulated a view of climate, slavery, and bodily difference that would have been familiar to his listeners. He maintained that the lowcountry climate excluded any possibility of white labor because white bodies could not physically handle the intensity of hard work in hot, humid climates. Moreover, in Smith's view, lowcountry cultivation required forced labor, and slavery was implicitly Black. For Smith, the place of Black Americans was clear: they should be enslaved, and they should cultivate the South for the benefit of white Americans. By using the climatic argument to support slavery, Smith contributed to a rhetoric that separated Black people from white people by insisting that their bodies were physiologically different from one another.

To convince his listeners, Smith referenced colonial Georgia under the Trustees. According to Smith, Georgia's history had definitively demonstrated that the southern lowcountry could "only be cultivated by slaves" because its climate precluded the possibility of white laborers. "Experience convinces us of the truth of this," he elaborated. "Great Britain made every attempt to settle Georgia by whites alone and failed, and was compelled at length to introduce slaves." In Smith's telling, colonial Georgia without slavery had been a failure because white laborers could not stand the climate. This was, of course, a perfunctory interpretation of Georgia's history that deviated significantly from the actual story. It served Smith well, though, because this version of the story appeared to prove that the region could only be cultivated by enslaved Africans and their descendants.[4]

Smith's interpretation was not singular. His fellow South Carolinian, Charles Cotesworth Pinckney, had made similar arguments in the preceding years during the state's debates over the slave trade. Pinckney had claimed that the lowcountry climate "oblige[d]" planters to use Black laborers, and that, as the experience with Georgia had shown, "without them South Carolina would soon be a desert waste." Published histories from the preceding decades confirmed, or informed, Smith's and Pinckney's accounts. In 1768, the writer Oliver Goldsmith explained that in Georgia's early years the climate was "excessively hot, and field work very laborious." The labor, according to Goldsmith, "was too heavy for the White men, especially men who had not been seasoned to the country." The resulting "idleness" on the part of the settlers led to depopulation, a loss of the Trusteeship, and the government's reversal of the "error" of "prohibiting the use of Negroes." In Goldsmith's telling, the hard work involved in clearing and cultivating land in Georgia proved too much for unseasoned white people. In the years since the government had taken control of the colony and allowed white settlers to use enslaved Black laborers, Goldsmith wrote, the colony had begun to recover from "the difficulties that attended its first establishment." Readers of Goldsmith's text might reasonably conclude that slavery had saved the colony.[5]

Other eighteenth-century texts also recounted Georgia's history as one that proved the necessity of Black labor in warm places. One volume, published in 1770, specifically used Georgia's history to defend the transatlantic slave trade and African slavery in the Americas. According to the book, slavery was "a necessary but unfortunate circumstance." The trade and the institution were products of "the unfitness of Europeans" for cultivating plantations in the American South. The "nature of the climate, and of the labour to be performed," wrote historian John Huddlestone Wynne, were such that "no European constitution" could carry out such labor, at least not profitably. Experience offered proof. "By the original settlement of the colony of Georgia," wrote Wynne, "negro-slaves were totally excluded from it; but a very short experience made it appear, that this was an impracticable measure." The lesson of Georgia was clear: "It is certain that Africans, or their descendants, are better able to support severe labour in hot countries than any of European blood," Wynne concluded. For Wynne, Georgia offered proof positive that African slavery was "necessary" on American plantations.[6]

In the following years other historians repeated this story. In 1778 and 1779 several texts recounted Georgia's beginnings, all of them describing the colony's history as doomed from the start. The prohibition on slavery, according to one, "was made without a due attention to the climate and soil of Georgia, and the inconveniencies to which Europeans, unseasoned to the country, must be

exposed in clearing the lands." Another noted the "errors" that "had been com-
mitted in framing the constitution of the colony." Minister Alexander Hewatt
wrote of "the necessity of employing Africans" in the lowcountry, particularly
for laborious tasks like felling forests and cultivating rice. Hewatt, who had
emigrated from Scotland to South Carolina, was not especially sympathetic to
the institution of slavery, but offered Georgia's story as evidence that African
slavery was essential to southern cultivation. The colony's experiment with
European laborers failed, Hewatt explained, because the climate proved "dangerous to European constitutions." Unlike Africans and their descendants,
"whose natural constitutions were suited to the clime," the Georgia colonists of
the 1730s and 1740s "found labor in the burning climate intolerable." All these
interpretations confirmed that Africans and their descendants had bodies well-
suited to the lowcountry climate while Europeans would wither and collapse
in the heat. In Hewatt's telling, the "white people were utterly unequal to the
labours requisite," and only laborers of African descent could prevent the colony
from complete failure.[7]

These simplifications and reworkings of Georgia's history had an impact on
public perceptions not just of the colony's early years, but as lasting justifications
for racial slavery in the American South. In fact, the arguments in these texts did
not actually demonstrate the necessity of continued Black labor, because several
of them mentioned the "unseasoned" European settlers who had first arrived in
the colony. White people born in the lowcountry presumably would not need a
seasoning and would therefore be suited to labor in the region. In addition, some
of the texts that told Georgia's story explained that the issue was actually more
complicated. Goldsmith, for example, pointed out that all of Britain's North
American colonies had originally been "settled without the help of Negroes." In
these cases, he wrote, "The White men were obliged to the labour, and they underwent it, because they then saw no other way." Yet it was human nature, he
wrote, "not to submit to extraordinary hardships" if an alternative presented itself, and when slavery offered European laborers in Georgia "a much more easy
condition," it was inevitable that they would choose it.[8]

The Georgia experiment, then, had not actually demonstrated the "necessity"
of Black laborers in southern climates. Instead, it had shown that white laborers
preferred to force others to work for them rather than performing labor themselves. Nevertheless, in the late eighteenth century those looking to justify racial
slavery overlooked this caveat and reached the apparently obvious conclusion
that warm climates necessitated enslaved African laborers. Although the story
was not that simple, the rhetoric had gained enough traction by the end of the
eighteenth century that slaveholders could present it as such. As politicians
invoked this explanation for racial slavery, and as histories of colonial America
pointed to Georgia's "failed experiment" as an object lesson, the logic seemed

clear enough to white Americans. Even many of those opposed to slavery accepted the idea that dark skin was suited to hot places, and that white labor in those places was impossible.

Smith used a distorted version of Georgia's history to support his argument that Black laborers were essential to the cultivation of southern plantations. As a colony settled by white laborers, Smith argued, Georgia had "failed." This language was deliberate, as Smith attempted to convince his fellow lawmakers that without racial slavery the United States itself might fail. No American Congressman wanted to see the country fall into economic and political oblivion. And Smith had pointed to a powerful piece of history—colonial Georgia did indeed falter before the Trustees allowed enslaved Black labor—to stoke a fear of the new nation's failure. According to this construction of the climatic rhetoric, Black Americans belonged on southern plantations where they were enslaved, and the future of the union depended on Black slavery.

Smith's speech both reflected and helped to establish Georgia's narrative. In the decades following his climatic defense of slavery, advocates of racial slavery in the U.S. South continually argued that white people could not labor in the heat. These arguments became especially intense as the nation grew increasingly divided over the issue of slavery during the nineteenth century, particularly in the years leading up to the Civil War. Just as Smith had done decades earlier, slaveholding planters in mid-century predicted utter economic devastation should slavery end. In doing so, they leaned heavily on the climatic argument. Their language could be vaguely or overtly threatening, as slaveholders insisted on dire consequences for white people if slavery were to be abolished. If southern planters attempted to rely on white labor, defenders of slavery argued, they would be economically ruined, and white people—naturally unsuited to labor in hot climates—would lose their lives.

There are countless examples of slaveholders using this argument to defend racial slavery and, by extension, forced Black labor. One article in a South Carolina newspaper explained in 1857 that white labor in the South was impossible because "the constitution of the white man withers under the fury of a burning sun." Another article in a Georgia paper noted that Black laborers were "more capable than the white man," and an editorial from a newspaper along the Indiana–Kentucky border declared that "the black man is the proper laborer for these hot climes . . . he flourishes under them, while the white man degenerates and dies." In the weeks before the crucial 1860 election, Alabama politician William Yancey explained in a speech to New Yorkers that "No white man" could "work at laborious occupation under the fervid sun of the South," but "the black man" was "fitted for such a climate." Meanwhile, Democratic Vice-Presidential candidate Herschel Johnson defended and reiterated a speech he had delivered four years earlier in which he had declared that the climate of the South was "such that the whites cannot labor." While "the black man" could "live and work in that climate," he asserted, "Labor, in the heat of our Southern sun cannot be endured by the white men." Physicians, too, endorsed this position; one Georgia doctor wrote that "The Southern sun" was "congenial" to the nature of Black people. The "miasmatic atmosphere" that was "breathed with impunity by the negro," he added, was "insalubrious and fatal to the white population." Books as well as newspaper articles and speeches reiterated this claim. One argued that, while white men exposed to the southern sun died, it was a "fact that the African slaves are better adapted to labor" in warm places.[9]

All these speeches and publications repeated and disseminated the climatic rhetoric expressly to preserve racial slavery in the American South. For proslavery advocates, any threat to slavery was a threat to the Black labor force in the South because they insisted that Black laborers would never work if they were not enslaved. In addition, this particular manipulation of the climatic argument focused on white bodies and lives. If enslaved workers were emancipated, the logic went, southern planters would have to turn to white laborers. According to this version of the climatic rhetoric, these white laborers would suffer and die because their bodies would never withstand physical exertion in warm places. Thus, proslavery advocates argued that the end of slavery would pose a direct threat to white lives.

Significantly, in the decade preceding the Civil War, slavery's advocates returned once more to the history of Georgia, or to their rendition of the colony's past. In their urgent defense of racial slavery, mid-nineteenth-century planters repeated the popular portrayal of Georgia under the Trustees as insurmountable evidence that white men could not work in southern climates. In an essay addressed to slaveholders of the South, reprinted in the widely circulated *De Bow's Review* in 1851, Charlestonian E. B. Bryan explained Georgia's history. When the colony began, he wrote, the Trustees prohibited African slavery. But after several years, "It was found impracticable in such a climate, and without African labor, for the colony to flourish" because "White labor was found here to be incompatible with the climate." The "experiment" with white labor, he wrote, had "been fairly tried" and "proved a failure." This apocryphal, or at least incomplete, version of the story was exactly calculated to resonate with white slaveholders. According to this version of Georgia's history, the colony's experiment with white labor had clearly demonstrated the necessity of Black laborers in hot climates.[10]

Others repeated this argument. An article in the Georgia newspaper *Southern Field and Fireside* explained in 1859 that in the colony's early days, "The Europeans who attempted field labor under the hot sun, and debilitating climate of Southern Georgia, soon became exhausted, from their inability to endure it, and gave up in despair." The following year physician Joseph Jones delivered a speech to the cotton planters of Georgia. He presented the history of the colony as proof that "no white man can ever work with impunity in this climate—no race but the African can ever stand the burning heat and fatal miasms of the Rice fields, and of the Cotton fields." If slavery were abolished, he added, "millions" of white southerners would "be brought to absolute poverty and starvation." Following this line of reasoning, without racial slavery white people would experience utter devastation. White laborers would exhaust themselves or perish, and planters would starve with the collapse of their personal fortunes.[11]

These arguments demonstrate the enduring legacy of Georgia's Trustee period up through the brink of the Civil War. More than a century after the Malcontents had successfully established racial slavery in Georgia, slaveholders still relied on their arguments to defend the institution. Just as the Malcontents had themselves calculated their arguments to appeal to white people's "humanity," slavery's advocates made the same calculation over a century later. For slaveholders fearing the imminent dissolution of slavery, it was not enough to argue for Black peoples' ability to labor in warm places. They used the history of Georgia, along with the climatic rhetoric in general, to argue that white people would physically and financially suffer, with potentially deadly repercussions, should racial slavery come to an end.

Georgia's early colonial history, far from being an insignificant blip in the settler occupation of North America, became the default story for defenders of slavery through the nineteenth century. Every time writers or orators repeated the story, they contributed to a notion that Black and white bodies were different because they suited different climates. Writers who repeated Georgia's story, often by directly copying one another, made it seem as though Georgia's history offered proof of racial bodily difference, determined by climate and skin color.

"A Miserable Pretence": Colonization and Emigration

Black responses to this climatic rhetoric are not easy to discern. A lack of sources makes it difficult to determine the opinions of most Black inhabitants of plantation societies during the eighteenth century, although it seems safe to assume that Black people did not view white people's climatic arguments as reasonable justifications for racial slavery. Slave narratives, the most widely available form of written material recounting the experiences of formerly enslaved people during the late eighteenth and nineteenth centuries, focus on personal accounts and do not engage with planters' rhetorical defenses of slavery. By the nineteenth century, though, free Black Americans, particularly in the North, had begun to publish newspapers. These newspapers, written by and for Black Americans, are a valuable source for understanding the opinions of at least one subset of Black Americans during the nineteenth century. In most of these newspapers, the climatic rhetoric figured only briefly, but it is worth investigating the moments when it did appear. Although these instances were brief, they were not infrequent.[12]

Black Americans engaged with the climatic rhetoric because it was so pervasive. By the nineteenth century the language about climate and race had become part of an accepted lexicon; whether or not people subscribed to it or believed in it, they encountered it regularly. One of the ways free Black Americans engaged with climatic language was through public discussions about emigration out of the United States. As Black Americans considered whether or not they wanted to leave the country, and where they might want to go, they encountered tropes about race and climate. The question of emigration was bound up with the issue of colonization, or the idea that Black Americans should start a colony in Africa or Central or South America. The colonization movement operated under the assumption that formerly enslaved people could never live in harmony with their former enslavers and, more broadly, that Black and white populations could not exist together on equal footing. White proponents of colonization concluded that it would be better for both Black and white Americans if formerly enslaved peopled settled elsewhere. Although some Black Americans chose to leave the oppressive racism in the United States and try their luck abroad, most saw colonization schemes as racist attempts to exile them from their native land. Often proponents of colonization and other types of emigration used climatic language to advertise their ideas. Just as importantly, those resistant to these schemes used the same climatic language. In each of these cases, climatic rhetoric was central to discussions about the physical place of Black Americans.[13]

The fact that Black Americans themselves used the climatic rhetoric as they advocated for or against emigration demonstrates the extent to which these ideas infiltrated a common parlance and influenced people's actions. The first proposals for colonization gained popularity among some Black and especially among white Americans during the late eighteenth century. Colonization appealed to free Blacks because it offered an escape from white racism, while whites uneasy about living alongside free Blacks saw colonization as a solution to their anxiety. Racial antipathy lay behind much of this white enthusiasm, although some white abolitionists genuinely seem to have believed that their fellow white Americans would never treat Black Americans as equals and that free Blacks would be better off in a society without persistent and endemic racism. Although supporters of colonization were mostly white, one of the most strenuous early advocates was Paul Cuffe, a mariner from New England born to an Akan father and a Wampanoag mother. In the early nineteenth century Cuffe became involved with a group of evangelists who connected him to the founders of Sierra Leone, Britain's experimental free Black colony in West Africa. Cuffe's fervor for colonization grew with his visit, and upon his return he asked President James Madison and the U.S. Congress for funds to support a colony in Africa. At first Cuffe had significant support among free Blacks, especially in Philadelphia and Baltimore, but many Black northerners were not eager to uproot themselves to travel to an unfamiliar place.[14]

In 1816 a group of white enthusiasts formed the American Colonization Society to promote the emigration of Black Americans to Africa, and in 1821 they founded Liberia, directly south of Sierra Leone on the West African coast. Most Black Americans who supported colonization saw an African colony as an opportunity for them to create an American society in Africa, rather than as a way for them to adopt an African identity themselves. But Black support for colonization remained small, with only a few thousand free Black Americans traveling to the beleaguered colony over several decades. Many more believed the colonization scheme in Liberia was yet another forced migration motivated by racism. Some of those opposed to colonization believed that white advocates simply wanted to strengthen the institution of slavery by ridding the United States of free Blacks and that colonization plans undermined abolition movements. These Black writers, activists, and others opposed calls for their exodus repeatedly from the 1820s through the 1850s, viewing colonization as a way to dislodge them and to racially cleanse the United States. Notably, Black Americans resisted the suggestion put forward by white members of the American Colonization Society that they should migrate to Africa because it was their natural climatic home.[15]

In 1850 Frederick Douglass's newspaper *The North Star* ran an editorial condemning colonization. "If any one thing awakens in our inmost soul a detestation more intense and bitter than another, it is the idea that it is necessary to remove the colored man from this land," the piece asserted. The idea that "the colored man cannot prosper here, in the land of his birth, in a climate adapted to his health" Douglass considered "most scandalous and impudent." The climatic element was important here. Rather than embracing an unfamiliar climate in a place they had never been, Douglass pointed out that the climate in which they were born suited Black Americans perfectly well. Douglass reiterated this position across several different newspapers over the years: Black American bodies suited American rather than African climates. As he lamented in an 1858 editorial, American emigrants to Africa would find themselves "in a climate for which they have been unfitted by two hundred years residence in this temperate zone." This argument directly contradicted the essentialist positions of many of Douglass's white American contemporaries, who insisted that Blacks inherited an affinity for heat regardless of their birthplace.[16]

Black Americans opposed to emigration often grew exasperated with the climatic argument. In one editorial appearing in both the *Herald of Freedom* and

The Colored American, the author emphasized the absurdity of sending Black Americans to Africa on the basis that it was their native or natural home. Many Black Americans had been in the United States for generations, the writer pointed out, and some had white slaveholding fathers and grandfathers. Concluding that the "climate is deadly" in Africa, the author stressed that Black Americans had no wish to emigrate there.[17]

The American Colonization Society refuted these objections. Conceding that most migrants would suffer from fevers before they became "acclimated" to Liberia, the writers of an article in the Society's official journal downplayed people's fears. Because Africa was "the birth place of the black man," they wrote, Black migrants would, after acclimation, find themselves well suited to the Liberian climate. Another article claimed that migrants would actually "suffer less in their acclimation" to Liberia than inhabitants of the northern states would if they moved to the U.S. South. A few hedged on the expansiveness of their views, admitting that migrants' health would likely suffer if they relocated from parts of the United States to Liberia. "We wish it not to be understood," wrote the authors of one article, "that we believe colored persons from the northern, and the elevated regions of our middle states, can emigrate to Liberia without exposure to fever, which may, in some instances, prove fatal to life." Some Black Americans would be "exposed to suffering from the climate." More frequently, though, articles expounding upon the benefits of colonization noted the innate suitability of Black people for the Liberian climate.[18]

Black Americans opposed to colonization continued to rebut this argument. One editorial responding directly to a promotional piece for Liberia pointed out that the promoters themselves "tacitly acknowledged that the climate of Africa is one not suited to the constitutions of the mass of the slave population." This particular promotional piece had repeated a common suggestion at the time: that potential migrants spend "a number of years residence in Louisiana and the other southernmost States . . . in order to acclimate them, and prevent risk to their health and lives in Africa." Acclimation in the Deep South was not only undesirable for northern free Blacks, but it also seemed fairly strong evidence that Black Americans did not suit African climates merely by nature of being Black. Other anti-colonization pieces wrote of the "direful climate" in Liberia or the "unhealthy and unhospitable climate" in West Africa, where migrants would "find their graves far away from the land of their birth." One Liberian migrant, upon returning to America, "alluded to the extreme heat and unhealthfulness of that climate, the frightful mortality existing there among emigrants, rendering it nothing else but a magnificent grave yard to persons born in this climate."[19]

As these comments demonstrate, it was a white fiction that the climate in Africa would somehow naturally suit Black Americans. White proponents of colonization declared that moving to a hot place would be the best solution for free Blacks, but Black Americans themselves saw this reasoning as fraudulent. For them, suitability for a particular climate was not an inherited trait. Instead, people's bodies best fit the climate in which they were born. Notably, this view was more consistent with much of the British writing about climate and bodies around the Atlantic during the colonial period. The concept of seasoning was one of mutability; according to colonial-era white planters and physicians, bodies were adaptable. If people did not relocate, they suited the climate in which they were born. In the nineteenth century, Black Americans held this view. In contrast, white Americans embraced theories of biological bodily difference as evidenced by skin color. They vaunted a racialized model that reduced all descendants of Africans, no matter how far removed, to African, rather than American.

Apart from the various colonization schemes promoted by white Americans, Black Americans themselves considered migrating to other places. Haiti held considerable promise as a free Black republic, and during the 1820s more than 8,000 Black Americans emigrated there. But this wave of migration flagged after discouraging reports, and many of the migrants, frustrated with cultural and social differences on the island, returned to the United States. While some Black Americans remained opposed to the idea of leaving, others sought a place with fewer racist strictures and, most importantly, a place without racial slavery. During the late 1820s and the 1830s, African Americans looked both north to Canada and south to Mexico and, after emancipation in the 1830s, to the British West Indies. Advocates of Canada faced considerable skepticism, in large part because Black migrants had traveled there before. After the American Revolution, a group of Black Loyalists settled in Nova Scotia, only to face racism and other difficulties, including a climate inhospitable to farming. Many of these Loyalists later left for Sierra Leone, although they fared poorly there, and alarming numbers of people died in part from, in one person's words, "the unhealthiness . . . of the climate." But as increasing numbers of potential migrants weighed their options, they began to seriously consider both the West Indies and parts of Canada. In each case they sought advice about the climate.[20]

As handfuls of migrants began moving to these places, newspapers eagerly awaited reports to deliver to their readers. In early April 1840, Charles Bennett Ray, the editor of the New York paper *The Colored American*, informed his readers that, although he was still waiting for reliable reports from Black Americans in the Caribbean, he worried that "there may be too much summer, for people from this climate." Planters in the British West Indies who had lost much of their labor force after emancipation sought alternative sources and encouraged free Black Americans to immigrate, especially to Trinidad and Jamaica. A week later Ray wrote that he had "received intelligence from Trinidad" and was eager to share the opinions of Mr. Walker, a man who had gone to "investigate matters" before uprooting his family from New York. Walker's report was not promising. Notably, his first objection to Trinidad was "the unhealthy state of the climate." According to Walker, Black Americans could not perform field labor and "bear up under the climate" in the West Indies. In his estimation, "most of the emigrants that went, or all of them" were "sickly and extremely dissatisfied and disheartened." Walker reported that those emigrants would return to the States if they could save enough money for their passage, but that the labor conditions in Trinidad were so poor that saving that amount was nearly impossible.[21]

The following week Ray printed another article discussing the experiences of Trinidadian emigrants. Aware of the appeal of emigration to a place where slavery was no longer legal, a group of migrants in Trinidad had convened a committee to present the merits and drawbacks of emigration. The committee concluded that "emigration to this place will prove deeply detrimental to the health, happiness, and general prosperity of our American friends." Explaining that the only work available was difficult manual labor, the committee informed potential migrants that "human nature cannot endure such incessant toil in this excessively hot climate." It was not a matter of race, or of Black people in colder places finding their climatic home: laborious work in the West Indian climate was simply too difficult for anyone.[22]

The newspaper also reported on the experiences of migrants to Jamaica, who gave similarly discouraging assessments of the climate. Jamaica's heat was "intense" and "*protracted*," according to the Reverend C. S. Renshaw, who had moved there from the United States in the late 1830s. "You would have to undergo a severe acclimating process," the reverend informed prospective migrants. Noting that enslaved people moving only as far as Louisiana from Virginia "pass through an acclimating that kills many of them," Renshaw pointed out that the change in climate to Jamaica was considerably greater and therefore dangerous. "EMIGRATION TO JAMAICA WOULD RESULT MOST DISASTROUSLY TO THE EMIGRANTS," he warned readers. A few months later the paper ran "The Emigration Scheme," an article about the experience of a migrant who had returned from Jamaica. The migrant, Nancy Prince, had written a pamphlet recommending that Black Americans not emigrate to the West Indies. William Lloyd Garrison's newspaper *The Liberator* reported on Prince's pamphlet, and Charles Bennett Ray at *The Colored American* shared Garrison's conclusions: namely, that "we feel in duty bound to advise such of our colored friends, in this country, as think of emigrating to Trinidad or Jamaica, not to go." Conditions in the island were not good, Ray concluded from various reports, and if migrants chose to go, they would "speedily fall victims to the climate." As these reports show, Black Americans did not hold the same essentialist beliefs as whites about their bodies and warm climates. Their bodies were not suited to the heat of the West Indies, and they were unlikely to survive under the demanding labor conditions there.[23]

Canada also attracted both migrants and questions about the climate. Unlike the West Indies, Canada was cold—and Black Americans, accustomed to hearing that their bodies suited warm places, worried that it might be too cold for them. The climatic racial rhetoric had grown beyond slaveholder and planter circles, and many white physicians, politicians, and abolitionists, among others, adopted versions of it. One article in a medical journal, for example, explained to readers that "a cold climate is unfriendly to the health of a negro," and white abolitionists who supported Black migration tended to adhere to this climatic reasoning. Citing "the healthfulness of the climate" as "a very important consideration" for potential migrants, abolitionist Samuel Allinson thought that Jamaica would be a better option than a cold place because the warm climate would suit Black Americans. Similarly, another abolitionist thought that "the free negroes of America" (presumably those in the southern states) would find the climate of the West Indies "much more suitable to them than the Northern States or Canada." Black Americans, then, understandably felt unsure about whether they wanted to risk their health in a cold place; moving north seemed to go against all the inherited wisdom and climatic rhetoric they had encountered throughout their lives.[24]

Hoping to counteract this belief, some formerly enslaved people living in Canada shared their own stories with Black Americans. Others formed or joined societies to promote emigration to Canada, arguing that the climate was "more congenial" to health than that of Liberia or that it was similar to parts of several northern states. Mary Ann Shadd, who edited the Black Canadian paper *Provincial Freeman*, declared that, despite "the arguments generally promulgated throughout the States, misrepresenting the existing condition of our people and temperature of the climate," the areas on the north shore of Lake Erie were well suited to Black American bodies. Contrary to popular representations, Shadd argued that the climate in Canada, especially in more temperate parts, was entirely fit for Black people.[25]

Some writers portrayed the prevailing climatic rhetoric as a deliberate strategy employed by slaveholding and racist whites. Henry and Mary Bibb declared in their Canadian newspaper that "pro-slavery men" had perpetuated the "falsehood" that Canada was too cold for Black people. "Wherever a white man can live and prosper," they wrote, "a colored man can also, if he is given an equal chance." Meanwhile, Frederick Douglass linked the rhetoric with colonization schemes. "It is said that we cannot prosper in a cold climate," he wrote in January 1849. "There is no truth in the proposition." Black people could live wherever white people could, Douglass asserted during the depths of winter in upstate New York. "The idea that we cannot, is a miserable pretence, got up to afford a pretext for getting us out of this country." Black Americans could and did live in any and every American climate, and Blacks should not listen to any arguments by whites that cold climates were "unfavorable" to Black people. "We must banish all thoughts of emigration from our minds, and resolve to stay just where we are," Douglass concluded. For a number of Black writers, resistance to the climatic rhetoric functioned as an assertion of equality.[26]

The following year, Congress passed the brutal Fugitive Slave Act. This act, which essentially allowed slaveholders *carte blanche* to kidnap free Black Americans living anywhere in the United States, was an assault on the marginal freedoms that Black people had carved out for themselves in pockets of the country. Regardless of the increased danger this legislation posed for all Black Americans, most chose to stay, as one group in Cincinnati put it, in "the spot where our fathers, mothers, sisters and brothers have died." This group stated their position clearly: "we will never voluntarily leave the land of our birth." For them, emigration hewed too closely to colonization, and colonization schemes amounted to an unwanted forced removal from their home country. Some, however, felt differently and began to look anew at prospects of emigration and colonization. This time, both Blacks and whites championed plans for colonization in Central or South America.[27]

One of the most vocal advocates of colonization in these regions was Black activist Martin R. Delany. Delany had been born free in the United States, but grew tired of the overt, persistent racial discrimination he faced wherever he went. As his increasing exasperation turned to activism, Delany began to seriously consider emigration. In 1852, motivated in part by the passage of the Fugitive Slave Act, he published *The Condition, Elevation, Emigration and Destiny of the Colored People of the United States*, in which he promoted Central and South America as "the ultimate destination and future home of the colored race on this continent." Notably, Delany used the climatic rhetoric not as a means to assign Black bodies to particular regions, but rather to argue for the limitations of white bodies and the comparative strength of Black bodies. "Our oppressors, when urging us to go to Africa," he wrote, "tell us that . . . the constitution of colored people better endures the heat of warm climates than that of the whites." In Delany's assessment, this argument was true—but it was not the whole truth. He agreed that Black people withstood heat better than white people, adding that "they also stand *all other* climates, cold, temperate, and modified," better than white people did. According to Delany, then, Black people were therefore "a *superior race*" and could live wherever they chose because they suited all climates on earth.[28]

Although Delany's enthusiasm for colonization in Central America did not cause a mass exodus, his ideas reached the highest echelons of government. White anti-slavery advocates seized upon the vision of starting a colony in Central America, billing colonization as an alternative to slavery. In 1858, Missouri

Congressman Frank P. Blair suggested that a Central American colony of free Black laborers could supply the United States with products grown in warm regions, and once the United States had established a line of supply, slavery would become redundant and disappear. Racial prejudice held an important place in this plan, as Blair admitted no particular desire to live among free Blacks in his home state. Colonization, then, would accomplish two ends: it would thin the ranks of free Black Americans living in the United States, and, as Blair explained to the House of Representatives, it would provide white Americans with a source of tropical produce grown "by the labor of the only class of freemen capable of exertion in that climate." Endorsing this plan, an editorial in *The National Era* suggested that "some enterprising, sagacious black man organize a system of colored emigration" in order to "demonstrate that cotton, sugar, rice, can be profitably raised without slave labor."[29]

A number of white Americans felt these plans were a perfect solution to the problem of slavery and, in their minds, the problem of Blackness in America. Some believed that slavery was wrong, but they could not imagine living among free Black Americans. If Black Americans could just go elsewhere, these white people proposed, they would free white Americans from the social, political, and economic uncertainties of living in a racially mixed society. At the same time, their industry in a faraway colony would demonstrate that free Black laborers could indeed cultivate crops without enslavement. Either through some fantastically optimistic idea that slaveholders would realize that free labor was possible or else by paying free Black laborers so little as to make their crops competitive with those of slaveholding planters, white proponents of colonization predicted that a free Black colony would cause domestic slavery to simply dwindle away.

Speaking in favor of this plan, Wisconsin Senator James Doolittle explained that Central and South America had climates "well adapted to the constitution of the African race." Doolittle saw colonization as a way for free Blacks to escape racism and possible re-enslavement and a way for whites to create a more homogenous society. Doolittle's own state was home to the forced migration of Indigenous peoples both into and out of the region, as the U.S. government continued its violent removal of Indigenous people westward. Yet by the 1850s many white commentators believed that Indigenous people were on the verge of extinction and would thus pose no threat to their imagined white nation. Black Americans, on the other hand, were not yet subjects of a robust narrative of extinction. But just as the U.S. government removed Indigenous peoples from areas of white settlement, so too did government officials flirt heavily with the idea of removing Black Americans from these areas. Indeed, states across the Midwest and, later, the Pacific West, adopted laws segregating and excluding Black residents. In a concerted effort to whiten the country, proponents of colonization argued that Central and South America would be the ideal home for Black Americans because of the climate.[30]

A year into the Civil War, both Doolittle and Abraham Lincoln advocated for colonization in these regions. "The negro is the child of the tropics and of the sun," Doolittle insisted to the Senate in 1862. Temperate climes suited "the Caucasian race," he argued, while "the colored man" fared better in "the torrid zone." For Doolittle, skin color determined where a person should live. The physical place of Black Americans, according to this logic, was outside of the United States. "No laws of Congress or any other legislative power can reverse this great law stamped upon the earth and upon the constitution of man," he added. His reasoning was simple: the "African race" naturally suited hot climates, so Black people should go to the tropics. Abraham Lincoln adopted this same reasoning in his support for colonization. Influenced in large part by Blair's arguments, eight months into the war he recommended that Congress find a way to settle formerly enslaved people "at some place or places in a climate congenial to them." A year later he reiterated this position. "Applications have been made to me by many free Americans of African descent to favor their emigration," he informed Congress at the end of 1862. He had been in contact with "several states situated within the tropics, or having colonies there," he added, to try to open a path for free Black Americans who chose to emigrate. According to the logic of white politicians, even those who did not support slavery, the suitability of different people for different climates was an immutable and inherited condition.[31]

These colonization plans never materialized, however. Black communities across the nation denounced Lincoln's proposal, announcing their desire and intention to remain in the country. Martin Delany abandoned the notion of a Central American colony, preferring first to explore a new colonial venture on the African coast, and eventually settling in Canada. His contemporary and fellow Black activist James Theodore Holly re-introduced Haiti as an emigration haven during the 1850s, and about 2,000 Black Americans moved there between 1859 and 1862. Indeed, following the Supreme Court's 1857 decision in *Dred Scott vs. Sandford*, which denied them U.S. citizenship, Black Americans looked again at the possibility of moving abroad, although most decided to stay.[32]

Regardless of the size of these various waves of interest in colonization and emigration from the early decades of the nineteenth century through the Civil War, the climate remained a significant piece of the rhetoric. Formerly enslaved southerner Lott Cary, for example, who supported colonization in Africa, claimed in 1827 that Black Americans would naturally prefer a warm climate to the "Frigid Zone" of the North. Delany did not directly endorse, though neither did he condemn, the rhetoric about Black bodies, instead writing in 1852 that they were better suited to warm climates than white bodies were because they were so pliable and strong.[33]

Many Black northerners, though, disagreed and argued that Black Americans were no more suited to Africa than white Americans were. At the same time that Cary lobbied for Black southerners to relocate to Africa, the editors of one Black northern newspaper insisted that "The idea that the free population of the North are more fitted to the climate of Africa than the whites, is perfectly futile." It is possible that the differences between these viewpoints could be attributed to regionalism. Almost all the newspapers and other writings by free Blacks were northern in origin, and Black southerners' conceptions of bodies and climate largely went unrecorded. Some free Blacks in the South no doubt feared moving to a cold place. But many did move north, and when they arrived, they found that the climate was not actually deleterious to their health.[34]

The most significant piece of these arguments lies in the fact that Black Americans made use of climatic rhetoric to promote or oppose colonization and emigration. Whether they denounced the rhetoric—as most did—or agreed with it, Black Americans employed this language because it was so familiar and so widespread. The frequency with which it appeared demonstrates how prevalent, pervasive, and inescapable it had become in debates over the physical place that Black Americans occupied. For the most part, Black writers rejected the idea promulgated by whites that Black people naturally suited hot climates and that they suffered in colder places. Some Black Americans saw this argument as an affront to their very presence in the United States, concluding that it was a means to banish Black Americans from the country. Because this "miserable pretence" had long justified racial slavery, it seems almost inevitable that whites would expand the argument to encourage colonization and emigration. But just as white Americans had long used the climatic argument that Black bodies suited hot places, they continued to use the converse of this argument—that white bodies could not labor in these same places—to justify racial slavery as the United States expanded its reach.

"The Manifest Destiny of African Slavery"

In his argument for colonization, Doolittle referred to a "great law stamped upon the earth" that determined where people should live based upon their skin color. This language repeated the rhetoric espoused by white politicians who, in the preceding years, debated the expansion of slavery across the United States. As the federal government encroached onto more and more Indigenous land and the country added territories and states, the issue of slavery divided national politics. For white Americans, political power lay at the heart of the divide; slaveholding states wanted to ensure they would not be controlled by the interests of free states, and vice versa. For Black Americans, of course, the stakes were much higher as the political vitriol determined their lives.

Notably, arguments about climate surfaced repeatedly during the course of these debates. Politicians discussing the admission of a state or territory often considered the region's climate as an indicator of whether or not the place would have slavery. According to their logic, a climate conducive to the production of crops usually grown by enslaved laborers would "naturally" invite slavery, while a place with a different climate would "naturally" discourage or exclude the institution. For many whites, this logic seemed clear and obvious: if a place's climate encouraged the growth of cotton, for example, that place would have slavery. If the climate was too cold or did not support the growth of crops grown by enslaved laborers, there was no reason for that place to have slavery. Yet this logic demonstrated how deeply white Americans had internalized climatic justifications for racial slavery, as well as the implicit assumptions they made about climate, race, and labor. The way in which politicians articulated their arguments about racial slavery—in particular the way they automatically coupled Blackness with labor in warm climates—shows the extent to which they had accepted slaveholders' rhetoric. White Americans in both the North and the South accepted the climatic reasoning as truth.

The longstanding and repeated climatic arguments, in fact, gave rise to the development of a language naturalizing the relationship between race and climate. This rhetoric sanctified the bonds between slavery and climate as a supposed law of nature. By presenting this relationship as natural, white politicians made it appear as though the question of slavery was out of their hands; it was not something that could be regulated by human law, but rather was subject to a different set of laws entirely. By resorting to this language, politicians sought to appease slaveholders and absolve themselves of responsibility for limiting slavery's expansion. At the same time, this rhetoric clarified white views about the "natural" place of Black Americans, away from much of the territory the United States was rapidly seizing from Indigenous peoples and populating with white settlers. Black Americans, on the other hand, rejected this "climatic law" as nothing more than a poor excuse politicians used to release themselves from the responsibility of prohibiting slavery.

When California petitioned for statehood in 1849, its admission to the Union as a free state would have upset the balance of power between free and slave states. At the same time, the U.S. government was debating what to do with the lands taken from Mexico in the recent Mexican–American War. The political battle surrounding the eventual Compromise of 1850 focused on the extension of slavery into these areas. Massachusetts senator and supporter of colonization Daniel Webster argued that the decision about slavery was essentially a moot point for legislators, as it would be determined by the climate. Webster assumed that places with soils and climates unsuited for the production of crops usually grown by enslaved laborers would attract white settlers who would not bring enslaved people with them and who would not support slavery out of their own self-interest. According to this line of reasoning, there was no need for any legislation forbidding slavery because the "laws of nature" in New Mexico and California, both of which had cooler climates in mountainous regions, naturally excluded slave labor. This idea was not new; the same commentary had appeared repeatedly in the debates surrounding the Missouri Compromise in 1820 and continued to emerge as legislators discussed the admission of new territories and states. But this wording further naturalized slavery in warm places. According to this reasoning, neither politicians, abolitionists, nor anyone else could determine the bounds of slavery: it was a law of nature that cold places required white labor while hot places required Black labor—and, in these instances, slave labor.[35]

Politicians across the nation continually used this language while debating the expansion of slavery. James Rollins, who suffered a narrow defeat in his bid for the Missouri governorship in 1857, declared that he would leave the question of slavery "to the laws of climate." The editors of the New York Herald applauded this position, writing that it "teaches us the fundamental laws and the manifest destiny of African slavery." Leaving the future of racial slavery to these "fundamental laws," the paper's editors announced, would relegate "free white labor and black slave labor to their congenial climates." That same year, Governor Robert Walker of Kansas delivered an inaugural address printed in newspapers across the country. Regarding slavery, Walker announced that there was "a law more powerful than the legislation of man . . . that must ultimately determine the location of slavery in this country; it is the isothermal line, it is the law of the thermometer, of latitude or altitude, regulating climate." Northern climates, according to Walker, were "unsuited to the tropical constitution of the negro race" and would therefore naturally not have African slavery. This "great climatic law," Walker continued, determined and would continue to determine the status of slavery in every state. Journalists all over the country commented on this "great climatic law" and the "isothermal line," and Stephen Douglas, the Illinois senator who ran against Lincoln for president in 1860, used this same rhetoric when he explained that slavery would only expand to places where it was suited to the climate.[36]

Black Americans were unconvinced by the climatic reasoning. Unsurprisingly, they did not share the opinion that certain crops required slave labor. But they also did not believe that a "great climatic law" was sufficient to determine the bounds of slavery or to protect against its spread. As for the Compromise of 1850, several Black abolitionists roundly condemned Webster's argument. "What man, endowed with a common share of talents," asked the Black activist

Henry O. Wagoner in a public letter to Frederick Douglass, "would have ventured
to throw out to the scrutiny of the civilized world, such crooked and crippled-up
logic as that of Daniel Webster's on the exclusion of slavery from California and
New Mexico by the geography and climate of those territories[?]" While Webster
triumphantly maintained that these places could never sanction slavery because
plantation crops would not grow, to Wagoner the "silly and simple arguments"
about the climate were absurd and insufficient. The "natural" exclusion of slavery
on the basis of climate alone would not stop slaveholders from bringing enslaved
people to these places. Indeed, Douglass's paper *The North Star* reported in 1849
that white people had already begun leaving the East for California with Black
enslaved laborers in tow. This evidence, Douglass wrote, refuted the "pretence"
that California's climate naturally excluded slavery. For Black activists, the argument that legislation forbidding slavery was "superfluous" because of the climate
was merely a political maneuver.[37]

Several years later, the abolitionist newspaper *The National Era* ridiculed
the same reasoning while responding to Governor Walker's argument about
an "isothermal line" determining the boundaries of slavery. The editors of *The
National Era* wondered aloud about the existence of any natural law sanctioning
slavery at all. They were confident that "The law of temperature, of altitude,
or latitude, does not determine the location of Slavery," they wrote. Slavery
had "existed in all latitudes"; cotton grew in other places in the world without
slavery; and some places that had once had slavery had since abolished it,
demonstrating that there was in fact no "*uncontrollable* climatic law." Moreover,
if Walker believed that Africans and their descendants suited only particular
climates, the southern states were not tropical. "If the negro race be 'tropical' in
its constitution," the editors wrote, "its location *anywhere* in the United States is
against 'the isothermal line'" and "against the law of nature." A few years earlier,
Frederick Douglass's Paper (a later iteration of *The North Star*) had also attacked
the argument about "natural" barriers to slavery in Kansas. Those who believed
this rhetoric, wrote Douglass, "seem not to have learned the fact, that the cu-
pidity of slavery has no respect for climate, or soil, or geographical position."
Wagoner, Douglass, and other Black abolitionists drew attention to the fact that
slavery was not naturally determined; instead, slaveholders made a conscious
decision to hold slaves, and legislators decided upon its legality. As one newspaper pointed out in 1853, claims that Black people were better suited to hot
climates than white people "simply prove the adaptation of the black man's constitution to the climate, but not his fitness for slave labor." Blackness and slavery
were not the same, and arguments that only Black Americans could labor in the
South failed to address the essential issue of enslavement. While some white
northerners might satisfy themselves that they had shored up their own political power by admitting California as a free state, advocates of abolition saw

the argument of a "great climatic law" as affirming and sanctioning slavery in the South.[38]

Other abolitionist publications provided evidence of white people laboring in hot climates in an attempt to show the frailty of the climatic argument. An anti-slavery paper based in London reported on white laborers cultivating sugar in Cuba in 1854, and an Illinois newspaper published an article about whites cultivating crops in Honduras and New Orleans in 1857. The widely-circulated book *The Impending Crisis of the South*, published in 1857, contained reports of white people working in fields all across the South. Reviewing the book, an article in *The National Era* explained that "The idea is generally prevalent at the North, that the climate of the slave States is dangerously hot for white men. The author of this volume charges that this idea is erroneous." While not sympathetic to Black Americans, the book's author rejected the climatic argument as clearly untenable.[39]

Nevertheless, many white northerners as well as southerners tended to accept the theory of a "great climatic law." In some places, newspaper articles addressed northern white laborers' fears of potential competition from free Blacks using this same language. These articles promised white laborers that they need not fear competition because Black Americans would never choose a cold climate. "If liberated, negroes would not come North," the editors of one Connecticut newspaper assured their readers, "because they especially dislike a cold climate .... Their natural affinities are for the tropics." Other articles repeated this theory. "*Emancipation will bring no colored laborers to the North*," emphasized an article in the New York *Independent*. "The colored man is the creature of the tropics, and all his aptitudes fit him for a warm climate. Even the temperate zones are not temperate to his heat-loving constitution . . . he is fitted by nature for tropical latitudes." The article, which was reprinted in several other northern papers, reassured its readers that there would be no labor competition, although it was not convincing enough to stop white laborers in New York from rioting over their fear of Black migrants. Some papers went so far as to claim that if slavery were abolished, free Blacks in the North would actually move to the South so that they could be in a warmer climate. The language about climate was ubiquitous: white northerners and southerners alike subscribed to the "great climatic law" in various degrees. Even Black writers, who more often than not rejected this theory, still felt the need to engage with the climatic rhetoric because it was so pervasive.[40]

There were a few white politicians who pointed to the faulty premise of these arguments. Congressional representatives from Pennsylvania, for example, argued in January 1820 that there was no logical reason to expand slavery "over the boundless regions of the west" because the region's climate offered "none of the pretexts urged for resorting to the labor of natives of the torrid zone." While this claim still engaged with the climatic argument—the climate in the West was not conducive to crops grown by enslaved laborers—the notion that planters' arguments were a "pretext" is a notable departure from most politicians' acceptance of this notion. Just as Black Americans opposed to colonization had called the idea that Black people could not live in cold places a "pretext" for their removal, the Pennsylvania representatives also operated under the assumption that the climatic argument was a pretext for slavery. But this was a minority view. For the most part, white politicians in both the North and the South operated under the guise of a climatic law, beholden only to nature, that would determine the country's bounds of racial slavery.[41]

The language of climate, slavery, and nature was ubiquitous, even finding its way into Mississippi's statement of secession. The announcement in early January 1861 was short but telling. "Our position is thoroughly identified with the institution of slavery," it began. Mississippi's chief economic export was cotton, a product grown with slave labor, and one "peculiar to the climate verging on the tropical regions." Through "an imperious law of nature," the statement continued, "none but the black race can bear exposure to the tropical sun." According to Mississippi's politicians, the state's crops grew in a climate in which only Black people could labor. As they made their reasons for secession public, Mississippi's politicians enshrined the rhetoric of race and climate into the most powerful political statement since the state's formation. In doing so, they affirmed the potency of the climatic argument for racial slavery.[42]

During the Civil War the climatic rhetoric remained mostly unchanged. According to the logic of white politicians, even those who did not support slavery, the suitability of different people for different climates was an immutable and inherited condition. Politicians portrayed the link between climate and skin color as grounded in nature and beyond human control. Although abolitionists pointed out that in fact there was nothing whatsoever uncontrollable about slavery, white politicians continued to present their own helplessness in the face of a supposedly naturally ordained condition. Despite Black activists' clear arguments that no climate would automatically prevent white people from enslaving Black people, and that slavery was an institution entirely regulated by human laws, for much of the war both northern and southern whites continued to believe in this "great climatic law."

"Mistaken Ideas and Prejudice"

The abolition of slavery resulting from the Civil War sparked a dramatic shift in the climate rhetoric. Slaveholders who had leaned upon climatic language to justify their use of enslaved Black labor found themselves having to attract laborers to their plantations, and many were unsure of how to do so. In the wake of the Civil War, then, advocates of slavery performed an astonishing turnabout in their use of the climatic rhetoric. Instead of leaning heavily on it to bolster their defense of racial slavery, they disavowed it as they tried to lure white laborers to southern plantations. Planters who had strenuously argued that Black laborers were the only possible workers in the South swiftly denounced this characterization. These planters sought white laborers and attempted to assure them that the southern climate was mild and congenial to white bodies. Some of the more embittered southerners even portrayed the climatic rhetoric as the erroneous work of vitriolic northerners. In this depiction, the place of Black Americans had become ambiguous: according to southern planters, labor in the South was no longer the exclusive space of Black people.

As the war ended, journalists, politicians, and former slaveholders articulated their uncertainty in a time of change. One article, published in several southern newspapers in the summer of 1865, pointed out the deeply ingrained climatic rhetoric as the author posed the question of white labor on plantations. "The belief has been promulgated and acted upon for many years that the rice, cotton, and sugar fields of the South can be successfully cultivated only by negroes; the climate there being too hot for laboring white men," wrote the article's author. "The period is now rapidly approaching when the soundness of that belief will be fully tested." Despite generations of planters insisting the opposite, could whites labor in the southern heat after all? To encourage white workers, some newspaper editors published pieces insisting that white labor in the heat was entirely feasible. "We have been accustomed to believe, without questioning," wrote the editor of the *Houston Telegraph* in 1865, that whites could not live and labor in southern climates. "The theory that white men cannot stand the enervating heats of this climate has, we are told, been disproved most completely." It turned out, he clarified, that white people performed outdoor manual labor in cities across the Gulf South, so "we urge upon the people to dismiss all such unprofitable ideas as that white man cannot stand the Texas sun or breathe the Texas air and live. What good can possibly come," the editor asked, "from the acceptance of any false doctrine, and especially one so manifestly absurd and demonstrably false as this?" The editor's words are striking: by calling the idea that white men could not labor in hot places "manifestly absurd" and "demonstrably false," he implicitly questioned the defense of slavery that slaveholders had used for decades. Given that slavery was no longer legal, the Texas editor suggested that it would be prudent to abandon the "false doctrine" of climate and race because these ideas had become "unprofitable."[43]

The *Savannah Republican*, a Georgia newspaper taken over by the Union army late in the war and edited by Massachusetts journalist John E. Hayes, shared this editorial with its readers. Hayes pointed out—with notable sarcasm—that the

Telegraph editor had apparently experienced a "change of position." "If we mistake not," wrote Hayes, the editor of the *Telegraph* "was one of the most earnest adherents, at one time, of the doctrine that a white man could not, with health or success, cultivate Southern staples or do out-door labor here." It was not difficult to find a reason for the editor's "change of position." White employers across the South wanted to attract white migrant laborers and desperately needed to alter the prevailing rhetoric.[44]

Other articles also advocated for white labor in the South. In 1866, one reported that, although "it has been argued" that "the Southern climate is too hot for white labor," it turned out that white laborers cultivated cotton, rice, and tobacco in hot places abroad, and that in the states "it has since been proved that white labor will do in a number of the cotton raising regions." Another article lamented that "mistaken ideas and prejudice have turned aside from the South the great current of white labor," because "It has been maintained that white labor cannot produce cotton, and cannot live in such a climate as ours." The author of this article, which was published in a Georgia paper in March 1866, maintained that "The very reverse of this is proved by the fact that thousands of tenderly nurtured Southern men, marched, fought, and dug ditches under the very suns where it is said a white man cannot hoe a cotton field." For this article's writer, the experience of white men fighting in the Civil War counteracted any misgivings about white labor in the climate. If white men could march and fight on southern soil, surely they could cultivate it, too. Another article addressed readers still unsure of the prospect of white labor. The writer, a prominent southern physician who believed that Blacks and whites were two different species, explained that whites could easily cultivate cotton, sugar, tobacco, and even rice, because unlike Blacks whose bodies only suited tropical climates, whites had "a higher degree of *pliability* of constitution" and would adapt to southern climates. In other words, even if whites needed to adjust, their bodies were certainly capable of doing so. Notably, this explanation assured readers of the superiority of white bodies over Black bodies because of their greater capacity for adaptation.[45]

Remarkably, an essay addressed to the Georgia Convention of Planters in the fall of 1866 attributed the climate argument to Northern enemies of the South. "Northern speakers and newspapers," claimed the writer, had "produce[d] the conviction . . . that the South [was] no country for white laborers." The writer argued that this idea was a malicious misrepresentation. "It has been said at the North, and I have heard Southern men join in that opinion, that a white man cannot labor in our climate," he announced, adding that this was obviously untrue because white people had labored and continued to labor there. Even more incredibly, the writer turned to the history of Georgia as evidence. Unlike the other references to the history of Georgia in the years leading up to the Civil War, this writer chose to highlight a different part. Instead of relying on the arguments of the Malcontents, the writer pointed to the testimony of "the German and Highland settlers." He quoted letters from the Salzburgers, who had explained that they worked until ten in the morning and then again in the afternoon, with a midday break. Arguing that this testimony was "very strong," the writer suggested that white laborers—especially Germans—could labor in the South.[46]

These articles demonstrate a spectacular reversal of southerners' positions on the possibility of white labor. There was nothing particularly mysterious about this reversal. While slavery was legal, it was in planters' best interest to exploit unpaid, forced labor, so defending it made sense to them. Once racial slavery was no longer an option, planters wanting to entice laborers tried to convince whites that the climatic argument had all been a ruse (or at least a mistake). As it happened, planters continued to rely overwhelmingly on Black workers to labor on plantations. Nevertheless, the abrupt change in the rhetoric was a bold if desperate move as it seemed to undercut nearly a century's worth of unwavering climatic arguments for racial slavery. Georgia's history underwent a stark revision as planters no longer used it to justify slavery but instead suddenly altered it to demonstrate the feasibility of white labor in the South. Sometimes the authors of articles downplayed the novelty of white manual labor in southern climates. The writer of one 1866 article, for instance, assured his readers that white labor was "no new thing in the South." He wrote that he had worked "at all hours through the hottest of South Carolina summers" and that "the same has been done by thousands of Northern men" for years. For southern slaveholders, the challenge was to convince potential white laborers that the southern climate was no obstacle to working on their plantations after all.[47]

That challenge proved difficult to meet. Not only was the climatic rhetoric about the incompatibility of white bodies for warm climates so strong as to be almost overwhelming, but former slaveholders also had to combat social obstacles to white labor. Under slavery, white laborers who had attempted to work in the South found themselves confronting a deeply rooted hierarchical system, one in which many white planters preferred enslaved laborers. In 1845, for example, a Baltimore paper printed an article about a group of northerners who had gone to Virginia to work as farm laborers. Discouraged, the workers were returning north, the reporter wrote, "so strong is the influence of the odium resting on white labor." In this case, white workers found themselves pushed out by a system that ostensibly had no place for them. In other cases, white laborers themselves proved too averse to engage in work they considered to be slave labor. In 1848, during an address of the Free Soil Central Committee in Maryland, the speaker explained that it was "a fact known throughout all slave countries, that the free white man engages with great reluctance in that labor which can be, and generally is, performed by slaves." Encouraging white migration westward, the speaker noted that migrants to "the new and uncultivated territories, shall not there meet with slave labor to depreciate and degrade his own." The idea that slave labor "depreciated" and "degraded" free labor was a common refrain. In an 1853 lecture on white migration, a different speaker admitted that slavery was "a serious barrier to white immigration in the South. Free labor is too proud to mingle its labor with slave labor." According to this speaker, this pride accounted for the "sparse" white migration to the South.[48]

After the Civil War, former slaveholders in the South continued to confront barriers to white immigration. Social obstacles, coupled with continued misgivings about the southern climate, made potential migrants reluctant to pursue labor opportunities. Although slavery had been abolished, many planters turned to formerly enslaved people to fulfill their labor needs, and Black workers predominated in most places. But in some cases, Black laborers left plantations, and planters tried desperately to fill the resulting labor gaps. German workers were in particularly high demand, and several southerners spoke or wrote in favor of encouraging German immigration. But they felt frustrated by the tendency of Germans, along with Scandinavians, to move to "the West"—primarily Wisconsin and Minnesota—instead of settling in the South. Several former slaveholders feared that the climatic rhetoric had helped to deter potential immigrants from moving to the South.[49]

One article in the October 1867 issue of *DeBow's Review*, for example, expressed anger over "the persistent misrepresentations" of the South in Europe. Agents recruiting European migrants for the "Western States," the article alleged, had represented the South as "uniformly unhealthy," a place where almost every migrant would die either from acclimatization "or from the heat of the sun." These "agents" reported that "none but Africans can bear the exposure in the field," a characterization that indignant southern planters lamented as deterring migrants. Some planters turned to migrant workers from parts of South and East Asia, as West Indian planters had also done in the years following emancipation. Still, many continued to seek European laborers, but felt thwarted by the widespread reputation of the southern climate.[50]

In the wake of the Civil War, then, defenders of slavery disowned and refuted the climatic rhetoric because it had become antithetical to their purposes. After having leaned on it for so long to support racial slavery, former slaveholders and others quickly sought to distance themselves from the argument that white people could not labor in hot places. They tried instead to delegitimize the climatic rhetoric, claiming that it was a fabrication promoted by northerners and by European labor agents that held no basis in truth. Southern plantations, they argued, were actually perfectly healthy for white laborers. In an unexpected twist, one writer replaced the supposed suffering of colonial white laborers in

Georgia's early history with the success of the Salzburgers in order to attract Germans to the American South. This attempt to revise the history of Georgia, however, was a feeble contrast to the selective interpretations of the colony's history that earlier planters had used to buttress slavery. So too were former slaveholders' assurances that the southern climate was hospitable to white laborers. Most white immigrants went north and west, although some southern planters still tried to attract them by presenting the climatic rhetoric as an insidious falsehood.

* * *

The continuing significance of the climatic rhetoric in the nineteenth century revealed itself in multiple and varied ways related to the politics of slavery and race in the United States. While the climatic argument in defense of slavery may be familiar, placing it in the context of the larger Atlantic story shows the ways in which this rhetoric developed and spread over time. Different groups of people in nineteenth-century America manipulated the climate argument in slightly different ways as they attempted to impose or resist a racial hierarchy. Martin Delany, for example, argued that Black people's ability to labor in the heat, as well as in all other climates, demonstrated their racial superiority, and after the Civil War a white physician made the same argument about white bodies.[51]

Although on the surface the climate rhetoric may seem straightforward, politicians, journalists, physicians, and others exploited it to make subtly different arguments. Some used it to defend racial slavery by proposing alternatives dire to white imaginations: the certain death of white laborers, and/or an uncivilized wasteland. Both scenarios were calculated to raise fears of white Americans who hoped to assert their dominance over other people and over enormous spaces. If southern plantations became deserted wilderness, as Congressman Smith predicted in 1790, whites would be driven from the South instead of expanding across it. If white laborers died in high numbers from working under an intense sun, the white population would diminish. Each of these portrayals threatened the white nation that many white Americans imagined and tried to build by massacring and removing Indigenous and Black populations.

The racialized climatic language that supported the enslavement of Black people in the American South also helped propel colonization schemes encouraging the removal of Black Americans from the United States altogether. The argument that Black bodies belonged in tropical climates encouraged their exile from white society. This language, of course, was a bizarre reconceptualization of North America for white people, who tried hard to eliminate the region's actual inhabitants—who were not white—from the land. But as white Americans comforted themselves that Indigenous people would soon disappear altogether, they had difficulty imagining the place of free Black Americans. Their removal from the United States seemed an easy answer for whites anxious to reimagine the nation as a place for white people. Thus, the story of Georgia changed from one in which whites were utterly unable to labor in the heat to one in which industrious white laborers could easily reap harvests from the fertile lowcountry soil. The first version justified racial slavery before the Civil War, while the second version sought to encourage white migration—and the strengthening of an imagined white nation—afterward.

At the same time, situating the antebellum climatic rhetoric within a broader and longer Atlantic context demonstrates that there was nothing exceptional about American slaveholders' defense of racial slavery. Nineteenth-century white planters were not the first to make these claims, nor were they drawing upon established experience. It would be a mistake to conclude that their arguments were grounded in the experiences of former generations. Instead, as the post-bellum material so clearly reveals, the rhetoric slaveholders employed was, in the words of one newspaper editor, "manifestly absurd and demonstrably false." Earlier reports of white laborers working in Latin America, as well as in the American South, were not difficult to obtain as abolitionists enthusiastically promoted them. But racial slavery was ingrained in the South, established as an economic and cultural institution that planters had no intention of relinquishing without force. In some ways, the climatic argument was not the issue at hand: much deeper forces rooted racial slavery in American plantations. Yet planters still repeated the language about race and climate. In the end, this rhetoric served slaveholders not because it had any material grounding but because it was repeated so often as to become a maxim. Presented as a truism, the racialized climatic rhetoric provided a veneer for the brute force of slavery.[52]

Climatic language featured substantially in debates over slavery, as well as over emigration, and each time people used the rhetoric they reinforced it. Planters' arguments that white people could not labor in hot places, and that such places required Black laborers, became not just an excuse but an explanation for racial slavery. In addition, the rhetoric entered a common parlance. Tracking every single case is not necessary to show its persistence and its currency throughout this period. Even white abolitionists for the most part accepted the tenet that Black bodies suited hot places. The result was a validation and deepening of the idea that Black and white bodies were in fact fundamentally different from one another. If their bodies responded in different ways to different climates, the theory went, there must be some deep biological difference between them. The climatic racial language left no room for racial ambiguity; this was a binary racial formulation.

Crucially, slaveholders' insistence that Black and white bodies were suited to different climates drove an Anglo-American concept of race as an immutable bodily difference. The idea that Black and white bodies were physiologically different at their cores justified further racial exclusion and separation in the aftermath of slavery. The climatic rhetoric perpetuated these notions of biological race and remained an explanation for slavery long after emancipation.

Conclusion

In 1807, as both Britain and the United States moved to end their participation in the transatlantic slave trade, British writer Robert Renny published a history of Jamaica. Renny had spent time on the island at the turn of the century and suggested what seemed to him an obvious solution to the colony's imminent labor problems. "Turn your eyes, Ye legislators of Jamaica!" he wrote, to "the crowded shores of Scotland and Ireland! Here, an immense, an incalculable accession of strength, power, and security, awaits you." Renny urged Jamaicans to offer "allurements" to potential migrants "sufficient to counterbalance their terror of the climate." Populating the Caribbean with Scottish and Irish laborers, he reasoned, would increase the cultivation, industry, and security of the islands.[1]

Only sixteen years earlier St. Vincent inhabitant Thomas Fraser had marveled at the arrival of a "Scotch *Guinea man*," overflowing with "white negroes from Scotland enough to cultivate our plantations without buying them." Despite this influx of Scots in 1791, in 1807 planters would not have considered Renny's proposal viable. Even with the end of the slave trade, slaveholders firmly rejected the idea of relying on paid laborers to do the work of cultivating plantations. While some planters made desperate pleas to legislators about their own financial futures, others tried to sell previously lucrative plantations that had become a liability in their eyes. Few believed they could continue to turn a profit without a continued influx of enslaved African laborers. They had built an economy that relied on unpaid labor and could not imagine it otherwise. In addition, Caribbean slaveholders had just spent years arguing exhaustively in Parliament that white laborers could never work in the West Indian climate. That insistence rendered recruitment of these workers nearly impossible. Planters' Parliamentary testimony, which had been published and circulated around the Anglo-Atlantic, contributed a great deal to the narrative that these places were unhealthy for white bodies. Although earlier migrants knew the region's reputation as a dangerously unhealthy place, planters had worked hard to corroborate this view. By

The Nature of Slavery. Katherine Johnston, Oxford University Press. © Oxford University Press 2022.
DOI: 10.1093/oso/9780197514603.003.0008

the early nineteenth century, the climatic rhetoric planters used to justify racial slavery had become a widely accepted article of faith.[2]

In the United States, a thriving internal slave trade continued long after the official end to the transatlantic trade, and southern plantations remained dependent on enslaved Black workers to cultivate crops up through the Civil War. Here, too, defenders of racial slavery perpetuated a climatic rhetoric justifying their reliance on Black laborers in the southern lowcountry. After the war, former slaveholders eager to attract white laborers to their plantations insisted that the reputation of the South as "no country for white laborers" was unfair and inaccurate. Despite planters' efforts to recruit white laborers, a rhetoric linking race, climate, and labor had long since solidified, and white immigrants flocked elsewhere.[3]

Constructing Race

In the history of the development of African slavery in the Americas, climate played a minor role. In the seventeenth century, planters began to favor enslaved African laborers over indentured Europeans for reasons of economy and convenience. Africans were becoming easier to obtain than servants from the British Isles, and planters decided the long-term investment was economically prudent. Planters did not believe that Africans would be any healthier than Europeans on plantations; if the transition had anything to do with the Caribbean climate, it was only that servants may have heard rumors of its unhealthiness, increasing their reluctance to travel. The situation in Georgia during the 1730s and 1740s was similar: English settlers wanted enslaved Africans for economic and social rather than climatic reasons. The Malcontents turned to a climatic argument by appealing to existing British suspicions of hot climates only after their initial pleas went unheeded. In doing so, they deliberately manipulated an existing but inchoate set of ideas linking skin color, climate, and the ability to labor in order to achieve personal financial ends.[4]

Despite climate's minimal impact on the development of racial slavery in American plantation societies, the rhetoric irrevocably tying labor in hot climates to Black bodies became a significant part of the way this history was told. Half a century after the Malcontents clamored for racial slavery in Georgia, slaveholders arguing against the abolition of the slave trade insisted categorically that white people could not labor in hot climates. They made these arguments despite a history of European labor on plantations and regardless of their notions of seasoning. Planters knew that Africans did not suit American climates and that they needed to be seasoned over a period of time. They also knew that enslaved Africans fell ill and died at alarming rates. Yet they presented unified arguments insisting upon the need for enslaved African laborers because of the climate in plantation societies. Thus, this rhetoric consolidated in a relatively brief period of time around the close of the eighteenth century. It lasted well into the nineteenth century as a continued justification for racial slavery on plantations in the American South. White Americans also used it to promote colonization abroad and to encourage Black Americans to emigrate out of the United States. They relied on it to shape political battles over the expansion of slavery, and they portrayed it as a law of nature, as a naturally occurring physiological distinction between Black and white people.

Beyond these manipulations of the climatic argument, its legacy proved more damaging and lasting than planters could have imagined. This rhetoric solidified at the same time that white anatomists in the United States and in Europe searched for biological distinctions between Black and white bodies. As Africans and Europeans became seasoned to the same climate, as they suffered from the same environmental conditions, and as mixed-race populations exemplified the commonalities among all bodies, Euro-Americans looked for a way to assert bodily differences. Anatomical studies categorizing bodies developed precisely because Euro-Americans wanted a way to measure, define, and articulate physical difference. Historian Winthrop Jordan has observed that "as interest in man's physical structure grew, faith in his plasticity diminished." A less passive view of this occurrence might be that, as white people sought to assert the fixity of human bodies and to deny their plasticity, they turned to anatomical and physiological sciences to construct a sense of biological racial difference supposedly grounded in nature.[5]

Slaveholders who insisted that Black people could labor where white people could not attempted to maintain a strict divide between Black and white bodies, despite evidence to the contrary. White planters and settler-colonists sought to preserve a racial hierarchy in which certain types of difficult manual labor were associated with Blackness. They were eager to draw a distinction between Black and white bodies that their own experiences threatened to undermine. White anatomists who developed race sciences around categorizing bodies perpetuated a theory of biological race: the idea that bodies with different skin colors were categorically and fundamentally different at their cores. Planters' arguments about people suiting different climates fueled ideas about different bodies. In the nineteenth century, a growing number of scientists argued that people were biologically and racially distinct from one another.[6]

In addition to the connection with the development of biological race, the story about the labor transition became so ingrained in historical narratives that it became naturalized, shaping subsequent accounts of the history of Atlantic world slavery. More than half a century after the end of the Civil War, Vincent Harlow's *History of Barbados* (1926) and Lowell Ragatz's *The Fall of the Planter*

Class (1928) were influential scholarly books on the history of the Caribbean that discussed the labor transition to enslaved Africans. Explaining the seventeenth-century transition from European to African laborers in Barbados, Harlow wrote, "Successful white settlements can only take root in regions where the climate is sufficiently temperate for the European to work," and in the West Indies "the white man was an alien." As a result, he continued, planters "discovered" that "negro slaves, accustomed as they were to intense heat and sudden cold," were more efficient laborers in the Caribbean. "Consequently," he finished, "the British labourer in these islands gave place to the negro. It was the triumph of geographical conditions." In Harlow's telling, the climate was a major factor in precipitating the labor transition. Slaveholders' climatic rhetoric, articulated in the late eighteenth century to protect their interests, over time transformed into historical fact in the revised history of slavery.[7]

Ragatz began his book with a perfunctory explanation of laborers on West Indian plantations: "Climatic conditions made an economic system based on free European workers impossible," he wrote. He did not bother to elaborate; the theory that white people could not work in hot climates had become so established that historians took it as a matter of course. These histories continued the long tradition of using climatic explanations to describe the shift to African slavery in the Greater Caribbean. Histories of Georgia written in the 1760s and 1770s explained that the colony turned to enslaved Black laborers for climatic reasons, and in the 1790s through the 1850s those seeking to uphold racial slavery in the American South cited these texts as authoritative. Even those wishing to demolish slavery, including some Black people, reiterated this history. Black activist Martin R. Delany, for example, wrote in 1852 that the earliest Europeans colonizing the Americas found their bodies "inadequate to stand the climate." In "the warmer climates," he added, "the white race cannot work," so the early colonizers turned to Black people for a labor force. In each of these histories, white people's supposed inability to labor in hot climates became a historical explanation for racial slavery.[8]

Two decades after Harlow and Ragatz wrote, Eric Williams tried to dispel the argument that the West Indian climate was a central factor in the switch from European to African labor during the seventeenth century. He pointed out that England's Atlantic colonies had relied on the labor of European servants for years before the adoption of African slavery. "This white servitude," Williams argued, "completely explodes the old myth that the whites could not stand the strain of manual labor in the climate of the New World and that, for this reason and this reason alone, the European powers had recourse to Africans. The argument is quite untenable." The fact that Williams had to dismantle planters' propaganda over a century and a half after they disseminated it demonstrates the strength and persistence of the climatic argument's legacy.[9]

Yellow Fever and Seasoning

Despite the work of Eric Williams and a few others explicitly denouncing the climate argument, that legacy persists. In the three-quarters of a century since Williams wrote, the climatic argument has not disappeared, but rather reemerges as a justification for the transition to African slavery in colonial plantation societies far too often. These explanations are usually given in passing, with climate mentioned as a factor in the labor transition. In other cases, Euro-American planters are said to have switched from a majority of indentured European laborers to a majority of enslaved African laborers in part because they noted differing rates of illness among these populations, particularly malaria and yellow fever. This epidemiological claim deserves more careful scrutiny, predicated as it is on an incomplete analysis of the historical record.[10]

Because they perpetuate slaveholders' justifications for racial slavery, these assertions are problematic on several levels. No one in the seventeenth- or eighteenth-century Atlantic diagnosed malaria as an illness. Instead, physicians and laypeople alike described most illnesses simply as "fevers" for patients of all origins. Fevers could be "continued" or "intermittent," and historians often interpret descriptions of "intermittent" fever as malaria. But eighteenth-century inhabitants of the Greater Caribbean did not write about it as such, and making retroactive medical diagnoses for historical subjects is dangerous and unreliable.[11]

Most important, relying on differences in immunity to explain the transition to enslaved African labor in the Caribbean assumes that planters themselves noticed these differences and acted accordingly. But seventeenth- and eighteenth-century planters and physicians had fundamentally different conceptions of health and illness, grounded in environmental conditions. In their personal correspondence and in medical manuals, colonists and medical practitioners repeatedly blamed wet weather and exposure to dangerous air for illnesses in colonial plantation societies. Planters and other slaveholders explained that both Black and white populations who fell ill did so because of local environmental conditions: either because of "excessive rains" or because they were not yet "seasoned to the country." On the whole, planters did not tend to note that white people were especially more likely to fall ill than Black people were, nor did they mention differences in Black and white health in the Caribbean as a reason for African slavery until they felt the institution was under threat. Slaveholders and other settler-colonists did not usually align the causes of illnesses with skin color. Instead, they blamed fevers in general on environmental conditions, particularly wet weather.[12]

One exception worth examining is yellow fever. Although some physicians had trouble distinguishing yellow fever from other fevers, others recognized it as a particular disease.[13] Many eighteenth-century medical practitioners who did differentiate yellow fever believed it had environmental causes. Nevertheless, there are a few cases of physicians speculating that it affected Black and white people differently. Yellow fever recurred repeatedly throughout the Atlantic world in the seventeenth, eighteenth, and nineteenth centuries. Perhaps most famously, in a 1793 outbreak in Philadelphia, Dr. Benjamin Rush called upon the city's Black population to help care for the sick, assuring them that they would not become ill. The grounds for Rush's suspicion that Black people were immune to the disease lay in a letter written decades earlier by Dr. John Lining about a yellow fever outbreak in South Carolina. In the letter, which was published in 1754 in Scotland, Lining had suggested that Black people were "not liable to this fever." Taking Lining at his word, Rush encouraged free Black Philadelphians to care for and bury scores of white city residents. Of course, Black people were not immune, and they too fell sick and died from yellow fever, leaving Rush to lament his mistake. He quickly backtracked, realizing that his assertion was incorrect.[14]

A close look at Lining's letter, however, reveals more than a dichotomous racialized view of bodily susceptibility. Just before his comment implying Black immunity, Lining wrote that the people vulnerable to yellow fever included Indigenous Americans; people of both Indigenous and white heritage; "Mulattoes," or those with Black and white parents; and white people, "especially strangers lately arrived from cold climates." This observation is noteworthy on several levels. Lining did not simply present a Black–white opposition. Instead, he grouped Indigenous people and biracial people with white people in terms of susceptibility. His comment that the disease particularly affected "strangers" from cold places is essential to reframing understandings of eighteenth-century concepts of health and illness.[15]

Perhaps because the concept of seasoning has fallen out of use in current understandings of health and illness, a twenty-first century reader might be tempted to highlight the racial disparity, rather than the difference of seasoning, in Lining's comments. While the racial piece is noteworthy, it is also singular; his observation on seasoning aligned much more closely with that of other physicians and settler-colonists who placed enormous importance on seasoning in their conceptions of bodily health. In the eighteenth century, the "strangers" piece of Lining's observation was echoed over and over in medical and laypeople's descriptions of fevers, yellow fever included. In 1794, for example, Charles Cotesworth Pinckney of South Carolina wrote that there had been a "fever in Charleston; it proved fatal to strangers but not to the natives." In another letter a month later, he wrote, "To strangers & persons from the Country this City has during the Summer & Fall been generally fatal, but to the inhabitants it has been very healthy." In 1796, Simon Taylor wrote from Jamaica that usually "no people fell by the Yellow Fever but new comers." And in his 1791 medical treatise, physician Robert Jackson wrote that Europeans tended to contract yellow fever "soon after their arrival in the tropical countries." Seasoning altered people: after Europeans had "remained for a year or two in those hot climates," he wrote, only rarely did they contract yellow fever. Similarly, if "Creoles or Africans" traveled to a cold place, Jackson explained, they were entirely susceptible to yellow fever upon their return to the West Indies.[16]

According to these writings, seasoning, not race, affected people's susceptibility to fevers. Once Europeans had become accustomed to the Caribbean environment, Jackson wrote, they were no longer likely to contract yellow fever. Conversely, if natives of the West Indies, regardless of color, spent enough time away, they would be vulnerable to the illness upon returning to the Caribbean. Jackson was no particular exception; both personal correspondence and medical treatises show that many other planters and physicians who noted differences in people's susceptibilities distinguished not among skin colors, but between inhabitants of a particular place and "strangers" to that place.[17] They believed that fevers, yellow or otherwise, affected recent arrivals, or unseasoned people. To understand the nuances of eighteenth-century conceptions of health and bodily difference, then, it is important to distinguish between concepts of seasoning and those of race or skin color. Recognizing the importance of seasoning for historical subjects should lay to rest any speculation that health differences helped drive planters' reliance on enslaved African laborers.[18]

This emphasis on seasoning does not eliminate or negate any racism that white physicians, planters, or other settler-colonists displayed, either overtly or not, in their behaviors toward Black bodies. There is no question that racism undergirded these interactions. But white people who held racist attitudes and who exhibited racist behavior did not usually differentiate bodily illnesses based upon skin color, even when we might expect them to do so. Given how frequently "fevers" made their appearances in Greater Caribbean plantation societies during the eighteenth century, we would expect to find multiple references to differences of skin color in medical manuals, plantation correspondence, or other documents. Instead, these writings consistently portray fevers in non-racial terms: illnesses were environmental, or they attacked "strangers" to a place. The pattern holds in the nineteenth-century United States; white people in antebellum New Orleans, for example, thought of yellow fever as a "strangers' disease" for decades before eventually casting it in a racial light. These interpretations of fevers and of other illnesses demonstrate that planters did not turn to African laborers for health reasons, in large part because slaveholders did not observe racial differences in susceptibility to disease on a regular basis.[19]

* * *

Explanations for racial slavery based upon climatic suitability for labor and spec-ulative health differences between Black and white bodies end up perpetuating planters' self-serving rhetoric. The idea that planters turned to African laborers for health reasons is based on an anachronistic view of racialized health. Climate functioned as a convenient excuse for racial slavery, and it persisted as a veneer and a justification throughout slavery's existence in the Atlantic. It was not a reason for African slavery in the Americas, but it was a common defense. Plantation correspondence reveals no clear sense of biological bodily difference between Africans and Europeans. Instead, planters' and physicians' comments on the mutability of bodies reveal an understanding of bodies' capacity to change, particularly through the seasoning process.

It would be a mistake, though, to conclude that the climatic rhetoric that solidified around the end of the eighteenth century is unimportant. Slaveholders' arguments ingrained a rhetoric of climate and labor first as a colonial axiom and then as a historical explanation for racial slavery. The historiographical argu-ment that planters turned to enslaved Africans for health reasons downplays the racism at the heart of Atlantic slavery. Africans were enslaved because European planters valued African lives less than European lives. The continuance of cli-matic arguments merely propagates notions of biological race by suggesting that white planters had some physiological reason to enslave Africans. Such explanations soften the racism that propelled, and that grew in tandem with, Atlantic slavery in the Americas.

In addition, the climatic rhetoric helped transform concepts of bodily flu-idity into ideas about fixed racial difference. The notion of a fundamental differ-ence between Black and white bodies based upon their suitability for different climates diverged from the complex and nuanced understandings of climates and bodies that characterized eighteenth-century colonial experience and perspectives. Although these arguments began as strategic moves designed to protect planters' economic livelihoods, they grew into a rhetorical tool used to justify racial slavery and biological bodily distinctions for many years thereafter.

Repeated assertions that Black and white bodies suited different climates only became more dangerous as white politicians, physicians, and others imbued this rhetoric with a language of nature. In 1856, a prominent Southern physi-cian proclaimed that Black and white races were "originally made to suit the climate in which Nature placed" them. This language, which white politicians used freely to defend racial slavery in the American South, gave theories of bi-ological race the unquestionable authority of nature. The idea that Black and white bodies were biologically distinct steepened the climb for Black activists struggling against an oppressive racial system. As Frederick Douglass wrote in *The North Star* in 1850, this reasoning was "most scandalous and impudent." The climatic claim masked a socially constructed racial hierarchy, presenting it as a natural outcome of environment and biology when it was neither. Ultimately, the climatic rhetoric enabled the use of a language that sounded natural—physiological distinctions beyond human control—and that was essential to the perpetuation of racist ideas and practices.[20]

The legacy of this rhetoric had real and lasting effects. By portraying Black people as physiologically, fundamentally different from white people, the theory and language of biological race gave white people official license to exploit Black bodies even beyond slavery. White Americans could justify placing people of color in situations dangerous to their health by leaning on supposed racial differences and on the idea that Black bodies were particularly suited to demanding labor in unhealthy places. They have used the climatic racial rhetoric as a shortcut to support racist labor practices. The term environmental racism is usually used to describe situations where people of color are deliberately and systematically placed in environmentally hazardous situations, but studies have tended to go back only into the twentieth century to describe these situations. *The Nature of Slavery* has shown that the roots of environmental racism in the United States and the broader Anglo-Atlantic world go much deeper. The institution of racial slavery, particularly as practiced on plantations in the lowcountry and the West Indies, virtually guaranteed that Black bodies would be placed in these situations. While enslaved Black people were subjected to systematic and race-based exposure to dangerous environments, planters' rhetoric about the suitability of Black bodies for hard labor in hot climates gave license for these practices to continue long after slavery was abolished.

Defenders of slavery who used a language of climate and natural bodily difference helped to construct theories of biological race. By resorting to this climatic rhetoric and appealing to a language of nature, slaveholders and others constructed a nexus of ideas about race with consequences that have reverberated for centuries.

NOTES

Abbreviations

APS	American Philosophical Society, Philadelphia
BL	British Library, London
Bod.	Bodleian Library, Oxford
GHS	Georgia Historical Society, Savannah
HSP	Historical Society of Pennsylvania, Philadelphia
ICS	Institute of Commonwealth Studies Library, London
MHS	Massachusetts Historical Society, Boston
NLJ	National Library of Jamaica, Kingston
NLS	National Library of Scotland, Edinburgh
NRS	National Record Office of Scotland, Edinburgh
TNA	The National Archives, Kew, London

Introduction

1. Thomas Fraser to Simon Fraser, April 8, 1791, Simon Fraser Papers, HCA/D238/D/1/17/6, Highland Archive Centre, Inverness, Scotland. Fraser did not include other details about the ship, writing only that it was "a ship from Glasgow." For more on Scottish migrants to the Caribbean, see Alan L. Karras, *Sojourners in the Sun: Scottish Migrants in Jamaica and the Chesapeake, 1740–1800* (Ithaca: Cornell University Press, 1992).

2. On Parliamentary debates over the slave trade, see Srividhya Swaminathan, *Debating the Slave Trade: Rhetoric of British National Identity, 1759–1815* (Farnham, UK: Ashgate, 2009); David Beck Ryden, *West Indian Slavery and British Abolition, 1783–1807* (New York: Cambridge University Press, 2009); Roger Anstey, *The Atlantic Slave Trade and British Abolition, 1760–1810* (Atlantic Highlands, NJ: Humanities Press, 1975); Seymour Drescher, "Public Opinion and Parliament in the Abolition of the British Slave Trade," in *The British Slave Trade: Abolition, Parliament and People* ed. Stephen Farrell et al., (Edinburgh: Edinburgh University Press, 2007), 42–65. On low reproduction rates among enslaved populations in the Caribbean, see Jennifer L. Morgan, *Laboring Women: Reproduction and Gender in New World Slavery* (Philadelphia: University of Pennsylvania Press, 2004); Colleen A. Vasconcellos, *Slavery, Childhood, and Abolition in Jamaica, 1788–1838* (Athens: University of Georgia Press, 2015); Sasha Turner, *Contested Bodies: Pregnancy, Childrearing, and Slavery in Jamaica* (Philadelphia: University of Pennsylvania Press, 2017); Katherine Paugh, *The Politics of Reproduction: Race, Medicine, and Fertility in the Age of Abolition* (Oxford: Oxford University Press, 2017).

3. The term "planters" could refer to resident plantation owners, proprietors or absentee planters living primarily in Britain, or the managers or attorneys that plantation owners appointed to

serve in their stead and to direct the workings of a plantation. When absentee planters left resident managers in charge of a plantation, the owners tended to correspond regularly with the managers regarding the operations and events of plantation life. See Richard S. Dunn, *Sugar and Slaves: The Rise of the Planter Class in the English West Indies, 1624–1713* (Chapel Hill: University of North Carolina Press, 1972), 46–48; B. W. Higman, *Plantation Jamaica 1750–1850: Capital and Control in a Colonial Economy* (Kingston, Jamaica: University of the West Indies Press, 2005), 7–11. Although several historians have argued that by the late eighteenth century a significant proportion of planters were absentees, Trevor Burnard argues that scholars have overstated the case, and that many planters, at least in Jamaica, had genuine transatlantic connections. See Burnard, "Passengers Only: The Extent and Significance of Absenteeism in Eighteenth Century Jamaica," *Atlantic Studies* 1, no. 2 (2004): 178–195. For more on eighteenth-century Jamaican planters, see Christer Petley, *Slaveholders in Jamaica: Colonial Society and Culture During the Era of Abolition* (London: Pickering & Chatto, 2009).

4. Speech of William Loughton Smith, *Annals of Congress*, House of Representatives, 1st Congress, 2nd Session, 1510, March 17, 1790. Charles Cotesworth Pinckney made similar arguments in 1785 and 1788. See Elizabeth Donnan, ed., *Documents Illustrative of the History of the Slave Trade to America* (Washington, DC: Carnegie Institution, 1930), vol. 4, 482; Elliot, ed., *Debates in State Conventions*, vol. IV, 285.

5. John Huddlestone Wynne, *A General History of the British Empire in America* (London: W. Richardson and L. Urquhart, 1770), vol. II, 541. Several other writers and historians in the same period repeated these claims. For specific examples, see Chapter 6. For a few examples of historians in the early twentieth century repeating this history of Georgia, see Robert Preston Brooks, *History of Georgia* (Boston: Atkinson, Mentzer, & Co., 1913), 65–67; Ralph B. Flanders, "The Free Negro in Ante-Bellum Georgia," *North Carolina Historical Review* 9, no. 3 (1932): 250–272. On the West Indies, see Vincent T. Harlow, *A History of Barbados, 1625–1685* (New York: Negro Universities Press, 1969 [1926]); Lowell Joseph Ragatz, *The Fall of the Planter Class in the British Caribbean, 1763–1833* (New York: Century, 1928). More recently, historians have repeated the claim that planters turned to African laborers in part because they suited the disease environment in plantation societies better than Europeans did. See, for example, Gary Puckrein, "Climate, Health and Black Labor in the English Americas," *Journal of American Studies* 13, no. 2 (1979): 179–193; Trevor Burnard, "'The Countrie Continues Sicklie': White Mortality in Jamaica, 1655–1780," *Society for the Social History of Medicine* 12, no. 1 (1999): 45–72; Philip D. Curtin, "Epidemiology and the Slave Trade," *Political Science Quarterly* 83, no. 2 (1968): 190–216; Kenneth F. Kiple and Virginia Himmelsteib King, *Another Dimension to the Black Diaspora: Diet, Disease, and Racism* (Cambridge: Cambridge University Press, 1981). Other scholars have mentioned this explanation for the labor transition in passing without questioning the premise behind it. See, for example, Simon Newman, *A New World of Labor: The Development of Plantation Slavery in the British Atlantic* (Philadelphia: University of Pennsylvania Press, 2013), 76; Emily Senior, *The Caribbean and Medical Imagination, 1764–1834* (Cambridge: Cambridge University Press, 2018), 4; Ikuko Asaka, *Tropical Freedom: Climate, Settler Colonialism, and Black Exclusion in the Age of Emancipation* (Durham: Duke University Press, 2017), 7; Robin Blackburn, *The American Crucible: Slavery, Emancipation and Human Rights* (New York: Verso, 2011), 65.

6. On some of the ways abolition influenced the construction of racial theories, see Seymour Drescher, "The Ending of the Slave Trade and the Evolution of European Scientific Racism," *Social Science History* 14, no. 3 (1990): 415–450; Suman Seth, *Difference and Disease: Medicine, Race, and the Eighteenth-Century British Empire* (Cambridge: Cambridge University Press, 2018). This is not to say that there was no sense of bodily difference before the emergence of biological race. It is instead to argue that Britons and Anglo-Americans did not see these differences as immutable or unable to change through alterations in climate, culture, governing structure, or circumstances.

7. On the development of "race science" in the late eighteenth and early nineteenth centuries, see Nancy Stepan, *The Idea of Race in Science: Great Britain, 1800–1960* (London: Macmillan Press, 1982); Roxann Wheeler, *The Complexion of Race: Categories of Difference in Eighteenth-Century British Culture* (Philadelphia: University of Pennsylvania Press, 2000); Londa

Schiebinger, "Medical Experimentation and Race in the Eighteenth-Century Atlantic World," *Social History of Medicine* 26, no. 3 (2013): 364–382; Londa Schiebinger, "The Anatomy of Difference: Race and Sex in Eighteenth-Century Science," *Eighteenth-Century Studies* 23, no. 4 (1990): 387–405; Snait B. Gissis, "Visualizing 'Race' in the Eighteenth Century," *Historical Studies in the Natural Sciences* 41, no. 1 (2011): 41–103; Andrew S. Curran, *The Anatomy of Blackness: Science and Slavery in an Age of Enlightenment* (Baltimore: Johns Hopkins University Press, 2011). Bronwen Douglas argues that colonial endeavors were particularly responsible for this turn to scientific race; see Douglas, "Climate to Crania: Science and the Racialization of Human Difference" in Douglas and Chris Ballard, eds. *Foreign Bodies: Oceania and the Science of Race 1750–1940* (Canberra: Australian National University E Press, 2008): 33–96. James Delbourgo argues that scientific experiments in the Americas were crucial to this shift; see Delbourgo, "The Newtonian Slave Body: Racial Enlightenment in the Atlantic World," *Atlantic Studies* 9, no. 12 (2012): 185–207.

8. Scholars generally use the term environmental racism to refer to relatively modern situations. I argue, however, that racial slavery in the Americas exemplified environmental racism and that scholars should take these older examples into account. See Katherine Johnston, "Endangered Plantations: Environmental Change and Slavery in the British Caribbean, 1631–1807," *Early American Studies* 18, no. 3 (2020): 259–286. On environmental racism, see Robert D. Bullard, ed., *Confronting Environmental Racism: Voices from the Grassroots* (Cambridge, MA: South End Press, 1993). The term is generally attributed to Benjamin Chavis, who used it to describe a case of environmental injustice in North Carolina. See Eileen Maura McGurty, "From NIMBY to Civil Rights: The Origins of the Environmental Justice Movement," in *Environmental History and the American South*, ed. Paul S. Sutter and Christopher J. Manganiello (Athens: University of Georgia Press, 2009), 372–399. On the necessity of including environmental racism in environmental history more broadly, see Carolyn Merchant, "Shades of Darkness: Race and Environmental History," *Environmental History* 8, no. 3 (2003): 380–394.

9. On the influence of climate on European bodies in the Americas, see, for example, Rebecca Earle, *The Body of the Conquistador: Food, Race, and the Colonial Experience in Spanish America, 1492–1700* (Cambridge: Cambridge University Press, 2012); Jorge Cañizares Esguerra, "New World, New Stars: Patriotic Astrology and the Invention of Indian and Creole Bodies in Colonial Spanish America, 1600–1650," *American Historical Review* 104, no. 1 (1999): 33–68; Neil Safier, "The Tenacious Travels of the Torrid Zone and the Global Dimensions of Geographical Knowledge in the Eighteenth Century," *Journal of Early Modern History* 18 (2014): 141–172; Sean Quinlan, "Colonial Bodies, Hygiene, and Abolitionist Politics in Eighteenth-Century France," in *Bodies in Contact: Rethinking Colonial Encounters in World History* (Durham: Duke University Press, 2005), 106–121. On similar ideas in India, see Mark Harrison, *Climates and Constitutions: Health, Race, Environment and British Imperialism in India, 1600–1850* (New Delhi: Oxford University Press, 1999); E. M. Collingham, *Imperial Bodies: The Physical Experience of the Raj, c. 1800–1947* (Cambridge: Polity Press, 2001). On these ideas in Africa, see Philip D. Curtin, "'The White Man's Grave:' Image and Reality, 1780–1850," *Journal of British Studies* 1, no. 1 (1961): 94–110; Michael A. Osborne, "Acclimatizing the World: A History of the Paradigmatic Colonial Science," *Osiris* 15 (2000): 135–151; Emma Christopher, *A Merciless Place: The Fate of Britain's Convicts after the American Revolution* (New York: Oxford University Press, 2011); Emma Christopher, "A 'Disgrace to the very Colour': Perceptions of Blackness and Whiteness in the Founding of Sierra Leone and Botany Bay," *Journal of Colonialism & Colonial History* 9, no. 3 (2008).

10. Kourou, a short-lived settlement in French Guiana, faltered for non-climatic reasons, but its detractors blamed the climate. See Emma Rothschild, "A Horrible Tragedy in the French Atlantic," *Past and Present* 192 (2006): 67–108. As far as British colonization was concerned, the case of Sierra Leone is instructive: the beleaguered experimental colony on the West African coast also faltered for various reasons and ended up contributing to the climatic narrative. See Seymour Drescher, *The Mighty Experiment: Free Labor versus Slavery in British Emancipation* (New York: Oxford University Press, 2002), 91–100.

11. On the Greater Caribbean as a region, see Matthew Mulcahy, *Hubs of Empire: The Southeastern Lowcountry and British Caribbean* (Baltimore: Johns Hopkins University Press, 2014), 2–8. In the eighteenth century, British naval physician James Lind, whose work was often cited by

his contemporaries, explicitly argued for the similarity of the lowcountry and West Indian disease environments: "In the latitude of South Carolina, we find these diseases . . . much of the nature of those distempers which are so fatal to the newly arrived Europeans in West Indian climates. The same may be said of Georgia," he wrote. See James Lind, *An Essay on Diseases Incidental to Europeans in Hot Climates* (London: T. Becket and P.A. De Hondt, 1768), 37. On seventeenth-century concerns about English bodies in hot climates, see Karen Ordahl Kupperman, "Fear of Hot Climates in the Anglo-American Colonial Experience," *William and Mary Quarterly* 41, no. 2 (1984): 213–240. On European bodily health in West Africa, see Curtin, "'The White Man's Grave'"; Christopher, *A Merciless Place*. Elsewhere Christopher argues that in the late eighteenth century Europeans came to see West Africa as a completely inhospitable place for white bodies. See Christopher, "A 'Disgrace to the very Colour'. On the importance of the Greater Caribbean region to ideas about race during the eighteenth century, see Rana A. Hogarth, *Medicalizing Blackness: Making Racial Difference in the Atlantic World, 1780–1840* (Chapel Hill: University of North Carolina Press, 2017), 10. Other historians have also used the Greater Caribbean as a framework for understanding the development of bodily difference and as a way to think about disease environments. See J. R. McNeill, *Mosquito Empires: Ecology and War in the Greater Caribbean, 1620–1914* (Cambridge: Cambridge University Press, 2010). On the centrality of the West Indies to the British Atlantic as a whole, see Kathleen Wilson, *The Island Race: Englishness, Empire and Gender in the Eighteenth Century* (London: Routledge, 2003); Trevor Burnard, *Planters, Merchants, and Slaves: Plantation Societies in British America, 1650–1820* (Chicago: University of Chicago Press, 2015); Vincent Brown, *The Reaper's Garden: Death and Power in the World of Atlantic Slavery* (Cambridge, MA: Harvard University Press, 2008); Brooke N. Newman, *A Dark Inheritance: Blood, Race, and Sex in Colonial Jamaica* (New Haven: Yale University Press, 2018); Susan Dwyer Amussen, *Caribbean Exchanges: Slavery and the Transformation of English Society, 1640–1700* (Chapel Hill: University of North Carolina Press, 2007).

12. Joyce E. Chaplin, *Subject Matter: Technology, the Body, and Science on the Anglo-American Frontier, 1500–1676* (Cambridge, MA: Harvard University Press, 2001). See also David S. Jones, *Rationalizing Epidemics: Meanings and Uses of American Indian Mortality since 1600* (Cambridge, MA: Harvard University Press, 2004); Cristobal Silva, *Miraculous Plagues: An Epidemiology of Early New England Narrative* (New York: Oxford University Press, 2011); Kelly Wisecup, *Medical Encounters: Knowledge and Identity in Early American Literatures* (Amherst: University of Massachusetts Press, 2013).

13. On the difficulty of separating Indigenous from Black bodies in historical records, see Rebecca Anne Goetz, "Indian Slavery: An Atlantic and Hemispheric Problem," *History Compass* 14, no. 2 (2016): 59–70; Andrés Reséndez, *The Other Slavery: The Uncovered Story of Indian Enslavement in America* (Boston: Houghton Mifflin Harcourt, 2016).

14. English investors in Providence Island claimed that "English bodies" were "not fit for that work" as early as 1632, but these claims were clearly not based on experience, and relied only on inherited assumptions and racial prejudice. See Karen Ordahl Kupperman, *Providence Island, 1630–1641: The Other Puritan Colony* (New York: Cambridge University Press, 1993), 166.

15. On the nineteenth and twentieth centuries, see Asaka, *Tropical Freedom*; see also Warwick Anderson, "Immunities of Empire: Race, Disease, and the New Tropical Medicine, 1900–1920," *Bulletin of the History of Medicine* 70, no. 1 (1996): 94–118; Dane Kennedy, "The Perils of the Midday Sun: Climatic Anxieties in the Colonial Tropics," in *Imperialism and the Natural World*, ed. John M. MacKenzie (Manchester: Manchester University Press, 1990), 118–140.

16. On planters' economic decisions, see Joyce Chaplin, *An Anxious Pursuit: Agricultural Innovation and Modernity in the Lower South, 1730–1815* (Chapel Hill: University of North Carolina Press, 1993); Lorena Walsh, *Motives of Honor, Pleasure, and Profit: Plantation Managements in the Colonial Chesapeake, 1607–1763* (Chapel Hill: University of North Carolina Press, 2010); S. Max Edelson, *Plantation Enterprise in Colonial South Carolina* (Cambridge, MA: Harvard University Press, 2006); Caitlin Rosenthal, *Accounting for Slavery: Masters and Management* (Cambridge, MA: Harvard University Press, 2018).

17. Karen Ordahl Kupperman, "The Puzzle of the American Climate in the Early Colonial Period," *American Historical Review* 87, no. 5 (1982): 1262–1289; Sam White, *A Cold*

Welcome: The Little Ice Age and Europe's Encounter with North America (Cambridge: Harvard University Press, 2017). For a history of climatic ideas from ancient theories through the late eighteenth century, see Clarence J. Glacken, *Traces on the Rhodian Shore: Nature and Culture in Western Thought from Ancient Times to the End of the Eighteenth Century* (Berkeley: University of California Press, 1967).

18. Hippocrates, *On Airs, Water, and Places*; Conevery Bolton Valenčius, *The Health of the Country: How American Settlers Understood Themselves and Their Land* (Boston: Basic Books, 2002). On the influence of Hippocratic theories on early modern European medicine, see Seth, *Difference and Disease*, 30–44; Mark Harrison, *Medicine in an Age of Commerce and Empire: Britain and its Tropical Colonies, 1660–1830* (New York: Oxford University Press, 2010), 30–33; Andrew Wear, "Place, Health, and Disease: The *Airs, Waters, Places* Tradition in Early Modern England and North America," *Journal of Medieval and Early Modern Studies* 38, no. 3 (2008): 443–465.

19. Earle, *Body of the Conquistador*, 26–32.

20. Lind, *Essay on Diseases*, 198. On colonists changing their environments, see Anya Zilberstein, *A Temperate Empire: Making Climate Change in Early America* (New York: Oxford University Press, 2016); Karen Ordahl Kupperman, "Climate and Mastery of the Wilderness in Seventeenth-Century New England," in *Seventeenth-Century New England*, ed. David D. Hall and David Grayson Allen (Boston: Publications of the Colonial Society of Massachusetts 63, 1984): 3–37. Also see Kate Luce Mulry, *An Empire Transformed: Remolding Bodies and Landscapes in the Restoration Atlantic* (New York: New York University Press, 2021); Jan Golinski, "American Climate and the Civilization of Nature," in *Science and Empire in the Atlantic World*, ed. James Delbourgo and Nicholas Dew (New York: Routledge, 2008): 153–174; Larry Gragg, *Englishmen Transplanted: The Colonization of Barbados, 1627–1660* (New York: Oxford University Press, 2003); Edelson, *Plantation Enterprise*, Mart A. Stewart, *"What Nature Suffers to Groe": Life, Labor, and Landscape on the Georgia Coast, 1680–1920* (Athens, GA: University of Georgia Press, 1996) In his (excellently titled) book chapter "The Nature of Slavery," Max Edelson shows how enslaved people both threatened and enabled planters' desire to tame the lowcountry environment. See Edelson, "The Nature of Slavery: Environmental Disorder and Slave Agency in Colonial South Carolina," in *Cultures and Identities in Colonial British America*, ed. Robert Olwell and Alan Tully, (Baltimore: Johns Hopkins University Press, 2006), 21–44..

21. Seth, *Difference and Disease*, 19; Winthrop D. Jordan, *White Over Black: American Attitudes Towards the Negro, 1550–1812* (Chapel Hill: University of North Carolina Press, 1968), 259.

22. On illness as a moral failing, see Trevor Burnard and Richard Follett, "Caribbean Slavery, British Anti-Slavery, and the Cultural Politics of Venereal Disease," *Historical Journal* 55, no. 2 (2012): 427–451; Vladimir Jankovic, *Confronting the Climate: British Airs and the Making of Environmental Medicine* (New York: Palgrave Macmillan, 2010), 42–54. For more on slaveholders assigning behavioral causes to poor health of the enslaved, see Seth, *Difference and Disease*, 250–260.

23. On the seasoning process for Europeans, see Seth, *Difference and Disease*, 91–111; Kupperman, "Fear of Hot Climates," 215; Curtin, "Epidemiology and the Slave Trade," 211; Chaplin, *Subject Matter*, 151–152; Valenčius, *Health of the Country*, 22–34; Darrett B. Rutman and Anita H. Rutman, "Of Agues and Fevers: Malaria in the Early Chesapeake" *William and Mary Quarterly* 33, no. 1 (1976), 43; Jan Golinski, *British Weather and the Climate of Enlightenment* (Chicago: University of Chicago Press, 2007), 188–189. Most historians writing about African seasoning interpret it somewhat differently, but I show how slaveholders thought of the process as essentially the same as European seasoning in Chapter 4. Suman Seth also holds this interpretation; see Seth, *Difference and Disease*, 99. For more on seasoning enslaved Africans, see Chapter 4.

24. On notions of bodily fluidity during the eighteenth century, see Wheeler, *Complexion of Race*; Katy L. Chiles, *Transformable Race: Surprising Metamorphoses in the Literature of Early America* (New York: Oxford University Press, 2014); Susan Scott Parrish, *American Curiosity: Cultures of Natural History in the Colonial British Atlantic World* (Chapel Hill: University of North Carolina Press, 2006), 77–102. Scholars have also shown the ways in which colonists linked climate with identity. See in particular Jim Egan, "The 'Long'd-for Aera' of an 'Other

Race': Climate, Identity, and James Grainger's *The Sugar-Cane*," *Early American Literature* 38, no. 2 (2003): 189–212.

25. Charles Gordon Gray to father, June 11, 1812, MS 163, f. 23, NLJ. Francis Grant to Charles Gordon, April 6, 1789, Gordon Family Papers, MS1160/6/64/3, University of Aberdeen Library Special Collections, Aberdeen, Scotland. As the scholar Katy Chiles has noted, early Americans conceived of race as "an exterior bodily trait" that was "continuously subject to change." See Chiles, *Transformable Race*, 2. Also see Wheeler, *Complexion of Race*. Even in the nineteenth century, according to Valenčius, migrants from the East Coast to the western United States believed that acclimation transformed people's skin tone as well as their health. Through the process of seasoning, she writes, "racial and individual identity were vulnerable" as "white observers feared change in their very selves." See Valenčius, *Health of the Country*, 230, 243. Similarly, Linda Nash argues that throughout much of the nineteenth century, "most Euro-Americans believed that it was the very permeability of the body that created its race and that a person's race was liable to change in a new location." See Nash, *Inescapable Ecologies: A History of Environment, Disease, and Knowledge* (Berkeley: University of California Press, 2006), 13.

26. On racial prejudice before biological race, see James Sweet "The Iberian Roots of American Racist Thought," *William and Mary Quarterly* 54, no. 1 (1997): 167–192; Kim F. Hall, *Things of Darkness: Economies of Race and Gender in Early Modern England* (Ithaca: Cornell University Press, 1995); Morgan, *Laboring Women*; Wheeler, *Complexion of Race*; William B. Cohen, *The French Encounter with Africans: White Response to Blacks, 1530–1880* (Bloomington, IN: Indiana University Press, 1980); Jordan, *White Over Black*. On legislation strengthening or creating racial categories, see Kathleen Brown, *Good Wives, Nasty Wenches, and Anxious Patriarchs: Gender, Race and Power in Colonial Virginia* (Chapel Hill: University of North Carolina Press, 1996). On slavery and racial antipathy reinforcing one another, see Jordan, *White Over Black*, 80. Also see Betty Wood, *The Origins of American Slavery: Freedom and Bondage in the English Colonies* (New York: Hill and Wang, 1997); Eric Williams, *Capitalism and Slavery* (Chapel Hill: University of North Carolina Press, 1944); Edmund Morgan, *American Slavery, American Freedom: The Ordeal of Colonial Virginia* (New York: W.W. Norton, 1975). George Fredrickson distinguishes between racial prejudice and racism, arguing that the first existed long before the second, because racism depended on modern concepts of race. See Fredrickson, *The Black Image in the White Mind: The Debate on Afro-American Character and Destiny, 1817–1914* (New York: Harper & Row, 1971), 2. On the persistence and pervasiveness of racism, even without scientific race, for many centuries and across cultures, see Francisco Bethencourt, *Racisms: from the Crusades to the Twentieth Century* (Princeton: Princeton University Press, 2013). On race as a social construct that enables racism, see Jean-Frédéric Schaub, *Race Is about Politics: Lessons from History*, trans. Lara Vergnaud (Princeton: Princeton University Press, 2019).

27. The literature on this topic is sizable. For a few examples, see Ivan Hannaford, *Race: The History of an Idea in the West* (Washington, DC: Woodrow Wilson Center Press, 1996); Nicholas Hudson, "From 'Nation' to 'Race': The Origin of Racial Classification in Eighteenth-Century Thought," *Eighteenth-Century Studies* 29 (1996): 247–264; George Fredrickson, *Racism: A Short History* (Princeton: Princeton University Press, 2002); Kathryn Burns, "Unfixing Race," in *Rereading the Black Legend: The Discourses of Religious and Racial Difference in the Renaissance Empires*, ed. Margaret R. Greer, Walter D. Mignolo, and Maureen Quilligan (Chicago: University of Chicago Press, 2008), 188–202. For a brief overview of eighteenth-century racial theorists, see Bruce Dain, *A Hideous Monster of the Mind: American Race Theory in the Early Republic* (Cambridge, MA: Harvard University Press, 2002).

28. Aristotle, *Politics*, Book VII, Part VII. See, in particular, the debates between Bartolomé de Las Casas and Juan Ginés de Sepulveda in the middle of the sixteenth century over enslaving Native peoples in Spanish America. On Bodin, see Marian J. Tooley, "Bodin and the Mediaeval Theory of Climate," *Speculum* 28, no. 1 (1953): 64–83.

29. Delbourgo, "Newtonian Slave Body," 186. On eighteenth-century philosophies of climate and bodily difference, see Hannaford, *Race*; David Bindman, *Ape to Apollo: Aesthetics and the Idea of Race in the 18th Century* (London: Reaktion Books Ltd., 2002). On Montesquieu's influence, see Glacken, *Traces on the Rhodian Shore*, 565–581. On the famous dispute between

Thomas Jefferson and the Comte de Buffon over the supposed degeneration of all things American, see Lee Alan Dugatkin, *Mr. Jefferson and the Giant Moose: Natural History in Early America* (Chicago: University of Chicago Press, 2009). There is a great deal of scholarly work on Jefferson, even as Winthrop Jordan's account remains astute; see Jordan, *White Over Black,* 429–481.

30. As Kathleen Brown argues in her study of race and gender in the seventeenth century, "Concepts of racial difference . . . acquired rhetorical force as a consequence of English efforts to naturalize them." See Kathleen Brown, *Good Wives,* 110.

31. David Brion Davis, *Slavery and Human Progress* (New York: Oxford University Press, 1984), 65.

32. Matthew Lewis, *Journal of a West India Proprietor* (London, 1834), entry for February 3, 1818. On death in the seventeenth- and eighteenth-century West Indies, see Dunn, *Sugar and Slaves,* 301; Vincent Brown, *Reaper's Garden,* 13. David Eltis has also pointed out that life expectancies for Europeans and Africans in the Caribbean were similar during slavery, and that "Arguments that Africans could stand up to the epidemiology of the Caribbean are irrelevant." See Eltis, *The Rise of African Slavery in the Americas* (Cambridge: Cambridge University Press, 2000), 68. Winthrop Jordan has also noted the "enormous toll" that work in lowcountry rice swamps and West Indian plantations took on Black lives. See Jordan, *White Over Black,* 233.

33. Puckrein, "Climate, Health and Black Labor"; Burnard, "'The Countrie Continues Sicklie'"; Kiple and King, *Another Dimension to the Black Diaspora;* Kenneth F. Kiple, *The Caribbean Slave: A Biological History* (Cambridge: Cambridge University Press, 1984); Francisco Guerra, "The Influence of Disease on Race, Logistics and Colonization in the Antilles," *Journal of Tropical Medicine and Hygiene* 69, no. 2 (1966): 23–35.

Chapter 1

1. The first English Caribbean colonies, established in the 1620s and 1630s, were St. Christopher, Barbados, Nevis, Providence Island, Antigua, and Montserrat. For more on these early colonies, see Dunn, *Sugar and Slaves.* On ancient climatic theories influencing early European voyages to the Americas, see White, *A Cold Welcome;* Kupperman, "Puzzle of the American Climate." As Linford Fisher points out, English colonists learned how to cultivate crops such as tobacco, cotton, and cacao from Native people, many of whom were enslaved and transported to Barbados from elsewhere in the Anglo-Atlantic. Meanwhile, the English attacked native Caribs on other Caribbean islands. See Linford Fisher, "'Dangerous Designes': The 1676 Barbados Act to Prohibit New England Indian Slave Importation," *William and Mary Quarterly* 71, no. 1 (2014): 99–124.

2. On enslaved Africans' experiences in the middle passage, see Stephanie E. Smallwood, *Saltwater Slavery: A Middle Passage from Africa to American Diaspora* (Cambridge: Harvard University Press, 2007); Sowande' M. Mustakeem, *Slavery at Sea: Terror, Sex, and Sickness in the Middle Passage* (Urbana, IL: University of Illinois Press, 2016); Alexander X. Byrd, *Captives and Voyagers: Black Migrants Across the Eighteenth-Century British Atlantic World* (Baton Rouge: Louisiana State University Press, 2008).

3. Justin Roberts notes that mortality rates among enslaved African laborers on sugar plantations were highest during holing and dunging seasons; see Roberts, *Slavery and the Enlightenment in the British Atlantic, 1750–1807* (New York: Cambridge University Press, 2013), 176–177.

4. According to Hilary Beckles, "By 1652, some 12,000 servants were employed in Barbados sugar production." See Hilary McD. Beckles, "Plantation Production and White 'Proto-Slavery': White Indentured Servants and the Colonisation of the English West Indies, 1624–1645," *The Americas* 41, no. 3 (1985): 21–45, especially 35–36. Also see Beckles, *A History of Barbados: From Amerindian Settlement to Nation-state* (Cambridge: Cambridge University Press, 1990), 48. For more on the transition to sugar during the 1640s and 1650s, see John J. McCusker and Russell R. Menard, "The Sugar Industry in the Seventeenth Century: A New Perspective on the Barbadian 'Sugar Revolution'" in *Tropical Babylons: Sugar and the Making of the Atlantic World, 1450–1680,* ed. Stuart B. Schwartz (Chapel Hill: University of North Carolina Press, 2004), 289–330.

5. Goetz, "Indian Slavery"; Carolyn Arena, "Indian Slaves from Guiana in Seventeenth-Century Barbados," *Ethnohistory* 64, no. 1 (2017). For more on Indigenous slavery during this period, see Arne Bialuschewski and Linford D. Fisher's introduction to the special issue of *Ethnohistory* 64, no. 1 (2017).

6. It is important to note here that indentured European laborers were not the same as enslaved African laborers. Indentures were different from enslavement and noting the presence of Europeans laboring on plantations is not an argument equating the two groups of people. At the same time, discussing the existence—at times, even the abundance—of European laborers in Caribbean climates is essential to understanding the history of plantation labor. Late eighteenth-century planters insisted that Europeans could not have possibly labored in the West Indies, giving rise to the notion that planters turned to Africans for climatic reasons. This claim then entered the historiography.

7. In addition to those of Galen and Aristotle, Hippocratic theories were most influential during this period. Physician Thomas Trapham of Jamaica, for example, explained in his medical treatise that he always consulted "the Topicks of *Hippocrates, viz.,* the Air, the Place, and the Waters." See Trapham, *A Discourse of the State of Health in the Island of Jamaica. With a provision therefore calculated from the Air, the Place, and the Water: The Customs and Manners of Living, &c.* (London: R. Boulter, 1679). As Susan Scott Parrish notes, the English in the 1600s "had to selectively absorb classical sources" to fit their own agendas. See Parrish, *American Curiosity,* 81. For more on the application of Hippocratic theories in the British colonial context, see Seth, *Difference and Disease;* Harrison, *Medicine in an Age of Commerce and Empire,* 30–33. Other elements of early modern European medical thought maintained that the body's internal humors—blood, phlegm, black bile, and yellow bile—had to stay in balance with the external elements—earth, water, air, and fire. For more on humoralism in the early Anglo-American context, see Sharon Block, *Colonial Complexions: Race and Bodies in Eighteenth-Century America* (Philadelphia: University of Pennsylvania Press, 2018), 12. Historian Michael Stolberg explains that by the early modern period, medical practitioners in Europe embraced a model of health that was "founded on the continuous movement of fluids, spirits, and vapors within the body, as well as across the body's boundaries." Stolberg discusses the application of these ideas through practices, such as bloodletting, that encouraged the movement of bodily fluids. See Stolberg, *Experiencing Illness and the Sick Body in Early Modern Europe,* trans. Leonhard Unglaub and Logan Kennedy (New York: Palgrave Macmillan, 2011), esp. 83–105, 126–134 (quote on 127). Sharon Block also notes "the porousness of the human body" in English colonial understandings. See Block, *Colonial Complexions,* 13.

8. Aristotle, *Meteorology,* trans E.W. Webster (Blacksburg, VA: Virginia Tech, 2001 [350 BCE]), book II, section V. As Karen Kupperman has argued, the English in the seventeenth century "continued to question the wisdom of transplantation to strange lands on the basis of the Aristotelian claim that the 'burning' and the 'frozen' zones were equally uninhabitable." See Kupperman, "Puzzle of the American Climate," 1278.

9. José de Acosta, *Natural and Moral History of the Indies,* ed. Jane E. Mangan and trans. Frances M. López-Morillas (Durham, NC: Duke University Press, 2002), 39. Acosta, a Jesuit priest, explained in 1590 that Aristotle and other philosophers were mistaken in their belief that "the burning heat of the sun, which is always so close overhead" in the tropical latitudes would cause the entire region to dry up any water and vegetation, rendering it unfit for human habitation. In contrast, Acosta insisted that in fact, "men enjoy a beautiful climate in the Torrid Zone." See Acosta, *Natural and Moral History,* 34–39 (Book 1, chapters 9–10). Acosta's work was translated into English in 1604, and Andrew Fitzmaurice writes that his text was "enthusiastically received by promoters of early modern English colonization." See Fitzmaurice, "Moral Uncertainty in the Dispossession of Native Americans" in *The Atlantic World and Virginia, 1550–1624,* ed. Peter C. Mancall (Chapel Hill: University of North Carolina Press, 2007), 403. Also see Jorge Cañizares-Esguerra, *Nature, Empire, and Nation: Explorations of the History of Science in the Iberian World* (Stanford: Stanford University Press, 2006), 25–26.

10. See Hippocrates, *Airs, Water, Places,* especially sections 124–127, on the ways in which climate affected people's dispositions and bodies. As Susan Scott Parrish points out, the English worried that although the Spanish would be able to tolerate tropical heat, the English could not. See Parrish, *American Curiosity,* 83.

11. "The second voyage to Guinea set out by Sir George Barne, Sir John Yorke, Thomas Lok, Anthonie Hickman and Edward Castelin, in the yere 1554. The Captaine whereof was M. John Lok" in Richard Hakluyt, *The Principal Navigations* (London, 1910–1913 [orig. 1589–90; enlarged edition 1598–1600]), vol. IV, 57–66. Other accounts in the text casually mentioned the presence of "people without heads" who had "their eyes and mouth in their breast." Such descriptions harkened back to the widely circulated but wildly imaginative narrative attributed to John Mandeville, published in the fourteenth century. For Mandeville's description, see *The Travels of Sir John Mandeville*, trans. C. W. R. D. Moseley (New York: Penguin, 2005), chapter 22. In addition, the writer of the Hakluyt piece noted that his homeward bound ship carried "certaine blacke slaves," several of whom expressed dislike for the "colde and moyst aire" they encountered off the English coast. He hastened to assure his readers that the enslaved Africans would adapt, although English people would have a harder time adapting to hot places. For more on the likely status of these "certaine blacke slaves," see Michael Guasco, *Slaves and Englishmen: Human Bondage in the Early Modern Atlantic World* (Philadelphia: University of Pennsylvania Press, 2014), 67–68. Meanwhile, traveler George Best speculated that since Africans in England could "well endure" the cold after a brief period of adjustment, English people might be able to adjust to hot climates just as easily. See George Best, "A true discourse of the three Voyages of discoverie, for the finding of a passage to Cathaya, by the Northwest, under the conduct of Martin Frobisher Generall" in Hakluyt, *Principal Navigations*, vol. V, 172. For more on Best's writing and the presence of Africans in early modern England, see Hall, *Things of Darkness*, 11.

12. Henry Colt, "The Voyage of Sr Henrye Colt Knight to ye Ilands of ye Antilleas in ye Shipp called ye *Alexander* whereof William Burch was Captayne & Robert Shapton Master accompanied with Diuers Captaynes & Gentlemen of Note" in *Colonising Expeditions to the West Indies and Guiana, 1623–1667*, ed. V. T. Harlow (London: Hakluyt Society, 1925), 98–99; Richard Ligon, *A True and Exact History of the Island of Barbadoes* (London, 1657), 9, 27; Colt, "Voyage," 73. As far as historians know, Colt's account remained in manuscript form, prefaced by a letter to his son, until it was published in 1925.

13. Colt, "Voyage," 90, 101.

14. There were both voluntary and involuntary European indentured servants in the Caribbean during the seventeenth century. During the English Civil War (1642–1651) many political prisoners, as well as prisoners of war, were sent to Barbados as punishment. John Donoghue argues that the coerced laborers who were "spirited" away, especially during the English Revolution, should be thought of as bond slaves rather than servants; in this conceptualization he relies on seventeenth-century language. See John Donoghue, "'Out of the Land of Bondage': The English Revolution and the Atlantic Origins of Abolition." *American Historical Review* 115, no. 4 (2010): 943–974. In contrast, Jerome Handler and Matthew Reilly argue that white servants cannot be considered slaves in this period. See Handler and Reilly, "Contesting 'White Slavery' in the Caribbean: Enslaved Africans and European Indentured Servants in Seventeenth Century Barbados," *New West Indian Guide* 91 (2017): 30–55.

15. Ligon, *True and Exact*, 43–44, 27.

16. For more on the labor transition, see Hilary McD. Beckles, *White Servitude and Black Slavery in Barbados, 1627–1715* (Knoxville: University of Tennessee Press, 1989), 59–78, 115–39; Gragg, *Englishmen Transplanted*, 113–131; Newman, *A New World of Labor*, 71–107; Dunn, *Sugar and Slaves*, 67–73; Russell R. Menard, *Sweet Negotiations: Sugar, Slavery, and Plantation Agriculture in Early Barbados* (Charlottesville, VA: University of Virginia Press, 2006), 29–48. Hilary Beckles points out that the dearth in the servant pool resulting from the Navigation and Trade Laws of 1660 and 1661 contrasted with the 1650s, when Oliver Cromwell sent prisoners of war (including Scots) to Barbados. For more on the changing availability of laborers, see Eltis, *Rise of African Slavery*, and Richard S. Dunn, "Servants and Slaves: The Recruitment and Employment of Labor" in *Colonial British America: Essays in the New History of the Early Modern Era*, ed. Jack P. Greene and J. R. Pole (Baltimore: Johns Hopkins University Press, 1984): 157–194. For more on the transportation of English, Scottish, Irish, and Welsh laborers to the Caribbean, see Carla Gardina Pestana, *The English Atlantic in an Age of Revolution, 1640–1661* (Cambridge, MA: Harvard University Press, 2004), 186–192. On Irish laborers in particular, see Jenny Shaw, *Everyday Life in the Early English Caribbean: Irish,*

Africans, and the Construction of Difference (Athens, GA: University of Georgia Press, 2013); Hilary McD. Beckles, "A 'riotous and unruly lot': Irish Indentured Servants and Freemen in the English West Indies, 1644–1713," *William and Mary Quarterly* 47, no. 4 (1990): 503–522. On the existence of racial awareness or biases in Europe before African slavery in the Americas, see Hall, *Things of Darkness*; Guasco, *Slaves and Englishmen*; Morgan, *Laboring Women*; Sweet, "The Iberian Origins of American Racist Thought." On the way in which these existing racial biases hardened through the experience of slavery, see Jordan, *White Over Black*. For an explanation linking racial attitudes and economics, see Wood, *Origins of American Slavery*, 48–55.

17. As Carla Pestana points out, there is a "paucity of sources" on Atlantic migration for the 1640s and 1950s, but Barbados planters relied upon captured "criminals and the vagrant poor" from the British Isles in addition to enslaved Africans. See Pestana, *English Atlantic*, 185–187.

18. Robert Venables, "Relation Concerning the Expedition," published as *The Narrative of General Venables*, ed. C. H. Firth for the Royal Historical Society (London, 1900), 61: 26–27, 34. Carla Pestana explains that soldiers originally had three days' worth of provisions but landing and disembarking took so long that by the time they began on foot many soldiers had only enough food left for a day and a half. See Pestana, *The English Conquest of Jamaica: Oliver Cromwell's Bid for Empire* (Cambridge, MA: Harvard University Press, 2017), 72. For a brief account of the expedition, see Bernard Capp, *Cromwell's Navy: The Fleet and the English Revolution, 1648–1660* (New York: Oxford University Press, 1989), 88–90.

19. Venables, "Relation," 49. Although the English marked 1655 as the transition of power in Jamaica, the Spanish did not surrender in some areas of the island until years later. For more on the Western Design, see Carla Gardina Pestana, "English Character and the Fiasco of the Western Design," *Early American Studies* 3, no. 1 (2005): 1–31 and Pestana, *The English Conquest of Jamaica*. For the campaign's effects on labor patterns in England and abroad, see Abigail L. Swingen, *Competing Visions of Empire: Labor, Slavery, and the Origins of the British Atlantic Empire* (New Haven: Yale University Press, 2015), 32–55.

20. I. S., *A Brief and Perfect Journal of the Late Proceedings and Success of the English Army in the West-Indies, Continued until June the 24th, 1655: Together with Some Quaeres Inserted and Answered: published for satisfaction of all such who desire truly to be informed in these particulars* (London, 1655), 24. Although Cromwell tried to suppress accounts of the disastrous expedition in the press, the news spread. As Carla Pestana explains, two letters describing the failed expedition, one from a soldier to his wife and one from an officer, circulated in London in September 1655. The return of the soldiers also enabled the spread of verbal accounts in England, and one participant published a detailed description of the expedition, noted above. As Pestana writes of the pamphlet by I.S., "Any hope the government had of suppressing details of the disaster was effectively frustrated by its publication." She also notes that although Venables's own narrative was not published, "other accounts were available." See Pestana, *English Conquest*, 97, 115. Jamaica's reputation as an unhealthy place, she writes, was "earned initially with the deaths of so many soldiers in the first year." See Pestana, 220. On further English negative interpretations of Jamaica's climate following the Western Design, see Pestana, 144, 157–160, 219–220. On naval recruits, see Capp, *Cromwell's Navy*, 267. According to Capp, prior to this expedition the Navy still had to impress most of its sailors, although some willingly joined. For more on the recruiting process, see Capp, 258–292.

21. "Considerations about ye peopling & settling the island of Jamaica," Egerton MS 2395, f. 288, BL; "A Breife Discription of the Ilande of Barbados" in *Colonising Expeditions*, ed. Harlow, 43; "A Briefe Survey of Jamaica," Egerton MS 2395, BL; CO 1/18, no. 109, f. 260-61, TNA. Also see "A View of the Condition of Jamaica the 20th of October 1664," [Thomas Modyford], Add MS 11410, f. 20-21, BL. "Ague" was generally a term used to describe illnesses, often (but not always) in conjunction with fevers. It usually meant chills, aches, or general feelings of lassitude. The writers of "A Briefe Survey" noted that Jamaica was "allways cooled with the breezes that constantly blow Easterly, and refreshed with frequent showers of rain, and such dewes in the night." See "A Briefe Survey," f. 609. Ligon also commented appreciatively on the "coole breezes of wind" that arose each morning. See Ligon, *True and Exact*, 27.

22. Spain ceded control of the island in 1661, but it took several more years for Spanish settlers to leave. Michael Guasco notes that "English immigrants/invaders" suffered from high mortality rates, which kept the population down. See Guasco, *Slaves and Englishmen*, 196.

23. Petition of representatives of Barbados to King, September 5, 1667, CO 1/21, f. 207, TNA. Carla Pestana argues that "as working people became aware of problems in particular New World destinations, recruiters had more difficulty lining up volunteers to travel as laborers to those ports." See Pestana, *The English Atlantic*, 186. Also see Wood, *Origins*, 55.

24. Sir Jonathan Atkins to Council, October 26, 1680, CO 29/3, f. 46–47; "Proposals made by Richard Dutton to Lords of Privy Council appointed by Committee for Trade and Plantations," September 1, 1683, CO 29/3, f. 106, TNA. Atkins, however, also noted that planters were particular about which servants they wanted. According to historian Vincent Harlow, "Of servants from Ireland the planters apparently had had more than enough. 'They grow weary of them,' wrote Atkins, 'for they prove commonly very Idle, and they do find by Experience that they can keepe three Blacks, who work better and cheaper than one White man.'" Sir Jonathan Atkins to Lords of Trade and Plantations, August 15, 1676, quoted in Vincent T. Harlow, *A History of Barbados, 1625–1685* (New York: Negro Universities Press, 1969 [1926]), 309. Hilary Beckles argues that migration to Jamaica, recruitment to military service, and various "ill-fated settlement schemes" elsewhere in the Caribbean all contributed to a reduction in the numbers of white laborers in Barbados during this period. See Beckles, "A 'riotous and unruly lot'," 509.

25. Christopher Jeaffreson to William Poyntz, June 5, 1676; May 11, 1677; May 6, 1681 in J.C. Jeaffreson, ed. *A Young Squire of the Seventeenth Century: from the papers of Christopher Jeaffreson, 1676–1686* (London: Hurst & Blackett, 1878), vol. I, 186, 207–209, 255–259. Jeaffreson wrote that the indentures were generally four years, and that it was customary to promise three hundred pounds of sugar at the end of this term. "But for a good carpenter," he wrote, "I would allow him foure thousand of sugar, or a little more ... and the like to a good cooper, and soe to a mason." For more examples of seventeenth-century Caribbean inhabitants writing to relatives in England requesting servants, see Gragg, *Englishmen Transplanted*, 113–115.

26. Egerton MS 2395, f. 289–290, BL.

27. Jonathan Atkins to Council, October 26, 1680, CO 29/3, f. 46–47; Edwyn Stede to Council, March 1687/8, CO 29/3, f. 232, TNA.

28. Instructions from the Jamaica Council, signed by Andrew Langly and Edward Broughton, to agents Gilbert Heathcote, Bartholomew Gracodion, and John Tutt [1693], in "History of the Island of Jamaica," Henry Barham, 1722, Sloane MS 3918, f. 93, BL.

29. *A Brief Description of the Province of Carolina, on the Coasts of Floreda. And More perticularly of a New Plantation begun by the English at Cape Feare, on that River now by them called Charles-River, the 29th of May, 1664. Wherein is set forth The Healthfulness of the Air; the Fertility of the Earth, and Waters; and the great Pleasure and Profit will accrue to those that shall go thither to enjoy the same* (London: Robert Horne, 1666) in *Historical Collections of South Carolina*, ed. B.R. Carroll (New York: Harper & Brothers, 1836), vol. II, 13–17. For more on early Carolina promotional material, see Edelson, *Plantation Enterprise*, 16–23. Many of the earliest English settler-colonists in Carolina came from Barbados. For more on the Barbados–Carolina connection, see Jack P. Greene, "Colonial South Carolina and the Caribbean Connection," *South Carolina Historical Magazine* 88, no. 4 (1987): 192–210; Peter McCandless, *Slavery, Disease, and Suffering in the Southern Lowcountry* (New York: Cambridge University Press, 2011); Edelson, *Plantation Enterprise*, 43–44; and Justin Roberts and Ian Beamish, "Venturing Out: The Barbadian Diaspora and the Carolina Colony, 1650–1685," in *Creating and Contesting Carolina: Proprietary Era Histories*, ed. Michelle LeMaster and Bradford J. Wood (Columbia, SC: University of South Carolina Press, 2013), 49–72.

30. *A Brief Description*, 14–17.

31. Samuel Wilson, *An Account of the Province of Carolina, in America* (London, 1682), in *Historical Collections of South Carolina*, 27; T.A. Gent [Thomas Ashe], *Carolina; or a Description of the Present State of that Country, and the Natural Excellencies Thereof* (London, 1682), in *Historical Collections of South Carolina*, 62–63. These comments about Native bodies being particularly healthy are noteworthy. Literature on early colonial perceptions of bodily difference between English and Natives focuses on English portrayals of Native bodies as especially sickly or unhealthy. Moreover, Joyce Chaplin has argued that the English constructed a narrative of their own physical superiority for the North American climate as they dispossessed Native peoples of their land. See Chaplin, *Subject Matter*, 160. The above comment demonstrates that

not all early colonists held these sentiments, and in fact some colonists saw Native bodies as paragons of health.

32. Thomas Newe to father, May 29, 1682. Letters of Thomas Newe, Newberry Library [originals in Bodleian, MS. Rawlinson D. 810] Note: this particular definition of seasoning—involving a period of ill health—was one of several at the time.

33. John Archdale, *A New Description of the Fertile and Pleasant Province of Carolina* (London, 1707), in *Historical Collections of South Carolina*, 96; Peter Purry, *Proposals by Mr. Peter Purry, of Newfchatel, for Encouragement of such Swiss Protestants as should agree to accompany him to Carolina, to settle a new colony. And, also, a description of the Province of South Carolina, drawn up at Charles-Town, in September 1731* (1731) in *Historical Collections of South Carolina*, 135–136. On Purry's proposed settlement, see Arlin C. Migliazzo, "A Tarnished Legacy Revisited: Jean Pierre Purry and the Settlement of the Southern Frontier, 1718–1736," *South Carolina Historical Magazine* 92, no. 4 (1991): 232–252.

34. John Style to Council, CO 1/19/81; Thomas Modyford to Council, CO 1/19/127, TNA. Modyford began his Caribbean career as a planter in Barbados, then led the island politically in the 1650s before becoming royal governor of Jamaica in 1664. For more on Modyford, see Dunn, *Sugar and Slaves*, 81–82. Even Richard Ligon, who believed alcohol could strengthen exhausted bodies, cautioned that its excessive consumption could cause people to overheat and become ill. See Ligon, *True and Exact*, 27.

35. Trapham, *Discourse*, TOC, 5, 7, 10, 50, 67, chapter two. The physician William Hughes also warned that heat-producing substances like alcohol could cause the body to overheat, throwing it out of balance and causing illness. See William Hughes, *The American Physitian; or, a Treatise of the Roots, Plants, Trees, Shrubs, Fruit, Herbs, &c. growing in the English Plantations in America* (London, 1672), 141–142. Hughes advised that people consume hot food and drink only in summer, when pores would already be open, in order to minimize the dangers of overheating. For more on alcohol and temperance in the seventeenth-century West Indies, see Michael R. Hill, "Temperateness, Temperance, and the Tropics: Climate and Morality in the English Atlantic World, 1555–1705" (PhD dissertation, Georgetown University, 2013).

36. Sloane, *A Voyage to the islands*, vol. I, preface, viii–ix, xxxi, cxxxiv–cxxxvi; Sloane MS 3984, f. 282, BL. In his published text, a conglomeration of natural history and medical journal, Sloane claimed that he "never saw a disease in *Jamaica*, which I had not met with in *Europe*," although he did make an allowance for "some very few Diseases, Symptoms, &c. from the diversity of the Air, Meat, Drink, &c." See Sloane, *A Voyage to the Islands Madera, Barbados, Nieves, S. Christophers and Jamaica* (London, 1707), vol. I, preface, xc. Thomas Trapham believed that "*Jamaica* produces few Diseases in comparison of Northern Countries," Trapham, *Discourse*, TOC. Upon his return to England, Sloane went on to hold positions of authority in the Royal Society over the next fifty years. For more on Sloane see James Delbourgo, *Collecting the World: Hans Sloane and the Origins of the British Museum* (Cambridge, MA: Belknap Press, 2017).

37. Richard Blome, *The Present State of His Majesties Isles and Territories in America* (London: H. Clark, 1687), 22–23; "The History and State of Jamaica under Lord Vaughan, with the alterations of Government that have happened since the Appointment of the Earl of Carlisle (1679–1680)," MS 159, 4–5, NLJ. While one author explained that people who "seated themselves near great Marshes are subject to Agues," he added that those "who are so seated in England" had similar afflictions, and that settlers "who are planted more remote from Marshes or standing waters, are exceedingly healthy." See Wilson, *Account of the Province*, 26. Another claimed that the only "Epidemical or Mortal" illnesses colonists experienced arose from their excessive drinking. See Ashe, *Carolina*, 62.

38. [John Scott], "Some Observations on the Island of Barbados" (1667), CO 1/21, f. 334–335, TNA; John Taylor, *Jamaica in 1687: The Taylor Manuscript at the National Library of Jamaica*, ed. David Buisseret (Kingston: University of the West Indies Press, 2008), vol. II, 266; Ligon, *True and Exact*, 43–44. Also see Beckles, "A 'riotous and unruly lot,' " 511.

39. These differences in susceptibility to yellow fever, however, observers noted as being between seasoned and unseasoned bodies. For more on this, see this book's conclusion.

40. Taylor, *Jamaica in 1687*, 266–268. Others recorded cases of dropsy in both European and African bodies, remarking upon the high rates of the disorder in the Caribbean. See Sloane,

Voyage to the Islands, vol. I, preface, cxxxiv. In writing about Trapham's text, eighteenth-century historian James Knight claimed that Trapham thought some diseases struck Europeans but spared Africans because Africans bathed daily. Europeans could become healthier by bathing more often. See James Knight, "The Natural, Moral, and Political History of Jamaica," vol. II, Add MS 12419, f. 65, BL. Although Trapham's text did recommend that Europeans bathe more often, he did not mention differing rates of health between Africans and Europeans. See Trapham, *Discourse,* 136–137; 140–142.

41. Hans Sloane and Alvarez de Toledo, "A Letter from Hans Sloane, M.D. and S.R.S. with several Accounts of the Earthquakes in Peru October the 20th, 1687. And at Jamaica, February 19th, 1687/8, and June the 7th, 1692." *Philosophical Transactions of the Royal Society* 18, no. 207 (1694): 78–100. This article contains several accounts of the June earthquake, most of which, Sloane claimed, were from eyewitnesses, and the others were compiled secondary accounts. These quotes are from no. VI, March 6, 1693, and no. VIII, July 3, 1693. Two-thirds is a rough, but conservative estimate. One contemporary report claimed that nine-tenths of the town was submerged in the ocean. See Sloane and Toledo, "A Letter," no III, June 20, 1692. For more on Port Royal, see Nuala Zahadieh, "'The wickedest city in the world': Port Royal, Commercial Hub of the Seventeenth-century Caribbean," in *Working Slavery, Pricing Freedom: Perspectives from the Caribbean, Africa and the African Diaspora,* ed. Verene A. Shepherd (New York: Palgrave, 2002), 3–20.

42. Joseph Norris to Isaac Norris [summer 1692], MS 1662, NLJ; Sloane and Toledo, "A Letter," no. VI, March 6, 1693; no. VIII, July 3, 1693; no. IV, September 23, 1692.

43. Sloane and Toledo, "A Letter," no. VIII, July 3, 1693. Contemporary views held that earthquakes resulted from air escaping from under the earth. In the words of West Indian traveler Thomas Gage the "hollow" mountains in the islands trapped the wind, which then "shake the earth to get out," causing earthquakes. See Thomas Gage, *The English-American his Travail by Sea and Land: or, A New Survey of the West-India's* (London: R. Cotes, 1648), 44. Aristotle also believed that earthquakes were caused by a buildup of wind bursting out of the earth. See Aristotle, *Meteorology,* book II, chapter 8. The earthquake actually severed the connection between Port Royal and the Jamaican mainland temporarily, until enough sand accumulated to rebuild the land bridge between the two places. For more on this, and for a more extensive account of the earthquake, see Matthew Mulcahy, "The Port Royal Earthquake and the World of Wonders in Seventeenth Century Jamaica," *Early American Studies* 6, no. 2 (2008): 391–421.

44. See accounts in Sloane and Toledo, "A Letter." Trevor Burnard estimates that the quake caused the deaths, either directly or indirectly, of about two thousand people. See Burnard, "Not a Place for Whites? Demographic Failure and Settlement, 1655–1780," in *Jamaica in Slavery and Freedom: History, Heritage and Culture,* ed. Kathleen E.A. Monteith and Glen Richards (Kingston: University of the West Indies Press, 2002), 81.

45. Captain Crocket, *A True and Perfect Relation of that Most Sad and Terrible Earthquake, at Port Royal in Jamaica* (London, 1792 [1692]). For another account, see *The Truest and Largest Account of the Late Earthquake in Jamaica, June the 7th, 1692* (London: Thomas Parkhurst, 1693). This account, written by a "Reverend Divine" in Jamaica, emphasized the moral nature of the earthquake. For another moral interpretation, see Reverend Emmanuel Heath, *A Full Account of the Late Dreadful Earthquake at Port Royal in Jamaica; Written in two Letters from the Minister of that Place* (London, 1692).

46. James Knight, "History of Jamaica," vol. I, Add MS 12418, f. 149, BL; Robert Renny, *An History of Jamaica* (London: J. Cawthorn, 1807), 42–43. David Galenson has found a "complete absence of Jamaica as a stated destination" for indentured servants (based on a list of servants leaving from Liverpool) from the 1690s through the early 1700s and suggests there may have been "a temporary halt at the turn of the century." Evidence is inconclusive, but the tables he provides do suggest that either servants did not go to Jamaica during this period, or else did not list it as their stated destination, unlike earlier and later decades. See Galenson, *White Servitude in Colonial America: An Economic Analysis* (New York: Cambridge University Press, 1981), 82–85. According to Trevor Burnard, William Beeston complained in 1699 about the continued sickness and consequent difficulty of filling posts on the island. See Burnard, "A Failed Settler Society: Marriage and Demographic Failure in Early Jamaica." *Journal of Social History* 28, no. 1 (1994): 69. Elsewhere, Burnard has written about the decreasing European

population in Jamaica during the 1690s and early 1700s, in large part as a result of various disasters; Jamaica as a whole, and Port Royal especially, suffered a number of disasters around the turn of the century. See Burnard, "European Migration to Jamaica, 1655–1780," *William and Mary Quarterly* 53, no. 4 (1996), 771–772. After the 1692 earthquake, a large fire burnt much of the town in 1703, and major hurricanes struck in 1712 and 1722. For more on Port Royal, see Matthew Mulcahy, "'That fatall spot': The Rise and Fall—and Rise and Fall Again—of Port Royal, Jamaica," in *Investing in the Early Modern Built Environment: Europeans, Asians, Settlers and Indigenous Societies*, Carole Shammas (Boston: Brill, 2012), 191–218.

47. James Robertson notes that the legacy of the earthquake was "even more damaging" than the quake itself. See Robertson, "'Stories' and 'Histories' in Late-Seventeenth-Century Jamaica," in *Jamaica in Slavery and Freedom*, 42.

48. Sir Richard Dutton to Lords of Trade and Plantations, August 29, 1682, CO 1/49/33; also see CO 29/3, f. 66, TNA; Sir John Witham to Lord Sunderland, April 30, 1685, CO 1/57/107, TNA.

49. Journal of Council of Trade and Plantations, October 23/24, 1699, CO 391/12/218–223; Sir William Beeston to Earl of Nottingham, May 13, 1693, CO 137/44/31, TNA. Gilbert Heathcote resided served as the agent for Jamaica from 1692–1704. See Jacob M. Price's entry on Heathcote in the *Oxford Dictionary of National Biography*.

50. Beville Granville to Earl of Nottingham, June 4, 1703; to Lords Commissioners for Trade and Plantations, June 16, 1703; to Mr. Warre, August 3, 1703; to George Granville Esq., August 3, 1703; to Sir John Stanley, August 3, 1703, September 3, 1703, January 12, 1703/4; to George Granville Esq., January 12, 1703/4; to Bernard Granville, Esq., January 31, 1704/5, all in PRO 30/26/90, f. 5, 10, 12, 14, 16, 20–21, 35, 36, 96, TNA.

51. Charles Cox to Council, October 21, 1707, CO 28/10/37, TNA. The Council granted Cox's request for leave.

52. James Barclay to Charles Gordon, December 5, 1727, MS1160/5/1; Barclay to David Gordon, June 9, 1729, MS1160/5/2, Gordon Family Papers, University of Aberdeen Library.

53. See Beckles, "Plantation Production," 35–36.

54. Sidney Mintz makes a compelling argument for viewing the seventeenth-century sugar plantation as an "industrial enterprise" that preceded factory industries in England. Planters found that enslaved laborers worked more efficiently than servants did on large sugar plantations, particularly as those plantations turned towards proto-industrial factory operations in the late seventeenth century. See Sidney Mintz, *Sweetness and Power: The Place of Sugar in Modern History* (New York: Penguin, 1985), 50.

55. John Lawson, *A New Voyage to Carolina; containing the exact description and natural history of that country: together with the present state thereof* (London, 1709), 85, 87.

56. Wilson, *Account of the Province*, 26–31.

57. Hard labor, the pamphlet writer explained, was "not to be endur'd in such a sultry Climate by any but Negroes." See *A True State of the Present Difference Between the Royal African Company, and the Separate Traders* (London, 1710), 32, quoted in Swingen, *Competing Visions*, 180. On the Royal African Company and its competitors arguing for the centrality of African laborers to the West Indies and the empire as a whole, see Swingen, 143–195.

58. Alexander Baillie to Alexander Baillie, March 18, 1752, D456/A/1/28, Highland Archive Center, Inverness, Scotland.

Chapter 2

1. Alexander Hewatt, *An Historical Account of the Rise and Progress of the Colonies of South Carolina and Georgia* (London: Alexander Donaldson, 1779), vol. I, 120. Further examples from eighteenth-century histories are in Chapter 6. Winthrop Jordan and Betty Wood have both treated the Trusteeship in Georgia as an isolated incident because of the protracted, deliberate defense of Black slavery it entailed. Jordan concluded that the economic and social motivations behind the Malcontents' arguments were so obvious that they needed no further examination, and the story ended with the legalization of Black slavery in Georgia. See Jordan, *White Over Black*, 262–263; Betty Wood, *Slavery in Colonial Georgia, 1730–1775* (Athens, GA: University of Georgia Press, 1984). Other historians have focused on different

aspects of Georgia's colonial history and have not interrogated the climate argument deeply. Some have focused on the relationship between the colonists and Indigenous peoples; see Julie Anne Sweet, *Negotiating for Georgia: British-Creek Relations in the Trustee Era, 1733–1752* (Athens: University of Georgia Press, 2005); John T. Juricek, *Colonial Georgia and the Creeks: Anglo-Indian Diplomacy on the Southern Frontier, 1733–1763* (Gainesville: University Press of Florida, 2010). Others have argued either that the prolonged arguments over slavery between the Malcontents and the Trustees resulted from class divisions among whites (see Noeleen McIlvenna, *The Short Life of Free Georgia: Class and Slavery in the Colonial South* (Chapel Hill: University of North Carolina Press, 2015)) or, conversely, from a race consciousness among those same white settlers (see Andrew C. Lannen, "Liberty and Slavery in Colonial America: The Case of Georgia, 1732–1770," *The Historian* 79, no. 1 (2017): 32–55).

2. Peter Wood notes that early English colonists in Carolina tried planting cotton, indigo, ginger, grapes, olives, rice, tobacco, and tending livestock at the colony's outset, but in the mid-1690s "rice production took permanent hold." See Peter H. Wood, *Black Majority: Negroes in Colonial South Carolina from 1670 through the Stono Rebellion* (New York: Alfred A. Knopf, 1974), 27–28, 36. Emma Hart contends that after the 1690s, rice production in Carolina "continued to expand at an astonishing pace until 1740." See Hart, *Building Charleston: Town and Society in the Eighteenth-Century British Atlantic World* (Charlottesville: University of Virginia Press, 2010), 32. On enslaved Indigenous people in South Carolina, see Denise I. Bossy, "Godin & Co.: Charleston Merchants and the Indian Trade, 1674–1715," *South Carolina Historical Magazine* 114, no. 2 (2013): 96–131; D. Andrew Johnson, "Enslaved Native Americans and the Making of South Carolina, 1659–1739," (PhD dissertation, Rice University, 2018); D. Andrew Johnson and Carolyn Arena, "Building Dutch Suriname in English Carolina: Aristocratic Networks, Native Enslavement, and Plantation Provisioning in the Seventeenth-Century Americas," *Journal of Southern History* 86, no. 1 (2020): 37–74.

3. On the movement of enslaved Indigenous people, see Goetz, "Indian Slavery." For more on Indigenous slavery in the South, see Christina Snyder, *Slavery in Indian Country: The Changing Face of Captivity in Early America* (Cambridge: Harvard University Press, 2010). On the Yamasee War, see several of the essays in Denise I. Bossy, ed., *The Yamasee Indians: From Florida to South Carolina* (Lincoln, NE: University of Nebraska Press, 2018).

4. Peter Wood estimates that by approximately 1708, the number of South Carolina inhabitants of African descent outnumbered those of European descent. See Wood, *Black Majority*, 36. On free Black havens in Spanish Florida, see Jane Landers, *Black Society in Spanish Florida* (Urbana, IL: University of Illinois Press, 1999). A copy of the Georgia Charter from June 1732, which details the reasons for founding the colony, can be found at CO 5/681, f. 3–30, TNA.

5. According to Betty Wood, the Trustees, most of whom were "ministers, merchants, and parliamentarians," numbered twenty-one at the colony's outset but grew to seventy-one in total. See Wood, *Slavery in Colonial Georgia*, 2. For more on the Trustees' plan for the colony, see Wood, *Slavery*, 5–8. On Georgia as a silk colony, see Stewart, *"What Nature Suffers to Groe"*, 31–34.

6. On relationships between Georgia colonists and local Native groups, see Sweet, *Negotiating for Georgia*; Juricek, *Colonial Georgia and the Creeks*; Claire S. Levenson, "The Impact of Gifts and Trade: Georgia Colonists and Yamacraw Indians in the Colonial American Southeast," in Sophus A. Reinert and Pernille Røge, eds. *The Political Economy of Empire in the Early Modern World* (New York: Palgrave Macmillan, 2013), 147–172.

7. According to Betty Wood, Parliamentary aid accounted for about 90 percent of Georgia's funds during the Trustee period (1732–1752). See Wood, *Slavery in Colonial Georgia*, 10–11. A short 1732 tract explaining the purpose of the colony noted that the "useless Poor in *England*" could be put to work producing commodities which would serve manufacturers in Britain. Moreover, Georgia would form "a Barrier" keeping British colonies "safe from *Indian* and other Enemies." Finally, Georgia would "contribute greatly towards the Conversion of the *Indians*." See [Benjamin Martyn], *Some Account of the Trustees Design for the Establishment of the Colony of Georgia in America* (London, 1732). On some of the religious aspects of early Georgia, see McIlvenna, *Short Life of Free Georgia*; James Van Horn Melton, *Religion, Community, and Slavery on the Colonial Southern Frontier* (New York: Cambridge University Press, 2015).

8. The image, an engraving by John Pine, appeared in advertisements for the colony. See "Proclamation of colony of Georgia," June 9, 1732, GB233/Ch 2634, National Library of Scotland, Edinburgh. The image also appeared as the frontispiece for Benjamin Martyn's *Some Account of the Trustees*. For more on Martyn's tract, see Thomas D. Wilson, *The Oglethorpe Plan: Enlightenment Design in Savannah and Beyond* (Charlottesville, VA: University of Virginia Press, 2012), 63–64. On the image appearing in Martyn's work, see Leonard L. Mackall, "The Source of Force's Tract 'A Brief Account of the Establishment of the Colony of Georgia, under Gen. James Oglethorpe, February 1, 1733'," *American Historical Review* 30, no. 2 (1925), footnote on 305–306.

9. On the symbolism of palm trees, see Nancy Stepan, *Picturing Tropical Nature* (Ithaca: Cornell University Press, 2001), 19. Although this 1732 image pre-dates Stepan's argument that images of palm trees became "the ubiquitous sign of the tropics" by the nineteenth century, such images circulated early enough in England (they can be found in Ligon's 1657 *History of Barbados*, for example) that many viewers would have had some familiarity with them.

10. "*Paradise*," the tract proclaimed, "with all her Virgin Beauties, may be modestly suppos'd at most but equal to its Native Excellencies." See Robert Mountgomery, *A Discourse Concerning the design'd Establishment Of a New Colony to the South of Carolina, in the Most delightful Country of the Universe* (London, 1717), 5–6. For another pre-Georgia publication touting the benefits of a new colony to the South of Carolina, see [John Barnwell], *An Account of the Foundation, and Establishment of a Design, now on Foot, for a Settlement on the Golden Islands, to the South of Port Royal in Carolina* (London, 1720). On the promotional literature of early Georgia, see Julie Anne Sweet, "'The natural Advantages of this happy Climate': An Analysis of Georgia's Promotional Literature," *Georgia Historical Quarterly* 98, no. 1–2 (2014): 1–25; Randall Miller, "The Failure of the Colony of Georgia Under the Trustees," *Georgia Historical Quarterly* 53, no. 1 (1969), 2–3. On latitudinal thinking, see Kupperman, "Puzzle of the American Climate."

11. James Oglethorpe, *Some Account of the Design of the Trustees for establishing Colonys in America*, ed. Rodney M. Baine and Phinizy Spalding (Athens, GA: University of Georgia Press, 1990), 16–22. Baine and Spalding note that this text, which they attribute to Oglethorpe, informed Benjamin Martyn's tracts *Some Account of the Designs of the Trustees for establishing the Colony of Georgia in America* (1732) and *Reasons for Establishing the Colony of Georgia* (1733). See Baine and Spalding, xxix. On their identification of Oglethorpe as the author of the first tract, see xx–xxix. One 1735 account of the colony, *A New Voyage to Georgia, By a Young Gentleman*, described Georgia as having "the pleasantest Climate in the World, for it's neither too warm in the Summer, nor too cold in the Winter; they have certainly the finest Water in the World, and the Land is extraordinary good: this may certainly be called the Land of *Canaan*[.]" *A New Voyage to Georgia* (London: J. Wilford, 1735), 6–7.

12. In his promotional piece, Robert Mountgomery acknowledged that although "gay Descriptions of new Countries raise a Doubt of their Sincerity" he claimed to draw on "*English Writers*, who are very numerous, and universally agree, that *Carolina*, and especially in its *Southern Bounds*, is the most amiable Country of the Universe" (Mountgomery, *A Discourse*, 5). On the Trustees' savvy, see Stewart, "*What Nature Suffers to Groe*", 37. For more on conceptions of Edens in the New World, see Richard Grove, *Green Imperialism: Colonial expansion, Tropical Island Edens and the Origins of Environmentalism, 1600–1860* (Cambridge: Cambridge University Press, 1995), 16–72; Sarah Irving, *Natural Science and the Origins of the British Empire* (London: Pickering & Chatto, 2008), 52–56.

13. John Norris, "Profitable Advice for Rich and Poor in a Dialogue" (London, 1712) in Jack P. Greene, ed. *Selling a New World: Two Colonial South Carolina Promotional Pamphlets, by Thomas Nairne and John Norris* (Columbia, SC: University of South Carolina Press, 1989), 92.

14. Juricek, *Colonial Georgia and the Creeks*, 12, 38; Sweet, *Negotiating for Georgia*, 20–31; Oglethorpe to Trustees, August 12, 1733, Transcripts of Earl of Egmont Papers, ms1786, 14200, f. 39, Hargrett Rare Book and Manuscript Library, The University of Georgia Libraries (hereafter Egmont Papers). See https://dlg.usg.edu/collection/guan_ms1786.

15. Thomas Causton to wife, March 12, 1732/3, Egmont Papers 14200, f. 22.

16. Samuel Eveleigh to Trustees, April 6, 1733, Egmont Papers 14200, f. 26.

17. Samuel Eveleigh to Trustees, April 6, 1733, Egmont Papers 14200, f. 26.

18. Tailfer claimed that his land was seventy miles from the town, but this number seems high. Patrick Tailfer to Trustees, March 15, 1735, CO 5/636, f. 230, TNA.
19. John Brownfield to Trustees, June 19, 1737, CO 5/639, f. 367, TNA.
20. John Brownfield to Trustees, February 10, 1736/7, CO 5/639, f. 142, TNA. The Trustees did pay for some servants to build roads along with some public buildings, but these roads did not reach much of the outlying land. See Melton, *Religion, Community, and Slavery*, 206.
21. Joseph Avery to Trustees, October 27, 1742, CO 5/641, f. 178; Hugh Anderson to Earl of Egmont, March 3, 1739, CO 5/640, f. 288, TNA. For more on Anderson, see Mart A. Stewart, "'Policies of Nature and Vegetables': Hugh Anderson, the Georgia Experiment, and the Political Use of Natural Philosophy," *Georgia Historical Quarterly* 77, no. 3 (1993): 473–496.
22. Patrick Tailfer to Trustees, March 15, 1735, CO 5/636, f. 230, TNA.
23. Francis Bathurst to Trustees, April 15, 1735, CO 5/637, f. 53; Noble Jones to Oglethorpe, July 6, 1735, CO 5/637, f. 135; John Brownfield to Trustees, February 10, 1736/7, CO 5/639, f. 142, TNA.
24. Samuel Holmes to Trustees, August 22, 1738; William Stephens to Harman Verelst, January 19, 1737/8, CO 5/640, f. 154, f. 47, TNA; Entry for September 16, 1738 in Allen D. Candler, ed. *William Stephens's Journal, 1737–1740, The Colonial Records of the State of Georgia*, (CRG vol. IV) (Atlanta: Franklin Printing and Publishing Company, 1906), 201.
25. James Oglethorpe to Trustees, August 12, 1733, Egmont Papers 14200, f. 39. For his later thoughts about rum, see Oglethorpe to Trustees, February 12, 1742/3, MS 595, GHS. At Oglethorpe's urging, the Trustees amended the Charter to include "An Act to prevent the importation and use of rum and brandies in the province of Georgia," to take effect in 1735. See CO 5/681, f. 36, TNA. For more on rum and alcohol in early Georgia, see Julie Anne Sweet, "'That Cursed Evil Rum': The Trustees' Prohibition Policy in Colonial Georgia," *Georgia Historical Quarterly* 94, no. 1 (2010): 1–29.
26. "An Act for rendering the colony of Georgia more defencible by prohibiting the importation and use of Black Slaves or Negroes into the same" was added to the Georgia Charter in 1735. See CO 5/681, f. 39, TNA. Christina Snyder explains that Indigenous peoples and Europeans shared similar ideas about bodily difference in the colonial era; foremost among these ideas was "the fluidity of identity." See Snyder, *Slavery in Indian Country*, 123–126.
27. William Byrd to Earl of Egmont, July 12, 1736, in Elizabeth Donnan, ed., *Documents Illustrative of the History of the Slave Trade to America* (New York: Octagon Books, 1965), vol. IV, 131–132.
28. Oglethorpe to Trustees, (received July 26, 1736), CO 5/638, f. 350. Also see, for example, John Brownfield to Trustees, February 10, 1736/7, CO 5/639, f. 142; Brownfield to Trustees, May 17, 1737, CO 5/639, f. 355, TNA.
29. Samuel Eveleigh to Benjamin Martyn, September 10, 1735, CO 5/637, f. 224, TNA; Samuel Eveleigh to William Jeffreys, July 4, 1735, Egmont Papers 14201, f. 46.
30. Tailfer complained that servants were "generally indented for four or at most five Years one of which at least is lost by their frequent Sickness." Patrick Tailfer et al. to Trustees, received August 27, 1735, Egmont Papers 14201, f. 109–110.
31. Hugh Anderson to Trustees, March 3, 1739, CO 5/640, f. 288, TNA.
32. Despite Benjamin Martyn's assurances to South Carolina governor Robert Johnson that the Trustees had "sent none but people inured to labour" in the first transport to Georgia, in actuality most settlers had no such experience. Benjamin Martyn to Robert Johnson, January 24, 1732/3, CO 5/666, f. 2, TNA. Betty Wood notes that only three out of an initial transport of 44 British men sent to Georgia who stated their occupations "admitted to having any knowledge of agriculture." See Wood, *Slavery in Colonial Georgia*, 13; also see 94.
33. Patrick Tailfer, Andrew Grant, Hugh Stirling, Patrick Houston to Trustees, June 18, 1735, CO 5/636, f. 228, TNA.
34. Thomas Jones to Harman Verelst, February 17, 1738/9, CO 5/640, f. 282; P. Thickness to Mother, November 3, 1736, CO 5/639, f. 41, TNA; George Philip to William Nicoll, January 8, 1739; July 20, 1739, GB234/RH15/139, NRS.
35. Entry for April 21, 1739, in Candler, *Journal of the Earl of Egmont*, 155; Thomas Christie to Trustees, December 14, 1734, CO 5/636, f. 91, TNA. On the petition, see Wood, *Slavery in*

Colonial Georgia, 29 and Betty Wood, "A Note on the Georgia Malcontents," *Georgia Historical Quarterly* 63, no. 2 (1979): 264–278.

36. Samuel Eveleigh to Benjamin Martyn, September 10, 1735, CO 5/637, f. 224, TNA. Also in Egmont Papers 14201, f. 120.

37. Egmont Papers 14205, f. 241–242.

38. Egmont Papers 14205, f. 249–250.

39. The Malcontents claimed that Africans loved the heat; "Negroes . . . Welcome the rising Sun with their Songs," they wrote. See Egmont Papers 14205, f. 250.

40. For more on the Salzburgers, see George Fenwick Jones, *The Georgia Dutch: From the Rhine and Danube to the Savannah, 1733–1783* (Athens, GA: University of Georgia Press, 1992); Karen Auman, "'English Liberties' and German Settlers in Colonial America: The Georgia Salzburgers' Conceptions of Community, 1730–1750," *Early American Studies* 11, no. 1 (2013): 37–54; Melton, *Religion, Community, and Slavery.*

41. "John Martin Bolzius and Israel Christian Gronau to James Oglethorpe, March 13, 1739," in *The Clamorous Malcontents: Criticisms & Defenses of the Colony of Georgia, 1741–1743*, ed. Trevor R. Reese (Savannah: Beehive Press, 1973), 164–165. When the Salzburgers first arrived, Oglethorpe directed them to a plot of land northwest of Savannah, which they began clearing and planting almost immediately. The Salzburgers worked the land, trying to cultivate a mixture of European and local crops, but they found the soil too shallow and of too poor a quality to support extensive farming. After two years of fruitless efforts, in the spring of 1736 they relocated from Old Ebenezer to a new site six miles away, which they called New Ebenezer.

42. John Martin Bolzius to Harman Verelst, March 14, 1739, CO 5/640, f. 301, TNA. The Salzburgers impressed the Trustees so much, in fact, that the secretary Benjamin Martyn suggested that Samuel Eveleigh use German servants in place of either English servants or enslaved African laborers. In response to Eveleigh's complaints about the cost of white sawyers, Martyn wrote, "you will find it much to your advantage to have German servants rather than Negro slaves. The Germans are a sober, strong, laborious people." See Benjamin Martyn to Samuel Eveleigh, May 1, 1735, CO 5/666, f. 57, TNA. But Eveleigh remained unconvinced, in large part because his experience in South Carolina had taught him that slave labor could be easily procured relatively cheaply; Thomas Stephens argued that "a Man at the end of 8 years, who plants with white men is £715.9.9 worse, than he would be were he to use Negroes" (quoted in Wood, *Slavery in Colonial Georgia*, 36). For an extensive analysis of the comparative costs of indentured versus enslaved labor, see Ralph Gray and Betty Wood, "The Transition from Indentured to Involuntary Servitude in Colonial Georgia," *Explorations in Economic History* 13 (1976): 353–370. In their calculations, Gray and Wood estimate that the cost of maintaining a servant (food, clothes, and housing) was roughly four times that of a slave. See Gray and Wood, 356.

43. "The Petition of the Inhabitants of *New Inverness*," January 3, 1738/9, in Reese, *Clamorous Malcontents*, 169–170. The Darien settlers also worried that, should the Trustees allow slaves, the settlers would need to provide increased vigilance against potential insurgencies and desertions of enslaved people. For more on the Darien settlers, see Harvey H. Jackson, "The Darien Antislavery Petition of 1739 and the Georgia Plan," *William and Mary Quarterly* 34, no. 4 (1977): 618–631; Anthony W. Parker, *Scottish Highlanders in Colonial Georgia: The Recruitment, Emigration and Settlement at Darien, 1735–1748* (Athens, GA: University of Georgia Press, 1997), 52–67.

44. Deposition of Hugh Mackay, taken by Francis Moore, January 19, 1738/9, Egmont Papers 14203, f. 143. Another version, worded slightly differently, can be found in Allen D. Candler, ed. *Journal of the Earl of Egmont, first president of the Board of Trustees, from June 14, 1738 to May 25, 1744* (CRG vol. V) (Atlanta: Franklin-Turner Company, 1908), 96–97. On Oglethorpe's reported bribery, see Parker, *Scottish Highlanders*, 72–73. Betty Wood notes that a malcontent complained that Oglethorpe had obtained many of these signatures "under duress" so that they should not be taken as an indication of people's true feelings. At the same time, William Stephens argued for a similar situation regarding the Malcontents' petition—either people had been convinced to sign something they did not believe in, or they signed "out of spite" and not out of "genuine concern for Georgia." See Wood, *Slavery in Colonial Georgia*, 33, 41.

45. Egmont Papers 14203, f. 146; also see Candler, *Journal of the Earl of Egmont*, 97; "The Deposition of Lieutenant George Dunbar, taken upon the Holy Evangelists, before the Recorder of the Town of Frederica, Jan. 20, 1738-9," reprinted in Reese, *Clamorous Malcontents*, 17; also see Candler, *Journal of the Earl of Egmont*, 98.

46. Candler, *Journal of the Earl of Egmont*, 98. It is possible that the cultural makeup of the various settlements contributed to their views on slavery. At both Ebenezer and Darien the settlers worked from a community-oriented perspective and thus had less need to hire outside laborers. At Savannah, though, the residents tended to forego a communal approach in favor of a more competitive attitude. Unable to rely as much upon the help of their neighbors, then, these settlers had a greater need to hire laborers, and thus felt the servant shortage more strongly. On the clan nature of the Darien settlement, see Harvey Jackson, "The Darien Antislavery Petition," 624–631, and Parker, *Scottish Highlanders*, 24–37, 54–58.

47. John Vat to H. Newman, May 30, 1735, CO 5/637, f. 77, TNA; Egmont Papers 14200, f. 349; Salzburgers to Oglethorpe, March 13, 1738/9, Egmont Papers 14203, 395; John Martin Bolzius to Harman Verelst, December 29, 1740, CO 5/640, f. 547-48, TNA. The letter to Oglethorpe was signed by 50 Salzburgers.

48. Bolzius to Trustees, December 4, 1742 in Candler, *Journal of the Earl of Egmont, 1738–1744*, 674; "An Account of Charge and Benefits of Mr. Isaac Nunez Henriquez on the Improvements that he has made in the Colony of Georgia in America, from the 12th July 1733 it being the time of his Arrival," Egmont Papers 14205, f. 285–286; Bartholomew Londerbukler to Harman Verelst, August 2, 1748, CO 5/642, f. 181, TNA; Egmont Papers 14203, f. 137. See also a letter from Hugh Anderson to Adam Anderson, June 15, 1738, in which he explains that he cleared, fenced, and planted four acres of rice, among other crops. Candler, *Journal of the Earl of Egmont*, 38.

49. Entry for August 7, 1740, in Candler, *William Stephens's Journal, 1737–1740* (CRG vol. IV), 636; "A State of the Province of Georgia, attested upon oath in the court of Savannah, November 10, 1740," in *William Stephens's Journal, 1737–1740* (CRG vol. IV), 671. Also in Reese, *Clamorous Malcontents*, 11.

50. Oglethorpe to Trustees, January 14, 1738/9, in Candler, *Journal of the Earl of Egmont*, 94. Thomas Jones wrote to John Lyde from Savannah in the fall of 1740 explaining that the "several Falsehoods, which have been industriously spread in England, representing this Colony as Unfruitfull and Unhealthy" were "not worth the regard of the Government." Lyde wrote that these rumors had been generated by previously indentured servants whose "Indentures being expired, Poverty began to stare them in the Face," but unwilling to work for a living, they contrived to "raise discontents" and spread untruths about the colony. These were presumably the same ex-servants who signed the December 1740 petition to the Trustees. See Egmont Papers 14205, f. 132.

51. Entries for January 14 and March 16, 1738/9, in Candler, *Journal of the Earl of Egmont*, 93, 140. For letters, see Stephens to Trustees, January 2, 1738/9, CO 5/640, f. 247, TNA. For more on Robert Williams, see Carole Watterson Troxler, "William Stephens and the Georgia 'Malcontents': Conciliation, Conflict, and Capitulation," *Georgia Historical Quarterly* 67, no. 1 (1983), 5–6.

52. Entries for April 29 and June 6, 1739, in Candler, *Journal of the Earl of Egmont*, 158, 178.

53. Oglethorpe to Trustees, March 12, 1738/9, General Oglethorpe's Letters, MS 595, GHS. Also see CO 5/640, f. 297, TNA.

54. Entry for July 16, 1739, in Candler, *Journal of the Earl of Egmont*, 209. Also see Egmont Papers 14204, f. 10.

55. Stephens to Trustees, January 2, 1738/9, CO 5/640, f. 247, TNA. Several Savannah residents wrote to the Trustees about their debts, in some cases crediting Robert Williams with lending them money for other debts, thus indebting themselves to him. One such letter reads: "Mr. Robert Williams of this place who bought from the store for us every thing needfull & paid the debt I ow'd to the store without whose assistance I and all my family must have perish'd for want I am now working all the bricklayers business to endeav'r to pay him the am't of his acco't which is in all thirty five pounds Ster." Isaac Young to Trustees, March 29, 1738, CO 5/640, f. 69, TNA.

56. See testimony of George Philip, February 16, 1740, in Reese, *Clamorous Malcontents*, 305–306.

57. George Philip to William Nicoll, January 8, 1739; July 20, 1739, GB234/RH15/139, NRS.

58. Entries for November 16, 1739, February 4, 1740, in Candler, *Journal of the Earl of Egmont*, 254–255; 302, 304. For more on Thomas Stephens, see Betty Wood, "Thomas Stephens and the Introduction of Black Slavery in Georgia," *Georgia Historical Quarterly* 58, no. 1 (1974): 24–40.

59. Egmont Papers 14205, f. 174–176.

60. Patrick Tailfer et al., *A True and Historical Narrative of the Colony of Georgia in America* (Charlestown, SC, 1741), reprinted in Reese, *Clamorous Malcontents*, 57.

61. Tailfer in Reese, *Clamorous Malcontents*, 57–58.

62. Entries for January 8, 1741/2; October 5, 1741, in Candler, *Journal of the Earl of Egmont*.

63. Benjamin Martyn, *An Impartial Enquiry into the State and Utility of the Province of Georgia* (London: W. Meadows, 1741), reprinted in Reese, *Clamorous Malcontents*, 125, 129, 130.

64. Martyn in Reese, *Clamorous Malcontents*, 132, 141.

65. Thomas Jones to John Lyde, September 18, 1740, Egmont Papers 14205, f. 66/133. See Wood, *Slavery in Colonial Georgia*, 96, on the differences in price between seasoned and unseasoned enslaved laborers in 1750s South Carolina and Georgia. According to Wood, Georgians did not end up importing slaves directly for several years but kept up a trade instead with the West Indies and South Carolina (98). This would fit with Williams's business model if he lived in South Carolina and used his brother's ties in the West Indies to supply Georgia with enslaved laborers. While Gregory O'Malley notes that after about 1710 most enslaved Africans arriving in South Carolina came directly from Africa rather than from the Caribbean, the situation in Georgia was different. As Darold Wax shows, from 1750–1764, enslaved Africans arrived in Georgia from South Carolina and the West Indies. Among West Indian islands, St. Christopher held the largest share of the trade, sending nearly double the number of slaves as Jamaica, which commanded the next largest portion. This trend continued in the following decade (1765–1775), with St. Christopher importing the most enslaved laborers to Georgia (among places other than Africa). Although I have not found direct evidence of Robert Williams's (or his brother's) engagement in this trade, the St. Christopher connection is notable. See Gregory E. O'Malley, *Final Passages: The Intercolonial Slave Trade of British America, 1619–1807* (Chapel Hill: University of North Carolina Press, 2014), 176; Darold D. Wax, "'New Negroes Are Always in Demand': The Slave Trade in Eighteenth-Century Georgia," *Georgia Historical Quarterly* 68, no. 2 (1984): 193–220, especially 198–202.

66. Harman Verelst to James Oglethorpe, March 29, 1740, CO 5/667, f. 157; John Dobell to the Trustees' Secretary [Martyn], April 27, 1748, CO 5/642, f. 163, TNA. In May 1749 Benjamin Martyn informed William Stephens that the Trustees were considering a repeal of the ban on slavery, and in July he wrote again advising Stephens that the repeal had passed. In 1750 Georgia's officials agreed to the ban, which would take effect the following year. See Martyn to Stephens, May 19, 1749 and July 7, 1749, CO 5/668, f. 165 and f. 171, TNA. The act repealing the earlier ban on slavery can be found amended to the charter in CO 5/681, f. 45, TNA. For more details on the transfer to royal control, see Wood, *Slavery in Colonial Georgia*, 79–86. Also see Gerald Cates, "The Seasoning: Disease and Death Among the First Colonists of Georgia," *Georgia Historical Quarterly* 64, no. 2 (1980), 153; and Randall Miller, "The Failure of the Colony of Georgia," 13. The Trustees were not eager to give up control of the colony, writing to the king that they had fulfilled many of the original goals of the colony: to provide a place for "indigent British subjects, and persecuted foreign Protestants," "to secure the friendship of the Indians in Georgia," and to establish "a sufficient barrier for South Carolina," which the Trustees noted had prospered during Georgia's existence. See petition from the Trustees to the King in 1753, Add MS 33029, f. 72, BL.

67. Although William Stephens requested British servants who were "used to hard labour in the country," in actuality only a small portion of settlers had any farming experience. See Stephens, *A State of the Province of Georgia* quoted in Wood, *Slavery in Colonial Georgia*, 40. Betty Wood also notes that "the vast majority" of the Malcontents were either English or Lowland Scots, as opposed to the Highland Scots at Darien and the Salzburgers at Ebenezer, both of whom were presumably more familiar with agricultural labor. See Wood, *Slavery*, 51. On Georgia's

place in the Greater Caribbean from an economic perspective, see Paul M. Pressly, *On the Rim of the Caribbean: Colonial Georgia and the British Atlantic World* (Athens, GA: University of Georgia Press, 2013). For some explanations of the Trustees' reversal, see Milton Ready, "The Georgia Trustees and the Malcontents: The Politics of Philanthropy," *Georgia Historical Quarterly* 60, no. 3 (1976), 275–277; Miller, "The Failure of the Colony of Georgia," 13–15.

68. For more on these projects, see Golinski, "American Climate and the Civilization of Nature"; Stewart, *"What Nature Suffers to Groe"*.

69. Entries for August 26, 1738; May 25 and 26, 1739; June 27, 1739; July 27, 1739; September 18, 1739, in Candler, ed. *William Stephens's Journal, 1737–1740* (CRG vol. IV). Also see entries from August 24, 1738; September 7 and 8, 1738; November 1 and 2, 1739 and entries from October 23, 1740; April 10 and 11, 1741; July 23–August 24, 1742 in *Journal of Col. William Stephens, 1740–1741* (CRG supplement to vol. IV) and E. Merton Coulter, ed. *Journal of William Stephens 1741–1743* (Athens, GA: University of Georgia Press, 1958). The worst period of sickness, in the summer of 1742, Stephens described as "a Malignant Feaver of the worst sort, and near Epedemical." Entry for August 7, 1742, in Coulter, ed. *Journal*.

70. Candler, *William Stephens Journal* (CRG vol. IV), 438.

71. Betty Wood notes that once Europeans in Georgia began importing enslaved laborers they worried about imported Africans' "resilience during the seasoning period" because they "might fall ill or die before their owners had seen any return on their investment." See Wood, *Slavery in Colonial Georgia*, 101. Todd Savitt, who writes about later eighteenth- and nineteenth-century conceptions of racial susceptibility to disease in the American South, acknowledges that even Africans with some resistance to malaria required seasoning upon arrival in the Americas: "Even adult slaves from Africa had to go through a 'seasoning' period, because the strains of malarial parasites in this country differed from those in their native lands." Todd L. Savitt, "Slave Health and Southern Distinctiveness" in Todd L. Savitt and James Henry Young, eds., *Disease and Distinctiveness in the American South* (Knoxville: University of Tennessee Press, 1988), 124.

72. Despite Eveleigh's lack of experience with white people cultivating rice, several historians have cited Eveleigh's arguments about the inability of Europeans to work in rice fields as evidence of differences in racial immunity. See, for example, Wood, *Slavery in Colonial Georgia*, 17; Reese, *Colonial Georgia*, 48; Wood, *Black Majority*, 84. Also see Chaplin, *An Anxious Pursuit*, 119–122; on 119 she cites Peter Wood quoting Eveleigh. On the Salzburgers' frustrations with market pressure for rice, and the added difficulties of the 1740 war with Spain, see George Fenwick Jones, *The Georgia Dutch: From the Rhine and Danube to the Savannah, 1733–1783* (Athens, GA: University of Georgia Press, 1992), 214.

73. Egmont Papers 14205, f. 249–250; Reese, *Clamorous Malcontents*, 57. Betty Wood argues, "from first to last, [the Malcontents'] pro-slavery argument hinged on the economic necessity of employing slaves." Wood, *Slavery in Colonial Georgia*, 205. She also notes the Trustees' skepticism regarding the Malcontents' intentions; see Betty Wood, "The Earl of Egmont and the Georgia Colony," in *Forty Years of Diversity: Essays on Colonial Georgia*, ed. Harvey H. Jackson and Phinizy Spalding (Athens, GA: University of Georgia Press, 1984), 88. As some historians have noted, there were reports of enslaved Africans in Georgia in the 1740s, particularly in places remote from Savannah. See Wax, "New Negroes," 196.

Chapter 3

1. Anthony Stokes, *A View of the Constitution of the British Colonies in North America and the West Indies* (London, 1783), 414–415; "Journal of a Soldier," Kings MS 213, f. 51, BL; John Vaughan Papers, BV462, Series II, Commonplace book c. 1783, p. 16, APS; [George Millegan Johnston], *A Short Description of the Province of South-Carolina, with an account of the Air, Weather, and Diseases at Charles-town* (London: John Hinton, 1763), 44–45. Also see Lord Adam Gordon, "Journal," *Travels in the American Colonies*, edited by N. D. Mereness, 397, cited in Julia Cherry Spruill, *Women's Life and Work in the Southern Colonies* (Chapel Hill: University of North Carolina Press, 1938), 30. For more on lowcountry rice plantations, see Edelson, *Plantation Enterprise*, 74–79, 103–119; Stewart, *"What Nature Suffers to Groe"*, 97–116; Chaplin, *Anxious Pursuit*, 227–276; McNeill, *Mosquito Empires*, 57. On seasonal movement in

South Carolina, see Peter McCandless, *Slavery, Disease, and Suffering in the Southern Lowcountry* (New York: Cambridge University Press, 2011), 22, 30, 37, 249–252, 261–262; John Duffy, "The Impact of Malaria on the South," in *Disease and Distinctiveness in the American South*, ed. Todd L. Savitt and James Harvey Young (Knoxville: University of Tennessee Press, 1988), 38.

2. There were eight Lords Proprietors of Carolina at its founding, who received a charter from King Charles II in 1663 (but settlement did not begin until the following decade). Most of the early settlers arrived from Barbados. For more on Charles Towne (later Charleston), see Hart, *Building Charleston*. Hart argues that the Lords Proprietors' attentions to the town were in large part due to Shaftesbury witnessing the rebuilding of London after the Great Fire of 1666. For more on the initial settling of the colony, see Wood, *Black Majority*, 15–34.

3. Shaftesbury to Yeamans, September 18, 1671, PRO 30/24/48, vol. 2, f. 185; Jos. Dalton to Shaftesbury, January 20, 1671/2, PRO 30/24/48, vol. 3, f. 84, TNA. Max Edelson notes that the Native Cusabo people played a significant role in directing the colonists' place of settlement; see Edelson, *Plantation Enterprise*, 25–33.

4. Emma Hart puts the date of Charles Towne's relocation as 1678; Peter Wood writes that Oyster Point became the central settlement "by 1680." See Hart, *Building*, 1; Wood, *Black Majority*, 22. Oyster Point, though, was not without its disadvantages and colonists continued to suffer from ill health. In 1684 the Proprietors wrote that Charles Towne was "no healthy situation" and that all of the new arrivals who fell ill brought "a Disreputation upon the whole Country." It was some time before Charles Towne's reputation changed for the better. Quoted in Wood, *Black Majority*, 66.

5. James Oglethorpe to Trustees, February 10, 1732/3, MS 595, James Edward Oglethorpe Papers, Item 5, no. 13; "An account of a visit to Georgia, from Charlestown, in South Carolina, from whence it is dated, 22 March, 1732–3," Georgia History Extracts, MS 1038, GHS; Oglethorpe, *Some Account*, 33–36. In settling upon Savannah's location, Oglethorpe believed the colony would have the best chance of survival. Similarly, Oglethorpe thought carefully about the location of Frederica, the fort and principal town on the nearby island of St. Simon. As a visitor noted during the 1740s, Frederica was in an ideal location. "The air is pure and serene," he wrote, "and, perhaps never was a better situation, or a more healthful place." August 1745, William Bacon Stevens Papers, MS 759, Folder 14, Item 58, GHS.

6. Other historians have gone into greater detail about what constituted a healthy or an unhealthy place; Valenčius's *Health of the Country* has extensive descriptions. For the eighteenth century, see Jankovic, *Confronting the Climate*, 15–20, 87–89, 137–140; Golinski, *British Weather*, 62–63, 140–150, 158, 185–187; Simon Finger, *The Contagious City: The Politics of Public Health in Early Philadelphia* (Ithaca, NY: Cornell University Press, 2012), 7–20. On colonists believing they were changing the early American climate, see Zilberstein, *A Temperate Empire*. For more on clearing trees to improve air flow, and for how this practice changed the climate, see Grove, *Green Imperialism*, 65–67, 121–123, 208; McNeill, *Mosquito Empires*, 28–29, 80; Golinski, "American Climate and the Civilization of Nature", 155, 162–167; Stewart, "*What Nature Suffers to Groe*", 62–63, 140, 155; McCandless, *Slavery, Disease, and Suffering*, 33, 237. Draining swamps was another way of "improving" the air of a place; for more on this practice in the eighteenth-century lowlands, see Marion Stange, "Governing the Swamp: Health and the Environment in Eighteenth-Century Nouvelle-Orléans" in *French Colonial History* 11 (2010), 1–21. For more on colonists' disillusionment with their attempts to manage the land, see Matthew Mulcahy, *Hurricanes and Society in the British Greater Caribbean, 1624–1783* (Baltimore: Johns Hopkins University Press, 2006), 26–32. As other scholars have noted, English colonists in North America cleared land in an attempt to "tame" the land, and to lay claim to it based upon use: if Natives did not clear and cultivate the land, the argument went, they had no real claim to it, in contrast with European settlers. For more on this line of thought, see Golinski, *British Weather*, 4–5; David Armitage, *The Ideological Origins of the British Empire* (New York: Cambridge University Press, 2000), 97; Ken MacMillan, *Sovereignty and Possession in the English New World: The Legal Foundations of Empire, 1576–1640* (New York: Cambridge University Press, 2006), 8–10. Also see Nicholas Canny, *Kingdom and Colony: Ireland in the Atlantic World, 1560–1800* (Baltimore: Johns Hopkins University Press, 1988), 52–53 on British settlers "civilizing" forests and people in Ireland prior to North America.

7. On Kingston's dominance in Jamaica, especially for the slave trade but also for other merchant activities, see Trevor Burnard and Kenneth Morgan, "The Dynamics of the Slave Market and Slave Purchasing Patterns in Jamaica, 1655–1788," *William and Mary Quarterly* 58, no. 1 (2001): 205–228. On merchant activity in Kingston, see Trevor Burnard, "'The Grand Mart of the Island': The Economic Function of Kingston, Jamaica in the Mid-Eighteenth Century," in *Jamaica in Slavery and Freedom: History, Heritage and Culture*, ed. Kathleen E. A. Monteith and Glen Richards (Kingston: University of the West Indies Press, 2002), 225–241.

8. Add MS 33029, f. 185, BL. Knowles wrote first to the merchants, expressing his support for their idea, and then to the Board of Trade. See Charles Knowles to merchants, January 20, 1754, Egerton MS 3490, f. 28–30, BL. For Knowles's letter to the Board, see CO 137/60 f. 90–92. Knowles included his eagerness to have a new house in his letter of support. In a separate letter, Knowles argued that moving the capital would take some of the power away from Jamaica's planters, who opposed the move. See Knowles to "My Lord Duke," January 29, 1754, Add MS 32734, f. 87, BL. On the Spanish Town petition, see "Petition of residents of St Jago de la Vega," November 21, 1754, MS 1644, no. 3, NLJ. For a more extensive discussion of this debate, see Jack P. Greene, "'Of Liberty and of the Colonies': A Case Study of Constitutional Conflict in the Mid-Eighteenth-Century British American Empire" in *Liberty and American Experience in the Eighteenth Century*, ed. David Womersley (Indianapolis: Liberty Fund, 2006), 49–92; Jack P. Greene, *Settler Jamaica in the 1750s* (Charlottesville: University of Virginia Press, 2016).

9. Egerton MS 3490, f. 19–20, BL; also CO 137/27 f. 153–156, TNA.

10. Council and Assembly of Jamaica to King, May 17, 1755, Fuller Family Papers, SAS-RF/ 20/3/9, East Sussex Record Office, Brighton; Egerton MS 3490, f. 21, BL; also CO 137/27, f. 157–158, TNA.

11. MS 1644 no. 3, f. 151, 168, NLJ.

12. Add MS 22676, f. 11, BL.

13. MS 1644 no. 3, f. 176, 165, NLJ.

14. Add MS 33029, f. 186, BL. Mark Harrison writes about a similar case in the eighteenth-century Dutch East Indies, in which a physician determined the health of a port town by the direction of the prevailing winds; air from the sea would make it healthy, while breezes from the direction of the nearby marshes would bring ill health to the port. See Harrison, *Medicine in an Age of Commerce and Empire*, 37.

15. Add MS 33029, f. 183–186, BL.

16. Add MS 33029, f. 182–184, BL; "The Protest of President Grigory, Simon Clark and Henry Archbould Esq., members of the Council," CO 137/29, f. 35, TNA. For more on eighteenth-century understandings of yellow fever, see McCandless, *Slavery, Disease, and Suffering*, 61–83; 106–124. On yellow fever traveling around the Atlantic, see Billy G. Smith, Ship of Death: A Voyage that Changed the Atlantic World (New Haven: Yale University Press, 2013). On the population estimate in Jamaica, see Burnard, "Not a Place for Whites?" 82. Of course it is possible that European sailors, and not enslaved Africans, could carry yellow fever. But this scenario would still assume that sailors contracted the fever from Africans while on the coast.

17. Add MS 33029, f. 183, 192, BL.

18. Robert Stirling to Archibald Stirling, September 5, 1754, Stirling family papers, T-SK 11/ 3, The Mitchell Library, Glasgow; Journals of the Assembly of Jamaica, vol. IV (Jamaica, 1797), April 22, 1755 (508); Lord of Trades' Report to Privy Council, July 3, 1755, SAS-RF/20/3/10, Fuller Family Papers, East Sussex Record Office. Robert Stirling had recently arrived in Jamaica from Scotland and eventually sided with the Kingston faction because it was "agreeable to my own inclinations & the Govern. & most of my best friends are engaged in it." See Robert Stirling to Archibald Stirling, April 19, 1755, Stirling Family Papers; also see letter of July 1757 regarding the fallout with Knowles. On arguments about the safety of the colony's records, see Journals of the Assembly of Jamaica, April 22, 1755 (509). Also see letter of Stephen Fuller to gentlemen at Jamaica, February 9, 1757, in which he reported on the hearings on the matter at the Board of Trade. According to Fuller, the Board found "That what had been alledg'd against the safety of keeping the records in St Jago de la Vega could have but little weight, when they had been there near an hundred years without the least accident." SAS-RF/21/93, Fuller Family Papers. On the merchant forces, see James Robertson, *Gone*

is the Ancient Glory: Spanish Town, Jamaica, 1534–2000 (Kingston: Ian Randle Publishers, 2005), 90, although Robertson mentions Glasgow, not Lancaster, as the fifth of these cities.

19. For more on the debates about rebuilding Port Royal after each disaster, see Mulcahy, "'That Fatall Spott.'"

20. PC/2/106, f. 179-90, TNA. For details of the Jamaica Assembly's proceedings, see Journals of the Assembly of Jamaica, vol. IV, 502–646; also see CO 137/29 and Fuller Family Papers, East Sussex Record Office. On Knowles's removal, see document dated July 7, 1756, SAS-RF/21/49; also see Stephen Fuller to Gentlemen at Jamaica, February 9, 1757, SAS-RF/21/93, Fuller Family Papers. Kingston continued to harbor yellow fever; in 1799 planter Simon Taylor wrote to a friend advising him that his son, who was preparing to travel to the island, should avoid Kingston entirely. "Should he come by the way of London," Taylor wrote, upon arrival in Kingston "he should have particular directions not to come on shore immediately" but instead write to a neighbor announcing his arrival. Once friends received word of the visitor's arrival, they would bring him directly from the ship to Taylor's house, "which is in the country about three miles and a half from Kingston and where there is no risque of getting" yellow fever. Simon Taylor to George Hill, June 15, 1799, Simon Taylor Letterbook C, ICS 120/1/C/10, ICS.

21. John Rollo, Observations on the means of preserving and restoring health in the West-Indies (London: C. Dilly, 1783), 29; Edward Long, The History of Jamaica, or, General Survey of the Antient and Modern State of the Island (London: T. Lowndes, 1774), vol. II, 132, 169, 107, 599; vol. I, 358. Long himself was unimpressed with Kingston, writing, "The contiguity of buildings, the frowzy atmosphere of many inhabitants assembled within a small compass, the lowness of their situation, the easy communication of infectious distempers": all contributed to an atmosphere rife with disease. See Long, History, vol. I, 425. Long was particularly frustrated with Kingston, as with other unhealthy towns in the Caribbean, because colonists had had the opportunity to take climatic variations into account when developing a region. "That a West-India town," he wrote, "should be irregularly planned is, indeed, almost inexcusable, not only on account of health, which ought to be principally regarded, but because it is formed as it were at once." For Long, it was inconceivable that anyone with the opportunity to plan and develop a town would ignore health factors. "In laying out the surveys of these townships," he wrote, "every convenience ought to be attended to, in respect of water, or springs, goodness of soil, and healthiness of situation." See Long, History, vol. II, 4; vol. I, 424. Richard Ligon recorded a similar complaint about Barbados over a century earlier. Bridgetown, the colony's capital, was situated entirely without regard to people's health, he wrote, "If they had considered health, as they did conveniency," he grumbled, the founders of the town "would never have set it there." Ligon refused to believe that anyone could "have been so improvident, as not to forsee the main inconveniences that must ensue, by making choice of so unhealthy a place to live." Instead, he explained, the town sprung up without regard to health, and he considered building a town "upon so unwholsome a place" to be a serious mistake. See Ligon, True and Exact, 25.

22. Long, History of Jamaica, vol. I, 359. Long argued that even seasonality was entirely inconsistent between the northern and southern parts of Jamaica: "On the North side of the island the climate and seasons are very different; it being dry weather in general on this side, when there is rain on the South side, and vice versa." See Long, vol. I, 365. William Beckford made a similar argument: "The seasons, on the southern and on the northern sides of Jamaica, are almost as opposite in their periods of harvest, as are their points upon the compass; insomuch that about the time that the crops are terminated on the former, the process of sugar-making begins in the latter." Beckford, A Descriptive Account of the Island of Jamaica (London: T. and J. Egerton, 1790), vol. II, 286. Others also wrote about the variations in environment within Jamaica. Bryan Edwards found that between Kingston and "a villa eight miles distant, in the highlands of Liguanea" there was a midday temperature difference "of ten degrees in eight miles; and in the morning and evening the difference was much greater." See Edwards, The History, Civil and Commercial, of the British Colonies in the West Indies (New York: Arno Press, 1972 [1793]), vol. I, 179–180. Robert Renny repeated this claim in his own history of Jamaica a decade and a half later. See Renny, History of Jamaica, 83. Letters from individuals also confirm this perception. As one person wrote from Jamaica in 1777, "the different parts of this

Island are as various in the weather or what they here call seasons as Green-Land & Bombay." J. Jackson to Henry Jackson, October 27, 1777, C 110/141, TNA.

23. [Johnston], *A Short Description*, 44–45; Robert Duff to George Duff, September 2, 1773, Duff Family Papers, MS 3175/Z/204/1, University of Aberdeen Library; George Ogilvie to Margaret Ogilvie, November 22, 1774, Ogilvie Family Papers, MS 2740/10/5/2, University of Aberdeen Library.

24. CO 101/1, f. 91; "Queries relating to his majesty's islands of America, Answered for Tobago 20 October 1773," CO 318/2, f. 51, TNA. Edward Long wrote that by the 1770s, the climate of Jamaica was "undoubtedly much altered from what it was at the first settlement by the English." "The clearing of the mountainous tracts," he explained, "has much contributed to this alteration;" specifically, the lack of rainfall. In contrast, he believed that some parts along the island's south coast which were newly covered in "thick woods" would soon "become the sources of unwholesomeness." See Long, *History of Jamaica*, vol. I, 357–358. Regarding the parish of Hanover in Jamaica, Long wrote that the air "is esteemed healthy, and will be more so, when greater progress is made in cutting down its woods." Long, *History of Jamaica*, vol. II, 211.

25. William Gerard de Brahm, *Report of the General Survey in the Southern District of North America*, Kings 210, f. 94, BL.

26. John Farquharson to James Farquharson, August 20, 1788; John Farquharson to William Farquharson, December 25, 1790, Farquharson of Invercauld Papers, Box 115, Braemar, Scotland. For more on the St. Vincent preservation, see Grove, *Green Imperialism*, 293–296.

27. "An Act, to appropriate for the Benefit of the Neighbourhood the Hill, called the King's Hill, in the Parish of St. George, and for enclosing the same, and preserving the Timber and other Trees growing thereon, in order to attract Rain." February 9, 1791, in *The Laws of the Island of Saint Vincent and its dependencies, from the first establishment of a legislature to the end of the year 1787* [addendum] (Saint Vincent, 1788). Deforestation had serious consequences for Caribbean islands. Some animal species disappeared, other invasive species proliferated, and soil erosion became widespread. Rainstorms could result in massive soil loss to hilly areas, and all over some islands soil nutrients quickly depleted. For more on this, see McNeill, *Mosquito Empires*, 28–29. On the King's Hill preserve, see Richard Grove, "The Island and the History of Environmentalism: The Case of St. Vincent," in *Nature and Society in Historical Context*, ed. Mikulás Teich et al. (New York: Cambridge University Press, 1997): 148–162.

28. "Hints drawn up for the use of a gentleman on the point of making a tour through the West India Islands," Benjamin Vaughan papers, series III, APS.

29. Samuel Martin to Samuel Martin Esq., February 24, 1775, Add MS 41348, f. 210, BL. For more on Antigua's lack of rivers, and ponds dug by enslaved laborers to collect rainwater, see David Barry Gaspar, "Sugar Cultivation and Slave Life in Antigua Before 1800," in *Cultivation and Culture: Labor and the Shaping of Slave Life in the Americas*, ed. Ira Berlin and Philip D. Morgan (Charlottesville, VA: University of Virginia Press, 1993), 116.

30. Samuel Martin, *An Essay on Plantership* (Antigua, 1765), 3. According to Richard Sheridan, Martin's *Essay* went through at least nine editions, beginning most likely in the 1750s, with the ninth appearing in 1802. The last two reprints were published with other texts, both of which noted the influence of Martin's work. See Richard B. Sheridan, "Samuel Martin, Innovating Sugar Planter of Antigua, 1750–1776," *Agricultural History* 34, no. 3 (1996): 126–139.

31. Simon Taylor to David Reid, March 10, 1801, Simon Taylor Letterbook D, ICS; Long, *History of Jamaica*, vol. II, 169, vol. I, 404; Simon Taylor to Chaloner Arcedeckne, May 1, 1787, Vanneck-Arc/3A/1787/5, ICS.

32. Long, *History of Jamaica*, vol. I, 424; Joshua Steele to Joseph Banks, June 20, 1786, Add MS 33978, f. 70–71, BL; John Hunter, *Observations on Diseases of the Army in Jamaica, and on the Best Means of Preserving the Health of Europeans, in that Climate* (London, 1788), 19.

33. Hunter, *Observations on Diseases*, 104; September 26, 1765, John Bartram Diary, APS. On ventilation in homes, including slave cabins, and its relationship to health and to slavery in the nineteenth-century American South, see Elaine LaFay, "'The Wind Can Blow Through and Through': Ventilation, Public Health, and the Regulation of Fresh Air on Antebellum Southern Plantations," in *Atlantic Environments and the American South*, ed. Thomas Blake Earle and D. Andrew Johnson (Athens, GA: University of Georgia Press, 2020), 38–62. By

the time Long, Bartram, and Hunter wrote, several residents of the lowcountry and the West Indies considered the climate when constructing homes and buildings. For many decades previously, however, inhabitants had insisted on replicating English-style buildings despite their unsuitability for hot climates. For more on some of the ways South Carolinians ignored or refused to adapt to the climate (particularly hurricanes) in building, see Matthew Mulcahy, *Hurricanes and Society*, 132136. In the sixteenth century, Richard Ligon complained about the tendency of Barbados planters to build homes in a style that he believed antithetical to the demands of the climate: rather than digging deep cellars and incorporating many windows and high ceilings for cooling, he found small homes, low to the ground, with windows concentrated on the western sides of buildings. This design, he wrote, turned homes into "Stoves, or heated Ovens." See Ligon, *True and Exact*, 40. It is possible that these residents built their homes low to the ground because of the potential damage to tall buildings from hurricanes; those lower to the ground were more likely to be spared damage from high winds, or at the very least be easier to re-build. As Hans Sloane explained about Jamaica, the Spanish purposely built low houses with posts deep in the ground to protect against hurricanes and earthquakes. See Sloane, *A voyage to the Islands*, vol. I, xlvii.

34. Justin Roberts explains that hot houses were literally "hot" enclosures, with "little fresh air and tightly packed quarters," for housing sick enslaved laborers on plantations. See Roberts, *Slavery and the Enlightenment*, 166. For more on plantation hospitals, see Richard B. Sheridan, *Doctors and Slaves: A Medical and Demographic History of Slavery in the British West Indies* (New York: Cambridge University Press, 1985), 268–291. During the eighteenth century in Europe, as well as in the hot climates of the Americas, the situation of hospitals caused a great deal of debate as physicians began to embark upon the new field of public health. Physicians, particularly in cities, declared that the situation of most hospitals was nothing short of abysmal: they bred disease much more rapidly and more thoroughly than they cured it, and they often lay next to overflowing graveyards which stank in the summer months. Following a line of thought that associated bad smells with disease, these physicians and public advocates insisted that hospitals be moved to healthier areas. On locating hospitals and other buildings in Saint Domingue away from tanneries, butcheries, and cemeteries, see Karol Weaver, *Medical Revolutionaries: The Enslaved Healers of Eighteenth-Century Saint Domingue* (Urbana, IL: University of Illinois Press, 2006), 29. Historian James Riley argues that in Britain, the 1733 publication of John Arbuthnot's *An Essay Concerning the Effects of Air on Human Bodies* marked the start of a public health campaign focused on the links between "bad air" and poor health; see James C. Riley, *The Eighteenth-Century Campaign to Avoid Disease* (New York: St. Martin's Press, 1987).

35. Samuel Cary to Charles Spooner, July 31, 1788, Samuel Cary Letterbook, volume 6, Ms. N-1997, MHS; Simon Taylor to Chaloner Arcedeckne, October 6, 1790, Vanneck-Arc/3A/1790/31, ICS.

36. H. W. Plummer to Joseph Foster Barham Jr., March 16, 1803, MSClardepc357, bundle 3, Bod.; Charles Gordon Gray to Father, August 4, 1814, MS 2008; November 15, 1815; February 22, 1816, MS 163, NLJ.

37. On "feigning illness" see Sheridan, *Doctors and Slaves*, 270; Weaver, *Medical Revolutionaries*, 4; Hogarth, *Medicalizing Blackness*, 155. On hospitals, see Pratik Chakrabarti, *Materials and Medicine: Trade, Conquest and Therapeutics in the Eighteenth Century* (New York: Manchester University Press, 2010), 66–69.

38. Campbell Dalrymple to Board of Trade & Plantations, August 1763, CO 101/1, f. 87, TNA; "Report of St Vincents, 27 April 1765," Add MS 13879, f. 12, BL; Robert Melville to Board of Trade, January 3, 1765, CO 101/1, f. 181, TNA. Dalrymple left Dominica immediately after issuing his report and did not stay long enough to oversee the move away from Roseau. Two years later, another colonial official reported that Roseau still acted as the capital of Dominica. It was situated on low, unhealthy ground, and its residents found the water there so bad that they refused to use it, preferring water from a source a mile away. The official credited Dalrymple with recognizing Roseau's unhealthiness, which "caused him to take the resolution to change the place of Trade from hence to the Bay of Loubiere, where he imagined all those inconveniencies were greatly remedied." See "Report of Dominica," July 12, 1765, Add 13879, f. 18, BL.

39. "State of the Island of Grenada, 1 April 1765," Add MS 13879, f. 7-8, BL. The aptly named Santeur presumably refers to the present-day town of Sauteurs, located in St. Patricks parish in the northern part of the island. Writing about places' effects on people's health, physician James Lind explained that "the temperature of the climate, the colour, strength and activity, the constitutions and health of the inhabitants greatly depend" upon "the nature of the soil" in any particular region. Lind, *Essay on Diseases*, 198.

40. Hunter, *Observations on Diseases*, 71–72; Robert Jackson, *A Treatise on the Fevers of Jamaica, with some observations on the Intermitting Fever of America, and an appendix, Containing some Hints on the Means of preserving the Health of Soldiers in hot Climates* (London: J. Murray, 1791), 86–88. John McNeill writes that British army officials in mid-eighteenth-century Jamaica and London did not "express any remorse over the sufferings and deaths of so many Britons and colonials" in spite of the "grim odds" of British soldiers' survival in the West Indies. See McNeill, *Mosquito Empires*, 166–168. On planters successfully keeping troops in unhealthier spots close to plantations, see *Mosquito Empires*, 81. Enslaved soldiers also served in mid-eighteenth-century British armed conflicts. Maria Bollettino argues that British officials valued these men "precisely because they died in the place of disciplined European regulars and sailors, whose lives they treasured more." See Bollettino, "'Of equal or of more service': Black Soldiers and the British Empire in the Mid-Eighteenth-Century Caribbean," *Slavery and Abolition* 43, no. 3 (2017): 510–533 (quote on 519).

41. Long, *History of Jamaica*, vol. II, 313, 190–191.

42. Lord George Germain to John Dalling, March 7, 1781, CO 137/80; Dalling to Germain, May 24, 1781, CO 138/29, TNA.

43. Lind, *Essay on Diseases*, 173–175. Edward Long also wrote about the hospital's history, often copying Lind verbatim. See Long, *History of Jamaica*, vol. II, 108. For more on this hospital, see Chakrabarti, *Materials and Medicine*, 61–70.

44. "Copy of a report made to the Lords of the Admiralty & ye rest of the Commanders of His Majestys ships stationed at Jamaica in 1748, concerning ye unhealthfulness of ye town of Kingston, & ye state of the Hospital belonging to His Majesty's Navy near that town," CO 137/29, f. 15–16, TNA.

45. CO 137/29, f. 11–12, TNA.

46. In the early nineteenth century, Robert Renny recounted in brief the story of Kingston and Spanish Town in the 1750s under Knowles. He claimed that for several reasons, including the fact that Kingston was "more unhealthful than Spanish-town," Knowles was "necessitated to abandon" the proposed move. See Renny, *History of Jamaica*, 64–65.

47. James Lind's *Essay on Diseases*, for example, was a popular text, and later natural histories and medical manuals cited it repeatedly.

48. Long, *History of Jamaica*, vol. I, 404; William Beckford, *A Descriptive Account of the Island of Jamaica*, 178–179.

49. "Journal of a Soldier," Kings MS 213, f. 51, BL; Anthony Stokes, *A View of the Constitution*, 414–415.

Chapter 4

1. Simon Taylor to Chaloner Arcedeckne, April 7, 1788, Vanneck-Arc/3A/1788/3; Taylor to Arcedeckne, May 29, 1788, Vanneck-Arc/3A/1788/10; Taylor to Arcedeckne, July 21, 1788, Vanneck-Arc/3A/1788/19, ICS. For more on Simon Taylor, see Christer Petley, *White Fury: A Jamaican Slaveholder and the Age of Revolution* (Oxford: Oxford University Press, 2018); Higman, *Plantation Jamaica*.

2. William Wright to Chaloner Arcedeckne, March 1, 1788, Vanneck-Arc/3G/3 and 3 (ii), ICS.

3. William Smalling to Joseph Foster Barham, March 30, 1771, Barham Papers, Ms.Clar. dep.c.357, bundle 1, Bod.

4. On the seasoning process for Europeans, see Seth, *Difference and Disease*, 91–111. For other descriptions of seasoning, see Kupperman, "Fear of Hot Climates," 215; Curtin, "Epidemiology and the Slave Trade," 211; Chaplin, *Subject Matter*, 151–152; Golinski, *British Weather*, 188–189; Valenčius, *The Health of the Country*, 22–34. On seasoning enslaved laborers, see Sheridan, *Doctors and Slaves*, 131–134; Byrd, *Captives and Voyagers*, 61, 70; Smallwood,

Saltwater Slavery, 193, 197; Edward Kamau Brathwaite, *The Development of Creole Society in Jamaica, 1770–1820* (Clarendon Press, 1971), 298; Vincent Brown, *The Reaper's Garden*, 50. Suman Seth's recent work is an important exception to the common interpretation of African seasoning. Seth notes that Africans had to be seasoned to the Caribbean climate; see *Difference and Disease*, 99. On medical interpretations of African seasoning, and the relationship with abolition debates, see Sean Morey Smith, "Seasoning and Abolition: Humoural Medicine in the Eighteenth-Century British Atlantic," *Slavery and Abolition* 36, no. 4 (2015): 684–703.

5. Seasoning was also linked to value in complicated ways elsewhere; Kathryn Olivarius, for example, explains how white residents of nineteenth-century New Orleans who survived an attack of yellow fever gained immunity, a form of seasoning that enhanced their status. See Olivarius, "Immunity, Capital, and Power in Antebellum New Orleans," *American Historical Review* 124, no. 2 (2019): 424–455.

6. As Joyce Chaplin has written, "A seasoned colonist was an altered person." See Chaplin, *Subject Matter*, 151–152.

7. There are many relevant histories of medicine; for a start, see Harrison, *Medicine in an Age of Commerce and Empire*; Claire Gherini, "'Experiment and Good Sense Must Direct You': Managing Health and Sickness in the British Plantation Enlightenment, 1756–1815," (PhD dissertation, Johns Hopkins University, 2016); Pablo F. Gómez, *The Experiential Caribbean: Creating Knowledge and Healing in the Early Modern Atlantic* (Chapel Hill: University of North Carolina Press, 2017); Londa Schiebinger, *Plants and Empire: Colonial Bioprospecting in the Atlantic World* (Cambridge, MA: Harvard University Press, 2004); Londa Schiebinger and Claudia Swan, eds., *Colonial Botany: Science, Commerce, and Politics in the Early Modern World* (Philadelphia: University of Pennsylvania Press, 2005); Chakrabarti, *Materials and Medicine*; Kathleen S. Murphy, "Translating the Vernacular: Indigenous and African Knowledge in the Eighteenth-Century British Atlantic," *Atlantic Studies* 8 no. 1 (2011): 29–48; Matthew Crawford, *The Andean Wonder Drug: Cinchona Bark and Imperial Science in the Spanish Atlantic, 1630–1800* (Pittsburgh: University of Pittsburgh Press, 2016); Weaver, *Medical Revolutionaries*; Delbourgo, *Collecting the World*; Zachary Dorner, *Merchants of Medicines: The Commerce and Coercion of Health in Britain's Long Eighteenth Century* (Chicago: University of Chicago Press, 2020).

8. Robert Pinkney to Joseph Foster Barham, May 16, 1766, MS.Clar.dep.c.357, bundle 1, Bod.; John Vanheelen to Joseph Foster Barham Jr., July 24, 1787, MS.Clar.dep.c.357, bundle 1, Bod.; John Graham to Joseph Foster Barham Jr., May 23, 1790, MS.Clar.dep.c.357, bundle 2, Bod; Charles Gordon Gray to father, September 8, 1814, MS 163, NLJ. For planters' letters explaining that dry weather caused good health, see John Graham to Joseph Foster Barham Jr., December 16, 1790, MS.Clar.dep.c.357, bundle 2, Bod.; Alexander West Hamilton to Hugh Hamilton, July 22, 1796, AA/DC/17/8, Hamilton Family Papers, Ayrshire Archives; Robert Pinkney to Joseph Foster Barham, May 16, 1766, MS.Clar.dep.c.357, bundle 1, Bod.

9. Hunter, *Observations on Diseases*, 15–17; Jackson, *Treatise on the Fevers of Jamaica*, 77–78; Thomas Trotter, *Medicina nautica: an essay on the diseases of seamen: comprehending the history of health in His Majesty's fleet* (London, 1797), 443; James Grainger, *An Essay on the more common West-India Diseases; and the remedies which that Country itself produces. To which are added, some hints on the management, &c. of negroes* (London: T. Becket and P.A. De Hondt, 1764), 12; William Sandiford, *An Account of a Late Epidemical Distemper, extracted from a letter addressed to Gedney Clarke, Esq.* (Barbados: Esmand and Walker, 1771), 3, 16; William Hillary, *Observations on the Changes of the Air and the Concomitant Epidemical Diseases, in the Island of Barbadoes* (London: L. Hawes et. al., 1766, 2nd ed.), 18.

10. Samuel Cary to Charles Spooner, January 30, 1788, Samuel Cary Letterbook, volume 6, MHS; Charles Gordon Gray to father, September 8, 1814, MS 163, f. 43, NLJ; Thomas Pinckney to Harriott Horry, June 25, 1789, Pinckney Family Papers, Box 3, folder 2, Library of Congress; Pierce Butler to William Page, June 26, 1798, Pierce Butler Letterbook Am. 0368, vol. 2, f. 242, HSP.

11. George Ottley to Clement Tudway, December 17, 1808, Tudway Family Archive, Box 11, bundle 7, Somerset Heritage Centre; Grace Campbell to Archibald Campbell of Knockbuy, December 30, 1766, Campbell Family Correspondence, The Mitchell Library, Glasgow; Samuel Cary to Charles Spooner, December 13, 1785, Samuel Cary Letterbook, volume

6, MHS; Samuel Martin to Samuel Martin Esq., March 30, 1769; April 26, 1769, Add MS 41348, f. 40, 44, BL.

12. John Graham to Joseph Foster Barham, Jr., June 25, 1792; August 8, 1792; January 6, 1793, MS.Clar.dep.c.357, bundle 2, Bod. Many people took sea voyages, hoping the air would restore them. Plantation manager Francis Farley left Antigua for Tobago in the spring of 1779 "for the benefit of the sea air," hoping that the salt and the "change of climate would recover him." Unfortunately, like Cupid and Jackie, Farley did not survive his voyage, dying "the third day after he was at sea," because he was apparently "too far gone to recover" when he set sail. Main Swete Walrond to Clement Tudway, April 18, 1779; Alexander Hillock to Clement Tudway, April 21, 1779, Tudway Family Papers, DD\TD Box 15/6, Somerset Heritage Centre.

13. James Chisholme to Doctor Ewart, February 16, 1795, Chisholme Papers, MS 5464, f. 174, NLS. Chisholme wrote in response to Ewart's inquiry about the case, which had begun several years earlier, in December 1787. By 1795 the man was still alive, and Ewart's inquiry demonstrates that the case was unusual enough to warrant multiple transatlantic letters.

14. Letter from John Radcliffe to the Duke of Ormonde, printed in the back of *The Practical Physician for Travellers, Whether by Sea or Land* (London, 1729), 238–239, copy at the New York Academy of Medicine; Hillary, *Observations*, viii; also see John Huxham, *An Essay on Fevers, And their Various Kinds, As depending on Different Constitutions of the Blood* (London: S. Austen, 1750), 117. For more on Hillary, see Seth, *Difference and Disease*, 57–87.

15. James Stormonth to Margaret Darling, October 27, 1791, Stormonth-Darling Papers, NRAS1881, bundle 56, NRS; George Brissett to John Tharp, June 10, 179[?], R55/7/128(c)/1/1; Brissett to Tharp, April 14, 1805, R55/7/128(c)/1/6, Tharp Papers, Cambridgeshire Archives, Cambridge; Samuel Martin to Samuel Martin Esq., May 31, 1769, Add MS 41348, f. 54, BL.

16. John Stirling to William Stirling, May 24, 1791, Stirling Family Papers, T-SK 11/3, The Mitchell Library, Glasgow; Simon Taylor to David Reid, March 10, 1801, Simon Taylor Letterbook D, ICS; Janet Schaw, *Journal of a Lady of Quality; Being the Narrative of a Journey from Scotland to the West Indies, North Carolina, and Portugal, in the years 1774 to 1776*, ed. E.W. and C.M. Andrews (New Haven: Yale University Press, 1921), 104.

17. Grainger, *West-India Diseases*, 11–13.

18. Charles Spooner to Samuel Cary, June 8, 1786, Samuel Cary Papers, Ms. N-1997, Box 2, MHS.

19. Samuel Cary to Charles Spooner, March 31, 1785; July 30, 1786; October 25, 1786; November 20, 1786, Samuel Cary Letterbook, volume 6, MHS.

20. Charles Gordon Gray to father, March 12, 1812, MS 2008, NLJ; Thomas Mills to Francis Graham, April 4, 1810, MS 132, f. 93, NLJ; James Kerr to Hugh Hall, September 24, 1777, MS 1069, no. 3, NLJ. On the average prices of seasoned versus unseasoned slaves in Jamaica, see Trevor Burnard and Kenneth Morgan, "The Dynamics of the Slave Market and Slave Purchasing Patterns in Jamaica, 1655–1788," *William and Mary Quarterly* 58, no. 1 (2001), 221.

21. John Blythe and James Grant to Joseph Foster Barham, Jr., September 12, 1813, MS.Clar. dep.c.358, bundle 1, Bod.; Charles Webb to Joseph Foster Barham, Jr., August 28, 1803, MS.Clar.dep.c.357, bundle 3, Bod.

22. Charles Rowe to Joseph Foster Barham, Jr., July 4, 1789, MS.Clar.dep.c.357, bundle 2, Bod.; Simon Taylor to Chaloner Arcedeckne, May 1, 1773, Vanneck-Arc/3A/1773/12, ICS.

23. On creolization, see Brathwaite, *The Development of Creole Society in Jamaica*; also see Trevor Burnard, "Thomas Thistlewood Becomes a Creole," in *Varieties of Southern History: New Essays on a Region and Its People*, ed. Bruce Clayton and John A. Salmond (Westport, CT: Greenwood Press, 1996), 99–118.

24. Beville Granville to George Granville Esq., August 3, 1703; Beville Granville to Sir John Stanley, August 3, 1703, PRO 30-26-90, f. 14, 16, TNA; Robert Hamilton to James Buchanan, November 29, 1736, AA/DC/17/2, Hamilton Family Papers, Ayrshire, Scotland; John Pinney to Harry Puncy, March 2, 1765; John Pinney to Edward Jessup Esq., May 2, 1765, Pinney Family Papers, volume 3, Letterbook of John Frederick Pinney I and John Pinney, f. 67, 70, University of Bristol.

25. Lind, *Essay on Diseases*, 3, 146–147. Mark Harrison points out that Lind's treatise "became a standard work of reference for half a century. It went through many editions (the last in 1811) and was translated into German, Dutch, and French." See Harrison, *Medicine in an Age of Commerce and Empire*, 72. Many contemporary writers also cite Lind, in both medical treatises and natural histories. See, for example, Long, *History of Jamaica*, vol. II, 506–508.

26. William Smalling to Joseph Foster Barham, March 30, 1771; November 10, 1772; February 2, 1774, Barham Papers, Ms.Clar.dep.c.357, bundle 1, Bod; Charles Gordon Gray to father, December 31, 1816, MS 163, f. 74, NLJ. For more on the Barham plantations in Jamaica, see Richard S. Dunn, *A Tale of Two Plantations: Slave Life and Labor in Jamaica and Virginia* (Cambridge, MA: Harvard University Press, 2014).

27. George Barclay to Charles Gordon, June 30, 1739, Gordon Family Papers, MS1160/5/3, University of Aberdeen Library.

28. Simon Taylor to Chaloner Arcedeckne, January 26, 1788, Vanneck-Arc/3A/1788/1; Simon Taylor to Robert Taylor, Esq., June 9, 1810, Simon Taylor Letterbook, Reel 9, ICS/120/1/J/9, ICS; John Pinney to Azariah Pinney, October 28, 1789, Pinney Family Papers, Letterbook 11, f. 254, University of Bristol Library; Samuel Martin to Samuel Martin Esq., January 31, 1774, Add MS 41348, f. 157, BL; Schaw, *Journal of a Lady of Quality*, 105. Also see letter of Francis Grant, who worried "whether Scotland would suit either my health or habits" after years spent in Jamaica. Francis Grant to Charles Gordon, April 4, 1785, Gordon Family Papers, MS1160/6/36, University of Aberdeen Library.

29. Samuel Martin to Samuel Martin Esq., January 15, 1768; March 22, 1768; January 27, 1770; April 25, 1771; January 31, 1774; June 10, 1774, Add MS 41348, ff. 2–3, 6, 99, 145, 157, 183, BL.

30. Schaw, *Journal of a Lady of Quality*, 153, 182, 116.

31. Long, *History of Jamaica*, vol. I, 526; vol. II, 435. Long explained that "new Negroes" should be "gradually seasoned to the change of climate." See Long, *History*, vol. II, 433. Notes that appear to be early drafts of his text are in the British Library; see Add MS 12407, BL. Long was born in England, but spent several years in Jamaica and had considerable family connections to the island, stretching back several generations to 1655. See Howard Johnson, 'Introduction' to Long's *History of Jamaica* (Montreal: McGill-Queen's University Press, 2002); also see Suman Seth, "Materialism, Slavery, and the History of Jamaica," *Isis* 105, no. 4 (2014): 764–772. Seth's work points to Long's contradictory and ambivalent stance on race.

32. Long, *History of Jamaica*, vol. II, 261–262. Long ascribed most, though not all, bodily changes to the climate: others resulted from diet. For example, Long wrote that Creoles, both white and Black, had particularly good teeth, which Long credited to the high quantities of sugar they consumed. See Long, *History*, vol. II, 273. Bryan Edwards seems to have copied this view in writing his own natural history a couple of decades later. According to Edwards, creoles displayed a "peculiar cast of character impressed by the climate." "I am of opinion," he wrote, "that the climate of the West Indies displays itself more strongly on the persons of the Natives . . . They are obviously a taller race, on the whole, than the Europeans; but I think in general not proportionably robust." They had supple joints, he explained, which enabled a gracefulness and ease of movement; they also had cold and pale skin, and their eye sockets were "considerably deeper than among the natives of Europe," a feature Edwards credited to protection from the "strong glare of sun-shine." See Bryan Edwards, *The History, Civil and Commercial, of the British Colonies in the West Indies* (London, 1793), vol. II, 11–12.

33. Long, *History of Jamaica*, vol. II, 274; 351–352. For more on Long's views about changeable versus fixed bodies in Jamaica, see Newman, *A Dark Inheritance*, 140–142.

34. Long, *History of Jamaica*, vol. II, 477, 261–262, 273.

35. Ann Appleton Storrow to sister, January 29, 1793, Ann Appleton Storrow Papers, MHS; Francis Grant to Charles Gordon, April 6, 1789, Gordon Family Papers, MS1160/6/64/3, University of Aberdeen Library; Charles Gordon Gray to father, May 16, 1811, MS 163, f. 18, NLJ; James Savage to Mary Lincoln, March 17, 1806, James Savage Papers II, MHS; William Leckie to Walter Ewing, 1783, Orr Ewing Papers, Bundle 36, Port of Menteith, Scotland. On creole complexions, see Senior, *The Caribbean and the Medical Imagination*, 95–100 and Wheeler, *The Complexion of Race*. On creole women in general—who received more criticism from British men than creole men did—see Hilary McD. Beckles, "White Women

and Slavery in the Caribbean," *History Workshop* 36 (1993): 66–82; Wilson, *The Island Race*, 129–168.

36. Simon Taylor to Chaloner Arcedeckne, June 26, 1783, Vanneck-Arc/3A/1783/23, ICS; Walter Tullidelph to Alexander Campbell, April 23, 1739, Walter Tullidelph Letterbook, f. 103, NRS; Stephen Blizard to Charles Tudway, October 26, 1766, Tudway Family Archive, DD\TD Box 15/6, Somerset Heritage Centre; Extracts from John Mair's journal, Barbados [August 1776], MS 1920, NLJ; Charles Gordon to Charles Tudway, March 30, 1767, Tudway Family Archive, DD\TD Box 15/6, Somerset Heritage Centre. Physician John Tennent also published a medical treatise in which he argued that cold air braced bodily fibers while hot air relaxed them. See John Tennent, *Physical Enquiries: Discovering the Mode of Translation in the Constitutions of Northern Inhabitants, on going to, and for some Time after arriving in Southern Climates* (London: R. Spavan, 1749, 2nd ed. [1742]), 1–4, 22.

37. Long, *History of Jamaica*, vol. I, 362; John Campbell to John Campbell, August 14, 1797, Campbell Family Papers, AGN 321, The Mitchell Library, Glasgow; Caleb Dickinson to wife, July 15, 1756, Dickinson Family Archive, DD\DN/231, Somerset Heritage Centre; Samuel Martin to Samuel Martin Esq., January 15, 1768, MS Add 41348, f. 2–3, BL; Simon Taylor to Lady Taylor, January 9, 1803, Simon Taylor Letterbook F, ICS; Simon Taylor to John Taylor Esq., August 1, 1799, Simon Taylor Letterbook C, ICS. Also see letters of Joshua Steele, who believed Barbados to have "perhaps the finest climate in the world." The "delightfull climate," he wrote, had "the wonderfull effect of making old men young." Joshua Steele to Joseph Banks, June 20, 1786, Add MS 33978, f. 71, BL.

38. Samuel Martin to Samuel Martin Esq., January 15, 1768, Add MS 41348, f. 2–3, BL; Alexander Hamilton, *Gentleman's Progress: The Itinerarium of Dr. Alexander Hamilton*, ed. Carl Bridenbaugh (Chapel Hill: University of North Carolina Press, 1948), 199.

39. Several scholars have written about the malleability of racial categories in early America and the Atlantic world. See, for example, Wheeler, *Complexion of Race*, 264; Parrish, *American Curiosity*, 102; Block, *Colonial Complexions*, 20–22.

40. This remained the case into the nineteenth century. See, for example, the letters of Charles Gordon Gray, who in 1814 wrote, "The Constant rain has made the Parish sickly, white as well as black." The week before, he noted, twenty-eight people had been in the plantation hospital; "fever is the complaint." A month later, with continued wet weather, the situation had not improved. The plantation's inhabitants had suffered "much sickness, fevers from the continual rains & sores from the same cause," he wrote to his father. Charles Gordon Gray to father, August 4, 1814; September 8, 1814, MS 163, NLJ.

41. Long, *History of Jamaica*, vol. III, 614; vol. II, 29; 336. See also Hillary, *Observations*, 18. Ideas about illness and bodily exposure to the environment remained into the nineteenth century. See, for example, the letters of Charles Gordon Gray, who in 1814 wrote, "The Constant rain has made the Parish sickly, white as well as black." The week before, he noted, 28 people had been in the plantation hospital; "fever is the complaint." A month later, with continued wet weather, the situation had not improved. The plantation's inhabitants had suffered "much sickness, fevers from the continual rains & sores from the same cause," he wrote to his father. Charles Gordon Gray to father, August 4, 1814; September 8, 1814, MS 163, NLJ. Long's ideas about race were complicated and contradictory. For example, a passage often cited as evidence of Long's virulent racism—his claim that mixed-race people could not reproduce— is called into question by his reference to a "Mulatto wet nurse." Women could only be wet nurses if they were themselves nursing a baby—a sure indication of their ability to reproduce. The same passage also discloses his hesitation about the human body's fixedness or racial divisions. Berating British creole women for neglecting their infants by "disdaining to suckle" them, Long expressed his discomfort with these women handing their children "to a Negroe or Mulatto wet nurse, without reflecting that her blood may be corrupted, or considering the influence which the milk may have with respect to the disposition, as well as health, of their little ones." See Long, *History*, vol. II, 276. Long's concern that women of color could transmit something of their "disposition" to white babies through their breast milk indicates the dubious nature of his insistence upon unbridgeable differences between Black and white bodies.

42. William Hind to Eliza and Mary Hind, February 1, 1792; John Taylor to Mary Hind, March 9, 1802, Powel Family Papers, collection 1582, Series 12, Box 59, folder 1, HSP.

43. Charles Gordon Gray to father, June 11, 1812, MS 163, f. 23, NLJ.
44. Lind, *Essay on Diseases*, 198; Edwards, *History of the West Indies*, vol. II, 58–71. Also see Long, *History of Jamaica*, vol. II, 403–404. Simon Taylor thought that "Eboe" women were "the best breeding people," while "Eboes" in general, along with "Coromantees or Gold Coast negroes" were "the only ones fitt for sugar works." Simon Taylor to Chaloner Arcedeckne, March 1, 1790, Vanneck-Arc/3A/1790/1; Taylor to Arcedeckne, August 20, 1783, Vanneck-Arc/3A/1783/35. Even so, Trevor Burnard and Kenneth Morgan argue that in Jamaica, slave purchasers "were relatively powerless in choosing specific ethnic groupings." See Burnard and Morgan, "Dynamics of the Slave Market," 208, 219. In South Carolina, the merchant Henry Laurens explained to several of his trading partners that "Callabars" were "not at all liked" but that Africans from Gambia or the Gold Coast were the most popular among planters in his region. If no one from these regions was available, Africans from "the Windward Coast" were "prefer'd to Angola's." See Henry Laurens to Smith & Clifton, July 17, 1755 in *The Papers of Henry Laurens*, vol. I, ed. Philip M. Hamer et al. (Columbia, SC: University of South Carolina Press, 1968), 294–295 and Laurens to Maxwell & Udney, January 7, 1757 in *Papers of Henry Laurens*, vol. II, ed. Philip Hamer and George C. Rogers, Jr. (Columbia, SC: University of South Carolina Press, 1970), 402. Although several other letters from Laurens express similar preferences, others conveyed different ones, especially concerning the relative desirability of "Gambias" and "Angolas." See Laurens letters of November 18, 1755, May 17, 1756, January 31, 1756, February 12, 1756, April 7, 1756, all in *Papers*, vol. II, 16, 186, 83, 93, 143.
45. See, for example, Testimonies of Councils of Barbados, Jamaica, and Grenada, in BT/10 and BT/11, TNA (see Chapter 5).

Chapter 5

1. For a detailed study of the various West India Committees, Societies, and Associations, which together comprised the "West India interest," see Alexandra Franklin, "Enterprise and Advantage: The West India Interest in Britain, 1774–1840" (PhD dissertation, University of Pennsylvania, 1992). For a brief overview of British abolitionism, see Robin Blackburn, *The Overthrow of Colonial Slavery, 1776–1848* (New York: Verso, 1988), 131–160. For more extensive studies of abolitionist movements, see Christopher L. Brown, *Moral Capital: Foundations of British Abolitionism* (Chapel Hill: University of North Carolina Press, 2006); David Brion Davis, *The Problem of Slavery in the Age of Revolution, 1770–1823* (Ithaca: Cornell University Press, 1975); Manisha Sinha, *The Slave's Cause: A History of Abolition* (New Haven: Yale University Press, 2016); Anstey, *Atlantic Slave Trade*; Ryden, *West Indian Slavery*. On the extensive pamphlet war between the two sides, see Swaminathan, *Debating the Slave Trade*. On petitions to Parliament over abolition, see James Walvin, "The Public Campaign in England Against Slavery, 1787–1834" in *The Abolition of the Atlantic Slave Trade: Origins and Effects in Europe, Africa, and the Americas*, ed. David Eltis and James Walvin (Madison: University of Wisconsin Press, 1981), 63–79.
2. Testimony of Dr. Adair, May 16, 1788, BT 6/10, f. 435; Testimony of Council and Assembly of Grenada, May 30, 1788, read by the Privy Council September 23, 1788, BT 6/11; "The report drawn up by Stephen Fuller Esquire, with the Assistance of Messrs Long and Chisholme in Answer to the several heads of enquiry transmitted by their Lordships order to Mr Fuller— delivered in the 1st April 1788" (hereafter Jamaica Report), BT 6/10, f. 54; Testimony of Council of Barbados, read by the Privy Council September 23, 1788, BT 6/11, TNA.
3. Williams, *Capitalism and Slavery*, 20. Still, as Alexandra Franklin pointed out, the climatic argument (along with the benevolence of Britons rescuing Africans from Africa) became "the standard defense of slave and bonded labor in the Caribbean for the next century." See Franklin, "Enterprise and Advantage," 131. On the political context of abolition, see Brown, *Moral Capital*. On economic arguments regarding the prudence of abolition to the British economy, see Williams, *Capitalism and Slavery*; Seymour Drescher, *Econocide: British Slavery in the Era of Abolition* (Pittsburgh: University of Pittsburgh Press, 1977); David Eltis, *Economic Growth and the Ending of the Transatlantic Slave Trade* (New York: Oxford University Press, 1987); Ryden, *West Indian Slavery*. For arguments regarding British fears of strengthening slave rebellions in the colonies and their contributions to abolition, see Michael Craton, ed., *Empire, Enslavement*

and Freedom in the Caribbean (Kingston: Ian Randle Publishers, 1997); Gelien Matthews, *Caribbean Slave Revolts and the British Abolitionist Movement* (Baton Rouge: Louisiana State University Press, 2006); Claudius K. Fergus, *Revolutionary Emancipation: Slavery and Abolitionism in the British West Indies* (Baton Rouge: Louisiana State University Press, 2013).

4. By the time of the hearings, planters had already begun trying to improve living conditions and fertility rates on plantations to better insure their labor forces. For more on this process, known as amelioration, see Roberts, *Slavery and the Enlightenment*; J. R. Ward, *British West Indian Slavery, 1750–1834: The Process of Amelioration* (Oxford: Clarendon Press, 1988); J. R. Ward, "The Amelioration of British West Indian Slavery: Anthropometric Evidence," *Economic History Review* 71, no. 4 (2018): 1199–1226. On amelioration in Barbados, see Richard B. Sheridan, "Why the Condition of the Slaves was 'less intolerable in Barbadoes than in the other sugar colonies'" in *Inside Slavery: Process and Legacy in the Caribbean Experience*, ed. Hilary McD. Beckles (Kingston: Canoe Press, University of the West Indies, 1996), 32–50.

5. "The Examination of Charles Spooner, Esq., taken on the 1st of March, 1788," BT 6/9, f. 205, 208; Jamaica Report, BT 6/10, f. 103–106, TNA. Although he had never visited the Caribbean, Stephen Fuller had family plantations in Jamaica and represented the island's interests as its agent in London.

6. Jamaica Report, BT 6/10, f. 1–2, TNA.

7. "Additional information given in by Mr. Long relative to various matters, and tending to illustrate some of the answers in Mr. Fullers report dated the 28th of March 1788," BT 6/10, f. 202–204, 209, TNA (emphasis in original). For more on Indigenous slavery in the seventeenth-century Caribbean, see Goetz, "Indian Slavery"; Arena, "Indian Slaves"; Bialuschewski and Fisher, "Introduction," *Ethnohistory* 64, no. 1.

8. William Dickson, *Letters on Slavery* (London: J. Phillips, 1789), 60, 40–41 (emphasis in original); Dickson, *Mitigation of Slavery, in two parts* (London: R. & A. Taylor, 1814), 430 (emphasis in Dickson, though not in Ligon); for original, see Ligon, *True and Exact*, 43. Even more startling, Dickson claimed that women also labored in the heat: "in Barbadoes many whites *of both sexes*, till the ground, without any assistance from negroes, and poor white women often walk many miles loaded with the produce of their little spots, which they exchange in the towns for such European goods as they can afford to purchase." See Dickson, *Letters*, 41. Dickson spent over a dozen years in Barbados in the 1770s and early 1780s. See Sheridan, "Why the Condition of the Slaves," 36.

9. For more on enslaved women's low fertility rates in the Caribbean, see Turner, *Contested Bodies*; Paugh, *Politics of Reproduction*; Morgan, *Laboring Women*; Amanda Thornton, "Coerced Care: Thomas Thistlewood's Account of Medical Practice on Enslaved Populations in Colonial Jamaica, 1751–1786," *Slavery and Abolition* 32, no. 4 (2011): 543–546. Justin Roberts estimates that the enslaved population in eighteenth-century Jamaica decreased by 2–3.5 percent each year, and in Barbados by about 2 percent per year during the latter decades of the eighteenth century. See Roberts, *Slavery and the Enlightenment*, 162. According to David Brion Davis, "The black population of Barbados did not become self-perpetuating until after Britain had outlawed the slave trade; in Jamaica the deficit lasted until after emancipation." See Davis, *Problem of Slavery*, 56. These figures do not differentiate enslaved from free Black populations, but the vast majority of the Black population on each island was enslaved.

10. "The Examination of Charles Spooner, Esq., taken on the 1st of March 1788," BT 6/9, f. 176; Testimony of Dr. Adair, May 16, 1788, BT 6/10, f. 432–435; Testimony of Council & Assembly of Grenada; Testimony of Council of Barbados, BT 6/11; Testimony of Governor of St. Vincent, BT 6/11, TNA. Another copy of the St. Vincent testimony can be found in the Farquharson of Invercauld Papers, Box 115, "Answers," with letter dated June 17, 1788, Invercauld Estate Archive, Braemar, Scotland. Justin Roberts points out that the autumn was also the season of many enslaved laborers' heaviest labor, including cane holing and carrying heavy, wet loads of manure to fertilize fields. He argues that heavy labor contributed to the high death rates but also notes that planters themselves tended to blame wet weather for illness and death. See Roberts, *Slavery*, 175–177 and 190–199. Amanda Thornton notes that enslaved laborers also experienced higher mortality during the "hungry season," when food was less available. See Thornton, "Coerced Care," 547–551. On the change of climate, see, for example, "The Examination of Captain Hall," who testified on February 22, 1788 that

both Africans and British seamen suffered from the "change of climate" in traveling from the River Calabar to Jamaica, BT 6/9, f. 71, 78, TNA. Physician Robert Thomas, who lived in the Leeward Islands for nine years, explained that in traveling from Africa to the West Indies "the change of climate produces very great effects on the constitution of the negroes," and the Jamaica Council reported that Africans were "of inferior value" to creoles "because they enter into a new climate." See "The Examination of Mr. Robert Thomas" in *Abridgement of the Minutes of the Evidence, taken before a Committee of the Whole House, to whom it was referred to consider of the slave-trade,* Number II, 88–91; Jamaica Report, BT 6/10, f. 41, TNA.

11. Testimony of Council & Assembly of Grenada, BT 6/11; Jamaica Report, BT 6/10, f. 20, 22; Examination of Charles Spooner, BT 6/9, f. 176; Testimony of Governor of Barbados, BT 6/11; Testimony of Governor of St. Vincent, BT 6/11; Examination of Dr. Adair, BT 6/ 10, f. 432–435, TNA. On planters charging enslaved laborers with stealing, see Hilary McD. Beckles, "An Economic Life of Their Own: Enslaved Women as Entrepreneurs," in *Centering Woman: Gender Discourses in Caribbean Slave Society,* ed. Hilary McD. Beckles (Kingston: Ian Randle Publishers, 1999), 144–145. Trevor Burnard and Richard Follett argue that as aboli-tionist campaigns grew in strength in the 1780s, conceptions of illness changed from being largely humoral (with a notable early exception of Hans Sloane) to largely behavioral in cause. Venereal disease was especially telling, as it contributed to enslaved women's lack of fertility (and thus planters could blame enslaved women for low birth rates) but it also affected many planters, leading to Britons disassociating themselves from morally suspect planters. See Burnard and Follett, "Caribbean Slavery." Suman Seth also writes about planters and physicians blaming enslaved people for their own illnesses during the hearings over abolition of the slave trade; see Seth, *Difference and Disease,* 250–260.

12. Jamaica Report, BT 6/10, f. 21–26; Testimony of Governor of Barbados; of Council & Assembly of Grenada, BT 6/11; Examination of Charles Spooner, BT 6/9, f. 185, TNA; Benjamin Moseley, *A Treatise on Tropical Diseases; and on the Climate of the West-Indies* (London: T. Cadell, 1787), 509. All the questionnaires sent to colonial governors included these questions, as did many of the in-person examinations of witnesses. See, for example, the Examination of Charles Spooner Esq., March 1, 1788, BT 6/9, f. 182, 184, TNA. In March 1790, two years after Spooner referenced Moseley in his Parliamentary testimony, Simon Taylor wrote, "I cannot conceive of how the people in England have got the idea of Dr. Mosely, he was here a man in no manner of reputation in his profession, but a forward man, and fond of spouting." Simon Taylor to Chaloner Arcedeckne, March 31, 1790. Vanneck-Arc/3A/ 1790/5, ICS.

13. Testimony of Council of Barbados, BT 6/11; Jamaica Report, BT 6/10, f. 32–34; Examination of Charles Spooner, March 1, 1788, BT 6/9, f. 184–185, and Spooner's additions to his testi-mony, March 29, 1788, BT 6/9, f. 528–529, TNA. By "hereditary taints," the writers of this re-port meant smallpox, yaws, etc. Seymour Drescher also notes that these answers to questions of infant health focused on social and environmental factors. See Drescher, *The Mighty Experiment,* 83. In soliciting material for these answers, one member of the Jamaica Council wrote to William Wright, a physician who practiced in Jamaica from 1761–1786. Wright's confused answers may have contributed to the confusion in the official report. Wright, for example, answered the first question this way: "*The Negroe Slaves are subject to some diseases from which the White Inhabitants are exempted.* The seeds of such diseases are brought with them from Africa, and entailed on their posterity viz. the *Leprosy of the Greeks,* the *Leprosy of the Arabians,* and *Elephantiasis.* The Yaws *is an African complaint,* but now common in Jamaica and *many Negroes die under the best management* in that disease. *Negroes are not more sub-ject to diseases than White People or free Negroes.* Most of their disorders as *Fevers, Fluxes* and *Pleuriseys* are owing their going to distant parts to Negroe Plays in the night where they dance immoderately, drink to excess, sleep on the cold ground or commit many acts of sensuality and intemperance." See William Wright to Chaloner Arcedeckne, "Answers to Queries, con-cerning Negroe Slaves in the Island of Jamaica," March 1, 1788, Vanneck-Arc/3G/3 (ii), ICS. Wright's other answers also correspond closely with those of the Jamaica Council's as a whole.

14. Testimony of Governor of St. Vincent, BT 6/11, TNA.

15. Testimony of Governor of St. Vincent, BT 6/11, TNA.

16. John Farquharson to William Farquharson, June 17, 1788, Farquharson of Invercauld Papers, Box 115, Braemar.

17. John Farquharson to William Farquharson, June 17, 1788, Farquharson of Invercauld Papers, Box 115.

18. Testimony of Council and Assembly of Grenada, May 30, 1788, BT 6/11, TNA.

19. Aside from those illnesses that colonial governors attributed to behavioral causes, the reports insisted that there was no difference in the health of enslaved and free children. The Council of Barbados, for example, wrote that there were "no diseases to which slaves are subject, which Free Negroes or white inhabitants are not liable to" and the Governor of the island answered that slaves were "not peculiarly subject to any disease which does not also attack the white inhabitants." See testimonies, BT 6/11, TNA.

20. Testimony of Council of Barbados and of Governor of Barbados, BT 6/11; Jamaica Report, BT 6/10, f. 53; the Examination of John Braithwaite Esq., continued, March 15, 1788, BT 6/9, f. 402; Testimony of William Hutchinson, BT 6/10, f. 503; Testimony of R. Hibbert, Esq., and of James Tobin, Esq., in *Minutes of the Evidence*, Number II, 134, 92.

21. Testimony of Council & Assembly of Grenada, BT 6/11; William Beckford Esq., *A Descriptive Account of the Island of Jamaica* (London: T. and J. Egerton, 1790), vol. II, 322; Testimony of Alexander Willock, Esq. in *Minutes of the Evidence*, Number II, 130–131; Testimony of Doctor Samuel Athill in *Minutes of the Evidence*, Number II, 127; Henry Ellis to Lord Hawkesbury, March 27, 1788, BT 6/10, f. 218, TNA; Testimony of Thomas Norbury Kerby in *Minutes of the Evidence*, Number II, 114. Kerby later worked as a plantation manager for Clement Tudway in Antigua, and in 1805 wrote to Tudway about allowing a "mulatto man named Mick" to purchase his own freedom. Kerby was passing along the request from someone else, and did not know the man, but wrote, "I presume the man in question is merely a house servant & under this situation he may be parted with, under less detrimental circumstances than if he was a tradesman or field negro." The man would have worked in a house instead of the field because of his skin color. Thomas Norbury Kerby to Clement Tudway, Esq., September 11, 1805, Tudway Family Archive, Box 11, bundle 7, Somerset Heritage Centre. Cane holing was often considered the most difficult labor on plantations. For more on this, see David Barry Gaspar, "Sugar Cultivation and Slave Life in Antigua Before 1800," in *Cultivation and Culture: Labor and the Shaping of Slave Life in the Americas*, ed. Ira Berlin and Philip D. Morgan (Charlottesville, VA: University of Virginia Press, 1993), 104–105; Sheridan, *Doctors and Slaves*, 149–150.

22. According to some witnesses, such as William Dickson, poor whites in Barbados had cultivated land since the seventeenth century. For more on the poor whites of Barbados, sometimes known as "redlegs," see David Lambert, *White Creole Culture, Politics and Identity During the Age of Abolition* (New York: Cambridge University Press, 2005), 100–102. Hilary Beckles writes that Barbadian planters "knew that in the formative years of sugar cultivation, 1644–50, white servants working in field gangs were the backbone of the industry. Indeed, on some sugar estates, gangs of poor-whites were still to be found in the cane fields during the second half of the eighteenth century." Beckles argues that planters had "no ideological problem" with the substitution of white laborers for African slaves during the abolition debates, though from the sources I have found, it seems that these planters were not actually keen to make these opinions known to Parliament. See Hilary McD. Beckles, *A History of Barbados: From Amerindian Settlement to Nation-state* (Cambridge: Cambridge University Press, 1990), 48.

23. Testimony of William Hutchinson, BT 6/10, f. 486, TNA; Testimony of Alexander Campbell Esq., in *Minutes of the Evidence*, Number II, 72; Testimony of Lord Admiral Shuldham in *Minutes of the Evidence*, Number II, 157. Other sources also note the expense of European laborers throughout the eighteenth century. John Frederick Pinney, for example, wrote to the attorney on his Nevis estate in 1755 complaining about the high cost of paying a "white cooper" for a job. "For God's sake, Sir," he wrote, "buy me a negroe cooper or two," or "put out two or three young Negroe Boys prentice to that trade immediately." Otherwise, he added, he would rather buy casks already made than pay the extravagant wages of a white cooper. See J. F. Pinney to James Browne, October 27, 1755, John Frederick Pinney Letterbook, vol. I, Pinney Family Papers, University of Bristol Library. And in the 1760s, promotional material encouraging Britons to settle in Florida noted "the excessive price of labour in the West-Indies." "In

the islands, the wages of a carpenter, mason, &c. run up as high as ten shillings a day;" the author wrote, explaining that in Florida settlers would face no such prices for laborers. See William Stork, *An Account of East-Florida. With Remarks on its future Importance to Trade and Commerce*, (London: G. Woodfall, [1766]), 61–62.

24. Rowland Ash to Charles Tudway, July 22, 1761; Main Swete Walrond to Clement Tudway, April 23, 1773, Tudway Family Archive, DD\TD Box 15/6, Somerset Heritage Centre.

25. Testimony of Alexander Campbell; Dr. Samuel Athill; and of Mr. Gilbert Francklyn, all in *Minutes of the Evidence*, Number II, 57, 123, 29–32.

26. Testimony of James Ramsay, BT 6/10, f. 621–622, TNA; Testimony of Lieutenant Baker Davison; Alexander Campbell; and Sir Ashton Warner Byam in *Minutes of the Evidence*, Number IV, 87; Number II, 64; Number II, 49, 54. James Ramsay testified that white men worked in the West Indies as blacksmiths, masons, carpenters, and sawyers. See BT 6/10, f. 622, TNA. Similarly, the Reverend Robert Boucher Nicholls testified that "Many whites in Barbadoes exercise handicraft trades; such as carpenters, joiners, masons, copper-smiths, blacksmiths, shoemakers, &c. and also some of the poorer whites spin cotton for the lamps in the boiling houses. Whites are also employed in the coasting vessels, and as fishermen." See Testimony of Nicholls in *Minutes of the Evidence*, Number III, 135. Other witnesses who sided with planters argued that Europeans only oversaw the work of Africans and did not physically exert themselves too much. Notably, Ramsay also testified that "White men labour as hard in the West Indies as negroes at particular trades," and "white men" had "cleared Barbados, Nevis and St. Kitts, which is much harder work than the present culture of them." See "Questions Concerning the State of Slaves in the Sugar Colonies," transcription of folios from Bodleian Library, in *The Slave Trade Debate: Contemporary Writings For and Against* (Oxford: Bodleian Library, 2007), 138. Although this notebook is undated, it is either from 1788 or 1789, as Ramsay died in 1789 after spending the last years of his life "in debilitating debate with the West India slave interests who sought to discredit him." See Manisha Sinha, *The Slave's Cause*, 100.

27. Testimony of James Baillie, Esq., and of Dr. Samuel Athill in *Minutes of the Evidence*, Number II, 79, 122; Testimony of Samuel Athill and of R. Hibbert in *Minutes of the Evidence*, Number II, 127, 134; Testimony of R. Hibbert, 137. For more on the use of the plow in the West Indies, see W. A. Green, "The Planter Class and British West Indian Sugar Production, before and after Emancipation." *Economic History Review* 26, no. 3 (1973): 449–451 and J. R. Ward, "The Amelioration of British West Indian Slavery, 1750–1834: Technical Change and the Plough," *New West Indian Guide* 63, no. 1–2 (1989): 41–58.

28. Edward East to Anna Eliza Elletson, May 16, 1776, June 16, 1779, Roger Hope-Elletson Letterbook, MS 29a, f. 23, 46, NLJ; Simon Taylor to Chaloner Arcedeckne, July 5, 1789, Vanneck-Arc/3A/1789/20, ICS. As Chapter Four noted, Taylor managed Arcedeckne's plantations as well as his own.

29. Simon Taylor to Chaloner Arcedeckne, July 5, 1789, Vanneck-Arc/3A/1789/20, ICS. Tyburn was the name of the site for public executions of British prisoners.

30. Simon Taylor to Chaloner Arcedeckne, November 14, 1789, Vanneck-Arc/3A/1789/27, ICS.

31. Simon Taylor to Chaloner Arcedeckne, October 10, 1794, Vanneck-Arc/3A/1794/19, ICS. Taylor explained that he did not want anyone from London because such men "have been used to too much good eating and drinking there, and love to talk and jaw away better than to work." Others agreed about Londoners' poor habits; in 1755, for example, Samuel Hewat wrote from Jamaica to his employer in London requesting a carpenter, a "sober industrious man" to work on the plantation, warning him that "Londoners generally turn out bad servants." Samuel Hewat to Gibson Dalzell, March 27, 1755, Duff Family Papers, MS 3175/Z/183/1, University of Aberdeen Library.

32. John Graham to Joseph Foster Barham Jr., August 11, 1795, MS.Clar.dep.c.357, bundle 2, Bod.

33. [Henry Beaufoy], *The speech of Mr. Beaufoy, Tuesday the 18th June, 1788, in a Committee of the whole House, on a Bill for regulating the Conveyance of Negroes from Africa to the West-Indies* (London: J. Phillips, 1789), 9–10.

34. Several formerly enslaved people also published narratives arguing for abolition, although they tended to focus more on telling their own stories and appealing to readers' humanity than on climatic arguments.

35. Testimony of James Ramsay, BT 6/10, f. 621–622, TNA; James Ramsay, "A Letter from Capt. J. S. Smith to the Revd Mr. Hill on the State of the Negroe Slaves. To which are added an introduction, and remarks on free negroes, &c. by the editor" (London, 1786), 41–43 (emphasis in original). Included in Thomas Day, *Fragment of an Original Letter on the Slavery of the Negroes* (London: John Stockdale, 1784).

36. Edward Long, additions to Jamaica Report, March 28, 1788, BT 6/10, f. 206–207, TNA. Long emphasized the phrase, but in Lind's original work the wording differs slightly. Lind wrote that clearing trees had "often proved destructive," not always. See Lind, *Essay on Diseases*, 133. For more on Long misquoting Lind in order to defend African slavery in the West Indies, see Johnston, "Endangered Plantations."

37. Anon., *Considerations on the Emancipation of Negroes and on the Abolition of the Slave Trade* (London: J. Johnson & J. Debrett, 1788), 13–19.

38. *Considerations*, 14.

39. James Ramsay, *Objections to the Abolition of the Slave Trade, with Answers*, 2nd ed. (London: J. Phillips, 1788), 6.

40. Ramsay, *Objections*, 43.

41. Ramsay, *Objections*, 18, 21. Others cited statistics for seasoning losses at anywhere from two-fifths to one-third or one-half. Ramsay was not the first to use Long's own work against him; abolitionist leader William Wilberforce cited Long's *History of Jamaica* in Parliamentary debates as evidence of planters' depravity. See Drescher, *Mighty Experiment*, 77.

42. Ramsay, "A Letter," 40. On abolitionism as a mass social movement, see Seymour Drescher, "History's Engines: British Mobilization in the Age of Revolution," *William and Mary Quarterly* 66, no. 4 (2009): 737–756.

43. Robert Boucher Nickolls, *A Letter to the treasurer of the society instituted for the purpose of effecting the abolition of the slave trade* (London: James Phillips, 1788), 17, 20–21.

44. G. Francklyn, *Observations, occasioned by the attempts made in England to effect the abolition of the Slave Trade; shewing, the manner in which Negroes are treated in the British Colonies in the West-Indies: and also, some particular remarks on a letter addressed to the treasurer of the society for effecting such abolition, from the Rev. Robert Boucher Nicholls, Dean of Middleham, by G. Francklyn, Esq.* (London: Logographic Press, 1789), 53–54, 85; Testimony of Gilbert Francklyn in *Minutes of the Evidence*, Number II, 29–32. Francklyn joined Edward Long, Chaloner Arcedeckne, Stephen Fuller, Charles Spooner, John Braithwaite, Simon Taylor, and others as part of a subcommittee of the Society of West India Planters and Merchants, formed in February 1788 in response to the abolition question. See Ryden, *West Indian Slavery*, 191. Others made similar claims regarding their property; see, for examples, testimonies of Alexander Campbell, James Baillie, and John Castles in *Minutes of the Evidence*, Number II, 55, 74, 80.

45. *Minutes of the Evidence*, Number II, 200. Emma Rothschild argues that nineteenth-century physicians attributed the deaths in Kourou largely to typhoid fever, which the European colonists brought with them, but that in the decades following the disaster many people interpreted the mass mortality as evidence that Europeans could not labor in place of Africans in the hot American climate. Notably, and perhaps particularly so for the Privy Council, Victor Malouet, a colonial administrator who surveyed the remains of the settlement in the 1770s, published an account in 1788 in which he concluded that Europeans could not "be substituted for slaves." Yet Rothschild also points out that "informed observers of the time" believed that blaming the climate for the European deaths was inaccurate; the climate of Guyana was not particularly unhealthy, and whites and Blacks suffered from the same illnesses. See Rothschild, "A Horrible Tragedy," including Malouet quote from his *Mémoire sur l'esclavage des nègres* (1788), Rothschild, 88. Nevertheless, the tragic event was widely interpreted to constitute evidence that Europeans could not survive in such a climate without enslaved Africans to perform heavy labor. Also on Kourou, see McNeill, *Mosquito Empires*, 123–135.

46. John Wesley, *Thoughts Upon Slavery* (Philadelphia: Joseph Cruckshank, 1774), 39–43.

47. William Bell Crafton, *A Short Sketch of the Evidence for the Abolition of the Slave Trade, delivered before a committee of the House of Commons* (London and Philadelphia, 1792). John Frederick Pinney, who owned estates in the Leeward Islands, wrote to a fellow planter expressing his concern over the sugar boycott, which the "demagogues for the abolition are now preaching" as the most effective means of destroying the slave trade. See J. F. Pinney to John Taylor, October 24, 1791, Pinney Family Papers, Letterbook 9, f. 248, University of Bristol Library. Christopher Brown argues that the abolitionist cause in Britain became a signifier of the empire's moral worth in the aftermath of the American Revolution (see Brown, *Moral Capital*, 258, 312, 456–457). Crafton's inclusion of the Highlanders' and Salzburgers' anti-slavery petitions as proof of the morality of some early American settlers may have been an attempt to call upon the moral worthiness of those in the U.S. as well.

48. *A Letter to Granville Sharp, Esq. on the Proposed Abolition of the Slave Trade* (London: J. Debrett, 1788), 9, 12.

49. Dickson, *Mitigation of Slavery*, 431, 164; Dickson, *Letters*, 41. Dickson quoted letters written by planter Joshua Steele of Barbados, who later became an abolitionist. Steele wrote in direct answer to the questions posed by the Privy Council about the theoretical ability of Europeans to labor in the West Indies, but his answers are not preserved in the Board of Trade papers with the pro-slavery answers. On abolitionists and the "change of climate" for transported Africans, see, for example, William Roscoe, *A General View of the African Slave-Trade, demonstrating its injustice and impolicy: with hints towards a bill for its abolition* (London: R. Faulder, 1788), 9.

50. Examination of Doctor Jackson, in *Minutes of the Evidence*, Number IV, 30–33; Sir John Moore to Sir Robert Brownvigg, September 4, 1796, Add MS 57321, f. 58–59, BL. On the frailty of white soldiers in hot climates, see Anon., *Thoughts on civilization, and the gradual abolition of slavery in Africa and the West Indies* (London: J. Sewell, 1789), 11.

51. Beckford, *Descriptive Account*, vol. II, 328–331.

52. Beckford, vol. II, 283–284, 307.

53. Beckford, vol. II, 65; Edwards, "Jamaica: Book the First" in *Poems, written chiefly in the West-Indies* (Kingston: Alexander Aikman, 1792), 5; Edwards, *A Speech delivered at a free conference between the Honourable the Council and Assembly of Jamaica, held the 19th November, 1789, on the subject of Mr. Wilberforce's Propositions in the House of Commons, concerning the Slave-Trade* (Kingston: Alexander Aikman, 1789), 23. David Brion Davis points out that Edwards was initially sympathetic to those wanting to end the slave trade. It was only later that Edwards became convinced that it was essential to Jamaica's continuance as a thriving colony and changed his mind. See Davis, *Problem of Slavery*, 185–187. For a different interpretation of this switch to portraying the West Indian climate as dangerous, see Burnard, "'The Countrie Continues Sicklie.'" Burnard argues that Europeans in the West Indies exaggerated the health-iness of the climate until "the onset of abolitionism in 1788 changed all the rules of the game" and planters began to acknowledge the climate's unhealthiness for Europeans (64). Yet my reading of personal correspondence suggests different reasons for the switch; in 1788, I argue, Europeans felt pressured to insist upon the climate's unhealthiness for Europeans because they were afraid of losing their access to enslaved African laborers. Rather than feeling forced to exaggerate healthiness earlier and then later admitting true unhealthiness, then, I see the later reports of unhealthiness as purposefully exaggerated.

54. Jackson, *Treatise*, 403. Jackson believed, as did several of his contemporaries, that the pres-ence of Afro-creoles as servants encouraged laziness on the part of European soldiers and that it would be better to let them serve as soldiers in the army. At the time Jackson wrote, the formation of a "black corps" to serve in the islands was a hotly debated topic. Sir John Moore, for example, wrote from St. Lucia of his frustrations commanding European soldiers there; "the greatest use may be made of black corps," he wrote, "they may be made, be assured of it, excellent soldiers." Moore to Brownvigg, September 4, 1796, Add MS 57321, f. 58–59, BL. A group in Jamaica sent a series of petitions to the British army and government, arguing that "Mulattos, being natives," would make good soldiers because they were "inured to the cli-mate," having been born in the Caribbean and so would not need seasoning. (See Memorial of William Henry Ricketts et al. to Major General John Dalling, CO 137/77, f. 78, TNA; another copy, addressed to Archibald Campbell, can be found in CO 137/82, f. 204, TNA; as well as other copies throughout the CO 137 series and beyond). Planters, though, fought

the proposal on the grounds that arming slaves was a dangerous proposition. As one person reflected, "I did highly approve the measures adopted by Government to raise black corps," but "How could they hope that planters could be brought to support such a measure? when it must be clear that a slave holder must dread to see a sword in the hands of a man who has been his slave." See Add MS 59239, f. 89, BL. For more on these regiments, see Roger Norman Buckley, *Slaves in Red Coats: The British West India Regiments, 1795–1815* (New Haven: Yale University Press, 1979).

55. Jackson, *Treatise*, 404, 406.

56. On the vote, see *The Debate on a Motion for the Abolition of the Slave-Trade, in the House of Commons, on Monday and Tuesday, April 18 and 19, 1791, reported in detail* (London, 1791), 123. On the issue of lived experience, Simon Taylor, for example, fumed that it was "the highest presumption" among Britons, "who know nothing about the West Indies, to give their opinions upon what they know nothing about." Simon Taylor to Chaloner Arcedeckne, December 30, 1792, and January 6, 1793, Vanneck-Arc/3A/1792/19, ICS.

57. Anon., *Considerations*.

58. John Frederick Pinney, for example, wrote to his plantation manager in Nevis with some concern. "The present alarming crisis, respecting, the abolition of the African trade," he wrote, "operates so strongly on my mind, that I am resolved to contract, with the utmost expedition, all my concerns in the West Indies. Never again, upon my own private account, will I enter into a new engagement in that part of the world." To another friend, he wrote that "If there should be a total abolition, I am afraid it will be attended with fatal consequences in some of our islands—at any rate it will be very injurious to West India credit and property. It will make me anxious to lessen my concern in that part of the world." A few years later, he wrote to another friend expressing his concern over the "truly alarming" situation in the West Indies. See J. F. Pinney to William Coker, February 9, 1788; J. F. Pinney to Ulysses Lynch Esq., January 29, 1788; J. F. Pinney to Thomas Pym Weekes, March 21, 1792, Pinney Family Papers, Letterbook 9, f. 17, 18, 319, University of Bristol Library.

59. F. Graham to Thomas Milles Esq., December 10, 1807, MS 132, f. 22, NLJ; George Ottley to Clement Tudway, February 1, 1809, Tudway Family Archive, Box 11, bundle 7, Somerset Heritage Centre; William Leigh, *Remarks on the Slave Trade, and the Slavery of the Negroes. In a series of letters* (London: J. Phillips, 1788), Letter the fourteenth, 68.

60. Simon Taylor to Chaloner Arcedeckne, March 23, 1793, Vanneck-Arc/3A/1793/4, ICS. Eighteenth-century medical treatises commonly blamed illnesses on people's exposure to wet weather; see, for example, Hillary, *Observations on the Changes of the Air*, 18, 26; Grainger, *Essay on the More Common West-India Diseases*, 12; Hunter, *Observations on Diseases*, 23, 45, 188. Simon Taylor wrote that he would "rather save Mr. Wilberforce or anyone else the trouble of abolishing the trade" but that it was "impossible in a wett country to keep up the stock of Negroes by birth." Simon Taylor to Chaloner Arcedeckne, March 31, 1790, Vanneck-Arc/3A/1790/5, ICS.

61. See, for example, Simon Taylor to Chaloner Arcedeckne, July 21, 1788, Vanneck-Arc/3A/1788/19, ICS.

Chapter 6

1. Inaugural address of Robert J. Walker, Governor of the Territory of Kansas, May 27, 1857. Reported in *The Constitutionalist* (Augusta, GA), June 9, 1857. The speech was also printed in newspapers all over the U.S.

2. Both during and after the Civil War formerly enslaved Black laborers were not always eager to labor under the terms white planters demanded, which were often a de facto extension of slavery. Although some Black laborers did not want to leave the land which they had farmed for years, others wanted to go elsewhere. White planters also expressed frustration with those who stayed, accusing them of "impudence." For more, see Julie Saville, *The Work of Reconstruction: From Slave to Wage Laborer in South Carolina, 1860–1870* (New York: Cambridge University Press, 1994), 21–23, 42. On the labor shortage after the Civil War, see Erin Stewart Mauldin, *Unredeemed Land: An Environmental History of Civil War and Emancipation in the Cotton South* (New York: Oxford University Press, 2018), 145–150.

3. *Annals of Congress,* House of Representatives, 1st Congress, 2nd Session, March 17, 1790. South Carolina reopened the transatlantic trade in 1803 until it was closed permanently by federal law on January 1, 1808. See Gregory E. O'Malley, "Beyond the Middle Passage: Slave Migration from the Caribbean to North America, 1619–1807," *William and Mary Quarterly* 66, no. 1 (2009): 125–172. On ideas about cultivation and sovereignty, see MacMillan, *Sovereignty and Possession;* Patricia Seed, *Ceremonies of Possession in Europe's Conquest of the New World, 1492–1640* (New York: Cambridge University Press, 1995). On improvement projects in colonial English America, see Mulry, *An Empire Transformed.* On fears of wilderness, particularly fears that the American South would return to wilderness in the nineteenth century, see Lisa M. Brady, "The Wilderness of War: Nature and Strategy in the American Civil War," *Environmental History* 10, no. 3 (2005): 421–447.

4. *Annals of Congress,* House of Representatives, 1st Congress, 2nd Session, March 17, 1790. For an account of Georgia's history under the Trustees during the 1730s and 1740s, see Chapter 2.

5. Donnan, *Documents Illustrative of the History of the Slave Trade* vol. 4, 482; Elliot, ed., *Debates in State Conventions,* vol. 4, 285; [Oliver Goldsmith], *The Present State of the British Empire in Europe, America, Africa and Asia* (London: W. Griffin et al., 1768), 333–335.

6. Wynne, *A General History of the British Empire,* vol. II, 540–541.

7. William Russell, *The History of America, from Its Discovery by Columbus to the Conclusion of the late War* (London: Fielding and Walker, 1778), vol. II, 305; Jonathan Carver, *The New Universal Traveller* (London: G. Robinson, 1779), 607; Alexander Hewatt, *An Historical Account of the Rise and Progress of the Colonies of South Carolina and Georgia* (London: Alexander Donaldson, 1779), vol. I, 120; vol. II, 58, 150–151.

8. [Goldsmith], *Present State,* 333.

9. "Slave Labor and Hireling Labor—Climate and Competition," *The Marion Star,* October 6, 1857; *The Southern Recorder,* March 29, 1859; *The New Albany Daily Ledger,* December 5, 1856; "The Impending Crisis: Speech of Hon. William L. Yancey: The Commercial Side of the Irrepressible Conflict: The Right and Duty of Secession," October 10, 1860, printed in *The Old Line Guard,* October 18, 1860; "Herschel V. Johnson Refutes a Black Republican Slander," speech delivered in Rome, NY, on October 25, 1860, printed in *The Oshkosh Courier,* November 2, 1860; "Hygienic Management of Negroes, Being an Essay Written for, and submitted to, the First Annual Fair of the 'Georgia Cotton Planters' Convention,' held at Macon, Ga., December 1860, by J. Dickson Smith, M.D. of Macon, Ga.," *Georgia Weekly Telegraph,* February 21, 1861; Marvin T. Wheat, *The Progress and Intelligence of Americans; Collateral Proof of Slavery, from the first to the eleventh chapter of Genesis, as founded on organic law . . .* (Louisville, KY: 1862), iv.

10. "Decline of Northern and Growth of Southern Slavery," from essay by E. B. Bryan, "The Rightful Remedy," *DeBow's Review* (April 1851).

11. "The Early Settlers of Georgia—a Contrast," *The Southern Field and Fireside,* June 25, 1859; "Agricultural Resources of Georgia. Address Before the Cotton Planters' Convention of Georgia, at Macon, Dec. 13, 1860. By Joseph Jones, M.D., Chemist of the Association, and Professor of Medical Chemistry in the Medical College of Georgia at Augusta," *Daily Chronicle and Sentinel,* December 21, 1860.

12. There are limitations, of course, to using newspapers to present the views of free Black Americans. On this issue, see Kwando Mbiassi Kinshasa, *Emigration vs. Assimilation: The Debate in the African American Press, 1827–1861* (Jefferson, NC: McFarland, 1988), 1–3.

13. On Black emigration and colonization in the nineteenth century, see Asaka, *Tropical Freedom;* Ousmane K. Power-Greene, *Against Wind and Tide: The African American Struggle Against the Colonization Movement* (New York: NYU Press, 2014); Elena K. Abbott, *Beacons of Liberty: International Free Soil and the Fight for Racial Justice in Antebellum America* (New York: Cambridge University Press, 2021); Floyd J. Miller, *The Search for a Black Nationality: Black Emigration and Colonization, 1787–1863* (Urbana: University of Illinois Press, 1975); Kinshasa, *Emigration vs. Assimilation.*

14. Paul Cuffe to James Madison, June 6, 1813, Library of Congress. On Cuffe, see Nicholas Guyatt, *Bind Us Apart: How Enlightened Americans Invented Racial Segregation* (New York: Basic Books, 2016), 260–267; James Sidbury, *Becoming African in America: Race and Nation in the Early Black Atlantic* (New York: Oxford University Press, 2007), 11–13; Miller, *The Search for a Black Nationality,* 21–53. Elena Abbott argues that Cuffe's efforts

paved the way for the decades-long, hotly contested issue of Black emigration. See Abbott, *Beacons of Liberty*, 28–32. The first proposals for colonization came from New England in the 1770s—one from a small group of enslaved people who petitioned for gradual emancipation, declaring they would move to Africa if freed, and one from a white minister who encouraged evangelizing in Africa. Thomas Jefferson was also an early and vocal supporter of colonization. See Guyatt, *Bind Us Apart*, 210–215; and John Saillant, "The American Enlightenment in Africa: Jefferson's Colonizationism and Black Virginians' Migration to Liberia, 1776–1840," *Eighteenth-Century Studies* 31, no. 3 (1998): 261–282. On white attitudes toward colonization, see Eric Foner, *Free Soil, Free Labor, Free Men: The Ideology of the Republican Party Before the Civil War* (New York: Oxford University Press, 1995), 269; Guyatt, *Bind Us Apart*, 7–8. Paul Polgar notes that many northern proponents of colonization believed that free Black people were a menace to society, and that colonization would help to rid American society of their threatening presence. See Polgar, *Standard-Bearers of Equality: America's First Abolition Movement* (Chapel Hill: University of North Carolina Press, 2019), 230. On Sierra Leone, see Byrd, *Captives and Voyagers*, 200–243; Cassandra Pybus, *Epic Journeys of Freedom: Runaway Slaves of the American Revolution and Their Global Quest for Liberty* (Boston: Beacon Press, 2006), 139–155, 169–202.

15. On numbers of migrants to Liberia, see Sidbury, *Becoming African in America*, 182. Nicholas Guyatt notes that "barely 10,000" migrants moved to Liberia in the forty years preceding the Civil War; see Guyatt, *Bind Us Apart*, 327. Power-Greene estimates this figure at "nearly 13,000." See Power-Greene, *Against Wind and Tide*, xviii. For more on the experiences of some of those migrants, see Claude A. Clegg III, *The Price of Liberty: African Americans and the Making of Liberia* (Chapel Hill: University of North Carolina Press, 2004); Robert Murray, *Atlantic Passages: Race, Mobility, and Liberian Colonization* (Gainesville: University Press of Florida, 2021). On colonization skeptics, see Sidbury, *Becoming African in America*, 168–170; Polgar, *Standard-Bearers*, 261–262. Winthrop Jordan argues that although the earliest colonization movement in the late eighteenth century "was supported only by men of genuine antislavery feeling," by the 1820s and 1830s "some, perhaps most, of the support for colonization came from men interested in perpetuating slavery." See Jordan, *White Over Black*, 548, 566. It is notable that the move to establish a colony in West Africa followed the significant failures of Sierra Leone as well as disastrous British attempts at a penal colony there in the late eighteenth century. See Cassandra Pybus, "'A Less Favourable Specimen': The Abolitionist Response to Self-Emancipated Slaves in Sierra Leone, 1793–1808," *Parliamentary History* 26, no. 4S (2007): 97–112 and on the penal colonies see Emma Christopher, *A Merciless Place*. For more on the American Colonization Society, see Eric Burin, *Slavery and the Peculiar Solution: A History of the American Colonization Society* (Gainesville: University Press of Florida, 2005). Only months after the Society was founded, a group of several thousand Black Philadelphians met and voiced their opposition to it. See Abbott, *Beacons of Liberty*, 36–37.

16. "Editorial Items," *The North Star*, February 22, 1850; *Frederick Douglass's Paper*, September 17, 1858. On Black American identity and its relation to African colonization, see Sidbury, *Becoming African in America*.

17. *The Colored American*, July 7, 1838. Notably, a white pro-slavery writer agreed with this part of the climate argument. Thomas Roderick Dew, the president of the College of William and Mary and a firm and vocal defendant of slavery, opposed colonization because he feared it would encourage emancipation. Writing against the idea of Black Americans emigrating to Liberia, Dew explained that the climate in Africa was "deleterious" and "destructive." The insalubrious climate would negatively affect black Americans because "the lapse of ages has completely inured him to our colder and more salubrious continent." See Dew, "Abolition of Negro Slavery," in Drew Gilpin Faust, ed., *The Ideology of Slavery: Proslavery Thought in the Antebellum South, 1830–1860* (Baton Rouge: Louisiana State University Press, 1981), 43.

18. *African Repository and Colonial Journal*, January 1, 1832; February 1, 1845; "Health of Liberia," *African Repository and Colonial Journal*, July 1, 1831.

19. *The National Era*, December 2, 1847; *Frederick Douglass's Paper*, February 5, 1852; August 31, 1855; "Mass Anti-Slavery Convention in Rochester," *The North Star*, March 20, 1851. James Sidbury also notes Black Americans who returned from Liberia with unfavorable reports; see Sidbury, *Becoming African in America*, 194–196.

20. John Clarkson, *Clarkson's Mission to America*, 52, https://blackloyalist.com/cdc/docume nts/diaries/mission.htm. Clarkson, a British man who traveled to Nova Scotia to conduct migrants to Sierra Leone, had earlier noted in his diary that one Black Loyalist, Thomas Peters, had expressed his desire to travel to Sierra Leone with his family because it would be "much better suited to their constitutions than Nova Scotia." See Clarkson, *Clarkson's Mission*, 33. On arguments about the Canadian climate regarding Black Loyalists as well as Jamaican Maroons in the 1780s and 1790s, see Zilberstein, *A Temperate Empire*, 118-147. For one Black Loyalist's first-hand account of Nova Scotia and Sierra Leone, see Boston King, *Memoirs of the Life of Boston King* (1798). A second wave of Black Loyalists ventured to Nova Scotia after the War of 1812. See Asaka, *Tropical Freedom*, 31-33. On the earlier settlers in Nova Scotia (and especially the links with Sierra Leone), see Maya Jasanoff, *Liberty's Exiles: American Loyalists in the Revolutionary World* (New York: Alfred A. Knopf, 2012), 172-175, 279-294. On Canada more broadly, see Abbott, *Beacons of Liberty*, esp. 99-120 and 168-192; Sharon A. Roger Hepburn, *Crossing the Border: A Free Black Community in Canada* (Urbana: University of Illinois Press, 2007). On numbers of migrants to Haiti, see Power-Greene, *Against Wind and Tide*, xviii. On migrants' disillusion, see Miller, *The Search for a Black Nationality*, 55. For more on Haiti, see Miller, 74-90; Abbott, *Beacons of Liberty*, 39-64; Power-Greene, *Against Wind and Tide*, 16-45; Kinshasa, *Emigration vs. Assimilation*, 133-157. Haiti reemerged as an option for Black emigration during the 1850s; see Miller, 232-249. On migration to Mexico, see Abbot, *Beacons of Liberty*, 75-82, 118-126; Sarah E. Cornell, "Citizens of Nowhere: Fugitive Slaves and Free African Americans in Mexico, 1833-1857," *Journal of American History* 100, no. 2 (2013): 351-374; S. Charles Bolton, *Fugitivism: Escaping Slavery in the Lower Mississippi Valley, 1820-1860* (Fayetteville, AR: University of Arkansas Press, 2019), 82-86.

21. *The Colored American*, April 4, 1840; "News from Trinidad," *The Colored American*, April 11, 1840. On West Indian planters' encouragement, see Asaka, *Tropical Freedom*, 87.

22. "Important News from Trinidad," *The Colored American*, April 18, 1840.

23. "Letter from Rev. C. S. Renshaw, Fern Hill, St. Andrews, Jamaica, May 10th, 1840," *The Colored American*, July 18, 1840; "The Emigration Scheme," *The Colored American*, November 13, 1841.

24. "Effects of Mercury on the Constitution of Negroes," *Boston Medical and Surgical Journal*, November 26, 1834; "Jamaica—its Advantages as a Home for Colored Emigrants," *The National Era*, October 4, 1852; Charles Tappan, "Free Labor in Tropical Productions: Emancipation in the British West Indies," *The National Era*, August 5, 1858. Allinson stressed that migrants to Jamaica should adhere to behavioral guidelines, such as avoiding the "improper use of fruit, great fatigue in the sun, and exposure to night air from marshes."

25. "Public Meeting in Boston," *The North Star*, February 25, 1848; *Voice of the Fugitive*, June 1, 1851; *Provincial Freeman*, March 1, 1856. Shadd had migrated to Canada herself and promoted Canada as a haven for African Americans during her time as the paper's editor. See Jane Rhodes, "The Contestation over National Identity: Nineteenth-Century Black Americans in Canada," *Canadian Review of American Studies* 30, no. 2 (2000): 175-186; Abbott, *Beacons of Liberty*, 256. For more examples of Black Canadians refuting the climate argument, see Asaka, *Tropical Freedom*, 153-154.

26. *Voice of the Fugitive*, June 1, 1851; *The North Star*, January 19, 1849.

27. "Anti-Colonization," report from "a very large and respectable meeting of the colored citizens" of Cincinnati, *The North Star*, March 21, 1851.

28. Martin R. Delany, *The Condition, Elevation, Emigration and Destiny of the Colored People of the United States* (1852), 178, 202. Delany registered his objections to Liberia as being, "in the first place," too "unhealthy" for potential migrants. See Delany, *Condition*, 169. For more on Delany, see Sidbury, *Becoming African in America*, 205-206; Abbott, *Beacons of Liberty*, 252-260; Power-Greene, *Against Wind and Tide*, 140-141; Miller, *The Search for a Black Nationality*, 115-133.

29. "Speech of Hon. Frank P. Blair, Jr., of Missouri, on the Acquisition of Territory in Central and South America, to be Colonized with Free Blacks, and hold as a Dependency by United States, Delivered in the House of Representatives, Jan. 14, 1858," printed in *The National Era*, May 13, 1858; "Tropical Production—Slavery and the Slave Trade," *The National Era*, June

10, 1858. *The National Era* also printed a summary of Blair's speech under "Congressional Proceedings" on January 21, 1858. On the Blairs, see Foner, *Free Soil*, 268–269.

30. *A Century of Lawmaking for a New Nation: U.S. Congressional Documents and Debates, 1774–1875: Journal of the Senate of the United States of America*, vol. 49, p. 710, June 14, 1858. On Black exclusion, see Asaka, *Tropical Freedom*, 134–135. For some of the laws in the Midwest, see Stephen Middleton, *Black Laws in the Old Northwest: A Documentary History* (Westport, CT: Greenwood Press, 1993). Nicholas Guyatt argues that white plans for Indigenous removal and for Black colonization should be considered together. See Guyatt, *Bind Us Apart*. On an imagined Indigenous extinction, a sentiment especially prevalent in New England, see Jean O'Brien, *Firsting and Lasting: Writing Indians out of Existence in New England* (Minneapolis: University of Minnesota Press, 2010).

31. "Speech of Hon. J. R. Doolittle, of Wisconsin, in the Senate, March 19, 1862," *Congressional Globe, Senate*, 37th Congress, 2nd Session, Appendix, 83; *Journal of the Senate of the United States of America, 1789–1873*, December 3, 1861; *Journal of the Senate*, December 1, 1862.

32. Power-Greene, *Against Wind and Tide*, 187–188; Abbott, *Beacons of Liberty*, 279. Delany hoped to establish a free Black colony in the Niger Valley. See Miller, *The Search for a Black Nationality*, 183–216; Abbott, *Beacons of Liberty*, 260, 274–275.

33. "Notes and Documents," *Virginia Magazine of History and Biography* 104, no. 4 (1996): 481–504, quote on p. 496. For more on Lott Cary, see the accompanying article by John Saillant. Delany, *Condition*, 202.

34. *Freedom's Journal*, June 8, 1827. Charles Bolton examines southern newspapers extensively for evidence of enslaved people self-emancipating, some of whom went to Mexico, but these newspapers were written and published by white editors and did not contain Black southerners' thoughts on climate. See Bolton, *Fugitivism*. Historian Eric Burin argues that in contrast to Cary, most Black Southerners distrusted and opposed the American Colonization Society. See Burin, *Slavery and the Peculiar Solution*, 16.

35. Stephen E. Maizlish, *A Strife of Tongues: The Compromise of 1850 and the Ideological Foundations of the American Civil War* (Charlottesville: University of Virginia Press, 2018), 18. In a speech the following year Webster told a crowd in Buffalo, NY, that the "snow hills, the eternal mountains, and the climate . . . would never support slavery" in California. "Speech of Mr. Webster, at Buffalo, N.Y., May, 1851," *Weekly Chronicle and Sentinel*, September 1, 1852.

36. *New York Herald*, August 13, 1857; Inaugural address of Robert J. Walker, Governor of the Territory of Kansas, delivered May 27, 1857. Published (among other places) in *The Constitutionalist*, June 9, 1857. In Baltimore, for example, Douglas gave a speech in September 1860 arguing that slavery would not extend into places with "cold" and "rigorous" climates where "the white man is in his natural element." *The Herald*, September 19, 1860. For more on Douglas's theory, see James Oakes, *The Scorpion's Sting: Antislavery and the Coming of the Civil War* (W.W. Norton, 2014), 77.

37. "Letter from H. O. Wagoner, Chicago, Ill., March 3d, 1851," *The North Star*, March 20, 1851; "Slavery in California," *The North Star*, February 23, 1849.

38. "The 'Great Climatic Law'—'Isothermal Line,'" *The National Era*, June 18, 1857; "Kanzas and Slavery" (*sic*), *Frederick Douglass's Paper*, December 15, 1854; *The National Era*, October 6, 1853.

39. *The Anti-Slavery Reporter* 2, no. 11 (Nov. 1854); "Free and Slave Labor," *Daily Whig*, April 11, 1857; "The Impending Crisis of the South," review in *The National Era*, July 23, 1857.

40. "Negro Competition," *Hartford Daily Courant*, March 29, 1860; "The True Southern Laborers," *The Independent*, October 9, 1862. On the New York riots see Williston H. Lofton, "Northern Labor and the Negro During the Civil War," *Journal of Negro History* 34, no. 3 (1949): 251–273; Leslie M. Harris, *In the Shadow of Slavery: African Americans in New York City, 1626–1863* (Chicago: University of Chicago Press, 2003), 280–287. The newspaper article was directed especially to "the Irish," who played the most significant role in the riots. For more on the Irish during this period, see Brian Kelly, "Gathering Antipathy: Irish Immigrants and Race in America's Age of Emancipation," in Johanne Devlin Trew and Michael Pierse, eds., *Rethinking the Irish Diaspora: After the Gathering* (Palgrave McMillan, 2018): 157–185. On white labor movements during the Civil War, see Mark A. Lause, *Free Labor: The Civil War and the Making of an American Working Class* (Urbana: University of Illinois Press,

2015). For an example of an article arguing that Black northerners would move south, see "The War Against the Black Man," *Hartford Daily Courant*, August 9, 1862. On white southern labor managers and race, see David R. Roediger and Elizabeth D. Esch, *The Production of Difference: Race and the Management of Labor in U.S. History* (New York: Oxford University Press, 2012), 21–25, 37–38.

41. "Resolutions relative to preventing the introduction of Slavery into new States," January 5, 1820, *Journal of the Senate of the United States of America*, vol. 9, 79; *The North Star*, January 19, 1849.

42. "A Declaration of the Immediate Causes which Induce and Justify the Secession of the State of Mississippi from the Federal Union." Accessed through the Avalon Project: Documents in Law, History and Diplomacy, Lillian Goldman Law Library, Yale Law School.

43. "The Future of Emancipated Negroes," *The Daily Intelligencer*, July 29, 1865; *Savannah Republican*, July 29, 1865. "The Future" appeared in several other Georgia papers in the following weeks.

44. *Savannah Republican*, July 29, 1865. See Richard H. Abbott, "The Republican Party Press in Reconstruction Georgia, 1867–1874," *Journal of Southern History* 61, no. 4 (1995): 725–760.

45. "White Labor in the Tropics," *The Sun*, January 3, 1866; "White Labor in the South," *The Rome Weekly Courier*, March 16, 1866; J. C. Nott, "Climates of the South in Their Relations to White Labor," *DeBow's Review* 5, issue 2 (Feb 1866): 166–173. Josiah Nott practiced medicine in South Carolina, Alabama, and Louisiana before the Civil War, and wrote extensively on medicine and ethnology. In a book he co-wrote in 1854, Nott argued that white people "certainly deteriorate physically" in hot climates. See J.C. Nott and George R. Gliddon, *Types of Mankind* (Philadelphia, 1854), 63. According to Robert Wald Sussman, this book went through ten printings in less than two decades. See Sussman, *The Myth of Race*, 34. For more on Nott, see Faust, *Ideology of Slavery*, 206–208.

46. "An Essay: With Special Reference to the Introduction of German Agriculturalists and Laborers to the State of Georgia," submitted to the Convention of Planters, from the State of Georgia, Convened at Macon, Georgia, Sept. 6, 1866, printed as "On the Labor Question at the South," *Georgia Weekly Telegraph*, October 22, 1866. For more on the Salzburgers and the early history of Georgia, see Chapter 2.

47. "The White Labor Question," *American Phrenological Journal* 44, no. 4 (Oct 1866).

48. *The Baltimore Sunday Visitor*; reprinted in *The True American* (Lexington, KY), July 22, 1845; *The National Era*, November 2, 1848; "Lecture on Migration: Applying the Principles of a previous Lecture on the same subject to the Black Race in America," delivered April 2, 1853, printed in *The National Era*, June 16, 1853.

49. "The Negro and the South," *New-York Tribune*, November 29, 1867; *DeBow's Review* 4, no. 4 (October 1867).

50. *DeBow's Review* 4, no. 4 (October 1867). Laborers from China and India began arriving in the British West Indies early in the nineteenth century and grew in number during the 1830s and 1840s. With the end of slavery in the United States, some planters—especially those with sugar plantations in Louisiana—turned to Asian laborers too. See Moon-Ho Jung, *Coolies and Cane: Race, Labor, and Sugar in the Age of Emancipation* (Baltimore: Johns Hopkins University Press, 2006). On the Caribbean, see B.W. Higman, "The Chinese in Trinidad, 1806–1838," *Caribbean Studies* 12, no. 3 (1972): 21–22; David Northrup, *Indentured Labor in the Age of Imperialism, 1834–1922* (New York, 1995), esp. 16–17; Verene A. Shepherd, "The 'Other Middle Passage?': Nineteenth-century Bonded Labour Migration and the Legacy of the Slavery Debate in the British-Colonised Caribbean," in *Working Slavery, Pricing Freedom: Perspectives from the Caribbean, Africa, and the African Diaspora*, ed. Verene A. Shepherd (New York: Palgrave Macmillan, 2002): 343–376; Walton Look Lai, *Indentured Labor, Caribbean Sugar: Chinese and Indian Migrants to the British West Indies, 1838–1918* (Baltimore: Johns Hopkins University Press, 1993). For examples of white planters feeling frustrated in their attempts to attract European laborers, see "The Negro and the South," *New-York Tribune*, November 29, 1867; *Tri-Weekly Constitutionalist*, March 30, 1866. Some persisted, hoping to attract Irish immigrants, but others foresaw a continued spiral into poverty if southerners tried to rely on white labor.

51. Delany, "Condition"; J. C. Nott, "Climates of the South."

52. *Savannah Republican*, July 29, 1865.

Conclusion

1. Renny, *History of Jamaica*, 183–184. Between 1791, when Parliament decided to continue the transatlantic slave trade and 1806, when its members voted to abolish it, the Haitian Revolution transformed the Atlantic world. On the links between the Haitian Revolution and British abolition, see Claudius Fergus, "'Dread of Insurrection': Abolitionism, Security, and Labor in Britain's West Indian Colonies, 1760–1823," *William and Mary Quarterly* 66, no. 4 (2009): 757–780.

2. Thomas Fraser to Simon Fraser, April 8, 1791, Simon Fraser Papers, HCA/D238/D/1/17/6, Highland Archive Centre, Inverness. Historian Seymour Drescher notes that in Adam Smith's 1776 *An Inquiry into the Nature and Causes of the Wealth of Nations*, which "furnish[ed] a distinctive economic argument to the British abolitionist movement," Smith "did not challenge the general climatological rationale for the utility of African slaves in tropical areas." See Drescher, *The Mighty Experiment*, 21, 26. On anti-abolitionist literature, see Swaminathan, *Debating the Slave Trade*, 127–170; Ryden, *West Indian Slavery*, 202–207.

3. "On the Labor Question at the South," *Georgia Weekly Telegraph*, October 22, 1866.

4. On the shrewd economic calculations planters made, see Walsh, *Motives of Honor, Pleasure, and Profit*; Chaplin, *An Anxious Pursuit*; Rosenthal, *Accounting for Slavery*.

5. Jordan, *White Over Black*, 537.

6. On the development of anatomy and other biological sciences at the end of the eighteenth century, see Schiebinger, "Medical Experimentation and Race"; Curran, *Anatomy of Blackness*; Stepan, *The Idea of Race in Science*. On the further development of phrenology during the nineteenth century, see Ann Fabian, *The Skull Collectors: Race, Science, and America's Unburied Dead* (Chicago: University of Chicago Press, 2010); Cynthia S. Hamilton, "'Am I Not a Man and a Brother?': Phrenology and Anti-Slavery," *Slavery and Abolition* 29, no. 2 (2008): 173–187; James Poskett, *Materials of the Mind: Phrenology, Race, and the Global History of Science, 1815–1920* (Chicago: University of Chicago Press, 2019); John D. Davies, *Phrenology, Fad and Science: A 19th Century American Crusade* (New Haven: Yale University Press, 1955). On Black responses and contributions to these arguments, see Britt Rusert, *Fugitive Science: Empiricism and Freedom in Early African American Culture* (New York: New York University Press, 2017).

7. Harlow also concluded that it was "inevitable" that labor in tropical regions would be performed by people of color. See Vincent T. Harlow, *A History of Barbados, 1625–1685* (New York: Negro Universities Press, 1969 [1926]), 292–293, 307, 310, 328.

8. Lowell Joseph Ragatz, *The Fall of the Planter Class in the British Caribbean, 1763–1833* (New York: Century, 1928), 3; Delany, *Condition, Elevation, Emigration*, 53, 214. Ragatz's characterization of people of color in general was profoundly, even breathtakingly, racist; see especially p. 27. Ragatz also expressed the view that planters were themselves degenerate both because "the white man in tropical America was out of his habitat" and because his "Constant association with an inferior subject race blunted his moral fibre and he suffered marked demoralization." See Ragatz, *Fall of the Planter*, 5.

9. Williams, *Capitalism and Slavery*, 20. In his 1988 Elsa Goveia Memorial Lecture, Barry Higman noted the fact that Williams was himself a student of Harlow and a close acquaintance of Ragatz. See B. W. Higman, "Ecological Determinism in Caribbean History" in *Inside Slavery: Process and Legacy in the Caribbean Experience*, ed. Hilary McD. Beckles (Kingston: Canoe Press, 1996), 52–77.

10. For a nuanced explanation of this theory of the turn to African labor, see Philip R.P. Coelho and Robert A. McGuire, "African and European Bound Labor in the British New World: The Biological Consequences of Economic Choices," *Journal of Economic History* 57, no. 1 (1997): 83–115. In 1974, Peter Wood suggested that the "epidemiological advantages" of West Africans over Europeans in the Lowcountry should not "be taken lightly with regard to the creation, or analysis, of a colonial labor force." See Wood, *Black Majority*, 91. Others have repeated this theory of immunity; see Stewart, *"What Nature Suffers to Groe"*, 63–64; Curtin, "Epidemiology and the Slave Trade," 207; Burnard, "'The Countrie Continues Sicklie'"; Puckrein, "Climate, Health and Black Labor"; Kiple and King, *Another Dimension to the Black Diaspora*. For recent examples of this immunological explanation for the labor

transition made in passing, see Newman, *A New World of Labor*, 76; Senior, *The Caribbean and Medical Imagination*, 4; Asaka, *Tropical Freedom*, 7; Blackburn, *The American Crucible*, 65.

11. As Betty Wood points out, most ailments in the early part of the eighteenth century "were lumped together under such headings as 'pestilential fevers' and 'malignant diseases.'" See Wood, *Slavery in Colonial Georgia*, 150.

12. Robert Pinkney to Joseph Foster Barham, May 16, 1766, MS.Clar.dep.c.357, bundle 1, Bod.; Simon Taylor to David Reid, March 10, 1801, Simon Taylor Letterbook D, ICS.

13. Yellow fever manifested itself in travelers' descriptions as a particular illness from about the seventeenth century, although precise diagnoses by historians are impossible. Some of its symptoms resemble those of other illnesses, and physicians also used a number of different names to describe their observations. Urmi Engineer Willoughby notes that mild symptoms of yellow fever resemble those of malaria, dengue fever, chikungunya, typhoid, and other diseases, and that Atlantic physicians "often conflated yellow fever, dengue, malaria, and other diseases." See Willoughby, *Yellow Fever, Race and Ecology in Nineteenth-Century New Orleans* (Baton Rouge: Louisiana State University Press, 2017), 17. Similarly, Ari Kelman also explains that yellow fever in nineteenth-century New Orleans was difficult to diagnose; see Kelman, *A River and Its City: The Nature of Landscape in New Orleans* (Berkeley: University of California Press, 2003), 90–91. Writing about the eighteenth century, Peter McCandless explains that "sources refer to yellow fever by a bewildering variety of names, including malignant fever, pestilential fever, putrid bilious fever, Siam distemper, black vomit, or simply plague, pestilence, or sickness." See McCandless, *Slavery, Disease, and Suffering*, 62. Mark Harrison writes that most eighteenth-century physicians found yellow fever "difficult to distinguish from common varieties of fever"; see Harrison, *Medicine in an Age of Commerce and Empire*, 257; and Philip Curtin argues that in the nineteenth century, "'Fevers' as a category covered yellow fever, malaria, typhoid, and a great deal more . . . because medical men could not always make valid distinctions between them." See Philip D. Curtin, "Epidemiology and the Slave Trade," 208. With such an enormous variety, it seems anachronistic and does not do justice to historical subjects to apply modern diagnoses to past illnesses.

14. John Lining, *A Description of the American Yellow Fever, which Prevailed at Charleston, in South Carolina, in the Year 1748* (Philadelphia: Thomas Dobson, 1799), 7. On the Lining-Rush connection, see Wood, *Black Majority*, 82, note 70; Mariola Espinosa, "The Question of Racial Immunity to Yellow Fever in History and Historiography," *Social Science History* 38, no. 3–4 (2014): 437–453 (see 441); Hogarth, *Medicalizing Blackness*, 22–40. For a first-hand account of Black Philadelphians' role in the 1793 outbreak, see Absalom Jones and Richard Allen, *A Narrative of the Proceedings of the Black People, During the Late Awful Calamity in Philadelphia, in the Year 1793* (Philadelphia, 1794). For a detailed account of the outbreak, see Smith, *Ship of Death*, 147–241. Rush himself believed that yellow fever had environmental causes; he thought that Philadelphia's 1793 outbreak could be traced to foul air connected with rotting coffee beans on a wharf. See Smith, *Ship of Death*, 198–199.

15. Lining, *A Description of the American Yellow Fever*, 7. John McNeill also notes that visitors to the Americas from various parts of Europe throughout the eighteenth century noted the yellow fever affected "newcomers." See McNeill, *Mosquito Empires*, 65.

16. Charles Cotesworth Pinckney to Thomas Pinckney, September 13, 1794, October 5, 1794, Pinckney Family Papers, Charles Cotesworth Papers, Box 1, Container 1, Folder 3, Library of Congress; Simon Taylor to Chaloner Arcedeckne, November 26, 1796, Vanneck-Arc/3A/1796/22, ICS; Robert Jackson, *Treatise on the Fevers of Jamaica* (1791), 249–251. Also on yellow fever as a "strangers' disease" in the eighteenth century, see McCandless, *Slavery, Disease and Suffering*, 106–124.

17. John Hunter, another military physician in Jamaica, wrote in 1788 that "Europeans, after remaining some time in the West Indies, are less liable to be affected by the causes of fevers than on their first arrival" because over time they acquired some resistance. "The negroes afford a striking example," he continued, "of the power acquired by habit of resisting the causes of fevers." See Hunter, *Observations on Diseases*, 24. In 1797, the physician George Davidson suggested the reason that "the Yellow Fever [was] so fatal to Europeans just arrived" was because cold air "brace[d] and invigorate[d]" the body. See "Observations Upon the Yellow Fever, and its Proximate Cause," *Medical Repository* (Nov 1, 1797): 165–171 (quote on

168). In the 1820s, James Johnson noted that "Europeans, within the first eighteen months after their arrival" in the West Indies were the most likely to contract yellow fever, and it also afflicted those people who had "resided some years in England" before returning to the Caribbean. See James Johnson, *The Influence of Tropical Climates on European Constitutions*, 3rd ed. (New York: W. E. Dean, 1826), 361.

18. Mariola Espinosa has expertly dismantled the suspicion among scholars that Black and white people suffer differently from yellow fever. She has also shown conclusively that there was no consensus among physicians even as late as the nineteenth century that racial differences in immunity existed. See Espinosa, "The Question."

19. On New Orleans, see Willoughby, *Yellow Fever, Race, and Ecology*, 80; Kelman, *A River and Its City*, 98–99; Olivarius, "Immunity, Capital, and Power."

20. Josiah C. Nott, "Thoughts on Acclimation and Adaptation of Races to Climates," *American Journal of the Medical Sciences* (October 1856): 320–334 (quote on 325); "Editorial Items," *The North Star*, February 22, 1850. Rana Hogarth notes that medical practitioners today continue to assume that biological and physiological differences between Black and white bodies are grounded in "nature" rather than in the experience of racism; see Hogarth, *Medicalizing Blackness*, 187–193. On the fallacy of biological race, see C. Loring Brace, *"Race" is a Four-Letter Word: The Genesis of the Concept* (New York: Oxford University Press, 2005); Robert Wald Sussman, *The Myth of Race: The Troubling Persistence of an Unscientific Idea* (Cambridge, MA: Harvard University Press, 2014).

SELECTED BIBLIOGRAPHY

Manuscript Collections

American Philosophical Society, Philadelphia
Ayrshire Archives
Bodleian Library, University of Oxford
Bristol Record Office
British Library, London
Cambridgeshire Archives, Cambridge
Cardross House, Port of Mentieth, Scotland
East Sussex Record Office, Brighton
Georgia Historical Society, Savannah
Highland Archive Centre, Inverness
Historical Society of Pennsylvania, Philadelphia
Huntington Library, San Marino
Institute of Commonwealth Studies Library, Senate House, London
Invercauld Estate, Braemar, Scotland
Leicestershire Record Office, Leicester
Library of Congress, Washington DC
Massachusetts Historical Society, Boston
The Mitchell Library, Glasgow City Archives
The National Archives at Kew, London
National Library of Jamaica, Kingston
National Library of Scotland, Edinburgh
National Records of Scotland, Edinburgh
Newberry Library, Chicago
Somerset Heritage Centre, Taunton
University of Aberdeen Special Collections
University of Bristol Library
University of Exeter Special Collections

Published Primary Sources

Acosta, José de. *Natural and Moral History of the Indies*, edited by Jane E. Mangan, translated by Frances M. López-Morillas. Durham: Duke University Press, 2002.

Adams, Francis, trans. *Hippocrates on Airs, Water, and Places: The received Greek Text of* Littré, *with Latin, French, and English Translations by Eminent Scholars.* London: Mssrs. Wyman & Sons, 1881.

Anon. *A Letter to Granville Sharp, Esq. on the Proposed Abolition of the Slave Trade.* London: J. Debrett, 1788.

Anon. *Abridgement of the Minutes of the Evidence, taken before a Committee of the Whole House, to whom it was referred to consider of the slave-trade.* Numbers I–IV. 1789–1791.

Anon. *An Abstract of the Evidence Delivered Before a Select Committee of the House of Commons in the years 1790, and 1791; on the part of the Petitioners for the Abolition of the Slave-Trade.* 1st and 2nd ed. London: James Phillips, 1791; Edinburgh, J. Robertson, 1791.

Anon. *An Apology for Negro Slavery: or, the West-India Planters Vindicated from the Charge of Inhumanity.* London: Stuart and Stevenson, 1786.

Anon. *Considerations on the Emancipation of Negroes and on the Abolition of the Slave Trade.* London: J. Johnson & J. Debrett, 1788.

Anon. *Debates in the British House of Commons, Wednesday, May 13th, 1789 on the Petitions for the Abolition of the Slave Trade.* Philadelphia: Joseph Crukshank, 1789.

Anon. *Journals of the Assembly of Jamaica.* Vol. IV, 1745–1756. Jamaica: Alexander Aikman, 1797.

Anon. *Substance of a Speech Intended to have been made on Mr. Wilberforce's Motion for the Abolition of the Slave Trade, on Tuesday, April 3, 1792.* London: J. Owen, 1792.

Anon. *The Laws of the Island of Saint Vincent and Its Dependencies, from the first establishment of a legislature to the end of the year 1787.* Saint Vincent: Joseph Berrow, 1788.

Anon. *The Truest and Largest Account of the Late Earthquake in Jamaica, June the 7th, 1692.* London: Thomas Parkhurst, 1693.

Aristotle. *Meteorology,* translated by E. W. Webster. Blacksburg, VA: Virginia Tech, 2001.

Ashe, Thomas. *Carolina: or A Description of the Present State of that Country, and the Natural Excellencies Thereof.* London, 1682.

Atwood, Thomas. *The History of the Island of Dominica.* London, 1791.

Beaufoy, Henry. *The Speech of Mr Beaufoy, Tuesday the 18th June, 1788, in a Committee of the whole House, on a Bill for regulating the Conveyance of Negroes from Africa to the West-Indies.* London: J. Phillips, 1789.

Beckford, William Esq. *A Descriptive Account of the Island of Jamaica, with Remarks Upon the Cultivation of the Sugar Cane, Also Observations and Reflections Upon What Would Probably Be the Consequences of an Abolition of the Slave Trade, and of the Emancipation of the Slaves.* 2 vols. London: T. and J. Egerton, 1790.

Blome, Richard. *The Present State of His Majesties Isles and Territories in America.* London: H. Clark, 1687.

Candler, Allen D., ed. *William Stephens's Journal, 1737–1740. The Colonial Records of the State of Georgia,* CRG vol. IV. Atlanta: The Franklin Printing and Publishing Company, 1906.

Candler, Allen D., ed. *Journal of the Earl of Egmont, first president of the Board of Trustees, from June 14, 1738 to May 25, 1744,* CRG vol. V. Atlanta: Franklin-Turner Company, 1908.

Carroll, B.R., ed. *Historical Collections of South Carolina.* New York: Harper & Brothers, 1836.

Carver, Jonathan. *The New Universal Traveller.* London: G. Robinson, 1779.

Catesby, Mark. *The Natural History of Carolina, Florida and the Bahama Islands.* London, 1731.

Chalmers, Lionel. *An Account of the Weather and Diseases of South Carolina.* London: Edward & Charles Dilly, 1776.

Clarkson, Thomas. *The Substance of the Evidence of Sundry Persons on the Slave-Trade collected in the course of a tour made in the Autumn of the year 1788.* London: James Phillips, 1789.

Coleman, Kenneth, ed. *Trustees' Letter Book, 1738–1745,* CRG vol. 30. Athens, GA: University of Georgia Press, 1985.

Colt, Henry. "The Voyage of Sr Henrye Colt Knight to ye Ilands of ye Antilleas" in *Colonising Expeditions to the West Indies and Guiana, 1623–1667,* edited by V.T. Harlow. London: Hakluyt Society, 1925.

Coulter, E. Merton, ed. *Journal of Col. William Stephens, 1740–1741; 1741–1743; 1743–1745.* Athens, GA: University of Georgia Press, 1958, 1959.

Crafton, William Bell. *A Short Sketch of the Evidence for the Abolition of the Slave Trade, delivered before a committee of the House of Commons.* London & Philadelphia, 1792.

Crocket, Captain. *A True and Perfect Relation of that Most Sad and Terrible Earthquake, at Port Royal in Jamaica.* London, 1792 [1692].

Day, Thomas. *Fragment of an Original Letter on the Slavery of the Negroes; written in the year 1776, by Thomas Day, Esq.* London: John Stockdale, 1784.

De Brahm, John W. G. *Report of the General Survey in the Southern District of North America,* edited by Louis De Vorsey, Jr. Columbia, SC: University of South Carolina Press, 1971.

Delany, Martin R. *The Condition, Elevation, Emigration and Destiny of the Colored People of the United States.* 1852.

Dickson, William. *Letters on Slavery.* London: J. Phillips, 1789.

Dickson, William. *Mitigation of Slavery, in two parts.* London: R. & A. Taylor, 1814.

Donnan, Elizabeth, ed. *Documents Illustrative of the History of the Slave Trade to America.* 4 volumes. New York: Octagon Books, 1965.

Edwards, Bryan. *The History, Civil and Commercial, of the British Colonies in the West Indies.* 2 volumes. New York: Arno Press, 1972 [London, 1793].

Fothergill, John. *Rules for the preservation of health.* London: John Pridden, 1762.

Francklyn, Gilbert. *Observations, occasioned by the attempts made in England to effect the abolition of the Slave Trade.* London: Logographic Press, 1789.

Gage, Thomas. *The English-American his Travail by Sea and Land: or, A New Survey of the West-India's.* London: R. Cotes, 1648.

Goldsmith, Oliver. *The Present State of the British Empire in Europe, America, Africa and Asia.* London: W. Griffin et al., 1768.

Grainger, James. *An Essay on the more common West-India Diseases; and the remedies which that Country itself produces. To which are added, some hints on the management, &c. of negroes.* London: T. Becket & P.A. De Hondt, 1764.

Hakluyt, Richard. *The Principal Navigations: Voyages, Traffiques and Discoveries of the English Nation, made by sea or overland to the remote & farthest distant quarters of the Earth at any time within the compass of these 1600 yeares.* London: J.M. Dent, 1910–1913. [1589–1590; 1600].

Hamilton, Alexander. *Gentleman's Progress: The Itinerarium of Dr. Alexander Hamilton, 1744,* edited by Carl Bridenbaugh. Chapel Hill: University of North Carolina Press, 1948.

Heath, Reverend Emmanuel. *A Full Account of the Late Dreadful Earthquake at Port Royal in Jamaica; Written in two Letters from the Minister of that Place.* London, 1692.

Hewatt, Alexander. *An Historical Account of the Rise and Progress of the Colonies of South Carolina and Georgia.* 2 volumes. London: Alexander Donaldson, 1779.

Hillary, William. *Observations on the Changes of the Air, and the Concomitant Epidemical Diseases in the Island of Barbadoes.* London: C. Hitch and L. Hawes, 1759.

Hughes, Griffith. *Natural History of Barbados.* London, 1750.

Hughes, William. *The American Physitian; or, a Treatise of the Roots, Plants, Trees, Shrubs, Fruit, Herbs, &c. growing in the English Plantations in America.* London: J.C., 1672.

Hunter, John. *Observations on the Diseases of the Army in Jamaica; and on the best Means of Preserving the Health of Europeans, in that Climate.* London: G. Nicol, 1788.

Huxham, John. *An Essay on Fevers, And their Various Kinds . . . .* London: S. Austen, 1750.

Jackson, Robert. *A Treatise on the Fevers of Jamaica, with some observations on the Intermitting Fever of America . . . .* London: J. Murray, 1791.

Jeaffreson, John Cordy, ed. *A Young Squire of the Seventeenth Century: From the Papers of Christopher Jeaffreson, 1676–1686.* 2 volumes. London: Hurst & Blackett, 1878.

Jefferson, Thomas. *Notes on the State of Virginia.* Baltimore: W. Pechin, 1800.

Johnson, James. *The Influence of Tropical Climates on European Constitutions.* 3rd ed. New York: W. E. Dean, 1826.

Johnston, George Millegan. *A Short Description of the Province of South-Carolina, with an account of the Air, Weather, and Diseases at Charles-town.* London: John Hinton, 1763.

Laurens, Henry. *The Papers of Henry Laurens.* 16 vols, edited by Philip M. Hamer. Columbia, SC: University of South Carolina Press, 1968.

Lawson, John. *A New Voyage to Carolina . . . .* London, 1709.

Leslie, Charles. *A New and Exact Account of Jamaica.* Edinburgh: R. Fleming, 1740.

Lewis, Matthew Gregory. *Journal of a West India Proprietor.* London: John Murray, 1834; reprinted New York: Negro Universities Press, 1969.

Ligon, Richard. *A True and Exact History of the Island of Barbadoes . . . .* London, 1657.

Lind, James. *An Essay on Diseases Incidental to Europeans in Hot Climates, with the Method of Preventing their Fatal Consequences.* London: T. Becket & P. A. De Hondt, 1768.

Lind, James. *An Essay on the Most Effectual Means of preserving the Health of Seamen, in the Royal Navy.* London: D. Wilson, 1762.

Lining, John. *A description of the American yellow fever, which prevailed at Charleston, in South Carolina, in the year 1748.* Philadelphia, 1799.

Long, Edward. *The History of Jamaica, or General Survey of the Antient and Modern State of that Island.* 3 volumes. London: Frank Cass & Co., 1970 [London: T. Lowndes, 1774].

Martyn, Benjamin. *Reasons for Establishing the Colony of Georgia.* London: W. Meadows, 1733.

Martyn, Benjamin. *An Impartial Enquiry into the State and Utility of the Province of Georgia.* London: W. Meadows, 1741.

Moseley, Benjamin. *A Treatise on Tropical Diseases; and on the Climate of the West-Indies.* London: T. Cadell, 1787.

Mountgomery, Robert. *A Discourse Concerning the design'd Establishment Of a New Colony to the South of Carolina, in the Most delightful Country of the Universe.* London, 1717.

Nickolls, Robert Boucher. *A Letter to the treasurer of the society instituted for the purpose of effecting the abolition of the slave trade.* London: James Phillips, 1788.

Nott, Josiah C., and George R. Gliddon. *Types of Mankind.* Philadelphia: Lippencott & Co., 1854.

Oglethorpe, James. *Some Account of the Trustees for establishing the colony of Georgia in America,* edited by Rodney M. Baine and Phinizy Spalding. Athens, GA: University of Georgia Press, 1990.

Pringle, John. *Observations on the Diseases of the Army.* London: A. Miller, 1768.

Ramsay, David. *A Dissertation on the Means of Preserving Health in Charleston, and the Adjacent Lowcountry.* Charleston, SC: Markland & M'Iver, 1790.

Ramsay, James. *Objections to the Abolition of the Slave Trade, with Answers.* 2nd ed. London: J. Phillips, 1788.

Reese, Trevor R., ed. *The Clamorous Malcontents: Criticisms and Defenses of the Colony of Georgia, 1741–1743.* Savannah, GA: Beehive Press, 1973.

Reese, Trevor R., ed. *The Most Delightful Country of the Universe: Promotional Literature of the Colony of Georgia, 1717–1734.* Savannah, GA: Beehive Press, 1972.

Renny, Robert. *An History of Jamaica.* London: J. Cawthorn, 1807.

Rollo, John. *Observations on the means of preserving and restoring health in the West-Indies.* London: C. Dilly, 1783.

Roscoe, William. *A General View of the African Slave-Trade, demonstrating its injustice and impolicy: with hints towards a bill for its abolition.* London: R. Faulder, 1788.

Russell, William. *The History of America, from its Discovery by Columbus to the Conclusion of the Late War.* 2 volumes. London: Fielding & Walker, 1778.

S., I. *A brief and perfect journal of the late proceedings and success of the English army in the West-Indies, continued until June the 24th, 1655: together with some quaeres inserted and answered: published for satisfaction of all such who desire truly to be informed in these particulars.* London, 1655.

Sandiford, William. *An Account of a Late Epidemical Distemper, extracted from a letter addressed to Gedney Clarke, Esq.* Barbados, 1771.

Schaw, Janet. *Journal of a Lady of Quality: being the narrative of a journal from Scotland to the West Indies, North Carolina, and Portugal, in the years 1774–1776*, edited by Evangeline Walker Andrews and Charles McLean Andrews. New Haven: Yale University Press, 1921.

Sloane, Hans. *A Voyage to the Islands Madera, Barbadoes, Nieves, St. Christophers, and Jamaica*. 2 volumes. London, 1707 (vol. I), 1725 (vol. II).

Sloane, Hans, and Alvarez de Toledo. "A Letter from Hans Sloane, M.D. and S.R.S. with several Accounts of the Earthquakes in Peru October the 20th, 1687. And at Jamaica, February 19th, 1687, and June the 7th, 1692." *Philosophical Transactions* 18, no. 209 (1694): 78–100.

Smith, Samuel Stanhope. *An Essay on the Causes of the Variety of Complexion and Figure in the Human Species*. Edinburgh: C. Elliot & T. Kay, 1788.

Stokes, Anthony. *A View of the Constitution of the British Colonies in North America and the West Indies*. London, 1783.

Stork, William. *An Account of East-Florida. With Remarks on its future Importance to Trade and Commerce*. London: G. Woodfall, [1766].

Tailfer, Patrick, Hugh Anderson, and David Douglas. *A True and Historical Narrative of the Colony of Georgia in America, from the first settlement thereof until this present period*. Charles-town, SC, 1741.

Taylor, John. *Jamaica in 1687: The Taylor Manuscript at the National Library of Jamaica*, edited by David Buisseret. Kingston, Jamaica: University of the West Indies Press, 2008.

Tennent, John. *Physical Enquiries: Discovering the Mode of Translation in the Constitutions of Northern Inhabitants, on going to, and for some Time after arriving in Southern Climates*. London: T. Gardner, 1742.

Trapham, Thomas. *A Discourse of the State of Health in the Island of Jamaica*. London: R. Boulter, 1679.

Trotter, Thomas. *Medicina nautica: an essay on the diseases of seamen: Comprehending the history of health in His Majesty's fleet, under the command of Richard Earl Howe, admiral*. London, 1797.

Venables, Robert. "Relation concerning the expedition," [1655], published as *The Narrative of General Venables*, edited by C.H. Firth. *Royal Historical Society Publications* 61 (1900): 1–105.

Wesley, John. *Thoughts Upon Slavery*. Philadelphia: Joseph Crukshank, 1774.

Wheat, Marvin T. *The Progress and Intelligence of Americans*. Louisville, KY, 1862.

Williamson, Hugh. *Observations on the Climate in different parts of America, compared with the climate in corresponding parts of the other continent*. New York: T. & J. Swords, 1811.

Wynne, John Huddlestone. *A General History of the British Empire in America*. 2 volumes. London: W. Richardson and L. Urquhart, 1770.

Secondary Sources

Abbott, Elena K. *Beacons of Liberty: International Free Soil and the Fight for Racial Justice in Antebellum America*. New York: Cambridge University Press, 2021.

Amussen, Susan Dwyer. *Caribbean Exchanges: Slavery and the Transformation of English Society*. Chapel Hill: University of North Carolina Press, 2007.

Anderson, Warwick. "Immunities of Empire: Race, Disease, and the New Tropical Medicine, 1900–1920." *Bulletin of the History of Medicine* 70, no. 1 (1996): 94–118.

Anstey, Roger. *The Atlantic Slave Trade and British Abolition, 1760–1810*. Atlantic Highlands, NJ: Humanities Press, 1975.

Arena, Carolyn. "Indian Slaves from Guiana in Seventeenth-Century Barbados," *Ethnohistory* 64, no. 1 (2017): 65–90.

Armitage, David. *The Ideological Origins of the British Empire*. New York: Cambridge University Press, 2000.

Arnold, David, ed. *Warm Climates and Western Medicine: The Emergence of Tropical Medicine, 1500–1900*. Amsterdam: Rodopi B.V., 1996.

Asaka, Ikuko. *Tropical Freedom: Climate, Settler Colonialism, and Black Exclusion in the Age of Emancipation*. Durham: Duke University Press, 2017.

Ballantyne, Tony, and Antoinette Burton. *Bodies in Contact: Rethinking Colonial Encounters in World History*. Durham: Duke University Press, 2005.

Beckles, Hilary McD. *White Servitude and Black Slavery in Barbados, 1627–1715*. Knoxville: University of Tennessee Press, 1989.

Beckles, Hilary McD. *A History of Barbados: From Amerindian Settlement to Nation-state*. Cambridge: Cambridge University Press, 1990.

Bethencourt, Francisco. *Racisms: from the Crusades to the Twentieth Century*. Princeton: Princeton University Press, 2013.

Bindman, David. *Ape to Apollo: Aesthetics and the Idea of Race in the 18th Century*. London: Reaktion Books Ltd., 2002.

Blackburn, Robin. *The American Crucible: Slavery, Emancipation and Human Rights*. New York: Verso, 2011.

Blackburn, Robin. *The Overthrow of Colonial Slavery, 1776–1848*. New York: Verso, 1988.

Block, Sharon. *Colonial Complexions: Race and Bodies in Eighteenth-Century America*. Philadelphia: University of Pennsylvania Press, 2018.

Bollettino, Maria Alessandra. "'Of equal or of more service': Black Soldiers and the British Empire in the Mid-Eighteenth-Century Caribbean." *Slavery and Abolition* 43, no. 3 (2017): 510–533.

Bolton, Charles. *Fugitivism: Escaping Slavery in the Lower Mississippi Valley, 1820–1860*. Fayetteville, AR: University of Arkansas Press, 2019.

Bossy, Denise I., ed., *The Yamasee Indians: From Florida to South Carolina*. Lincoln, NE: University of Nebraska Press, 2018.

Brace, C. Loring. *"Race" is a Four-Letter Word: The Genesis of the Concept*. New York: Oxford University Press, 2005.

Brathwaite, Edward Kamau. *The Development of Creole Society in Jamaica, 1770–1820*. Oxford: Clarendon Press, 1971.

Brown, Christopher Leslie. *Moral Capital: Foundations of British Abolitionism*. Chapel Hill: University of North Carolina Press, 2006.

Brown, Kathleen. *Good Wives, Nasty Wenches, and Anxious Patriarchs: Gender, Race and Power in Colonial Virginia*. Chapel Hill: University of North Carolina Press, 1996.

Brown, Vincent. *The Reaper's Garden: Death and Power in the World of Atlantic Slavery*. Cambridge, MA: Harvard University Press, 2008.

Buckley, Roger Norman. *The British Army in the West Indies: Society and the Military in the Revolutionary Age*. Gainesville: University Press of Florida, 1998.

Buckley, Roger Norman. *The British West India Regiments, 1795–1815*. New Haven: Yale University Press, 1979.

Bullard, Robert D., ed. *Confronting Environmental Racism: Voices from the Grassroots*. Cambridge, MA: South End Press, 1993.

Burnard, Trevor. "'The Countrie Continues Sicklie': White Mortality in Jamaica, 1655–1780." *Social History of Medicine* 12, no. 1 (1999): 45–72.

Burnard, Trevor. "Passengers Only: The Extent and Significance of Absenteeism in Eighteenth Century Jamaica." *Atlantic Studies* 1, no. 2 (2004): 178–195.

Burnard, Trevor. "Not a Place for Whites? Demographic Failure and Settlement in Comparative Context: Jamaica, 1655–1780." In *Jamaica in Slavery and Freedom*, edited by Kathleen E. A. Monteith and Glen Richards, 73–88. Kingston: University of the West Indies Press, 2002.

Burnard, Trevor. *Planters, Merchants, and Slaves: Plantation Societies in British America, 1650–1820*. Chicago: University of Chicago Press, 2015.

Burnard, Trevor, and Richard Follett. "Caribbean Slavery, British Anti-Slavery, and the Cultural Politics of Venereal Disease." *The Historical Journal* 55, no. 2 (2012): 427–451.

Burns, Kathryn. "Unfixing Race." In *Rereading the Black Legend: The Discourses of Religious and Racial Difference in the Renaissance Empires*, edited by Margaret R. Greer, Walter D. Mignolo, and Maureen Quilligan, 188–202. Chicago: University of Chicago Press, 2008.

Burin, Eric. *Slavery and the Peculiar Solution: A History of the American Colonization Society*. Gainesville: University Press of Florida, 2005.

Byrd, Alexander X. *Captives and Voyagers: Black Migrants Across the Eighteenth-Century British Atlantic World*. Baton Rouge: Louisiana State University Press, 2008.

Cañizares Esguerra, Jorge. "New World, New Stars: Patriotic Astrology and the Invention of Indian and Creole Bodies in Colonial Spanish America, 1600–1650." *American Historical Review* 104, no. 1 (1999): 33–68.

Capp, Bernard. *Cromwell's Navy: The Fleet and the English Revolution, 1648–1660*. New York: Oxford University Press, 1989.

Cates, Gerald L. "'The Seasoning': Disease and Death Among the First Colonists of Georgia." *Georgia Historical Quarterly* 64, no. 2 (1980): 146–158.

Chakrabarti, Pratik. *Materials and Medicine: Trade, Conquest and Therapeutics in the Eighteenth Century*. New York: Manchester University Press, 2010.

Chaplin, Joyce E. *Subject Matter: Technology, the Body, and Science on the Anglo-American Frontier, 1500–1676*. Cambridge, MA: Harvard University Press, 2001.

Chaplin, Joyce E. *An Anxious Pursuit: Agricultural Innovation and Modernity in the Lower South, 1730–1815*. Chapel Hill: University of North Carolina Press, 1993.

Chiles, Katy L. *Transformable Race: Surprising Metamorphoses in the Literature of Early America*. Oxford: Oxford University Press, 2014.

Christopher, Emma. *A Merciless Place: The Fate of Britain's Convicts after the American Revolution*. New York: Oxford University Press, 2011.

Clegg, Claude A., III. *The Price of Liberty: African Americans and the Making of Liberia*. Chapel Hill: University of North Carolina Press, 2004.

Coelho, Philip R. P., and Robert A. McGuire. "African and European Bound Labor in the British New World: The Biological Consequences of Economic Choices." *Journal of Economic History* 57, no. 1 (1997): 83–115.

Cohen, William B. *The French Encounter with Africans: White Response to Blacks, 1530–1880*. Bloomington, IN: Indiana University Press, 1980.

Crawford, Matthew. *The Andean Wonder Drug: Cinchona Bark and Imperial Science in the Spanish Atlantic, 1630–1800*. Pittsburgh: University of Pittsburgh Press, 2016.

Curran, Andrew S. *The Anatomy of Blackness: Science and Slavery in an Age of Enlightenment*. Baltimore: Johns Hopkins University Press, 2011.

Curtin, Philip D. "'The White Man's Grave': Image and Reality, 1780–1850." *Journal of British Studies* 1, no. 1 (1961): 94–110.

Curtin, Philip D. "Epidemiology and the Slave Trade." *Political Science Quarterly* 83, no. 2 (1968): 190–216.

Dain, Bruce. *A Hideous Monster of the Mind: American Race Theory in the Early Republic*. Cambridge, MA: Harvard University Press, 2002.

Davis, David Brion. *Slavery and Human Progress*. New York: Oxford University Press, 1984.

Davis, David Brion. *The Problem of Slavery in the Age of Revolution, 1770–1823*. Ithaca: Cornell University Press, 1975.

Delbourgo, James. "The Newtonian Slave Body: Racial Enlightenment in the Atlantic World." *Atlantic Studies* 9, no. 12 (2012): 185–207.

Delbourgo, James . *Collecting the World: Hans Sloane and the Origins of the British Museum*. Cambridge, MA: Belknap Press, 2017.

Dew, Nicholas, and James Delbourgo, eds. *Science and Empire in the Atlantic World*. New York: Routledge, 2008.

Donoghue, John. "'Out of the Land of Bondage': The English Revolution and the Atlantic Origins of Abolition." *American Historical Review* 115, no. 4 (2010): 943–974.

Douglas, Bronwen. "Climate to Crania: Science and the Racialization of Human Difference." In *Foreign Bodies: Oceania and the Science of Race 1750-1940*, edited by Bronwen Douglas and Chris Ballard, 33–96. Canberra: Australian National University E Press, 2008.

Drescher, Seymour. "White Atlantic: The Choice for African Slave Labor in the Plantation Americas." In *Slavery and the Development of the Americas*, edited by David Eltis, Frank D. Lewis, and Kenneth L. Sokoloff, 31–69. New York: Cambridge University Press, 2004.

Drescher, Seymour. *The Mighty Experiment: Free Labor versus Slavery in British Emancipation.* New York: Oxford University Press, 2002.

Drescher, Seymour. *Econocide: British Slavery in the Era of Abolition.* Pittsburgh: University of Pittsburgh Press, 1977.

Drescher, Seymour. "The Ending of the Slave Trade and the Evolution of European Scientific Racism." *Social Science History* 14, no. 3 (1990): 415–450.

Dugatkin, Lee Alan. *Mr. Jefferson and the Giant Moose: Natural History in Early America.* Chicago: University of Chicago Press, 2009.

Dunn, Richard S. *Sugar and Slaves: The Rise of the Planter Class in the English West Indies, 1624–1713.* New York: W.W. Norton & Company, 1973.

Dunn, Richard S. *A Tale of Two Plantations: Slave Life and Labor in Jamaica and Virginia.* Cambridge, MA: Harvard University Press, 2014.

Earle, Rebecca. *The Body of the Conquistador: Food, Race, and the Colonial Experience in Spanish America, 1492–1700.* Cambridge: Cambridge University Press, 2012.

Edelson, S. Max. *Plantation Enterprise in Colonial South Carolina.* Cambridge, MA: Harvard University Press, 2006.

Edelson, S. Max. "The Nature of Slavery: Environmental Disorder and Slave Agency in Colonial South Carolina." In *Cultures and Identities in Colonial British America*, edited by Robert Olwell and Alan Tully, 21–44. Baltimore: Johns Hopkins University Press, 2006.

Eltis, David. *The Rise of African Slavery in the Americas.* Cambridge: Cambridge University Press, 2000.

Eltis, David. *Economic Growth and the Ending of the Transatlantic Slave Trade.* New York: Oxford University Press, 1987.

Esch, Elizabeth D. *The Production of Difference: Race and the Management of Labor in U.S. History.* New York: Oxford University Press, 2012.

Espinosa, Mariola. "The Question of Racial Immunity to Yellow Fever in History and Historiography." *Social Science History* 38, no. 3–4 (2014): 437–453.

Eze, Emmanuel Chukwudi. *Race and the Enlightenment: A Reader.* Cambridge, MA: Blackwell, 1997.

Fabian, Ann. *The Skull Collectors: Race, Science, and America's Unburied Dead.* Chicago: University of Chicago Press, 2010.

Fergus, Claudius K. *Revolutionary Emancipation: Slavery and Abolitionism in the British West Indies.* Baton Rouge: Louisiana State University Press, 2013.

Fields, Barbara Jeanne. "Slavery, Race and Ideology in the United States of America." *New Left Review* I/181 (1990): 95–118.

Finger, Simon. *The Contagious City: The Politics of Public Health in Early Philadelphia.* Ithaca, NY: Cornell University Press, 2012.

Fisher, Linford. "'Dangerous Designes': The 1676 Barbados Act to Prohibit New England Indian Slave Importation," *William and Mary Quarterly* 71, no. 1 (2014): 99–124.

Foner, Eric. *Free Soil, Free Labor, Free Men: The Ideology of the Republican Party Before the Civil War.* New York: Oxford University Press, 1995.

Franklin, Alexandra. "Enterprise and Advantage: The West India Interest in Britain, 1774–1840." PhD diss., University of Pennsylvania, 1992.

Fredrickson, George. *Racism: A Short History.* Princeton: Princeton University Press, 2002.

Fredrickson, George. *The Black Image in the White Mind: The Debate on Afro-American Character and Destiny, 1817–1914.* New York: Harper & Row, 1971.

Galenson, David. *White Servitude in Colonial America: An Economic Analysis.* New York: Cambridge University Press, 1981.

Gaspar, David Barry. "Sugar Cultivation and Slave Life in Antigua Before 1800." In *Cultivation and Culture: Labor and the Shaping of Slave Life in the Americas*, edited by Ira Berlin and Philip D. Morgan, 101–123. Charlottesville: University Press of Virginia, 1993.

Glacken, Clarence J. *Traces on the Rhodian Shore: Nature and Culture in Western Thought from Ancient Times to the End of the Eighteenth Century.* Berkeley: University of California Press, 1967.

Gissis, Snait B. "Visualizing 'Race' in the Eighteenth Century." *Historical Studies in the Natural Sciences* 41, no. 1 (2011): 41–103.

Goetz, Rebecca Anne. "Indian Slavery: An Atlantic and Hemispheric Problem," *History Compass* 14, no. 2 (2016): 59–70.

Golinski, Jan. *British Weather and the Climate of Enlightenment.* Chicago: University of Chicago Press, 2007.

Gómez, Pablo F. *The Experiential Caribbean: Creating Knowledge and Healing in the Early Modern Atlantic.* Chapel Hill: University of North Carolina Press, 2017.

Gragg, Larry. *Englishmen Transplanted: the English Colonization of Barbados, 1627–1660.* New York: Oxford University Press, 2003.

Greene, Jack P. "'Of Liberty and of the Colonies': A Case Study of Constitutional Conflict in the Mid-Eighteenth-Century British American Empire." In *Liberty and American Experience in the Eighteenth Century,* edited by David Womersley, 21–102. Indianapolis: Liberty Fund, 2006.

Grove, Richard H. *Green Imperialism: Colonial Expansion, Tropical Island Edens and the Origins of Environmentalism, 1600–1860.* New York: Cambridge University Press, 1995.

Guasco, Michael. *Slaves and Englishmen: Human Bondage in the Early Modern Atlantic World.* Philadelphia: University of Pennsylvania Press, 2014.

Guyatt, Nicholas. *Bind Us Apart: How Enlightened Americans Invented Racial Segregation.* New York: Basic Books, 2016.

Hall, Kim F. *Things of Darkness: Economies of Race and Gender in Early Modern England.* Ithaca: Cornell University Press, 1995.

Handler, Jerome S., and Matthew C. Reilly. "Contesting 'White Slavery' in the Caribbean: Enslaved Africans and European Indentured Servants in Seventeenth Century Barbados." *New West Indian Guide* 91 (2017): 30–55.

Hannaford, Ivan. *Race: The History of an Idea in the West.* Washington, DC: Woodrow Wilson Center Press, 1996.

Harlow, Vincent T. *A History of Barbados, 1625–1685.* New York: Negro Universities Press, 1969 [1926].

Harris, Leslie M. *In the Shadow of Slavery: African Americans in New York City, 1626–1863.* Chicago: University of Chicago Press, 2003.

Harrison, Mark. *Climates and Constitutions: Health, Race, Environment and British Imperialism in India, 1600–1850.* New Delhi: Oxford University Press, 1999.

Harrison, Mark. *Medicine in an Age of Commerce and Empire: Britain and its Tropical Colonies, 1660–1830.* New York: Oxford University Press, 2010.

Hart, Emma. *Building Charleston: Town and Society in the Eighteenth-Century British Atlantic World.* Charlottesville: University of Virginia Press, 2010.

Hepburn, Sharon A. Roger. *Crossing the Border: A Free Black Community in Canada.* Urbana: University of Illinois Press, 2007.

Higman, B. W. *Plantation Jamaica 1750–1850: Capital and Control in a Colonial Economy.* Kingston, Jamaica: University of the West Indies Press, 2005.

Higman, B. W. "Ecological Determinism in Caribbean History." In *Inside Slavery: Process and Legacy in the Caribbean Experience,* edited by Hilary McD. Beckles, 52–77. Kingston: Canoe Press, 1996.

Hogarth, Rana A. *Medicalizing Blackness: Making Racial Difference in the Atlantic World, 1780–1840.* Chapel Hill: University of North Carolina Press, 2017.

Hudson, Nicholas. "From 'Nation' to 'Race': The Origin of Racial Classification in Eighteenth-Century Thought." *Eighteenth-Century Studies* 29 (1996): 247–264.

Jackson, Harvey H., and Phinizy Spalding, eds. *Forty Years of Diversity: Essays on Colonial Georgia.* Athens, GA: University of Georgia Press, 1984.

Jankovic, Vladimir. *Confronting the Climate: British Airs and the Making of Environmental Medicine.* New York: Palgrave Macmillan, 2010.

Jasanoff, Maya. *Liberty's Exiles: American Loyalists in the Revolutionary World.* New York: Alfred A. Knopf, 2012.

Jones, David S. *Rationalizing Epidemics: Meanings and Uses of American Indian Mortality since 1600*. Cambridge, MA: Harvard University Press, 2004.

Jones, George Fenwick. *The Georgia Dutch: From the Rhine and Danube to the Savannah, 1733–1783*. Athens, GA: University of Georgia Press, 1992.

Jordan, Winthrop D. *White Over Black: American Attitudes Toward the Negro, 1550–1812*. Chapel Hill: University of North Carolina Press, 1968.

Jung, Moon-Ho. *Coolies and Cane: Race, Labor, and Sugar in the Age of Emancipation*. Baltimore: Johns Hopkins University Press, 2006.

Juricek, John T. *Colonial Georgia and the Creeks: Anglo-Indian Diplomacy on the Southern Frontier, 1733–1763*. Gainesville: University Press of Florida, 2010.

Karras, Alan L. *Sojourners in the Sun: Scottish Migrants in Jamaica and the Chesapeake, 1740–1800*. Ithaca: Cornell University Press, 1992.

Kelman, Ari. *A River and Its City: The Nature of Landscape in New Orleans*. Berkeley: University of California Press, 2003.

Kidd, Colin. *The Forging of Races: Race and Scripture in the Protestant Atlantic World, 1600–2000*. Cambridge: Cambridge University Press, 2006.

Kinshasa, Kwando Mbiassi. *Emigration vs. Assimilation: The Debate in the African American Press, 1827–1861*. Jefferson, NC: McFarland, 1988.

Kiple, Kenneth. *The Caribbean Slave: A Biological History*. Cambridge: Cambridge University Press, 1984.

Kiple, Kenneth F., and Virginia Himmelsteib King. *Another Dimension to the Black Diaspora: Diet, Disease, and Racism*. Cambridge: Cambridge University Press, 1981.

Kupperman, Karen Ordahl. "The Puzzle of the American Climate in the Early Colonial Period." *American Historical Review* 87, no. 5 (1982): 1262–1289.

Kupperman, Karen Ordahl. "Fear of Hot Climates in the Anglo-American Colonial Experience." *William and Mary Quarterly* 41, no. 2 (1984): 213–240.

Kupperman, Karen Ordahl. *Providence Island, 1630–1641: The Other Puritan Colony*. New York: Cambridge University Press, 1993.

Lambert, David. *White Creole Culture, Politics and Identity During the Age of Abolition*. New York: Cambridge University Press, 2005.

Landers, Jane. *Black Society in Spanish Florida*. Urbana, IL: University of Illinois Press, 1999.

Lause, Mark A. *Free Labor: The Civil War and the Making of an American Working Class*. Urbana: University of Illinois Press, 2015.

LeMaster, Michelle, and Bradford J. Wood, eds. *Creating and Contesting Carolina: Proprietary Era Histories*. Columbia, SC: University of South Carolina Press, 2013.

Look Lai, Walton. *Indentured Labor, Caribbean Sugar: Chinese and Indian Migrants to the British West Indies, 1838–1918*. Baltimore: Johns Hopkins University Press, 1993.

MacMillan, Ken. *Sovereignty and Possession in the English New World: The Legal Foundations of Empire, 1576–1640*. New York: Cambridge University Press, 2006.

Maizlish, Stephen E. *A Strife of Tongues: The Compromise of 1850 and the Ideological Foundations of the American Civil War*. Charlottesville: University of Virginia Press, 2018.

Matthews, Gelien. *Caribbean Slave Revolts and the British Abolitionist Movement*. Baton Rouge: Louisiana State University Press, 2006.

Mauldin, Erin Stewart. *Unredeemed Land: An Environmental History of Civil War and Emancipation in the Cotton South*. New York: Oxford University Press, 2018.

McCandless, Peter. *Slavery, Disease, and Suffering in the Southern Lowcountry*. New York: Cambridge University Press, 2011.

McIlvenna, Noeleen. *The Short Life of Free Georgia: Class and Slavery in the Colonial South*. Chapel Hill: University of North Carolina Press, 2015.

McNeill, J. R. *Mosquito Empires: Ecology and War in the Greater Caribbean, 1620–1914*. New York: Cambridge University Press, 2010.

Melton, James Van Horn. *Religion, Community, and Slavery on the Colonial Southern Frontier*. New York: Cambridge University Press, 2015.

Menard, Russell R. *Sweet Negotiations: Sugar, Slavery, and Plantation Agriculture in Early Barbados.* Charlottesville, VA: University of Virginia Press, 2006.

Miller, Floyd J. *The Search for a Black Nationality: Black Emigration and Colonization, 1787–1863.* Urbana: University of Illinois Press, 1975.

Mintz, Sidney W. *Sweetness and Power: The Place of Sugar in Modern History.* New York: Penguin Books, 1985.

Monteith, Kathleen E. A., and Glen Richards, eds. *Jamaica in Slavery and Freedom: History, Heritage and Culture.* Kingston: University of the West Indies Press, 2002.

Morgan, Edmund. *American Slavery, American Freedom: The Ordeal of Colonial Virginia.* New York: W.W. Norton, 1975.

Morgan, Jennifer L. *Laboring Women: Reproduction and Gender in New World Slavery.* Philadelphia: University of Pennsylvania Press, 2004.

Mulcahy, Matthew. *Hubs of Empire: The Southeastern Lowcountry and British Caribbean.* Baltimore: Johns Hopkins University Press, 2014.

Mulcahy, Matthew. *Hurricanes and Society in the British Greater Caribbean, 1624–1783.* Baltimore: Johns Hopkins University Press, 2006.

Mulry, Kate Luce. *An Empire Transformed: Remolding Bodies and Landscapes in the Restoration Atlantic.* New York: New York University Press, 2021.

Murray, Robert. *Atlantic Passages: Race, Mobility, and Liberian Colonization.* Gainesville: University Press of Florida, 2021.

Mustakeem, Sowande' M. *Slavery at Sea: Terror, Sex, and Sickness in the Middle Passage.* Urbana, IL: University of Illinois Press, 2016.

Nash, Linda. *Inescapable Ecologies: A History of Environment, Disease, and Knowledge.* Berkeley: University of California Press, 2006.

Newman, Brooke N. *A Dark Inheritance: Blood, Race, and Sex in Colonial Jamaica.* New Haven: Yale University Press, 2018.

Newman, Simon P. *A New World of Labor: The Development of Plantation Slavery in the British Atlantic.* Philadelphia: University of Pennsylvania Press, 2013.

O'Brien, Jean. *Firsting and Lasting: Writing Indians out of Existence in New England.* Minneapolis: University of Minnesota Press, 2010.

O'Malley, Gregory E. *Final Passages: The Intercolonial Slave Trade of British America, 1619–1807.* Chapel Hill: University of North Carolina Press, 2014.

Oakes, James. *The Scorpion's Sting: Antislavery and the Coming of the Civil War.* W.W. Norton, 2014.

Olivarius, Kathryn. "Immunity, Capital, and Power in Antebellum New Orleans," *American Historical Review* 124, no. 2 (2019): 424–455.

Parker, Anthony W. *Scottish Highlanders in Colonial Georgia: The Recruitment, Emigration, and Settlement at Darien, 1735–1748.* Athens, GA: University of Georgia Press, 1997.

Parrish, Susan Scott. *American Curiosity: Cultures of Natural History in the Colonial British Atlantic World.* Chapel Hill: University of North Carolina Press, 2006.

Paugh, Katherine. *The Politics of Reproduction: Race, Medicine, and Fertility in the Age of Abolition.* New York: Oxford University Press, 2017.

Pestana, Carla Gardina. *The English Atlantic in an Age of Revolution, 1640–1661.* Cambridge, MA: Harvard University Press, 2004.

Pestana, Carla Gardina. *The English Conquest of Jamaica: Oliver Cromwell's Bid for Empire.* Cambridge, MA: Harvard University Press, 2017.

Petley, Christer. *Slaveholders in Jamaica: Colonial Society and Culture During the Era of Abolition.* London: Pickering & Chatto, 2009.

Petley, Christer. *White Fury: A Jamaican Slaveholder and the Age of Revolution.* Oxford: Oxford University Press, 2018.

Pettigrew, William A. "Free to Enslave: Politics and the Escalation of Britain's Transatlantic Slave Trade, 1688–1714." *William and Mary Quarterly* 64, no. 1 (2007): 3–38.

Polgar, Paul. *Standard-Bearers of Equality: America's First Abolition Movement.* Chapel Hill: University of North Carolina Press, 2019.

Power-Greene, Ousmane K. *Against Wind and Tide: The African American Struggle Against the Colonization Movement.* New York: NYU Press, 2014.

Pressly, Paul M. *On the Rim of the Caribbean: Colonial Georgia and the British Atlantic World.* Athens, GA: University of Georgia Press, 2013.

Pybus, Cassandra. *Epic Journeys of Freedom: Runaway Slaves of the American Revolution and Their Global Quest for Liberty.* Boston: Beacon Press, 2006.

Ragatz, Lowell J. *The Fall of the Planter Class in the British Caribbean, 1763–1833: A Study in Economic and Social History.* New York: Century, 1928.

Reese, Trevor R. *Colonial Georgia: A Study in British Imperial Policy in the Eighteenth Century.* Athens, GA: University of Georgia Press, 1963.

Reséndez, Andrés. *The Other Slavery: The Uncovered Story of Indian Enslavement in America.* Boston: Houghton Mifflin Harcourt, 2016.

Roberts, Justin. *Slavery and the Enlightenment in the British Atlantic, 1750–1807.* New York: Cambridge University Press, 2013.

Robertson, James. *Gone is the Ancient Glory: Spanish Town, Jamaica, 1534–2000.* Kingston, Jamaica: Ian Randle Publishers, 2005.

Rosenthal, Caitlin. *Accounting for Slavery: Masters and Management.* Cambridge, MA: Harvard University Press, 2018.

Rothschild, Emma. "A Horrible Tragedy in the French Atlantic." *Past and Present* 192 (2006): 67–108.

Rusert, Britt. *Fugitive Science: Empiricism and Freedom in Early African American Culture.* New York: New York University Press, 2017.

Ryden, David Beck. *West Indian Slavery and British Abolition, 1783–1807.* New York: Cambridge University Press, 2009.

Saakwa-Mante, Norris. "Western Medicine and Racial Constitutions: Surgeon John Atkins' Theory of Polygenism and Sleepy Distemper in the 1730s." In *Race, Science and Medicine, 1700–1960*, edited by Waltraud Ernst and Bernard Harris, 29–57. London: Routledge, 1999.

Saville, Julie. *The Work of Reconstruction: From Slave to Wage Laborer in South Carolina, 1860–1870.* New York: Cambridge University Press, 1994.

Savitt, Todd L. *Medicine and Slavery: The Diseases and Health Care of Blacks in Antebellum Virginia.* Urbana, IL: University of Illinois Press, 1978.

Savitt, Todd L., and James Harvey Young, eds. *Disease and Distinctiveness in the American South.* Knoxville: University of Tennessee Press, 1988.

Schaub, Jean-Frédéric. *Race Is about Politics: Lessons from History*, translated by Lara Vergnaud. Princeton: Princeton University Press, 2019.

Schiebinger, Londa. *Nature's Body: Gender in the Making of Modern Science.* Boston: Beacon Press, 1993.

Schiebinger, Londa. *Plants and Empire: Colonial Bioprospecting in the Atlantic World.* Cambridge, MA: Harvard University Press, 2004.

Schiebinger, Londa. "Medical Experimentation and Race in the Eighteenth-Century Atlantic World." *Social History of Medicine* 26, no. 3 (2013): 364–382.

Schwartz, Stuart B., ed. *Tropical Babylons: Sugar and the Making of the Atlantic World, 1450–1680.* Chapel Hill: University of North Carolina Press, 2004.

Senior, Emily. *The Caribbean and the Medical Imagination, 1764–1834: Slavery, Disease and Colonial Modernity.* Cambridge: Cambridge University Press, 2018.

Seth, Suman. *Difference and Disease: Medicine, Race, and the Eighteenth-Century British Empire.* Cambridge: Cambridge University Press, 2018.

Shaw, Jenny. *Everyday Life in the Early English Caribbean: Irish, Africans, and the Construction of Difference.* Athens, GA: University of Georgia Press, 2013.

Shepherd, Verene A., ed. *Working Slavery, Pricing Freedom: Perspectives from the Caribbean, Africa, and the African Diaspora.* New York: Palgrave, 2002.

Sheridan, Richard B. *Doctors and Slaves: A Medical and Demographic History of Slavery in the British West Indies, 1680–1834.* New York: Cambridge University Press, 1985.

Sidbury, James. *Becoming African in America: Race and Nation in the Early Black Atlantic.* New York: Oxford University Press, 2007.

Silva, Cristobal. *Miraculous Plagues: An Epidemiology of Early New England Narrative.* New York: Oxford University Press, 2011.

Sinha, Manisha. *The Slave's Cause: A History of Abolition.* New Haven: Yale University Press, 2016.

Smallwood, Stephanie E. *Saltwater Slavery: A Middle Passage from Africa to American Diaspora.* Cambridge, MA: Harvard University Press, 2008.

Smith, Billy G. *Ship of Death: A Voyage that Changed the Atlantic World.* New Haven: Yale University Press, 2013.

Snyder, Christina. *Slavery in Indian Country: The Changing Face of Captivity in Early America.* Cambridge: Harvard University Press, 2010.

Spruill, Julia Cherry. *Women's Life and Work in the Southern Colonies.* Chapel Hill: University of North Carolina Press, 1938.

Stepan, Nancy. *The Idea of Race in Science: Great Britain, 1800–1960.* London: Macmillan Press, 1982.

Stepan, Nancy. *Picturing Tropical Nature.* Ithaca: Cornell University Press, 2001.

Stewart, Mart A. *"What Nature Suffers to Groe": Life, Labor, and Landscape on the Georgia Coast, 1680–1920.* Athens, GA: University of Georgia Press, 1996.

Stewart, Mart A. "'Let Us Begin with the Weather?': Climate, Race, and Cultural Distinctiveness in the American South." In *Nature and Society in Historical Context*, edited by Mikulás Teich, Roy Porter, and Bo Gustafsson, 240–256. New York: Cambridge University Press, 1997.

Stolberg, Michael. *Experiencing Illness and the Sick Body in Early Modern Europe*, translated by Leonhard Unglaub and Logan Kennedy. New York: Palgrave Macmillan, 2011.

Sussman, Robert Wald. *The Myth of Race: The Troubling Persistence of an Unscientific Idea.* Cambridge, MA: Harvard University Press, 2014.

Sutter, Paul S., and Christopher J. Manganiello, eds. *Environmental History and the American South.* Athens: University of Georgia Press, 2009.

Swaminathan, Srividhya. *Debating the Slave Trade: Rhetoric of British National Identity, 1759–1815.* Farnham, UK: Ashgate, 2009.

Sweet, James H. "The Iberian Roots of American Racist Thought." *William and Mary Quarterly* 54, no. 1 (1997): 143–166.

Sweet, Julie Anne. *Negotiating for Georgia: British-Creek Relations in the Trustee Era, 1733–1752.* Athens: University of Georgia Press, 2005.

Sweet, Julie Anne. "'That Cursed Evil Rum': The Trustees' Prohibition Policy in Colonial Georgia." *Georgia Historical Quarterly* 94, no. 1 (2010): 1–29.

Swingen, Abigail L. *Competing Visions of Empire: Labor, Slavery, and the Origins of the British Atlantic Empire.* New Haven: Yale University Press, 2015.

Thornton, Amanda. "Coerced Care: Thomas Thistlewood's Account of Medical Practice on Enslaved Populations in Colonial Jamaica, 1751–1786." *Slavery and Abolition* 32, no. 4 (2011): 535–559.

Trouillot, Michel-Rolph. *Silencing the Past: Power and the Production of History.* Boston: Beacon Press, 1995.

Turner, Sasha. *Contested Bodies: Pregnancy, Childrearing, and Slavery in Jamaica.* Philadelphia: University of Pennsylvania Press, 2017.

Vasconcellos, Colleen A. *Slavery, Childhood, and Abolition in Jamaica, 1788–1838.* Athens: University of Georgia Press, 2015.

Valenčius, Conevery Bolton. *The Health of the Country: How American Settlers Understood Themselves and Their Land.* New York: Basic Books, 2002.

Walsh, Lorena. *Motives of Honor, Pleasure, and Profit: Plantation Management in the Colonial Chesapeake, 1607–1763.* Chapel Hill: University of North Carolina Press, 2010.

Ward, John Robert. *British West Indian Slavery, 1750–1834: The Process of Amelioration.* Oxford: Clarendon Press, 1988.

Wear, Andrew. "Place, Health, and Disease: The *Airs, Waters, Places* Tradition in Early Modern England and North America." *Journal of Medieval and Early Modern Studies* 38, no. 3 (2008): 443–465.

Weaver, Karol. *Medical Revolutionaries: The Enslaved Healers of Eighteenth-Century Saint Domingue.* Urbana, IL: University of Illinois Press, 2006.

Wheeler, Roxann. *The Complexion of Race: Categories of Difference in Eighteenth-Century British Culture.* Philadelphia: University of Pennsylvania Press, 2000.

White, Sam. *A Cold Welcome: The Little Ice Age and Europe's Encounter with North America.* Cambridge, MA: Harvard University Press, 2017.

Williams, Eric. *Capitalism and Slavery.* Chapel Hill: University of North Carolina Press, 1944.

Willoughby, Urmi Engineer. *Yellow Fever, Race, and Ecology in Nineteenth-Century New Orleans. The Natural World of the Gulf South.* Baton Rouge: Louisiana State University Press, 2017.

Wilson, Kathleen. *The Island Race: Englishness, Empire and Gender in the Eighteenth Century.* New York: Routledge, 2003.

Wilson, Thomas D. *The Oglethorpe Plan: Enlightenment Design in Savannah and Beyond.* Charlottesville, VA: University of Virginia Press, 2012.

Wisecup, Kelly. *Medical Encounters: Knowledge and Identity in Early American Literatures.* Amherst, MA: University of Massachusetts Press, 2013.

Wood, Betty. *Slavery in Colonial Georgia, 1730–1775.* Athens, GA: University of Georgia Press, 1984.

Wood, Betty. *The Origins of American Slavery: Freedom and Bondage in the English Colonies.* New York: Hill and Wang, 1997.

Wood, Peter H. *Black Majority: Negroes in Colonial South Carolina From 1670 through the Stono Rebellion.* New York: Alfred A. Knopf, 1974.

Zilberstein, Anya. *A Temperate Empire: Making Climate Change in Early America.* New York: Oxford University Press, 2016.

INDEX

For the benefit of digital users, indexed terms that span two pages (e.g., 52–53) may, on occasion, appear on only one of those pages.

Tables, figures, and boxes are indicated by an italic *t*, *f*, and *b* following the page number.

climate, race argument (*cont.*)
   in West Indies, 2, 3, 7, 16–18, 23–24, 25–26,
      34–35, 41–43, 105–6, 125–26, 127–30, 132,
      134, 135–36, 138–39, 141, 142, 143–44,
      145–48, 149–55, 168–70, 187–88, 189–
      90, 194–95
coffee, 1, 128
Compromise of 1850, 175–77
corn, 52, 53, 59–60, 61, 63–64
Colt, Henry, 24–25, 26, 27
Cooper, Lord Anthony Ashley, 77
cotton, 19, 24–25, 127–28, 163–64, 171–72, 175,
      177–78, 179, 180, 181
Council of Foreign Plantations, 28–30,
      32–33, 39
Council of Trade and Plantations, 39–41
Crafton, William Bell, 148–49
creoles, 99, 110–11, 113–14, 117–20, 121–22,
      125, 130–31, 133–34, 135, 137–38,
      154, 192–93
Cuba, 178
Cuffe, Paul, 165–66

death rates, 13–14, 20, 27, 33–34, 36–37, 38, 76,
      92, 96–97, 126, 132–33, 134–35, 142, 143–
      44, 149–50, 151
Delany, Martin R., 171–72, 173, 184, 190
diets, 1, 19–20, 24, 26–28, 34, 69–70, 81, 107–8,
      120–21, 125, 131–32, 134, 137–38
distempers, 33, 40, 56–57, 59–60, 68, 69, 71–72,
      73, 84, 96–97, 121–22, 132–33
Dominica, 78, 87–88, 93–94, 143
Doolittle, Senator James, 172–73, 174–75
Douglas, Stephen, 176
Douglass, Frederick, 166, 170–71, 176–
      78, 194–95
Dred Scott vs. Sandford, 173
dropsy, 33, 34–35, 54
Dutton, Richard, 28–29, 39
dysentery, 105–6, 130–31

Edwards, Bryan, 122, 151–52
Egmont, Earl of, 64, 65, 67–68, 69
earthquakes, 21–22, 35–38, 36f, 40, 41, 79,
      80, 81, 85
England, 19, 26–27, 37–38
   climate, 114–15, 116, 120, 151
   economic opportunities in, 25–26
   health, 27–28, 33, 67–68, 120
   hot climate fears in, 21, 23–24, 39
   servants from, 28–29, 30–31, 54, 138,
      145, 154–55
   settlers from, 31–33, 39–41, 60, 91, 114
English Navigation and Trade Laws, 25–26
environmental racism, 4–5, 13–14, 18, 73,
      153, 195
Eveleigh, Samuel, 52–53, 56, 59, 63, 73

Farquharson, John, 88–89, 134–35
fevers, 24, 27–28, 33–34, 36–37, 41, 50–51, 59,
      68–69, 71–73, 75, 77, 87–88, 95, 96–97,
      105–6, 107–8, 114, 122, 130–31, 167. *See
      also* yellow fever.
Florida, 47, 48, 72–73
fluxes, 26–27, 68–70, 71–72, 73, 96–97, 130–31
Francklyn, Gilbert, 138–39, 146–47, 149
French Guiana, 147–48
Fugitive Slave Act, 171
Fuller, Stephen, 127–29

Garrison, William Lloyd, 169–70
Georgia:
   anti-slavery movement, 3, 62–63, 68, 148–
      49, 160–61
   climate, 2–3, 13, 45–46, 48–51, 55, 62–63, 67–
      68, 69, 69–71, 148, 159–61, 163–64, 180–82
   climate, race argument in, 3, 56–57, 58–62, 63,
      64, 70, 73–74, 148, 159–66, 180–82, 183–
      85, 188–89, 190
   Convention for Planters, 181–82
   demand for servants, 56, 58
   demand for slavery, 45–46, 52, 57, 58, 59–60,
      65–67, 68, 188
   economic problems, 58, 59–60
   health, 5–6, 51–52, 54–55, 57, 58–59, 61–63,
      68–70, 71–73
   labor problems, 54–56, 57
   rice crops, 59, 60, 61, 63–64, 73, 75
   seasoning in, 50–51, 54–55, 56–57, 58, 59, 69–
      70, 71, 73, 74, 160–61, 188–89
   settlers, 47–48, 51, 52–54
   transition to slavery, 161–64, 190
ginger, 127–28
Grainger, James, 110–11
Granville, Beville, 40–41, 114
Gray, Charles Gordon, 93, 106, 114–15, 118–
      19, 122
Grenada:
   Council and Assembly of, 125, 130–31, 132–
      33, 135, 136–37
   climate, 111, 125, 130–31, 135
   health, 92–93, 94, 106–7, 111, 130–31, 132–
      33, 135
   racial hierarchy in, 136–38

Haiti, 168, 173
Hewatt, Alexander, 46, 160–61
Highlanders, 17–18, 62–63, 69–70, 148–
      49, 181–82
Hillary, William, 105–6, 109
Hippocrates, 7–8
Hispaniola, 26–27
Honduras, 178
Hunter, John, 91–92, 94–95, 105–6
hurricanes, 22, 38, 79, 81, 85, 133